FASHION RETAILING
a multi-channel approach

FASHION RETAILING

a multi-channel approach

third edition

Jay Diamond
Ellen Diamond
Sheri Litt

Fairchild Books
An Imprint of Bloomsbury Publishing Inc.

B L O O M S B U R Y

LONDON • NEW DELHI • NEW YORK • SYDNEY

Fairchild Books
An imprint of Bloomsbury Publishing Inc

1385 Broadway	50 Bedford Square
New York	London
NY 10018	WC1B 3DP
USA	UK

www.bloomsbury.com
FAIRCHILD BOOKS, BLOOMSBURY and the Diana logo are trademarks of Bloomsbury Publishing Plc

© Bloomsbury Publishing Inc, 2015
The Second Edition was published by Pearson Prentice Hall in copyright year 2006

Library of Congress Cataloging-in-Publication Data
Diamond, Ellen.
 Fashion retailing : a multi-channel approach. -- Third edition / Jay
Diamond, Ellen Diamond, Sheri Litt.
    pages cm
  ISBN 978-1-60901-900-6
1. Fashion merchandising--United States. I. Diamond, Jay. II. Litt,
Sheri. III. Title.

 HD9940.U4D53 2015
 687.068'8--dc23

                            2014020050

ISBN: 9781609019006
EISBN: 9781609019051

Typeset by Saxon Graphics Ltd, Derby
Cover Design: Untitled
Printed and bound in the United States of America

contents

extended contents

section three   MANAGEMENT AND CONTROL

preface

In a *Retailing Today* article, David Sisco asked, "What's changing consumers' expectations?" The conclusion was that

> The retail world is seeing significant shifts in consumer expectations and behaviors. Today's online shoppers have higher expectations than ever before. Consumers want the ability to shop anywhere at any time and are looking for retailers that offer multiple options. In particular, the flexibility to choose a delivery date can impact consumer loyalty and future spending with a brand. There are a number of recent trends that affect these delivery expectations, including omni-channel fulfillment, customized deliveries and free shipping—the latter of which has evolved to include free returns. E-tailers have to be quick to rethink their business strategies to accommodate these dramatic shifts in consumer behavior, or lose ground to others who will.

It is particularly notable that many changes are, in fact, taking place in fashion retailing. Although brick-and-mortar operations still account for the lion's share of consumer sales for fashion merchandise, they continue to be challenged by the increased competition of off-site ventures. Catalog sales continue to soar, e-tailing maintains a steady increase in sales every year, home shopping networks are breaking sales records, and mobile purchasing is fast becoming an excellent vehicle for those on the go. A major direction in the industry is omni-channel retailing, where merchants participate in every aspect of reaching the consumer.

Traditional retailing is facing more competition than ever before from the off-pricers, discounters, and value operations. The profitability of the traditionalists continues to decrease, resulting in many stalwarts closing their doors. The industry has shifted, in many instances, from the brick-and-mortar operations to new, Internet-only companies. Without the environments in which consumers shop, these businesses operate from warehouses where orders are placed on the Internet and sent to the purchaser. Their profit margins are generally excellent since the expense of running their stores is less.

Competition remains so fierce that present-day companies must meet these challenges with every bit of imagination and expertise they can muster. The playing field continues to be a bumpy one.

This third edition of *Fashion Retailing* offers the latest in up-to-date information while still retaining the wealth of past theoretical information that was experienced in the last edition. The innovative concepts that are obvious in today's operations are carefully examined, including omni-channel retailing, sustainable fashion merchandise practices, the greening of retailing, environmental innovation, new approaches to advertising, and the continuing influence of social media like Facebook and Pinterest. The all-new Chapter 17 is devoted to the ways that retailers use electronic media to interact with consumers. These include the in-store multimedia approaches that merchants are using to motivate customers to buy when they come into the store. Some of the tools used are full media walls that are made up of numerous screens that feature the latest up-to-the-minute fashions, and smaller screens throughout the store to alert the shopper with what's new at the point of purchase, etc. An excellent example of the major installation of these devices is found in the Fifth Avenue Uniqlo store, and is carefully presented in Chapter 17.

Attention is also focused on showrooming, a happening where many consumers come to the store to compare its prices with online offerings, to check on quality, and so forth. Discussion features the benefits of showrooming to shoppers and to retailers who are beginning to change the negativity to positives.

Text messaging is yet another plus for retailers to increase business. Through this instant communication delivery system, they can alert users to flash sales, new markdowns, messages that might be of interest, etc.

The use of blogs has given both the retailer and interested consumers information that, although the opinion of the blogger, provides the future endeavors of the industry, predictions, fashion forecasts, and the like. Some of these blogs, as discussed, are the brainchild of industry professionals who have spent as many as 30 years honing their retail skills.

To address the rapidly changing face of fashion retailing, this new edition features a new organization in addition to the aforementioned new chapter. Chapter 1, The Nature of the Fashion Retailing Industry, offers a look at both on-site and off-site ventures instead of breaking it into two chapters as in the previous edition. In this way the reader can make comparisons between the two classifications. With the significant growth of the multicultural consumer market, greater emphasis has been placed on this market.

Chapter 9, The Significance of Visual Merchandising to Stores, has been moved to Section Two since it plays an even more important role in retailing than ever before.

Chapter 17, Communicating to Customers through Electronic Media, a new chapter, concentrates on the Internet, social media, text messaging, digital signage, and blogging, all playing an important role in contemporary retailing in the United States and abroad.

A brief explanation of the full coverage and organization of the text follows.

SECTION ONE: INTRODUCTION TO FASHION RETAILING

The emphasis is on such topics as organizational structuring, global retailing, consumer differences, research for problem solving and the role of social responsibility for retailers.

Chapter 1 The Nature of the Fashion Retailing Industry A historical and present-day look at retailing, offering the different classifications from brick-and-mortar to multi-channel.

Chapter 2 The Global Impact of Fashion Retailing Emphasis is on the present and future trends that are becoming the norm in the retail industry.

Chapter 3 Organizational Structures The reasons for needing a specific structure for both on-site and off-site retailers and the trends that have caused many to restructure their organizations.

Chapter 4 The Fashion Consumer An analysis that includes such concepts as consumer behavior and social class groupings. Also provided is how to reach the multicultural shopper.

Chapter 5 Retail Research Directions in Today's Retail Environment The complete research process is explored along with the areas in retailing that often warrant research.

Chapter 6 Ethical Practices and Social Responsibility by Retailers Discussed are the importance of ethics and how social responsibility is taking the lead in many retail operations. Included are such topics as sustainable fashion and eco-friendliness.

SECTION TWO: THE FASHION RETAILER'S ENVIRONMENTS

Emphasized is the classification of shopping districts and the factors that are considered for choosing an appropriate specific site, the designing of brick-and-mortar environments, and the role visual merchandising plays.

Chapter 7 On-Site and Off-Site Locations Choosing the brick-and-mortar locations and off-site locations, the considerations for occupancy, and designing the store's premises.

Chapter 8 Designing and Fixturing Brick-and-Mortar Premises Included are planning concepts, fashion department classifications and designs, and the decorative and functional materials used in their installation.

Chapter 9 The Importance of Visual Merchandising to Stores A complete analysis of window and interior visual presentations and the elements necessary to enhance the merchandise as well as the principles of design.

SECTION THREE: MANAGEMENT AND CONTROL

Coverage in this section begins with the many different roles played by the Human Resources Division and its importance to the retail organization, followed by merchandise distribution methodology and concluding with loss prevention techniques that are intended to bring shoplifting and employee theft to lower incidence.

Chapter 10 The Human Resources Division The many hats that those in human resources wear include recruitment, training, compensation methodology, employee benefits and dealing in the labor relations negotiations.

Chapter 11 Merchandise Distribution and Loss Prevention Examined are the various aspects of merchandise distribution that includes methods of getting the products from the receiving room to the selling floor, quantity and quality checking, and the significance of addressing reducing loss prevention.

SECTION FOUR: MERCHANDISING FASHION PRODUCTS

The manner in which buyers plan their purchases both at home and abroad are thoroughly discussed and includes in-house preparation and outside assistance. Also carefully covered is the significance of private labels and brands, and the manner in which retail prices are determined.

Chapter 12 Planning and Executing the Purchase Included are the various responsibilities that buyers have that include a wealth of different aspects of their jobs.

Chapter 13 Purchasing in the Global Marketplace Featured are the domestic and off-shore markets. The importance of timing the purchase, where in the marketplace orders are written, and the actual writing of the orders are examined.

Chapter 14 Private Label Importance to the Merchandise Mix The different advantages that national brands and private brands offer by using each classification in the retailer's merchandise mix.

Chapter 15 Inventory Pricing Emphasis centers on the pricing considerations that retailers address before making their decisions, and the mathematical concepts of pricing.

SECTION FIVE: COMMUNICATING WITH AND SERVICING THE FASHION CLIENTELE

Advertising's importance to fashion retailers, promotional programs that they utilize, and the publicity they often achieve that all lead to better customer communication are covered. Also featured are today's trends in customer communication.

Chapter 16 The Importance of Advertising and Promotion The emphasis of this chapter is on advertising's approach to motivating shoppers to buy, the various promotional programs that could motivate shoppers to come to the store, and the positive publicity the retailer tries to achieve.

Chapter 17 Communicating to Customers through Electronic Media In this totally new addition to the book, it is shown how retailers are using social media, text messaging, in-store digital signage and blogs to reach their customers. Also featured are the trends in electronic media that are starting to play significant roles in the retailing playing field.

Chapter 18 Servicing the Fashion Shopper With personal selling still a very important service that retailers use to improve sales, beginning with a perfected sales presentation and offering other services in stores and off-site can also contribute to more sales.

A new feature for this edition is *Happening Now*, a chapter-by-chapter offering that examines up-to-the-minute snapshots of the latest in the fashion retailing arena that are making headlines in the trade papers, editorial press columns, trade association news, and the like. It is an exciting way for readers to keep abreast of the present-day industry.

They are all present-oriented making them one way to glimpse into the marketplace. Some of the companies discussed in these happenings include Uniqlo, a Japan-based retailing giant; Zara, a major Spanish retailer with hundreds of stores all over the world; and Massimo Dutti, which delivers fashion merchandise to worldwide retail outlets, and others of equal importance.

Maintained from the previous edition are such pedagogical tools as chapter highlights, terms of the trade, discussion questions, case problems, and exercises and projects.

Complete new artwork and ancillary materials such as an instructor's manual, computerized test bank, and a PowerPoint presentation are also available.

acknowledgments

The third edition of this text was written with the assistance of numerous professionals in the field of retailing, advisory consultants, and the major blogs that are becoming more and more important to the industry.

They include The Doneger Group; Carol Milano, Blogging for Retailers; Brad Tuttle, Time Inc.; Bill Loller, V.P. at IBM Smarter Conference; adweek.com; Kristina Datta, CBRE; mashable.com; CloudTags; Zara; Massimo Dutti, USA; Uniqlo; Allan Ellinger, MMG; Amy Meadows; Rootstein Mannequins; H&M; www.mymarket researchmethods.com; U.S. Bureau of Labor Statistics; Mike Ullman, J. C. Penney; Ken Doctor, industry analyst; WWD Digital Forums; Association of Image Consultants International.

In addition the authors would like to thank the reviewers of this edition for their numerous suggestions: Kate Campbell, The Art Institute of Tampa; Julie Crawley, The New England Institute of Art; Diane Ellis, Meredith College; Priscilla Fong, City College, C.U.N.Y.; Andrea Kolasinski Marcinkus, The Illinois Institute of Art—Schaumburg; Derry Law, Hong Kong Polytechnic University; Robert Ogilvie, Yorkville University; Joy H. Royal, Art Institute of Atlanta.

dedication

To the Special Six
Alex, Michael, Matthew, Amanda, Abby, and Sophia

chapter one

THE NATURE OF THE FASHION RETAILING INDUSTRY

After reading this chapter, you should be able to:

- Explain the differences between specialty retailers and department stores.

- Discuss why some merchants are opting for expansion through the spin-off store concept.

- Describe the differences between off-price retailing and discounting.

- Explain how some fashion organizations have expanded their companies without making their own investments.

- Assess the state of globalization for fashion retailers.

- Examine multi-channel retailing and identify its components.

- Describe the status of e-tailing as a tool to attract consumers.

- Explain why some consumers are flocking to catalog usage instead of brick-and-mortar visitation for their purchases.

- Determine the impact of the home shopping channels.

- Summarize some of the trends in fashion retailing.

Fashion merchants all over the world have made dramatic moves by extending their consumer reach far beyond their borders. When one looks at today's fashion retailing news it very often speaks of the changes, namely conducting business globally. Their quest for international expansion has motivated many of these businesses, in most parts of the world, to plan their growth into markets that were once considered poor company strategy. Now that many fashion arenas have proven themselves as destinations for offshore fashion retailers, merchandise assortments and emerging markets have started to join these lists of countries, the scene promises to become an exciting one and an opportunity for merchants to reach new markets.

An analysis and historical overview of the retailers who sold fashion goods to consumers actually began with the introduction of the **limited line store** also known later on as the **specialty store**. It was the late 1880s when manufactured merchandise became available to the average citizen, only the wealthy could afford to have fashion items produced for them by designers and dressmakers. For those who had the skills of sewing, fabrics were sometimes purchased and turned into wearable clothing. The era of the specialty store paved the way for affordable fashion items that were within the means of the consumer. Its popularity grew quickly alongside the growth of manufactured goods.

The popularity of the specialty store grew. Some merchants were quick to spread their business to include more than one location, leading to the beginning of the **chain store organization**. Retailers began to open more and more units that primarily featured one item such as apparel, shoes, jewelry, and so forth. Today, the specialty chains are considered to be the most popular places for shopping. Companies like The Gap Stores, Inc., with its global presence, are among the more profitable enterprises in fashion retailing. With the success of the limited lines operations, some merchants decided if they could satisfy the needs of their consumers in this manner, it might be feasible and profitable to expand their merchandise offering to more than one classification. Some of the more successful of these retailers broadened their inventories to include a variety

figure 1.1
Macy's is the largest department store in the world. It carries hard goods and soft goods and both national products and private labels and brands.

of products under one roof. It was the birth of the **department store**. Like the specialty store, the department store was a huge success and expansion would take place with **branch** stores that were opened to make shopping easier for those who found it too difficult to patronize the main or **flagship store**, a term used today to signify the first store in the organization. Macy's was an early entry in the department store and still commands tremendous recognition by fashion consumers. Figure 1.1 features Macy's flagship store in New York City.

Some department stores also expanded their customer base with the development of catalog divisions. Early on it was Sears who offered catalogs to shoppers who couldn't come to their premises. Among the many products featured was fashion merchandise. It was an easy approach that quickly caught the attention of a new market segment and helped to make the company more profitable. It was the forerunner of what today is known as **multi-channel retailing** that will be fully discussed later in the text.

Other brick-and-mortar fashion retailing enterprises in operation today, in addition to the department stores and specialty chains include **discounters, off-pricers, manufacturer's outlets, boutiques, warehouse clubs, pop-up stores,** and a multitude of off-site classifications that include e-tailers, and numerous social media formats such as Facebook and Pinterest, email, television shopping networks, and mobile devices.

The trend in retailing is for the merchants to reach their customers and to increase their consumer base through a combination of many of the enterprises already noted. The concept is known as multi-channel retailing in which the vast majority of retailers reach their markets with the use of many different means. It is typical of the giants in the field to use a combination of brick-and-mortar locations, catalogs, **e-tailing**, social networking, and mobile devices to broaden their reach.

Each of those entities that have been introduced thus far will be fully discussed in the next section of the chapter, culminating with a section on the strengths of the multi-channel retailing concept.

AN ANALYSIS AND HISTORICAL OVERVIEW OF FASHION ORGANIZATIONS

With so many people to serve in the global marketplace, the majority of the major fashion merchants engage in a number of the different enterprises. Each serves a unique purpose to the organization. Some, although few, today concentrate on just one classification, **brick-and-mortar**, while others might just be online ventures. For example, one major retailer of fashion footwear, and now apparel, whose exclusive selling method is online is the American-based Zappos.

Brick and Mortar Operations

Although the online companies are continually gaining customer support, it is the brick-and-mortar operations that continually record the highest sales in retailing. Numerous reasons are cited for their success. Being able to see the merchandise and try it on in the stores, the feel of the products, comparison with other items, and the service that these stores offer.

Fashion Specialty Stores

The stores that are attracting shoppers in record numbers are the fashion specialty stores. These stores concentrate on apparel, home fashions, wearable accessories and one major product classification. Globally, this retail segment is spreading from the countries in which they originated. It is not unusual for specialty chains with a beginning in the United States to have a worldwide presence. Gap, for example has entered China with its namesake store and Banana Republic, a Gap member has entered France with an outlet in Paris.

The global expansion is not only for American retail organizations but also from others around the world. Inditex, for example, now the world's largest fashion organization, is based in Spain but has made significant inroads in fashion with two of its operations, Zara and Massimo Dutti. The former has become a global empire since its inception in Spain in 1975, and the latter has also taken international fashion centers by storm since its launch in 1985. Each has outlets in more than 50 countries around the world. The Zara group will be discussed under franchising later in the chapter since it has numerous franchisees. Other major fashion chains with a global base are Mango, with representation in more than 100 countries, and H&M with outlets present in more than 50 countries. Others with a global presence include The TJX Companies, Inc., with exposure in Canada, Germany, the U.K. and many other countries. Table 1.1 features the ten major global specialty chains in operation at the present time.

Table 1.1

THE TEN LEADING GLOBAL FASHION SPECIALTY CHAINS

Company	Country of Origin	Global Presence*
Wal-Mart Stores, Inc.	United States	Brazil, Canada, China, U.K.
ÆON Co., Ltd.	Japan	Canada, China, U.K., U.S.
Intermarché	France	Belgium, Portugal, Spain
El Cortes Inglés	Spain	Belgium, Greece, Mexico
The TJX Companies, Inc.	United States	Canada, Germany, U.K.
Inditex	Spain	Austria, Germany, U.S.
The Gap Stores, Inc.	United States	Canada, France, Japan
H & M Hennes & Mauritz AB	Sweden	Austria, China, U.S., U.K.
L Brands, Inc.	United States	Canada
Fast Retailing Co., Ltd.	Japan	Belgium, Hong Kong, U.S.

* This is only a small percentage of the countries that the companies market in, other than the country of origin.
Extracted from Top 250 Global Retailers, *Stores* Magazine.

In addition to the specialty store concept as we know it, some of those with significant success have entered into the **subspecialty store** arena. The Gap Stores, Inc., for example, has expanded with stores that appeal to a specific, smaller market. They now operate BabyGap, GapBody, GapMaternity, and GapKids.

Department Stores

The department store soon followed on the tails of the specialty organizations with their own concept. By carrying a large assortment of **hard goods** (furniture and appliances) and **soft goods** (clothing) under one roof, they made shopping easier and were able to accommodate shoppers under it. Those that follow this traditional merchandise approach are called **full-line department stores**. Macy's and Bloomingdale's in the United States, Harrods and Selfridges in the U.K., and Printemps and Galeries Lafayette in France are very popular full-line department stores. In addition to their flagship operations they have **branches** all over their countries of origin. The branches, smaller versions of the flagships, have spread to a variety of locations within their respective trading areas and have proven to be financial successes.

There has been some global expansion for some department stores. Their success, however, has not been positive. Galeries Lafayette tried but failed with their entry on New York City's Fifth Avenue, a fashion mecca. Printemps entered the Colorado arena but failed in a mere 16 months. J. C. Penney Company, Inc., American based, operates a store in Puerto Rico that is still in operation.

Even though the success rate for upscale fashion department stores has been dismal thus far, two American fashion emporiums are in the planning stages for global expansion. Bloomingdale's is headed for one Canadian unit, and Nordstrom, with a more ambitious endeavor, for four anticipated locations in Vancouver, Toronto, Ottawa, and Calgary.

In addition to full-line department stores, **specialized department stores**, those that specialize in some merchandise classifications, found their place in fashion retailing. Widely known stores of this nature such as Saks Fifth Avenue and Neiman Marcus opened stores of this classification and have expanded throughout the United States.

Another way in which the department store expands its brick-and-mortar footprint is with the **spin-off** startup. In lieu of opening full-fledged branches, the concept involves the dedication of one merchandise classification to a particular location. Oftentimes, department stores have full-line brick-and-mortar stores and spin-offs in the same city. Bloomingdale's, for example, operates a full-line department store in Chicago along with a spin-off that exclusively sells home furnishings in the same city. Similarly, the Bloomingdale's flagship in New York City, and a home furnishings spin-off in Greenwich Village, New York City are examples of this type of fashion retailing.

Couture and Designer Fashion Boutiques

For the upscale fashion consumer, more and more **marquee label** couturiers and designers are opening their own boutiques across the globe. They are internationally based and are reaping the benefits of their fashion recognition. This concept began about 20 years ago when the only way to purchase designer collections was in department stores. Given the continuing sales growth, these world fashion-leaders embarked upon opening their own brick-and-mortar outlets. Initially, their first stores were located in the countries in which they designed their collections. Soon after, **boutiques** bearing their names began to spring up all over the world. For example, as of this writing, Ralph Lauren, based in the United States, operates 388 stores around the world and Chanel, from its headquarters in France, is home to more than 300 units that are globally located. Others with international exposure include Armani, based in Italy, Louis Vuitton, headquartered in France, Vera Wang, based in the United States, Dolce & Gabbana, an Italian company, Roberto Cavalli, also based in Italy, and Donna Karan, an American organization. Figure 1.2 is a Giorgio Armani specialty store spin-off, Emporio Armani.

Their worldwide growth is attributed to international travel that brings attention to the brands, vast exposure from the Internet, and the need for couture-level products in the upper-class consumer base.

Off-Price Merchants

Relatively new as a brick-and-mortar entity, Frieda Loehmann, operating out of her home's bedroom in Brooklyn, New York in the early 1950s is generally credited with off-price merchandising. What has now become a major force in fashion retailing began with Frieda searching the garment center on Seventh Avenue for apparel that was available at less than the original wholesale prices. She offered cash to vendors, many of whom were anxious to rid themselves of unwanted goods. The overwhelming response to her collection led to the opening of a store. The rest is history.

Today, off-price retailing is a profitable mainstay in the field. While the United States is the leader in this type of merchandising, other countries such as the U.K., Ireland, Germany, and Poland operate under the TJX umbrella, a well-known retail conglomerate in Europe, and Canada boasts successful operations like Marshalls and Winners.

Products that bear such instantly recognizable labels as Calvin Klein, Ralph Lauren, and DKNY make up a good proportion of the off-price names.

Independent **off-pricers** and privately held **manufacturers' outlets** make up this retail classification. Stocking these privately held units is a matter of location. Manufacturers who are ready to dispose of slow-sellers, past season's merchandise that hadn't been sold, or overruns by manufacturers, use these outlets. The task for these merchants is to locate these products as soon as they are for sale at reduced wholesale

figure 1.2
Emporio Armani is a lower priced partner of the Giorgio Armani family of stores. It gets the name across to many who love the Armani label but have spending limitations.

prices so that they can get them on their shelves as quickly as possible. Many have established relationships with vendors who often contact them when closeouts become available. In this way they often have the pick of the lot. Some rely upon **market specialists** such as Henry Doneger Associates which maintains Price Point Buying, a division that specializes in off-price merchandise. Unlike the traditional fashion retailers who purchase in advance of a season to make certain they have the latest products, the off-pricers are **opportunistic purchasers** where price is the most important facet of their merchandise assortments.

More and more off-price facilities are owned and operated by fashion design manufacturers. High fashion producers that primarily appeal to the upper-middle class have joined the off-pricers in record numbers. They are generally grouped in **outlet centers** that are void of traditional retailers. Couture organizations such as Gucci, Chanel, Ralph Lauren, Donna Karan, Calvin Klein, and Louis Vuitton are among the companies that run their own retail outlets in the United States and in foreign countries. One of the better known of these global outlet centers is right outside of Florence, Italy where couture apparel is sold. In the United States, these outlet centers are across the nation. Two of the better-known operations are Fashion Outlet Malls, two of which are located in Las Vegas and the suburbs of Chicago, and Premium Malls with its main operation, Woodbury Commons in Woodbury, New York and Orlando, Florida.

Department Store Clearance Outlets

No matter how successful some department stores are, merchandising is extremely difficult. With the best planning tools, expert buyers and merchandisers, outside fashion organizations such as resident buying offices and impeccable record-keeping, the possibility of selling out a season's merchandise is improbable. Today, companies like Saks Fifth Avenue operate OFF 5TH discount centers across the United States, as does Neiman Marcus with its Last Call units and Nordstrom that operates Nordstrom Rack. While these outlets are dominant in the U.S., other countries have their share of them as well: Tanger Outlets in Canada, Aubonne Outlet Center in Switzerland, Quai des Marques in France, Barcelona Roca Village in Switzerland and Ashford Designer Outlet in England.

While these fashion organizations run end-of-season and periodic sales, they still cannot completely dispose of unwanted inventory. In order to make way for the next season's fashion silhouettes, they have opted to move merchandise, at greatly reduced prices, through their own outlet centers.

Warehouse Clubs

For those consumers who wish to buy household products in bulk at desirable prices, heading to **warehouse clubs** such as Costco, Sam's and B.J.'s are routine. They are, however, retail arenas that also stock fashion merchandise at prices that are generally far below similar goods at other companies. Marquee names such as Ralph Lauren and Tommy Hilfiger are featured in abundance alongside their own private brands. Some of the fashion items are closeouts purchased from the manufacturer, or specially made products are in stock that have been made to the warehouse club's directions.

The warehouse club is a unique component of the retail industry in that membership is required from shoppers. While it started in the United States, it continues to spread to other countries. One of the leaders in international warehousing is PriceSmart, based in the United States. It also has numerous locations in Honduras, the Caribbean, Panama, Costa Rica, Trinidad, and Guatemala to name a few.

Discount Operations

Companies like Target and Wal-Mart are exemplary of the **discounters**. Their goal is to reach the mass markets with fashion and other merchandise in significant numbers. Once primarily selling lesser-known brands at affordable price points, in the last five years they have entered a new fashion arena with designer-label brands that are exclusive for their use. The second largest American discounter is Target. The regular addition of new units has given them significant recognition in the United States and Canada, where they presently operate more than 100 stores in the provinces. Adding great excitement to their **merchandise mix** is the addition of high fashion designer labels that are exclusive for their use. Names like Alexander McQueen, who died in 2010, created a collection for Target as did Proenza Schouler in 2007 or Rodarte in 2009. The designer collaborations have continuously grown. Names like Marc Jacobs, Tory Burch, Diane von Furstenberg, and Jason Wu—among others—have met with great success.

Sales records indicate that discounters continue to be a favorite among consumers. Their impact in the fashion industry suggests that this retail classification will continue to grow. With more and more of these discounters entering into exclusive contractual arrangements, it indicates that the fashion industry that produces the goods is realizing a new venue for profitmaking. Known to be timely reliable payers, the major discounters such as Target and Kohl's have helped design operations and manufacturers to make it easier for their companies to turn a profit. Also joining the bandwagon for marquee designers, Kohl's has joined forces with such fashion stalwarts as Narciso Rodriguez and Derek Lam.

Not strictly a discount operation, but a value merchant and one that also offers couture designed fashion merchandise at affordable prices is Sweden-based H&M. With 2,900 stores all across the globe at this time, the company has been a leader in the acquisition of labels that once were only available in luxury boutiques. Through negotiated contracts with designers such as Karl Lagerfeld, the first of many to come since 2004, others have been Jimmy Choo, Anna Dello Russo, Stella McCartney, Versace, and the latest entry Isabel Marant.

As part of the H&M expansion, the company became a multi-channel operation in the United States in 2013 much like the company's European models. In the section later in this chapter titled "Multi-Channel Retailing," this H&M expansion, just announced at the time of this writing, will be discussed in the *Happening Now* feature on page 13.

Franchises

Names like McDonald's and Burger King are immediately recognizable by most consumers as reliable fast-food companies. What few know is that the fashion retail industry also follows that concept, except it's fashion not food. The franchiser owns the right to offer franchisees "a piece of the pie" for an initial startup fee, and subsequent payments based upon such factors as merchandise acquired from the company, profitability, and others that vary from franchiser to franchiser.

While such arrangements have been successful in fashion retailing, many have not. Benetton, for example was the hottest franchiser when it began in Italy in 1965; its expansion into the United States in the 1970s was an unparalleled success. With growth in the U.S. and other countries reaching 6,500 stores, the operation was hailed as a model franchise until its collapse began. Today it is trying to resurrect the fashion image it once held and gain profitability. Time will tell if it can iron out the problems that caused its demise. Others have reached millions of consumers across the globe with franchised operations. Zara, a vertically integrated company based in Spain, expands through self-ownership and franchising. It enjoys a total of approximately 850 stores internationally, with a vast number in the United States, making it one of the faster growing, successful organizations. With its motto "High Fashion At An Affordable Price," it is able to produce a significant number of designs and bring them to the stores in two weeks, a business model that is capable of bringing the goods to the stores much faster than any other group. With fashion such a constantly changing business, the timeliness of this approach allows for a constant flow of new styles, an ideal situation for fashion merchandise.

Another very successful franchised operation is also based in Spain. Mango has approximately 1,300 stores in 91 countries, and by 2019 it expects to have 5,200 stores according to an article in *Women's Wear Daily* (*WWD*), June 23, 2013. Sales expectancy is $5.85 billion or 4.5 billion euros by then. Its franchise concept offers individuals a "ready-to-go" business with experts in merchandising, display, management and everything it takes for a successful operation. Their ultimate goal is to be "present in every city in the world." Like other franchisers, the company designs the products, manufactures them and markets the entire line. The store interiors are carefully designed, each with similar dimensions, to make it possible for image and product display so that shoppers can enjoy their shopping experience. With access to corporate service, training, and logistical expertise, the franchise, according to management, usually turns profit by the end of the first year. Table 1.2 features some of the fashion **franchises** now in operation.

Pop-Up Shops

These new retail operations are temporary outlets that have been growing in significant numbers. They are popping up in so many different kinds of places with each day revealing yet another type of location. Even some major retailers with permanent stores have entered the pop-up world of retailing. Target, for example, has taken temporary facilities in neighborhoods, malls, and on college campuses to sell clothing and other items to college students. Other big brands to use **pop-up shops** are Levi's, Adidas, and Gap.

The success of these outlets has been continuously growing according to IBIS World, a research firm that reported that the number of pop-up stores have increased 16 percent from 2,043 in 2009 to 2,380 in 2012. Some of the reasons for their success are low rent, a short-term commitment rather than the signing of long leases, and being places where brands can test-market their products. In addition to the storefront is the

Table 1.2		
FASHION APPAREL AND ACCESSORIES FRANCHISES[a]		
Company	Products	Startup Costs[b]
Bijoux Terner, LLC	Fashion accessories	233–494
Clothes Mentor	Women's resale fashion	155–239
fab'rik Boutique, Inc.	Women's clothing	120–200
Mainstream Fashions, Inc.	Women's fashions	43–129
Mode®	Designer apparel	108–139

[a] Extracted from www.entrepreneur.com/franchises/categories/rtapp.html#
[b] Costs given in thousands of dollars.

shipping container. Huge containers have been seen to feature merchandise in highly trafficked areas. This is an easy concept since the containers can be closed up and moved elsewhere. Old buses, no longer in service have also been used, having the advantage of being easy to drive to another spot and start all over again.

Off-Site Retailing

Change has been taking place in global retailing with the advent of numerous forms of off-site entries. Some are very old, as old as the early giant merchants such as Sears whose catalog dates back to the 1800s. Others such as e-commerce or e-tailing are relatively new for fashion merchants with most of the copy concentrating on company sales, special promotions, or short-term offerings. Other off-site ventures include social media such as Facebook and Pinterest, mobile devices, sites such as eBay which are engaged in fashion items in addition to a variety of other products, and television programming such as QVC and HSN.

Catalogs

The granddaddy of off-site retailing is the printed catalog. As briefly referred to earlier in the chapter, Sears used this device to reach shoppers who were either too far from their stores or didn't have the time to make the visit. Throughout the years the printed catalog had its ups and downs. According to the Direct Marketing Association more than 12.5 billion catalogs were sent to U.S. households in 2013 with the success rate of approximately 29 percent making purchases. Restoration Hardware, the fashion home products retailer, featured a catalog that was 992 pages long in its last edition. Figures like these indicate that consumers are still interested in paper catalogs.

Also prominent in reaching the shopper, the production of digital catalogs continues to grow. Shoppers of all ages are making use of digital catalogs with women in the 35–44 age group driving this trend. Figure 1.3 features catalog users.

There are different retailer classifications that use catalogs to reach shoppers. Catalog-only retailers such as Horchow and Lillian Vernon that offer a variety of fashion merchandise, and brick-and-mortar catalog divisions such as those featured by Macy's and Bloomingdale's that not only sell merchandise by mail, email, and hard-copy catalogs but also use them as incentives to attract shoppers to their stores. Some of the benefits to consumers of catalog purchasing include:

- The convenience of shopping without having to leave the confines of the home.
- The availability of seeing and purchasing some merchandise that isn't available at the brick-and-mortars such as Restoration Hardware and Pottery Barn where many bulk items are for purchase only through their catalogs.
- Quality color reproduction that lends reality to the merchandise.
- Returns are simplified with most catalog purchases returnable for full credit and free-of-charge shipping.
- The ability to speak with a representative to get further information about the goods.

figure 1.3
Two women looking through a fashion catalog. This off-site retail division enables people with little time to shop to make purchases in the comfort of their home or anywhere they choose.

E-tailing

Selling on the Internet has become a staple in fashion merchandising and sales. Most major retailers have online departments or divisions with France's Printemps, Canada's Holt Renfrew, and Russia's GUM opting out of selling in this manner according to a survey by New York University's think tank Luxury Lab in July 2013. Aside from the traditional retailers such as department stores and specialty chains, some companies have impacted the retail scene with online only operations. Companies that subscribe to this method of reaching the consumer are featured in Table 1.3. Some are major organizations with recognizable names and others are just making their way in the field. Those listed have some fashion merchandise in their offerings while other are exclusively fashion operations.

Table 1.3

ONLINE ONLY RETAILING	
Company	Product Mix
Amazon.com	Assorted merchandise classifications
eBay.com	Most every classification including fashion
Bluefly.com	Off-price couture and designer fashion
Overstock.com	Overruns of fashion merchandise
Zappos.com	Fashion shoes and apparel
Tobi.com	Trendy affordable fashion
GoJane.com	Fashion forward styles
Nastygal.com	New and vintage fashion
ASOS.com	U.K. company featuring trendy clothing
Threadsence.com	Trendy fashion

There are numerous reasons for the success of Internet sites. Among those that bring shoppers to the website are:

- Global reach is a major factor in this form of retailing. People in remote places throughout the world with online capability can shop for merchandise that they wouldn't otherwise be able to reach.
- Assortments are generally more plentiful since warehousing, rather than brick-and-mortar with limited space, can generally offer greater product diversity.
- Having found a particular style or company to purchase from, they can be reached either through particular Web sites or search engines that lead to a vast number of choices.
- Unlike traditional catalogs that infrequently change their offerings, the e-tailer can quickly change the Web site when merchandise is no longer available, when new items become part of the company inventory, and so forth.

Social Networking

The statistics alone show the worth of **social networking** to retailers according to Mediabistro. In 2012 ad revenues were $7.72 billion, increasing to $10.24 billion in 2013 and ultimately reaching an estimated $11.87 billion in 2014. The goals include raising brand awareness, and product sales. Table 1.4 features the top ten most popular social networking sites.

Table 1.4

THE TOP TEN MOST POPULAR SOCIAL NETWORKING SITES*	
Site	Monthly Visitors
1 - Facebook	750,000,000
2 - Twitter	250,000,000
3 - Linkedin	110,000,000
4 - Pinterest	85,000,000
5 - Myspace	70,500,000
6 - Google Plus	65,000,000
7 - deviantART	25,500,000
8 - LiveJournal	20,500,000
9 - Tagged	19,500,000
10 - orkut	17,500,000

* Extracted from Top 15 Most Popular Social Networking Sites, August 13, 2013, eBizMBA.com.

Figure 1.4 shows a young woman checking her facebook pages.

Social networking attracts millions of consumers. The ads that are placed on such networks as Facebook and Twitter are targeted to specific demographics and interests that often turn into sales. According to L2 Think Tank, retailers are gaining an increase in sales through search engines and direct web browsing. In the U.K. social shopping is expected to grow by 44 percent in 2014. For the fashion luxury retailer, the use is exploding. Social networking's latest applications allow for two-way communication, for customers to give their opinions on products, which has enabled retailers of this nature to make better decisions. At Zappos, the fashion shoe organization that also retails other fashion products, a third of its associates are employed on its Twitter account each day. The prescreening of new styles that are considered ready for the market is often used before actual selling is attempted.

Finally, while many have signaled eventual death to the brick-and-mortars, a large number of retailers have reported in a KPMG report that retail brick-and-mortars have increased foot traffic by embracing social media marketing.

Email

Many industry professionals conclude that the use of **email selling** has increased their sales volume. It is a fact that consumer households receive as many as 20 retail-oriented emails a day. Marketwired.com reports that 89 percent of respondents at least occasionally click through to a retail site after reading an email or visit the store immediately after reading the message. Fashion retailers, among numerous others such as Nordstrom, KateSpade.com, J.Jill, Saks Fifth Avenue OFF 5TH and Brooks Brothers make regular use of e-tailing to reach customers. They obtain email addresses from in-store visits, online purchases, and so forth. It gives them a continuous communication outlet to keep the name of the company in the shopper's mind. In Figure 1.5 is Gap, a major user of email to reach customers.

figure 1.4
Facebook user checking her account's pages on the beach. Wherever the user goes, and no matter the time of day, Facebook is always there to keep her abreast of anything new that is being offered by retailers.

The content most always is expected to pique the shopper's interest. For example, a **flash sale** has very limited time, perhaps a few hours or a day, for customer action. Special promotions, discounted pricing, etc. are typically used in flash sales.

Television Shopping Networks

The retail phenomenon that allows for purchasing from television viewing continues to grow. The major players are QVC and HSN, providing round the clock offerings for viewers. The two shows had approximately $10,000,000 in combined sales in 2012. For QVC, as reported by their management, jewelry accounts for between 25 percent and 30 percent of its sales. The number of households that watch the programming range from 12–16 million any time of the day.

Multi-Channel Retailing

Today's fashion retailing picture is far different from what we once knew. Not too long ago, as we studied early in the chapter, merchants chose one format to sell to their customers. It was the in-house ventures such as department stores and specialty shops that led the way, followed by the other on-site operations that we examined.

It is a totally different playing field that fashion merchants now negotiate to reach their customer bases and to attract new shoppers to their companies. Except for a few holdouts such as the aforementioned France's Printemps, it has become commonplace to utilize the multi-channel approach. Different variations are employed to maximize increased sales volume. Some have separate divisions or departments handling the tasks for each channel, others using their traditional methodology, such as relying on brick-and-mortar to fulfill their multi-channel needs, or something inbetween. It has steadily moved in the direction of separate management and merchandising for major fashion retailers. That is, in the area of buying and merchandising, there are often separate teams that purchase the merchandise for each channel. Those fully engaged in the multi-channel approach will break down the tasks for those involved in brick-and-mortar, e-commerce, catalogs, etc. H&M, a global chain, has just announced its entry into multi-channel retailing in the United States.

THE EXPANSION OF H&M AS A GLOBAL RETAILER

In August 2013, the Sweden-based retailer announced that it will soon be embarking on a U.S. e-commerce program. While its multi-channel approach is not new to the company, it will be a first for it in the United States. Since its arrival in America in 2000, it has branched out all across the country with brick-and-mortar stores. Thirty-two regions including New York, New York City; Massachusetts, Boston; Louisiana, New Orleans; and Washington D.C.'s Georgetown, among others, have H&M representation.

Included in the expansion are a mobile app, e-commerce site, brick-and-mortar stores and a catalog. Expectancy from management indicates that the four channels will reach 300,000,000 people in the United States. Not divulging sales projections, but stating "for sure online will be the biggest store. It has huge potential." They will offer American online shoppers the first glimpse of the Paris Show, a semi-annual presentation. The Paris Show is a trendier collection than H&M's main line, similar to their designer collaborations. The e-commerce site offers more colors and sizes than the stores.

Brick-and-mortar expansion will be an integral part of this new approach to retailing. They plan to open its largest store in the world, a six-level 57,000 square foot flagship on New York City's Fifth Avenue and a 42,500 square foot unit in Times Square, New York City as part of its new multi-channel endeavor.

TRENDS IN ON-SITE AND OFF-SITE FASHION RETAILING

There are indications from trade papers such as *WWD*, the editorial press, fashion organizations like market consultants (also known as **resident buying offices**) such as Henry Doneger Associates, and so forth that many changes are on the way for both the brick-and-mortar stores and the wealth of off-site ventures that are already in operation. Some of those include:

1. A continuation of globalization for fashion retailers based around the world. It may be the opening of brick-and-mortar stores in places far off from their flagships and a number of different off-site operations such as e-commerce, mobile device selling, etc. At this time, and for the future, Lands' End is bullish on its global business and is reaching out to more countries, and The Gap Stores, Inc. is growing its European base. The expansion plans are for Europe, Latin America, Asia, and Australia.

2. The use of **joint ventures** to enter the overseas markets. This partnership arrangement enables the company to obtain some of the money needed to expand, familiarize themselves with the nuances of doing business in countries other than their own, and so forth. Global expansion often requires the joint venture approach since some countries do not permit foreigners to open privately held companies.

3. It is expected that pop-up stores "will sprout like weeds" according to The Zimmerman Blog research. It will not only be the boutiques but some major retailers will inhabit these types of premises for short-lived periods such as before back-to-school or Black Friday that has turned into more than one shopping day.

4. Haute Wheels will be at the forefront of small fashion retail operations. The use of old trucks to move from one potentially hot spot to another has already shown

some success. Taking their cues from the ever-popular food trucks, they are currently in use in New York City, Boston, and Los Angeles. Other mobile sales emporiums are destined for entry in all the major cities in the United States. These **boutiques on wheels** have limited space and can only serve a few shoppers at a time, giving individual personalized service.

5. The E-Mall is showing signs of expansion and is expected to grow in the near future. It will be a social shopping experience: people can go to shopping sites where stylish goods are compiled from shops around the web, and shopping can be shared with friends, a very important part of brick-and-mortar purchasing. These sites, according to Jenna Wortham, founder and C.E.O. of Wanelo are somewhat like bazaars where people can browse at their leisure. Sites such as Polyvore, Fancy, and Fab are already online. Shoppers who have joined free-of-charge can peruse merchandise from all over the web. The sites generally tell the friends of someone online what she is seeing with the click of a button. A few can then look at the goods and give their opinions. It is much like the groups of young women who frequent traditional malls.

6. Spin-off stores have started to make an impact on fashion retailers. Saks Fifth Avenue already has a few in operation that occupy much less space than its traditional stores. Another that has had success with spin-offs has been Bloomingdale's with small units in SoHo, New York City and in Chicago in the landmark Medinah Temple where they only feature fashion furnishings. In addition to department stores, chain store organizations are joining this trend. Some include Target, Kohl's, and Gap who maintain their original names. Others have opted for new marquees such as Gymboree that now operates Crazy 8 and G by Guess from the parent Guess. H&M's spin-off is a digital entry called "& Other Stories" which is in ten European countries at the time of this writing.

Chapter Highlights

1. More and more fashion retailers are expanding their operations with use of digital social networking such as Facebook and Pinterest. Mobile devices are now bringing in additional sales to retailers.

2. Fashion retailers are joining the concepts of Saks Fifth Avenue and Bloomingdale's with the opening of spin-off stores. Target, Kohl's, and Gap have followed suit with the latest entries being Crazy 8 by Gymboree and G by Guess. In Europe, H&M is spinning off a digital division called "& Other Stories."

3. Global expansion is not only for U.S. companies but also for foreign retailer fashion operations. Inditex, a major Spanish fashion organization continues to expand its presence with such retailers as Zara and Massimo Dutti all over the world, with the U.S. as one of its major expansion countries.

4. "Online only" merchants continue to broaden their fashion merchandise assortments. Zappos, best known for its shoe inventory, has added apparel and other accessories to its roster as has Amazon.com with its expansion to include fashion merchandise. Those in the off-price online classification such as Bluefly.com will continue their presence in selling to consumers.

5. Social media such as Facebook and Twitter will continue to gain importance in advertising fashion items to consumers.

6. Television shopping networks such as QVC and HSN have made a significant impact on viewers in search of fashion items. Jewelry continues to be the major product featured on these channels.

7. Multi-channel retailing has become a surefire approach for retailers to generate more business. Except for a very few major companies, selling in this manner enables the merchants to reach shoppers that they otherwise would not be able to.

8. H&M, the Sweden-based fashion retailer has expanded its reach in the United States with an e-commerce division. Up until the time of this writing, the company reached Americans exclusively through its brick-and-mortar outlets.

Terms of the Trade

boutiques	manufacturer's outlets
boutiques on wheels	market specialists
branches	marquee labels
brick-and-mortar operations	merchandise mix
chain store organizations	multi-channel retailing
couture boutiques	off-pricers
department stores	online only companies
designer boutiques	opportunistic purchasing
discounters	outlet center
email selling	pop-up shops
e-tailing	resident buying offices
flagship	social media
flash sales	soft goods
franchises	specialized department stores
full-line department stores	specialty stores
hard goods	spin-off stores
joint ventures	subspecialty stores
limited line stores	warehouse clubs

For Discussion

1. How did the department store distinguish itself from the specialty or limited line store?

2. In what way did the specialty store expand throughout the United States to become one of the more important fashion retail classifications?

3. How are department store branches different from their spin-off operations?

4. Who is credited with originating off-price retailing, and why is this technique of doing business called off-price?

5. How are discount operations different than off-pricers?

6. What are pop-up shops and why have merchants resorted to their use?

7. By what means have companies like Sweden-based H&M upgraded their fashion image?

8. What is the difference between catalog-only retailers and department store catalog operations?

9. Why have some fashion operations expanded through the franchising arrangement rather than relying on company-owned stores?

10. Instead of expanding globally with wholly owned operations, what is a major reason for partnering in joint ventures?

11. What are some of the reasons for the continued growth of catalog shopping?

12. What is a flash sale?

13. What are some of the outlets used in multi-channel retailing?

14. Give some reasons for the success of online only retailing.

15. What is social networking and how has it increased retail sales?

Case Problem

Questions

1. Do you think Sanborns should follow its usual approach and hope for better times?
2. Might there be some changes to its methods of reaching more shoppers? How?

Sanborns is a major department store that had its roots established in 1920. It never reached the size and scope of the better-known department stores in the United States, but it admirably served its clientele in Nebraska with its flagship and 18 branches in its trading area. Being a traditionally organized department store with conservative concepts at the core of its existence, Sanborns has confined its operation to brick-and-mortar stores. Until last year sales were brisk but eventually started to decline. For the company, a privately held organization, with no dependence on the whims of shareholders that often takes place in public corporations, solving the problem lies primarily with C.E.O. John Sanborn, C.F.O. Casey Sanders, and company president, Rick Pauley.

The objective of the company is to reverse its downslide and to return to the position of profitability it enjoyed. Some of the conditions that might have affected Sanborns include:

- The opening of an off-price retail operation that is close to the flagship and that offers prices that are lower than Sanborns.
- Many stores of a competitive nature are using expanded catalogs to reach Sanborns' customer base.
- More and more of its shoppers have returned to the workplace and do not have the time they once spent for shopping.
- Some of its departments, particularly appliances, have had to compete with a discount operation in its proximity.

At the present time, the company has yet to decide upon a course of action to bring Sanborns' profitability up to that of its more productive years.

Exercises and Projects

1. Visit, write to, or use the Internet to compare a major department store with a
   major off-pricer to determine their differences and/or similarities in their operations
   for the following area:

	Department Store	*Off-Pricer*
Merchandise assortment		
Services offered		
Sales assistance		
Visual presentation		
Price points		

chapter two

THE GLOBAL IMPACT OF FASHION RETAILING

After reading this chapter, you should be able to:

- Establish how retailers from all over the world are expanding globally.

- Explain how retail globalization is curtailing local competition.

- Assess how mobile usage will expand retail sales.

- Discuss the global expansion of retailers that are based in France and the U.K.

- Differentiate between the three types of expansion methods for retailers pursuing overseas markets.

Many of today's fashion retailers are expanding their customer reach to places they never before considered to be viable options. Typically, the focus of most merchants was their brick-and-mortar operations, with some using catalogs as an alternate method of doing business. Since walk-ins were their primary focus, they used a variety of techniques to capture the browsers and those ready to shop. Visual merchandising was a mainstay with store windows regularly "dressed" to bring excitement to what would be seen inside the store. Of course, as we will learn in a later chapter, visual merchandise is still many retailers' priority, but the emphasis has somewhat changed.

The advent of the Internet and the enormous growth of social media have made retailers broaden their horizons and explore globalization as a means of attracting shoppers who may have never visited their stores. The reach has proven to be what many agree was once impossible. Now, countries all over the world can be introduced to a company that is several thousand miles away from the store's home base.

Opening units all over the world continues to be "smart retailing" so that those not attracted to the off-site components can make their treks to the brick-and-mortar facilities.

Today, without globalization considerations, many retailers are missing the boat and are finding that their profitability isn't maximized.

PRESENT AND FUTURE TRENDS

At the time of this writing, and in the future, fashion retailers will have more and more options to pursue in their global planning. Practically not a day goes by when one technique or another is showing promise in globalization. Although global reach is not an entirely new concept, its present interest is far beyond what has already taken place. Some of the trends provide significant potential growth for the retail operation. They include the following:

The Gaining of International Prominence

Europe has steadily been pursued by American retailers as has the United States by the Europeans. Gap, for example, has made significant gains in reaching most of the European countries. Likewise, companies such as Topshop, a British organization, has entered many offshore countries, the U.S. being one of them, and have gained **international prominence**.

Today, and for the future, the trend is for retailers to enter new markets like Asia Pacific, Africa, and South America. Many of these are emerging markets for international fashion merchants to fill the present void. It is especially looking to market upscale fashion to these countries. According to recent research from Accenture that produces the Accenture Globalization Index, retailers from around the world entered 25 new markets in 22 countries in 2013. The trend is expected to continue due to the competition retailers face in their home markets. These emerging markets include Indonesia, Kazakhstan, Malaysia, Pakistan, and Thailand. Luxury brands are the ones that most often take the first action of globalization. They seek out locales where there are affluent consumers, like Russia, where there is enormous growth in high net worth individuals. Retailers like Ralph Lauren continue to invade such arenas and benefit from the exposure.

Curtailing the Problem of Local Competition

In today's global landscape merchants of all sizes and classifications are facing the realities of competition. It might be a traditional specialty chain that has lost revenue due to the competitive nature of an off-pricer that has taken residence in the trading area. Trying to compete with lower prices rarely helps to solve this type of situation. Eliminating many of the product lines that the competitor merchandises often leads to turning away from marquee brands that gave the store its reputation. Developing private brands to entice the clientele with more exclusivity is an approach taken to differentiate the inventory from the competitor. Figure 2.1 shows three designers collaborating on private label merchandise.

figure 2.1
Some designers specialize in creating private label merchandise. Fashion designers often work as a group to discuss the advantages and disadvantages of potential new additions to the private label merchandise mix. This merchandise helps the retailer to establish a merchandise mix that is different from the competition.

To Generate Greater Sales Volume Through Multi-Channel Strategies

Every retailer's goal is to maximize profits for its organization. Remaining a "local" retailer with an operation that only offers sales outlets that have limited geographical appeal can lead to the inevitability of stagnant sales. For those major retailers with brick-and-mortar stores as their main method of conducting business, the finding of new locations that provide excellent consumer markets is very rare. These companies already have the best locations for their stores. The Gap Stores, Inc., for example, already has units in just about every prime location. A department store such as Macy's already boasts more than 800 locations in the United States with little potential for locating some new units in the U.S.

The use of a comprehensive multi-channel plan is a major approach to the increase of sales. Except for very few major retailers this is the expansion direction they are taking and are expected to continue with this endeavor. According to Deloitte, in a *Stores* magazine article in its January 2012 issue, the multi-channel strategy planning "will become more important than ever."

Customization of the Merchandise Mixes

To carry the same-old-same-old product assortments, especially in fashion, has already proven to be the downfall of many fashion retailers. Today, merchants are using different research techniques to study their inventories to learn of fast and slow sellers. More than ever it has become a merchandising necessity to improve performance. What many chain store organizations are finding is that they cannot rely upon the same product offerings for all of their units. They will continue to study the local consumers in their different trading areas to evaluate their wants and needs and will customize their product lines to fit each trading area.

Mobile Usage Will Become a Very Important Component of Multi-Channel Retailing

The introduction of the iPhone has generated sales rarely ever seen before for a product. According to the research division of Deloitte, a significant number of shoppers have yet to reach their shopping age. This untapped market will continue to grow and attract those in the 18–24 age bracket. In addition to the expected new-user market, mobile consumers are in most age categories. In order to maximize profits from the mobile users they must carefully plan presentations to make certain they understand the "apps", and make certain that usage will not affect privacy. Figure 2.2 shows a smart phone user.

Growth of the "Mobile" Retail Shops

As was referred to in the first chapter, pop-up-shops have seen significant growth. As part of this "catch-all" concept, the one that is reaching new heights is the mobile fashion truck. The introduction was on the West Coast of the United States where some young entrepreneurs took a cue from the taco and barbecue trucks that attracted hordes to their vehicles. Many small retailers who merchandised "niche" items, borrowed the concept and tailored it to their own needs. The increase in this type of venture has surpassed what was once thought of as a temporary retailing arena. Today the craze has spread to cities like Nashville, Portland, and Annapolis.

figure 2.2
Mobile users generate sales rarely ever seen. It allows them to make purchases from any location wherever it is, such as the office, in transit, or at home.

One of the outcomes of the mobile retail shop is the formation of the American Mobile Retail Association that has more than 60 members. From their reporting, the concept is expected to realize significant growth.

Consignment Website Growth

What was once an industry that most consumers frowned upon has become an important player in retailing. Pre-worn items would be resold in stores. Now and in the future, this sector has become one of, and will remain one of, the fastest growing in e-commerce according to Rachel Strugatz in a *WWD* article on Tuesday, March 5, 2013. In 2008 there wasn't a demand for pre-owned upscale and couture fashion, but today that has all changed. Digital marketing consultant Macala Wright reports that people will spend thousands for these items. Oftentimes, the representatives from such consignment websites as Material Wrld, Vaunte, and Closet Rich will call upon a potential consignor to meet at her home to select from the merchandise that will be shown on an e-commerce platform.

Growth of Sustainable Fashion

Throughout print and other media there has been a growing concern for the protection of the environment. The "green movement" continues to escalate as more and more consumers are willing to take a new look at clothing and are purchasing products that deliver sustainability. Companies like Patagonia that manufacture and sell their products in their own stores have been setting the standard for environment protection.

The topic is so significant for retailers that it will be further discussed in Chapter 6, Ethical Practices and Social Responsibility by Retailers.

TODAY'S MAJOR GLOBAL CENTERS FOR FASHION RETAILING

All around the world fashion retailers are placing more emphasis than ever before on having a presence in the major fashion retailing countries and cities. With globalization moving briskly along, some of the once-leading merchants in this arena have moved out of the top 20 locales where expansion is still taking place. Among the more notable cities in the United States are New York City and Los Angeles according to CBRE, a real estate global research and consulting organization. Annually it provides detailed information on globally hot fashion retail markets. Its findings are based on the study of markets and those considered to be *mature* or *emerging*. **Mature markets** are those that are steady fashion retail winners while **emerging markets** are those that are making significant strides in the global arena.

In this section discussion will center on the mature markets that have regularly been regarded as steady leaders, with the next section concentrating on the emerging markets.

The leaders are the United Kingdom, United Arab Emirates, and the United States. Table 2.1 features the top 20 fashion retailing countries and their chief cities, along with their rankings that make them excellent arenas for fashion retailers around the world to target for their own expansion.

Table 2.1

TOP 20 COUNTRIES — GLOBAL RANKINGS[a]

Ranking	Country	Top City
1	United Kingdom	London
2	United Arab Emirates	Dubai
3	United States	New York City
4	Spain	Madrid
5	China	Beijing
6	Germany[b]	Berlin
=	France[b]	Paris
8	Russia	Moscow
9	Italy	Rome
10	Hong Kong	Hong Kong
11	Saudi Arabia	Riyadh
12	Singapore	Singapore
13	Kuwait	Kuwait City
14	Turkey	Istanbul
15	Belgium	Brussels
16	Japan	Tokyo
17	Austria	Vienna
18	Switzerland[c]	Zurich
=	Canada[c]	Toronto
20	Czech Republic	Prague

[a] This table includes both mature and emerging markets.
[b] Germany and France are tied for 6th place.
[c] Switzerland and Canada are tied for 18th place.

Ranking culled from CBRE 2013 report.

High-End Global Fashion Leaders in Retailing and Design

The following countries are representative of the **high-end fashion leaders** that will be explored to give the action that is taking place in global retailing as well as their emphasis on the designers who are native to them.

United Kingdom

London and other U.K. outposts have been actively involved as an arena where other countries have established branches, as well as a region that has entered foreign locations itself. Retailers such as Gap, Banana Republic, Abercrombie & Fitch, H&M, Victoria's Secret, J.Crew, Bottega Veneta, and Ralph Lauren are among the major players and are planning to increase their presence. In their overseas expansion, the U.K. continues to add Topshop and Topman freestanding stores in the United States as well as boutiques in Nordstrom and other fashion department stores, but many have taken to online expansion to increase British sales. Merchants such as Debenhams, ASOS, N Brown, Next, Marks & Spencer, Ted Baker, and Reiss are using the online experience not only for immediate sales, but also to test the waters for brick-and-mortar expansion potential. Figure 2.3 shows the U.K., a prominent fashion center.

United States

New York City has long topped the list as the hottest U.S. city for fashion retailing, with the Location Group in Zurich confirming this standing. Not only have the permanent residents continued to be major fashion shoppers, but the more than 50 million tourists who visit every year have added to it becoming a fashion retailing leader. Areas other than Madison and Fifth Avenue, the traditional fashion locales, have

figure 2.3
Harrods in London is the center of high fashion designs from around the world. It is a visitor destination just as it is a British shopper mainstay.

added to this retail success. Foreign companies such as Sweden's H&M, Canada's Joe Fresh, Spain's Zara, and France's rash of marquee couturiers continually appeal to the fashion-oriented consumer.

Los Angeles has long been a fashion retailer's dream with the coveted prize going to Rodeo Drive. There, Beverly Hills residents and tourists alike have made this the place to purchase Christian Dior, Brioni, Hermès, Prada, Zegna, Burberry, and other elite design collections.

The overseas presence of American designer shops such as Ralph Lauren, DKNY, Calvin Klein, and Barneys New York is ever-growing with their offshore shops joining the retail landscapes of Europe, Asia, South America, and Australia. Of course the notable American designers such as Calvin Klein and Ralph Lauren have a global presence.

France

With Paris as its perennial fashion leader, France has maintained its distinction as the most important destination for luxury retailers. Even in the Charles de Gaulle airport, the likes of Prada and Gucci often motivate travelers to buy. Designers who have graced the fashion marquees for many years including Chanel, Balenciaga, Saint Laurent, and others also grace prime fashion locales. Even with the skyrocketing costs of retail space, merchants eagerly sign leases.

The French designers of distinction that include Yves Saint Laurent, Pierre Cardin, Christian Dior, and Coco Chanel are regularly exported to many of fashion's global arenas. Significant tourism has whetted the appetite for such couture offerings and has brought their presence to the tourists' many home countries. It is both the **couture designs** and **prêt-à-porter** (ready-to-wear) that propel their names.

Hong Kong

Most any tourist will quickly reveal that their major reasons for visiting Hong Kong are eating and shopping. In recent years a number of couture shops such as Lanvin, Marc Jacobs, and Phillip Lim have joined the frenzy of Hong Kong along with the more traditional shops such as Tommy Hilfiger, Coach, and Victoria's Secret. One of the reasons for the rise of popular shops is the consumers from mainland China who flock there to do their shopping.

As for setting up shop in other countries, Hong Kong designers, for the most part, have yet to achieve the international status afforded those from other fashion arenas. Although many do produce merchandise that is often sold as a retailer's **"private label,"** the achievement of worldwide recognition has yet to come.

Italy

Notably Milan, with Rome following close by, high-end fashion boutiques offer **luxe goods** from Italian designers as well as those from around the world. Armani, Gucci, Valentino, Prada, Ferretti, and Zegna are some of the homegrown couturiers that grace the fashion streets like Via Montenapoleone with a waiting list of companies eager to open. The biggest spenders are not the residents but the visiting Russians and Chinese. Also important to the luxury shopping scene are the tourists from Hong Kong, Japan, Singapore, Ukraine, United States, and many other countries.

Not only is the retail scene important to the economy of Italy, but also are the high fashion designers that grace the global landscape wherever fashion is of paramount importance. "Fashion streets" include New York City's Madison and Fifth Avenues, Los Angeles' Rodeo Drive, Palm Beach's Worth Avenue, Chicago's Oak Street, and Long Island's Miracle Mile in Manhasset.

Germany

With Germany's largest city as its leader in fashion retailing, Berlin has made significant strides as both a national and international player. One of the reasons for the relatively new success is the increase in tourism. The demand has pushed retail rental prices up to heights never seen before. The global fashion makers aren't there in the abundance they are in other cities around the world. Giorgio Armani, Dolce & Gabbana, Escada, Hugo Boss, and Louis Vuitton have a presence in Berlin, but it is the likes of companies such as H&M that have made major inroads as fashion retailers. The upscale fashion scene is centered in Munich where, among others, the wealthy Arab tourists are prominent shoppers. Many of the marquee labels in other countries also grace the fashion streets in Munich.

As for the creative designers, the number pales in comparison to other countries. Jil Sander, Karl Lagerfeld (who now designs French fashion collections like Chanel) and Wolfgang Joop are the names that are most recognized. A new breed that includes Michael Sontag, Vladimir Karaleev, and Perret Schaad is slowly but surely gaining a global reputation.

Spain

The country's most visited city is Barcelona where the tourists from all over the world fuel fashion retail growth. Most of the shops are moderately priced, except for some such as the country's own Loewe and overseas labels such as Stella McCartney, Louis Vuitton, and Bottega Veneta. The lower-priced fashion operations like H&M and Mango run 16 stores in Barcelona.

Some of world's most famous fashion designers came from Spain. Mariano Fortuny, with the long-heralded Delphos design, Cristóbal Balenciaga, a fashion icon of historical renown, and Manolo Blahnik whose shoe collections are found globally are Spain's most prestigious.

China

Although Beijing is often regarded as the hot spot for tourists, it has been joined by Shanghai, a city that is moving up the fashion-retailing ladder. Attracting tourists from all over the world, it is becoming a fashion mecca. Stores like Yves Saint Laurent and Louis Vuitton are freestanding brick-and-mortar entries with Reel Department Store merchandising such couture-level brands as Stella McCartney, Alexander Wang, Balenciaga and Lanvin. In addition to the global visitors, it is the nouveau riche tourists from second-, third-, and fourth-tier Chinese cities that travel to Shanghai to purchase fashion products.

Japan

As Asia's most important country for fashion retailers, Tokyo is by far its most important city. Not only has the Ginza remained a fashion-shopping street, but it has been joined by numerous venues such as the trendy Aoyama district, where Comme des Garçons and Prada are located, and Omotesando, where Emporio Armani maintains a shop.

Native to Japan are the marquee designers Rei Kawakubo, Issey Miyake, Hanae Mori, and Yohji Yamamoto. Not only have they reigned supreme in Japan's retail scene, but also in global environments such as New York City and Paris.

What has put Japan on the fashion merchandising map today was the introduction of Uniqlo, a unique company with enormous global reach. It is further discussed in *Happening Now*.

HAPPENING NOW

UNIQLO IS EXPANDING IN THE UNITED STATES

Uniqlo is a Japanese company that promotes **fast fashion**, a contemporary term that is used in the fashion industry to identify those companies that move design from the runways very quickly to capture the top current fashion trends and bring them to the stores in record time. Organizations such as Zara and H&M have been the leaders in this type of fashion merchandise but today face the ever-present competition from Uniqlo. In Japan it was the first company to establish an SPA model meaning "specialty store retailer of private label apparel." They incorporate the entire clothes-making process from materials procurement, product planning, development and manufacture through distribution and retail to inventory management. Figure 2.4 features a Uniqlo store.

From the moment a shopper enters the store, there is an immediate friendliness by the staff waiting to greet them. "Hello! How are you today? My name is Uniqlo! Let me know if you need any assistance. Thank you for waiting!"

With a reputation for design and service, the company has become the fourth largest fashion retailer in the world. In the United States, at the time of this writing, there are only seven stores, but the company is preparing to have 200 by the end of the decade. The company is expecting to achieve $50 billion in sales by the end of 2020, $10 billion of which should be in the United States. Their goal, according to the C.O.O. is to become the number one apparel retailer in the world.

Innovation is what is happening now at Uniqlo to help them achieve this goal. One exciting unique addition to many of the stores is the "magic mirror." The customer tries on an outfit, stands in front of this mirror, and with the touch of an LCD screen can change the color. This speeds up the operation since the customer doesn't have to try on more than the one item.

This and other innovative ideas are *happening now* to make Uniqlo a profitable enterprise with enormous global reach.

figure 2.4
Uniqlo now has stores all over the globe and is rapidly expanding to capture the fast fashion market. Through its use of multimedia display it has taken retail promotion to a new level.

The fashion retailing markets in the previous section dealt with those that have demonstrated that they are here to stay. The combination of inhabitants and visitors have made them destinations for those wishing to seek the latest in fashion. Along with these fashion merchants of moderate to high-end merchandise offerings, other countries have joined the fray. Some are competitive in nature to the mature markets while others are just reaching their potential.

Most prominent emerging countries and cities are Chile, Brazil, Mexico, Ho Chi Minh City, São Paulo, United Arab Emirates, Kuwait, New Delhi, and Saudi Arabia. The U.A.E.'s Dubai has just about achieved mature status with its very wealthy people and the sometimes equally wealthy visitors from around the world.

The following are selected emerging markets that will be explored.

Chile

One of the more successful fashion arenas in South America is Chile. It has emerged as a market where Chileans can purchase with ease and comfort, something they look for when shopping. The key players in this market are hypermarkets, department stores and shopping centers. The success can be exemplified by the presence of such international collections as Calvin Klein, Tommy Hilfiger, Zara, North Face, and H&M where they each have their own brick-and-mortar operations. Although Chile, and its main city, Santiago, is not a haven for upscale fashion merchandise, lower cost, volume-based fashion inventories are making its emergence a reality.

Mexico

After numerous years of foreign retailers' failure to enter the Mexican fashion retailing scene, many global retail organizations are coming there. Within 2012, Gap, Forever 21, and H&M arrived in Mexico City, joining Zara, which was the first foreign retail giant to enter the Mexican scene. With duties coming down, many overseas merchants are heading for Mexico.

Before this recent influx, Mexicans had to satisfy their fashion needs with two choices. Those in the lower class purchased at informal street-markets. The wealthy shopped at upscale shops such as El Palacio de Hierro also known as the Iron Palace, a company that was founded in 1891 to bring Paris fashion to the affluent ladies of the new world. It was the middle class with nowhere to shop. Now with the entry of the aforementioned fashion chains, the middle class is getting a chance to make better clothing purchases.

India

Recently relaxed limits on foreign investment rules have helped India, especially New Delhi, become an important venue for the apparel boom. India has the world's second largest population with 1.2 billion people, many of whom are in the middle class. There is significant evidence from Interbrand.com that with half the country's population under 25, and Internet savvy, retailers will embrace them as a major force in fashion retailing. Zara is already becoming a major player, and Gap is ready to face them with their own brands. Upscale malls with fashion brands like Burberry, Gucci, and Prada are showing that they too have a penchant to enlarge their footprint.

Brazil

In major cities such as the capital city, Brasília, and its primary center for fashion products, São Paulo, there is tremendous energy reported from marquee label companies such as Gucci, Chanel, Louis Vuitton, Missoni, and Burberry who have recently made large investments in urban centers. As reported at São Paulo Fashion Week, "Brazil is on fire!" With a booming economy the country is ready to take its place as a global fashion leader.

Kiev

Ukraine's modern fashion-conscious centers attract tourists from all over the world. Where it once was relegated to selling scarce basic products, Kiev's image is hardly recognizable. The main street, Khreschatyk, immediately reminds global shoppers of Oxford Street in London and Fifth Avenue in New York City. Gucci, Bulgari, Louis

Vuitton, and others represent upscale collections while the likes of Zara and Marks & Spencer feed the needs for medium priced merchandise.

The targeting of Europe for fashion retailers continues. In 2012 alone, new entries set a record for the region. Although to lesser degrees, Asia, the Middle East, North Africa, Latin America, North America, and the Pacific Rim were also of interest to foreign fashion retail organizations. It should be understood that North America has enjoyed mature status for so many decades that it is no longer considered an emerging market.

GLOBAL EXPANSION ARRANGEMENTS

When fashion retailers wish to expand beyond their native countries, today there are rarely any constraints put on them in terms of their expansion. Even in most countries if there are any constraints for foreign investment they are generally minimal. It is a matter for the merchant to abide by federal and municipal laws before they begin their new operations. The historical barriers that once were prevalent in foreign lands have generally eroded. It is still not just the signing of a lease and building the structure that is imperative to a successful offshore fashion retail opening. However, there is no single outreach that fits every situation.

There are three approaches to offshore retail expansion. They are **franchising**, joint venture, and **owned retail operations**. Each of these arrangements present advantages and disadvantages to the expanding company.

Franchising

In this situation, there is an agreement between the **franchiser** (the company that owns the brand) and the **franchisee** (the merchant who wants inclusion in the operation for a fee). It enables the franchisee to operate a single store or multiple stores in a specific trading area that is controlled by the franchiser. Some of the advantages of this arrangement include:

- proven track record of success
- markets have been researched to take guesswork out of expansion there
- a business model that has been tested
- training by the franchiser to educate the franchisee
- less investment than starting one's own company abroad
- potential for more than one unit
- immediate brand recognition
- franchiser knowledge of local market.

Some of the disadvantages of franchising include:

- often the start-up fees and terms of the contract are too rigid to make a success of the arrangement
- in order to expand, the franchiser has full control
- decision-making is in the hands of the franchiser
- product selection is most often in the hands of the franchiser
- strict adherence to franchiser rules and regulations.

Figure 2.5 shows "franchising" as a business concept.

figure 2.5
Franchising is one way for businesses to expand. Instead of companies opening their own units, for a fee they allow outsiders to open one or more units bearing the company name.

figure 2.5
Franchising is one way for businesses to expand. Instead of companies opening their own units, for a fee they allow outsiders to open one or more units bearing the company name.

Joint Ventures

As this approach implies, there is shared ownership. At the time of this writing, India doesn't allow for joint ventures between offshore and onshore retail businesses. Major merchants such as Mango, Marks & Spencer, Nike, and Zara use a variety of arrangements for global pursuits. Included are franchising, company-owned, and joint ventures.

Included in the advantages of joint venture expansion are:

- investment is shared
- if the partner has significant local experience it could benefit the global partner
- higher levels of control than franchising.

The disadvantages include:

- chance for disagreement among the partners
- accountability is sometimes questionable
- bureaucratic decision-making.

Owned

Since there are no others involved in this type of expansion, the merchant has only to use his or her experience, instincts, business acumen, knowledge, and previous success to open new units. Of course, if this is not allowed in foreign countries, there are no other choices than franchising or joint venture to expand the business. Typically, owning a company outright is the preferred expansion route. Some of the advantages include:

- higher degree of control
- if the company has a known image, it can play an enormous role in its expansion success

- it enables the retailer to purchase existing retail operations and change them to their own name
- complete control over merchandise inventories.

The disadvantages are also prevalent in fully owned companies and include:

- greater outlay of start-up expenses
- maintenance of costly office functions
- challenges of unfamiliar tax issues and labor laws
- costly advertising to promote the company to new shoppers
- possibility of competition from existing retail operations

Chapter Highlights

1. The advent of the Internet and the enormous growth of social media have contributed to expansion of retailing's globalization.

2. Fashion retailers are generating sales growth through the employment of multi-channel usage.

3. Mobile retail shops are making significant inroads in fashion retailing by "popping-up" wherever heavy consumer traffic warrants it.

4. The leading fashion retailers in the world are classified as mature, meaning they have achieved the top status, or emerging, signifying that they are about to reach the mature status.

5. The top three globally ranked fashion retailers are the U.K., United Arab Emirates, and the United States.

6. The goal for Uniqlo is to become the number one fashion retailer in the world.

7. Franchising, joint venture, and sole ownership are the three methods for a foreign merchant to enter another nation for the purpose of opening branches of their business there.

8. The advantages of franchising in a foreign land are less monetary commitments, the business plan has been tested, and training of employees.

Terms of the Trade

couture design	international prominence
emerging markets	luxe goods
fast fashion	mature markets
franchisee	owned retail operations
franchiser	prêt-à-porter
franchising	private label
high-end fashion leaders	

For Discussion

1. How far is the reach of the Internet for potential customers of the retailing community?

2. Does local competition among retailers contribute to their globalization practices?

3. What is multi-channel retailing and why is it important to today's retailer?

4. What age group is the major player in mobile purchasing?

5. Does sustainable fashion play an important part in fashion retailing? Why?

6. What is the difference between the classifications of mature and emerging markets?

7. Which fashion center in Italy has become the major one for upscale fashion design?

8. Two moderate-priced fashion leaders, Zara and H&M, are facing extreme competition from another fast-growing retailer. What is that retailer and what is its goal?

9. How has India started to emerge as a leader in foreign investment by retailers?

10. Why have so many retailers chosen the franchising route for overseas expansion?

11. What are some of the pitfalls of franchising for the franchisee?

12. Why have some retailers followed the joint venture approach for overseas expansion?

13. Are there any initial considerations before the choices of franchising and joint venture are made?

14. How do the local labor laws enter into a retailer's plan for complete ownership in a foreign country?

Case Problem

Questions

1. What are the pros and cons of each method?
2. If a checklist was developed to study the possibilities, what areas would be on it?

Lady Avidon has been in the fashion business as a prominent retailer in the southern tier of the United States. From its initial store opening in 1945 through 1987 it was an independent, family-owned business. In 1987 it considered a significant expansion which would add many locations in addition to its existing flagship and 30 branches. After numerous meetings and suggestions from family management, it was determined that the company should go public to maximize its potential as a fashion retailer.

In 1988 Lady Avidon became a public corporation and sold shares to investors. The decision was an immediate success and brought significant attention from the retail industry. With all of the necessities in place of transferring from private ownership to a public corporation the C.E.O., C.O.O., and other top decision-makers took the reins and began to explore expansion possibilities.

A major consideration was to enter the global marketplace and turn the company into an international player. With so much competition from other merchants in its trading area, global expansion would eliminate that competition.

Exploration of the three major expansion concepts, franchising, joint venture, and sole ownership were discussed. The governing board quickly learned that the decision would not be an easy one and have investigated the pros and cons of each method. At this point in the discussion phase the overseas expansion plans are still being discussed.

Exercises and Projects

1. Select a franchised fashion retail operation that has both outlets in the United States and abroad. The larger companies have information on the Internet that will give you some of the pertinent information about them.

   Using this information write a report that will offer such information as:

   a. initial capital investment
   b. merchandise offerings
   c. size of the operation in terms of units
   d. targeted market
   e. future expansion.

2. Choose a major "off-site only" fashion retailer for the purpose of learning which channels they use that produce sales for them. With the information garnered either through direct contact, a search engine, or both, prepare an oral presentation that will cover their operation.

chapter three

ORGANIZATIONAL STRUCTURES

After reading this chapter, you should be able to:

- Differentiate between line and staff positions as shown on organization charts.

- Describe how an organization chart is structured showing the lines of authority.

- Classify the different types of organizational structures presently used by retailers.

- Explain the beginnings of organization structuring for large department stores and how they have changed to suit today's companies.

- Cite the reasons why chain store organizations conduct their businesses as centralized operations, and explain why some chains have decentralized some of their functions.

- List the reasons for separating the buying and selling functions.

Once the decision has been made to begin a retail venture, it is necessary to plan its **organizational structure** in a way that maximizes efficiency and profitability. All of the duties and responsibilities of those in the company must be identified, and **lines of authority** must be carefully delineated so that all members of the organization will understand what their job responsibilities are. By doing so, everyone knows who will report to whom, who the decision makers are, and which advisory personnel is on hand to assist in the decision-making process. No matter how large or small the operation, whether it is a major department store or single-unit boutique, each company must be structured in such a way that best serves its needs and makes the business a success.

To clarify their organization's structure so that all employees can understand it, most companies prepare a graphic presentation called an **organization chart**. The chart clearly spells out the various **company divisions**, the roles they play, lines of responsibility and authority, decision-making positions, advisory roles (if there are any in the organization), and areas of responsibility. Such charts allow employees at any level of the organization to immediately learn their place in the company, to whom they are responsible, and, in turn, their own paths of responsibility.

Each retail classification has certain traditional organizational structures. Department store structures, for example, are somewhat dissimilar from those of the chain store organizations, as are small retail operations from their giant counterparts. Each company tailors a chart that best suits its specific needs. Often, companies undergo structural changes that fit their needs to address any new directions they take. Most department stores, for example, at one time exclusively brick-and-mortar operations, are now engaged in multi-channel retailing that necessitates placing their catalog and e-tail divisions on the organizational chart.

As small companies develop into larger ones, and as the giants expand their operations globally, their organizational structures must be adapted to fit their latest needs.

THE NEED FOR ORGANIZATIONAL STRUCTURES

Organizations need structuring so that lines of authority along with individual duties and responsibilities can be understood by every company member. There are, however, additional ways that these structures optimize the operation. Some of the more important ones, as offered by OrgPlus, a consulting firm that deals with the complexities of organizational structuring and chart creation, include:

- Turning groups of individuals into teams and getting everyone pointed in the same direction.
- Helping to orient new employees to the company and supplying them with career and succession plans.
- Understanding the complex nature of the structures and helping to simplify relationships.
- Empowering people to understand the strategic vision of the company by defining dependencies and relationships.

A wealth of additional information regarding organizational structuring is available on www.orgplus.com. Once the different company leadership, divisions, departments, and other components needed to efficiently run the organization have been identified, they must be laid out in chart form.

ORGANIZATION CHART COMPONENTS

At first glance, an organization chart looks like a stack of different boxes. They are positioned by job titles to depict the various company divisions or **company functions**, the relationships of these positions to each other, the decision-making positions as well as those that are advisory in nature (if they are present), lines of authority, and the overall size of the company.

To "read" organization charts and comprehend their meaning, it is necessary to understand the basic components and principles upon which they are based. Essentially, the charts are composed of only two major components: **line positions** and **staff positions**.

Line Positions

In every retail organization, no matter how large or small, decision making is a key to its success. Those who hold these positions are **company producers**, in that they are directly involved in making money for the company. Whether they are the merchandisers who have the responsibility for the buying function, the sales associates who sell the products, or those involved in advertising and promotion, they all have a hand in "producing" revenue for the company. Collectively, they are the holders of line positions.

By examining Figure 3.1, excerpted from a typical merchandising division of a department store, it is easy to understand **line relationships**. The most senior person is at the top, in this case the divisional merchandise manager, followed directly below by the buyer, who is next in command, and ultimately by the assistant buyer who is least senior. Each line position is presented in a rectangular box that is attached to the others with vertical lines.

The nature of the placement of the positions and the use of the traditional lines makes it easy for the observer to understand who is responsible to whom, who plays the most important decision-making roles, and the direct lines of authority and communication. Employees are expected to follow the formal delineations of communication when discussing company problems. For example, in Figure 3.1, the assistant buyer communicates only with the buyer, the immediate supervisor, and not with the divisional merchandise manager (DMM). Only the buyer has the authority to deal directly with the DMM. It is only appropriate to deal with someone in higher authority if one's immediate supervisor permits it. Of course, in some organizations, an informal structure might exist that enables some people to communicate with others out of the formal order.

Line Relationships

Divisional Merchandise Manager
Buyer
Assistant Buyer

figure 3.1
Line relationships.

In smaller companies, the use of a **line structure** is typical since there might not be a need to have employees other than decision makers operate the business. Small companies also generally do not have the funds to employ people other than those who are the company producers.

Staff Positions

Stores that have either grown from smaller companies into larger ones or were initially conceived to be large-scale operations often have the need for advisory or support positions, technically classified as staff positions. They are specialists within the organization who work at the behest of the line people to whom they report. An example of this type of relationship is depicted in Figure 3.2.

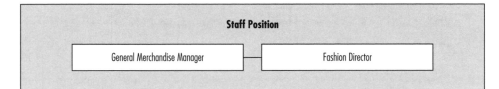

Staff Position

General Merchandise Manager	Fashion Director

figure 3.2
Staff positions.

In this example, the general merchandise manager (GMM), is a line executive who heads the merchandising division and has the ultimate power to determine guidelines and philosophies concerning product assortments for the entire company. Adjacent to the GMM box, connected by a horizontal line, is the fashion director. The fashion director is in a staff position and advises and makes suggestions to the GMM on areas such as fashion trends, silhouettes, fabric preferences, and color forecasts but does not have any decision-making powers. The GMM and the subordinates in the merchandising division make the actual merchandising selections.

Staff members play an important role in retail operations. Their salaries are often higher than those of many in line positions, and they are not lower-level employees even though they do not make the actual decisions. It is their advice and counsel that often makes an organization operate more efficiently and productively.

Large retailers that use a combination of line positions with staff positions are called **line and staff organizations**.

CONSTRUCTING AN ORGANIZATION CHART

The creation of the chart used to be a complex undertaking that required not only an understanding of the different components that needed placement on the graphic presentation but also the ability to draw the **organization chart boxes** in a manner that was visually meaningful. Today, with the numerous computer programs available to retailers, by inputting the information the charts are simple to construct. One of the leading organizations for the construction of producing organization charts is SmartDraw. In *Happening Now*, trends for the development of organization charts are discussed.

HAPPENING NOW

CHANGING SAKS FIFTH AVENUE'S STRUCTURE TO FIT WITHIN THAT OF THE HUDSON BAY COMPANY

As briefly discussed in the opening pages of this chapter, an organization chart is a tool that depicts all of the employee titles in the organization in a graphic presentation. Since this text is fashion-retailing oriented, the titles used reflect that industry.

One of the criticisms of some organization charts is that they become outdated for the present operation. Changes are sometimes necessary to fulfill a number of different factors. These include a merger or acquisition and the necessity to absorb the employees of the acquired or merged company into the organization that would be beneficial to the new structure. The acquisition of Saks Fifth Avenue by the Hudson Bay Company in November, 2013, for example, is presently undergoing changes in Saks' structure to make it more efficient. Happening now is the planning that will eventually provide the company with a new organization chart. The potential for the new structure is the avoidance of duplication of processes.

Also happening now is the reorganization of some companies due to the economic downturns caused by the latest recession. A careful study of the retail charts indicates that some stores made changes to address the downturn. If and when the economic predictors are positive, changes could be made to handle the potential for increased sales.

One of the means that retailers are presently using is the creation of an off-site operation in addition to their brick-and-mortar establishments. Discussion generally centers on whether or not the current organization chart will fit the needs of the new company structure, or if it must be changed to add new positions for the catalog and website additions. This is an ongoing problem for retailers that is happening now.

FASHION RETAILING ORGANIZATION CHARTS

Fashion retailers are divided into three main types:

- **on-site classifications**, which include the smallest operation, the single-unit small specialty store; the specialty store operation with several units; the small department store; large department stores; department store groups; and large chain store operations;
- the **off-site operations**, which include catalog and website-only retailers;
- and the multi-channel operations, which include brick-and-mortar retailers with catalog, social media and Internet divisions.

Each of their **tables of organization** is generally based upon a set of standardized practices that are tailored to fit specific company needs.

On-Site Classifications

The brick-and-mortar operations, or on-site retailers, use a variety of organizational structures based on the size of the company and the activities in which it is engaged.

Single-Unit Specialty Stores

These operations, which include boutiques, usually operate with a minimum number of people. Typically, the owner is the ultimate decision maker, with a few employees hired to perform more than one task, such as sort and ticket incoming merchandise, place the goods in the appropriate spots on the selling floor, make changes to existing visual presentations, and handle returns to vendors. The owner makes decisions that pertain to buying, store management, promotional endeavors, and the like. When stores are too big for their owners to handle all of the major decision-making responsibilities, they may hire managers to assist them.

The structure shown in Figure 3.3 is typical of single-unit specialty stores, and it follows the line organization concept in which each of the people in the company is either a decision maker or revenue producer. Figure 3.3 spells out the duties and responsibilities performed by each person.

In Figure 3.3, it is quite clear that the owner is in charge of the overall functioning of the operation, with the manager performing some specific tasks. The two sales associates on the chart, in addition to selling and merchandise sorting and ticketing, are required to assist in other areas.

When a company grows from a single-unit operation, not only does the number of employees increase but different types of people are generally hired to perform more specialized tasks.

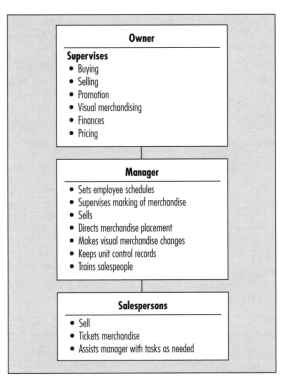

figure 3.3
Single-unit specialty store organization chart.

Small Multi-Unit Specialty Chains

Many small operations achieve success with their first stores and expand their operations with other units. Consequently, they must adjust their tables of organization to show the increased number of employees and their functions.

When the chain grows to five or more individual units, such activities as merchandising, advertising and promotion, store management, human resources, and receiving are centralized in one facility. The company management, led by the **chief executive officer (C.E.O.)** operates from this location and leaves the stores to attend to the selling of the merchandise.

Small Department Stores

The structure of many small department stores consists of two divisions. Headed by the company C.E.O., it often has a **chief financial officer (C.F.O.)** to handle areas such as accounting and credit, and a **chief operating officer (C.O.O.)** to deal with matters of store protection, traffic and facilities management, and so forth.

As shown in Figure 3.4, there are several departments within each of the two divisions, a fashion coordinator who operates in an advisory capacity and reports directly to the merchandising and promotions director, and a human resources specialist who works for both the C.E.O. and the two division heads.

This organizational structure allows for a certain degree of specialization in the company but guarantees coordinated store effort.

figure 3.4
Small department store
organization chart.

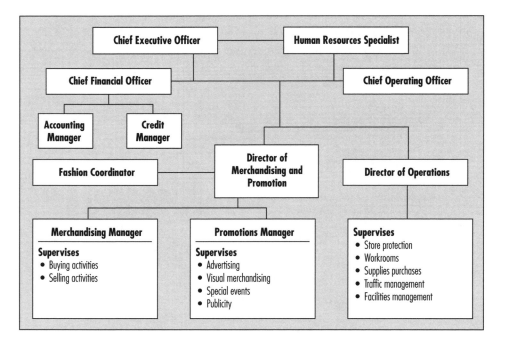

Large Department Stores

At the turn of the 20th century, department store expansion was at the forefront of retailing. Companies such as Macy's and Bloomingdale's recognized that they needed expanded organizational structures to handle the growth. Some companies went from the two-function format that they used in their early days, to four, five, and as many as eight divisional arrangements.

Early in the 20th century, the National Dry Goods Association, later to be called the National Retail Merchants Association and now known as the National Retail Federation (NRF), was called upon to suggest the best manner in which department stores would successfully operate. Under the direction of Paul Mazur, a management expert, the situation was studied and the four-function plan or Mazur Plan was introduced. For many years it was the basis of most major department store structures.

Today, relatively few department stores still use some of the Mazur Plan functions but have amended their structures to address the complexities of their organizations. Initially, the four-function plan had controller, merchandise, publicity, and store manager divisions. While these functions are still important to department store organizational structuring, some of the titles have changed—publicity is most often called promotion—and others have been added. By and large, the present-day department store's tables of organization generally utilize anywhere from five to eight divisions. They are described in the following sections.

MERCHANDISING

While each division is important to the overall success of the organization, the **merchandising division** is considered by most industry professionals to be the lifeblood of the retail operation. Most often, it has more upper-level and middle-management executives than any other division in a department store organization.

Merchandise planning and procurement takes a considerable amount of time and employs a variety of different line executives as well as staff positions such as fashion directors. The activities for which they are responsible are:

1. Purchasing merchandise from the four corners of the earth. With global acquisition so important to these companies, their buyers and merchandisers are in offshore markets year round.

2. Determining the product mixes not only for the brick-and-mortar operations but also for the off-site divisions such as the catalogs and websites. Since the off-site operations generally have no geographical boundaries, the items sold through these outlets are often different than those found in the stores.

3. Developing private brands and labels for their company's exclusive use. With the enormous amount of competition between department stores and the widespread use of similar marquee brands, the creative aspect has become commonplace for many buyers and merchandisers.

4. Determining the appropriate product mix in terms of price points that will best serve their clientele's needs.

5. Pricing the merchandise in a manner that provides the profitability necessary for the company to remain a viable business enterprise, while staying competitive with the prices of other retailers.

6. Establishing the proper rapport with vendors that assures the best possible buying terms, such as getting discounts, prompt delivery, accepting returns, and so on, to maximize profitability.

7. Obtaining the highest vendor allowances for advertising and promotional purposes that will help deliver their company's message to the consumer at a minimum of company expense.

8. Interacting with industry experts such as resident buyers and market consultants who provide information on color, fabric, style, and other fashion trends.

PROMOTION

Today's retail atmosphere has reached such competitive proportions that the dollar amounts that department stores spend to make themselves visible to their regular and potential customers have skyrocketed. Coupling this increase with the realities of budget shortfalls has made it necessary for the **promotional division** to apportion the funds spent on these areas with great care. Included among the activities that it oversees are the following:

1. Dividing the allocations for advertising among the various media available to them. Since not every medium provides the same return on the dollars invested, care must be exercised in making certain that expenditures are in line with the sales they are expected to generate.

2. Selecting the appropriate media outlets within a classification that promise the highest awareness rate. If, for example, the trading area has more than one daily newspaper, the one with the greatest potential for consumer response should merit the largest percentage of the newspaper advertising budget.

3. Developing distinctive advertisements that are appropriate for the store's image.

4. Choosing an advertising agency that specializes in department store promotion and has the ability to create signature ads for the company.

5. Designing special events that will capture consumers' attention and motivate shoppers to buy.

6. Creating and installing interior and window visual displays that will produce sales for the store.

7. Producing press releases and kits that will attract the attention of the fashion world's editorial press.

CONTROL

Behind the scenes in any department store operation are the people who make certain that the company's assets are protected and accurately spent. The **control division** serves in a multitude of capacities that include accounting, expense and control, and consumer credit. Specifically, its tasks are:

1. Developing the appropriate accounting procedures that address both account payables and receivables. In the establishment of these bookkeeping tasks, the best available computer programs must be procured or developed to fit the company's specific requirements.

2. Preparing reports for the merchandisers and buyers, human resources team, promotional executives, and other divisional managers as well as outside government agencies, as required by law.

3. Planning and supervising the taking of perpetual and physical inventories.

4. Establishing a credit card program that involves both in-house charge accounts and revolving credit, and third-party credit such as American Express, MasterCard, and Visa.

5. Developing a procedure that establishes customer credit card accounts in a timely manner.

Store Management

With department stores expanding through the opening of full-line branches and specialized units, the need for in-house managers continues to grow. The **store management division** is charged with overseeing the managerial positions and carrying out the practices that were established by the company's upper-level executives. Some of its responsibilities include:

1. Selecting the individual stores' managers, group managers, and department managers.

2. Determining the appropriate hours of operation for the flagship and branch stores.

3. Interfacing with the stores' managers to notify them of changes in corporate policies.

4. Communicating through means of personal contact, telephone, email, and faxes to learn about potential problems in the stores.

5. Managing the customer service departments.

Store Operations

The management of the store's physical operations are under the jurisdiction of the **store operations division**, developed by the company's top management team. It then carries out the specific tasks and responsibilities to which it has been assigned. These include:

1. Maintaining the physical plant.

2. Managing the security of the facility and protecting the merchandise from being stolen by shoplifters and employees.

3. Purchasing supplies that are used to run the stores such as light bulbs, cleaning compounds, and office materials.

4. Managing the receipt of incoming merchandise and the functions used in marking and ticketing.

Human Resources

All of the activities that relate to the company's personnel, such as recruitment, training, and labor relations, are in the domain of the **human resources division**. Its decision making is extremely important to the proper functioning of the company, and its duties and responsibilities include:

1. Establishing the job specifications of the various positions in the company so that the right person will be hired to perform the specific job.

2. Developing recruitment programs that will attract the best-qualified candidates for employment.

3. Training new employees and retraining those already employed with the latest in-house systems.

4. Designing benefits packages that will be competitive with other companies in the industry.

5. Evaluating employee performance.

6. Establishing compensation programs that will attract the best employees.

7. Participating in labor relations between management and rank-and-file employees.

Large Chain Store Organizations

Large chain store organizations have anywhere from 200 to more than 2,000 units. Among those with highly visible names are companies such as The Gap Stores, Inc., which operates many different retail concepts such as GapKids, BabyGap, Banana Republic, and Old Navy. Some are traditional stores, and others are either discount or off-price operations such as Target and Marshalls.

Their success is generally attributed to their centralized organizational structure that involves management from a home base or company headquarters. Typically, all of their decision making is accomplished there and includes buying and merchandising, advertising and promotion, warehousing, product development, human resources, accounting, purchasing of supplies, real estate development, and marketing research. In the giant chain store organizations, there is often some form of **decentralization** such as regional warehousing, which allows for shipments to stores to be accomplished in less time. In companies such as J. C. Penney, for example, some of the merchandising decisions are decentralized and left in the hands of the store managers and their in-store team. In this case, merchandise planning and procurement arrangements are left to the central buying team, which prepares "catalogs" of available products that store managers select from to develop their own merchandise mixes. In this way, each store in the chain can tailor the assortment to fit the needs of the individual trading areas.

In some chain store operations, associate buyers purchase lines that are earmarked for specific locations. For example, if a limited number of units in the chain have markets that are atypical from the rest of the company's stores, their unique merchandise requirements can be better satisfied with this type of buying arrangement.

Although **centralization** is and will always be the manner in which chains can control their entire operation and curtail costs, there will often be the need to decentralize their operations in some ways, as described above.

Off-Site Classifications

Just as the brick-and-mortar operations find the need to make changes in their tables of organization to address their present-day businesses, so do the "off-site only" companies. Many retail catalogers, for example, have opted to add websites as a means of attracting a broader marketplace. Conversely, so have the companies that initially entered retailing as online merchants. Some have opened catalog divisions to serve shoppers accustomed to that form of purchasing and have even developed "tie-ins" with brick-and-mortar operations that will sell their goods. Even the home shopping channels have entered the catalog arena to make certain that they have covered all bases in terms of marketing their goods.

The following organizational structures are examples of some of the various divisions and functions within each of the off-site operations.

Catalogs

Unlike brick-and-mortar retailers, which utilize stores to generate the greatest proportion of their sales, the catalog companies sell merchandise primarily through the pages of their "books," though they are using websites more and more. Thus, catalog retailer organization charts feature only those divisions and functions such as merchandising, product development, advertising, warehousing, transportation, and customer service.

Website Organizations

By and large, the websites with fashion orientations, such as Zappos, limit themselves to the Internet to reach potential customers. Their organization charts, like their cataloger counterparts, deal primarily with product acquisition, advertising, warehousing, transportation, research and customer services.

Home Shopping Organizations

The main distribution channel for the home shopping shows is on cable television. Some, however, have expanded their operations to include direct marketing through the Internet. In this way, they are able to appeal to the vast array of potential customers who shy away from on-site purchasing and prefer to make their purchases either by ordering goods that they see on products-oriented television programs or the Internet.

Multi-Channel Operations

Retailers, large and small, have become proponents of multi-channel retailing. Brick-and-mortar companies, in particular, have come to the conclusion that limiting themselves to in-store operations will prevent them from reaching wider trading areas.

In addressing these new opportunities, most have redirected their tables of organization to reflect all of the selling channels available to them. Typically, the addition of online offerings, mobile stores, and social networks are presented as separate divisions on their organization charts.

In retailing's rapidly changing playing field, the organizational structures that were "engraved in stone" are now flexible. To stay current and meet the challenges of the competition, retailers must restructure.

TRENDS IN ORGANIZATIONAL STRUCTURES

The growth in retailing, both on-site and off-site, has required merchants to readdress their tables of organization so that they will better serve the needs of their customers and make their companies more profitable. Some of today's trends in organizational structuring for the fashion-retailing arena are described in the following sections.

Restructuring to Accommodate Multi-Channel Expansion

When department stores in particular expanded their catalog operations, many initially opted to make this division part of their brick-and-mortar operations. Similarly, when retailers saw that the Internet had the potential to increase revenues, they changed their organizational structure to reflect this and to make the overall operation function more efficiently. Today, the trend is for the major multi-channel retailers to adjust and expand their tables of organization and separate the various channels they use into separate divisions.

Consolidation of Divisions

The acquisition of department stores by major retail groups has become a dominant trend. Canada's Hudson Bay, as an example, has purchased Lord & Taylor and merged it into its operation. Through this practice, fewer buyers and merchandisers were needed as were other executives who previously worked exclusively for one store. As this acquisition trend continues, the staff consolidation is likely to continue as well.

Decentralization

Much of the growth in large-scale retailing has come about by expansion into new trading areas. Although centralization was once the forte of the chain store organization, this expansion has necessitated some decentralization of functions in some companies. Merchandise distribution, for example, is now being decentralized by some very large chains. When stores are so far from the single distribution center, the time it took for merchandise to reach many of the units was both inefficient and costly.

Chapter Highlights

1. Both large and small companies should present their tables of organization on organization charts so that employees at all company levels may visualize the lines of authority.

2. Organization charts should not be left in place for long periods. They should be periodically reviewed and adjusted to fit the needs of the company as it changes.

3. An organization chart is a graphic presentation of the company and is presented in a series of boxes that are easy for everyone to understand.

4. Essentially, today's retailers utilize charts that feature line and staff positions, except in the cases where the companies are very small.

5. Line positions are used to indicate company producers and staff positions for the purpose of showing support personnel. The former group represents the company's decision makers; the latter, the advisory people.

6. Organization charts used to be hand drawn but are now computer generated.

7. As retail organizations grow, the need to add staff specialists also grows. This enables the company to use advisory personnel who can make a favorable difference in the running of the company.

8. Large department store organizations use a variety of different charts to depict their organizational structures, with the number of different divisions typically ranging from five to eight.

9. Most professionals agree that the merchandising division is the lifeblood of the retailing structure.

10. The promotional division of a major retailer is responsible for advertising, special events, visual merchandising, and publicity.

11. Department store acquisitions of other companies have accounted for the restructuring of their tables of organization. In many cases, some of the newly acquired stores are merged into existing divisions.

12. Large chains primarily operate under centralized organizational structures, with the result being more efficiency in their everyday operations.

13. Some chains have decentralized certain functions as they have moved into numerous geographical markets.

14. As major companies move toward multi-channel retailing, they have restructured their tables of organization.

Terms of the Trade

centralization
chief executive officer (C.E.O.)
chief financial officer (C.F.O.)
chief operating officer (C.O.O.)
company divisions
company functions
company producers
control division
decentralization
human resources division
line and staff organizations
line positions
line relationships

line structure
lines of authority
merchandising division
off-site operations
on-site classifications
organization chart
organization chart boxes
organizational structure
promotional division
staff positions
store management division
store operations division
tables of organization

For Discussion

1. Why is it important for all retail operations to graphically present their tables of organization?

2. What is meant by the term lines of authority?

3. In what way are the major components shown on an organization chart, and what are the traditional designations?

4. How do line positions differ from staff positions?

5. Why doesn't a small fashion retail operation, such as a boutique, use staff positions in its organizational structures?

6. What is the major function of a company producer in a retail operation?

7. What purpose do the boxes serve in an organization chart?

8. How does the structure of a small retail operation differ from a major company?

9. What are the major responsibilities of C.E.O.s, C.F.O.s, and C.O.O.s?

10. How many divisions are typically used in the structuring of large department stores, and what are they?

11. Why do many industry professionals consider the merchandising division to be the lifeblood of the company?

12. What are the areas of specialization that come under the jurisdiction of the promotional division?

13. How do the store operations and store management divisions differ from each other?

14. What is the key organizational principle on which large chain store operations are based?

15. Why has it become necessary for many department stores that have become multi-channel retailers to restructure their tables of organization?

Case Problem

Questions

1. With which partner do you agree? Why?
2. Briefly describe a new organizational structure you would suggest to the company.

Tailored Woman began as a small retail operation with one unit in New Hampshire in 1988. After only two years, the partners, Pam and Eleanor, decided to open another unit about 40 miles from the first store. There, too, the store was greeted with enthusiasm, and Pam and Eleanor were on their way to having a successful chain store operation.

With their third store, this one in Vermont, the partners began to realize that their informal approach to organizational structure was no longer appropriate for their business but still neglected to develop a formal structure for the company. All of the major decision-making responsibilities were handled by the two. Pam was the buyer, and Eleanor handled store operations for the three units. The only employees other than the sales associates were store managers for each unit.

At this time, Tailored Woman is considering additional units in Maine and Massachusetts.

Their profitability warrants the expansion but their informality in terms of organizational plans seems to be causing concerns for Pam. While she agrees that they have achieved more success in such a short time than either of them expected, she believes that a more formal approach would maximize profits. She envisions a small central warehouse for receiving, handling, and marking merchandise; an office for buying and merchandising; a computer installation for inventory control and other essential record keeping; and a shipping station for sending goods to the units. A small building that is central to the operation could be leased, and ultimately purchased, if the arrangements work well.

In contrast, Eleanor believes that the informal approach has been good to them and wants to continue that way. She still wants to use the first store's basement as their headquarters for record keeping. Merchandise would still be ordered separately for each unit, shipped directly to each by the vendors, and priced and marked by each. Each store would maintain its own computer for inventory purposes.

At this time, no decision has been made concerning any possible organization restructuring.

Exercises and Projects

1. Contact a member of a large retailer's management team to learn about its organizational structure. Make sure you identify yourself as a student who is preparing a research project for your class. Once you have the information, prepare an organization chart that features all of the divisions and departments of the company, making certain that the staff positions are included in the appropriate places on the chart.

2. Use any one of the many search engines such as www.google.com to learn about organizational structures and computer companies that provide software for graphically presenting the company's structure. One such company is SmartDraw. com, but there are many others that provide this service. After you choose a software company's website, prepare a report about the specific services it provides to retailers for organizational planning and structuring.

chapter four

THE FASHION CONSUMER

After reading this chapter, you should be able to:

- Identify the various factors that influence consumers with their fashion purchases.

- Differentiate between rational and emotional motives.

- Describe how demographic classifications affect fashion purchasing.

- Classify each of the social classes and their characteristics.

- List Maslow's Hierarchy of Needs and the implications of each stage in terms of purchasing ability.

- Describe the various stages of the family life cycle and each category's impact on the buying of fashion merchandise.

- Assess the importance of the multicultural consumer segments to fashion purchases.

The success of any fashion retail business rests with the company's ability to understand consumer needs and offer merchandise that will satisfy those needs. Too often retailers are unaware of the fundamental principles of needs assessment and enter into businesses that are destined for failure. The practice of selecting merchandise without having addressed the potential customers' needs often results in an abundance of unsalable merchandise and losses for the company. This is particularly commonplace with new small fashion operations, where inexperienced owners tend to "jump right in" without first learning the complexities of the marketplace.

Although all merchants are faced with the task of selecting merchandise, none has more **decision making** than the fashion merchant. With manufacturers and designers constantly introducing new styles that soon move out of favor with a fickle public, it is difficult to choose merchandise that will sell and make a profit. Companies that specialize in staples such as appliances do not have the same merchandising problems as their fashion-retailer counterparts. Color preferences for appliances do not change as rapidly or drastically as those for clothing and accessories, and the selling life for these products is comparatively long. A furniture operation generally relies on special-order merchandising and usually only carries samples in its showroom from which customers can choose. If some samples do not sell well, they are quickly replaced with others that might fare better.

In contrast fashion merchants must anticipate customer needs and place orders well in advance of the season, never knowing if the items will be popular. Since fashion consumers generally want their selections as soon as the new season approaches, stores must stock a complete inventory of the latest styles in a variety of colors, sizes, and price points to meet customers' expectations.

Because the dollar amounts expended for stocking such a fashion merchandise collection are often very large, the knowledgeable retailer should examine all of the principles of consumer behavior before deciding what styles to purchase.

Fashion merchants can make their businesses profitable if they understand the services that their customers want, the types of surroundings in which they want to shop, the time it takes for consumers to receive items ordered through catalogs and online, the different price points of fashion merchandise available for purchasing, the different types of brick-and-mortar environments, and the alternatives to shopping in-store by way of catalogs and websites. But in the face of increasing competition, fashion merchants also must understand what motivates people to buy fashion merchandise and how to appeal to those motivations to attract their target market and entice them to spend.

With the significant growth of African American, Hispanic, and Asian-American shoppers as well as designers, the turn of the 21st century began to show that retailers now understand there might be some differences between their traditional fashion consumer base and the ever-growing **multicultural consumer** segment. Many of the areas are the same for both classifications and will be fully explored.

In this first part of the chapter, attention will focus on the traditional consumer analysis techniques, and the theories that are assessed for retailer decision making, with the latter part concentrating on the multicultural consumer, and what areas of study are used to assess their importance as fashion consumers. It is the growth of ethnicities that is making fashion retailers refine their merchandising plans.

THE TRADITIONAL FASHION CONSUMER IDENTIFICATION AND ANALYSIS

Traditionally, fashion merchants have used numerous standard measurements to identify their target markets. Included are buying motives, assessment theories, consumer analysis methodology, and so forth.

Consumer Behavior

The motives that make consumers act and react in a particular way are broken down into **rational**, **emotional**, and **patronage motives**.

Rational Motives

People who consider such factors as price, care, serviceability, practicality, warranties, and safety when making a purchase are rationally motivated. In times when the economy is poor and consumers are either out of work or are experiencing difficulty in paying their bills, rational motives play an important part in how they satisfy their everyday needs. This is especially important when people buy fashion merchandise, because such purchases are not as important as necessities. Shoppers who head to such value-oriented operations such as Target, Marshalls, Walmart, and Kohl's to make their fashion purchases as well as those who go to the off-price emporiums—where marquee labels such as Ralph Lauren and Liz Claiborne are offered for prices that are substantially lower than at the traditional retail operations—are most motivated by the rational factor of price. Some people who have good jobs and spend a great deal of their disposable income on fashion goods but do not have to pay attention to price are affected by rational motives and are opting to buy from companies such as Old Navy, where style is available at an affordable price. Figure 4.1 shows Marshalls, a value-oriented store.

Emotional Motives

Striving to achieve prestige, status, romance, and social acceptance are emotionally driven motives. People often make fashion purchases to satisfy one or more of these needs. An important case in point is the "polo pony" that adorns much of the clothing in Ralph Lauren's collections. Does the insignia make the garment better than something comparable to it, or does it give the wearer a certain aura that implies prestige and status? Macy's Charter Club line features a polo shirt that rivals the Ralph Lauren design feature by feature. The only difference is the price. The Lauren shirt is significantly costlier than the Charter Club version.

How can merchants justify stocking their shelves with the higher-priced item? The answer is simple. A significantly large number of consumers are willing to pay higher prices for the "benefits" of status and prestige afforded them with such purchases.

A wealth of fashion merchandise is marketed solely on the basis of emotional appeal: couture creations from France and Italy that bear such names as Chanel, Armani, and Vuitton; cosmetics that bear names such as Estée Lauder and Bobbi Brown; footwear and handbag designs by Prada; and jewelry by David Yurman. There are many lower-priced versions of these items, but they cannot capture the attention of many fashion enthusiasts simply because the prestigious signatures are missing.

figure 4.1
Marshalls is a value-oriented store where bargain shoppers often satisfy their fashion needs. Their inventories are much less expensive than that of traditional retailers, but only available at a later date.

Patronage Motives

People have numerous places where they may purchase fashion merchandise, including brick-and-mortar outlets, catalogs, websites, and cable television programming. The factors that motivate shoppers to buy from these vendors include service, price, sales associate attention, personal shopping availability, convenience, and merchandise assortment. The more of these features a retailer offers, the more likely it is that shoppers will continue to return for future needs. These are called patronage motives.

Nordstrom, considered to be the benchmark in customer service, offers a wealth of these factors and has thus emerged as a primary destination for the fashion consumer. Shoppers who patronize Nordstrom have come to know exactly what to expect when paying a visit to their stores, buying from their catalogs, or purchasing through their website. Once customers begin to enjoy this comfort level, the store can expect repeat business.

With the wealth of competition that retailers face today, it is important to provide the right mix of merchandise and service that will appeal to a range of motivations and result in customer loyalty.

Consumer Assessment Theories

Several theories have been offered to retailers and other businesses to help them properly assess what prompts consumers to make decisions. These include **Maslow's Hierarchy**

of Needs, the concept of decision making, the **self-concept theory**, and **lifestyle profiling**, also known as *psychographic segmentation*. Each is described in the following sections.

Maslow's Hierarchy of Needs

Maslow's Hierarchy of Needs is based upon the belief that people follow a strict order when fulfilling their needs. People must first satisfy the needs of the lowest classification before moving on to the next, working their way up to the last level. The concept is represented in pyramid form, with the most basic needs at the bottom. The five levels are as follows:

1. *The basic needs of survival.* Cumulatively, these are considered physiological needs and consist of food, clothing, water, and shelter.

2. *The need for safety.* Once people have satisfied their physiological needs, they are concerned with the need for safety. They may make rational purchases such as sturdy athletic wear and sunscreen for bodily protection.

3. *Social needs—belonging and recognition.* Beginning with this level, people make purchases to gain acceptance by a group or to achieve recognition, and it is here that the fashion retailer plays an important role. Much of the purchasing people make is emotionally oriented, with apparel, accessories, and cosmetics leading the way. Clothing purchases are not merely for protection and serviceability but for attracting attention and feeling a sense of belonging to a particular social stratum.

4. *The need for esteem and status.* It is at this level that emotional purchasing plays the most important role. The need to be recognized as an achiever or member of an upper-class social segment prompts people to satisfy their emotional needs with such high-priced merchandise as designer or couture clothing, extravagant furs and accessories, and precious jewelry. Shops on America's fashionable shopping streets such as Madison and Fifth Avenues in New York City, Rodeo Drive in Beverly Hills, and Worth Avenue in Palm Beach all cater to the class that strives for self-esteem and status. Figure 4.2 shows a view of Rodeo Drive in Beverly Hills, CA.

5. *The need for self-actualization.* People who are the highest achievers reach this level. Their world involves self-fulfillment through acquiring artworks, traveling, and gaining knowledge. Their merchandise tastes very often turn to designers and couturiers who will assemble merchandise collections exclusively for them. Some people at this level, however, are so complete within themselves that they have no need for fashion.

It is apparent that the first two levels are of little importance to fashion merchants, since people's purchasing to meet these needs are totally rational and must provide for survival and security. The remaining levels have strong implications for fashion retailers, who must determine how they could best satisfy people's needs for recognition, acceptance, esteem, and status.

The Concept of Decision Making

The concept of decision making consists of five stages. By becoming familiar with how people make choices, the fashion merchants can gain still more insight into satisfying their customers' needs. The process involves the following:

1. *Awareness of need.* Some stimulus such as advertising, a visual presentation, or a special event ignites need for a product. For example, a woman receives a wedding invitation.

2. *Gathering information.* Once the woman determines that she wants to attend the wedding, she begins to gather the necessary information to satisfy the need. She may want to buy a dress to wear or buy a present for the newlyweds. She may know about places where she can buy these items from either print or broadcast advertisements; recollections of stores, catalogs; websites that had satisfied such needs in the past; or a friend's suggestion.

3. *Evaluating choices.* Oftentimes there are many dresses or gifts from which to choose. The woman must evaluate each before reaching a final decision.

4. *Making the decision.* The woman carefully measures each item against established criteria that might include price, attractiveness of the product, alternate uses, and so forth. Once she has studied the items in question she makes a decision to purchase or not to purchase. If she has not reached a positive decision to buy a dress or gift, she continues the process until the need is satisfied. It is at this level that the retailer plays an important role. Through understanding the principles of decision making, the retailer can apply various approaches to assist the customer with the selection.

5. *Satisfaction with the decision.* After the woman buys a dress to wear to the wedding, she may consider whether or not the decision was appropriate. Was the red dress she bought as practical as the black one left behind? Was the price reasonable or more than she should have spent? Will the selection satisfy her emotional needs, which is the underlying reason for most purchases of fashion merchandise? The answers the retailer can provide to these and other questions can either make the customer a "regular" or dissuade her from again patronizing the store. It is therefore important for the merchant to be as helpful as possible by assisting the customer, making suggestions that will be both beneficial to her, and assuring her that the red dress she chose is the best one for this wedding.

The Self-Concept Theory

The self-concept theory focuses on how the consumers perceive themselves. Fashion retailers can gain another perspective of their customers by applying this theory to how they stock their inventories. The four concepts are as follows:

1. *Real self.* This describes what the person really is in terms of ability, appearance, interest, and so forth.

2. *Ideal self.* This is what the person would like to be and is always trying to achieve. The fashion retailer attempts to satisfy this aspect by offering merchandise that would help that person attain his or her desired image. The woman who saves and saves so that she can purchase a new fur coat or a smashing piece of jewelry to make

herself feel successful and the man who uses the newest male-oriented line of cosmetics to achieve an impression of rugged, outdoors looks are two examples of this aspect.

3. *Other self.* This is a combination of the real self and ideal self; what the person's self-image is.

4. *Ideal other.* This is how others perceive the person and how the person would like to be perceived by others. It combines the first three aspects of real self, ideal self, and other self.

If the retailer can feature products that help people realize their ideal self, people will buy more of them. The cosmetics industry, in particular, offers products to make people appear as their ideal selves; fashion merchandisers selling luxury goods also help people achieve this image.

Lifestyle Profiling

By studying people's lifestyles and attitudes, fashion retailers are able to take even closer looks at their targeted markets. While **demographics** reveal a wealth of information regarding the groups of consumers, psychographic segmentation zeroes in on individual lifestyles.

One of the earliest proponents of lifestyle profiling was Standard Research Institute (SRI), a consulting firm that studied consumers through a number of different research tools. Today, the company is an employee-owned spin-off called SRI Consulting Business Intelligence (SRIC-BI.)

The VALS (Values, Attitudes, and Lifestyles) Segments table (Table 4.1) identifies each segment, defines specific individual characteristics of each, lists what motivates these types, and describes the nature of the purchases they are likely to make.

Table 4.1

THE VALS SEGMENTS

Segments	Characteristics	Motivations	Purchases
Innovators	Successful, sophisticated, high-esteem	Image, new ideas, technologies	Upscale, niche products and services
Thinkers	Mature, satisfied, comfortable, conservative, reflective	Open to new ideas	Durable, functional, value products
Achievers	Goal-oriented lifestyles; focus around family, place of worship, and work; politically conservative	Image, stability, self-discovery	Established, prestige products and services that demonstrate success to their peers
Experiencers	Young, enthusiastic, impulsive	Variety, excitement, risk	Fashion merchandise, entertainment, socializing
Believers	Conservative, conventional concrete traditions; established codes of religion, family	Ideals	Familiar products and established brands
Strivers	Trendy and fun loving, active consumers	Achievement, money, emulating purchases of people with greater material wealth	Stylish products
Makers	Practicality, self-sufficiency	Self-expression, tradition	Basic, practical, value products
Survivors	Few resources, cautious	Safety and security	Brands, discount prices

In analyzing the different VALS classifications, it is obvious that innovators, experiencers, achievers, and strivers are the best groups for fashion merchandisers to pursue. Each, to varying degrees, spends a considerable portion of its money on such purchases.

Consumer Analysis

It is imperative that merchants have a complete understanding of the characteristics of the marketplace from which they hope to attract consumers. The major research studies deal with a host of different areas, one of the most important of which is demographics, the study of population traits and characteristics. By analyzing population shifts, market size, family status, nationalities, age groups, and so forth, it is possible to gain a significant insight into potential markets. Social classes, and the ways each level views its income, goals, education, and attitudes, and the **family life cycle** and how the needs of people at each stage affect their purchasing potential are two other areas that merit attention.

Demographics

Demographics information is used differently by the various retail classifications. Brick-and-mortar organizations, for example, are more concerned with population density than are off-site operations such as catalogs and websites, because their customers come from the geographic trading areas in which their stores are located. Off-site retailers, in contrast, have no real boundaries, since consumers with computer access or a mailing address can examine their product assortment anywhere. Age classification, however, has implications for every type of retail classification. Therefore, retailers need to assess the population trends that most affect their consumer bases so they can determine the best use of their resources to attract them.

Population Concentration

Brick-and-mortar fashion retailers in particular must evaluate the areas in which their potential customers reside, because it can affect the specifics of the merchandise mix that they stock. People living in the suburbs, for example, might have more casual lifestyles than their urban counterparts, so their fashion needs are in the lines of informal, comfortable clothing. Those who live in the major urban cities have a busier, faster-paced lifestyle, so their dress is often more high fashion or career oriented.

Studying these different regions will help fashion managers determine which of these groups will buy their products. If people from more than one geographic concentration will patronize their stores, merchants should carefully assess their needs and lifestyles to determine which products might appeal to both types of customers. Often, major retailers with stores in downtown, central trading districts and suburban shopping malls tailor their merchandise mix to fit these communities' specific needs. The downtown flagship might, for example, stock a greater mix of career dress and the suburban branches might have a greater concentration of sportswear.

Climate Differences

If a store has its units in just one geographical climate, then merchandise emphasis and assortment are comparatively simple to determine. Those fashion retailers that exclusively operate southern outlets, for example, stock a mix that includes swimwear in each of their units.

Larger companies, such as The Gap Stores, Inc., that have stores that cross into different climate zones must address the different merchandise needs dictated by their locations. Lightweight clothing fits the everyday needs of customers shopping in the stores in the year-round warmer climates, and heavier garments are in demand during the winter months in such areas as the northeast. Fashion retailers must carefully consider their merchandise differentiation to make certain that the right assortment is available at the right time and place; improper merchandise allocation could adversely affect overall company profits. Figure 4.3 shows a Banana Republic store, part of The Gap group.

Age Groups

Although age consideration is an important factor in the merchandising of most retailers' assortments, it is fashion merchandise that offers more variables than any other product classification. A look at consumers on the street immediately reveals that dress varies considerably among the different age groups. Within the same geographical location, a teenage girl wearing a micro-mini skirt in the latest style can be seen walking along with her grandmother, who is attired in a more conservatively fashionable outfit.

Given the different needs of the many age classifications, it is vital that the right styles are being marketed to the right groups. By segmenting the consumer market into age categories, retailers are able to determine the size of each group, its potential for growth or decline, and its distinguishing characteristics. In this way, they can assess which groups are better to target for fashion merchandise and what their specific buying preferences are.

Age groups may be segmented in a number of different ways. Designations used by marketers to describe particular segments, especially as they concern fashion merchandise, include **baby boomers**, people born between 1945 and 1964, and **generation X** and **generation Y**, people who were ages 18–34 at the beginning of the twenty-first century. More traditional age classifications have been established by the U.S. Department of Commerce, and they are described below with their implications for fashion retailers.

CHILDREN

Ranging in age from birth to under 13, this group has become increasingly more important to the fashion retailer. Although newborns don't count as purchasers, children from such early ages as three begin to be important as those who influence those who do buy the products. Because these young children watch television, they are regularly inundated with commercials for a wide range of products, and they often badger their parents until they get what they want. Older children are also influenced by their favorite television characters and often want to emulate their favorite personalities by dressing as they do. Children aged 8 to 13 years are referred to as being in the mature boomlet stage. Companies such as The Gap Stores, Inc. and L Brands, Inc. have taken their cues from the potential of this market and have expanded their operations. As the size of this age group grows The Gap continues to open more units of BabyGap and GapKids.

figure 4.3
With stores in so many different climates, Banana Republic varies the merchandise mix to suit the climate. This makes their merchandise assortments different in each of their units.

TEENAGERS

When it comes to purchasing trendy fashion merchandise, this age classification has no rival. Teenagers tend to embrace everything that comes onto the fashion scene. If short skirts are the order of the day, they opt for the shortest; if it is ankle-length skirts that are being touted, then they will wear skirts that drag on the floor. No matter the shoes' color, the size, and the shape of its heel, teens will buy them if they're in style. Teens are often influenced by what is being worn on their favorite television shows. For example, *American Idol* significantly impacts the styles teenagers buy.

This group is a blessing for the merchant that primarily sells trendy fashions. Teenagers generally choose less-costly garments because they like to have a lot of clothes, but they stop wearing them once they are out of style. They make up their minds quickly because there are lots of styles in their sizes and they know what they want because their fashion appetites have been whetted by the fashion publications catering to them. Teens also buy in greater quantities than the other age groups. They patronize stores such as Old Navy, Abercrombie & Fitch, Wet Seal, and American Eagle. Figure 4.4 shows a teenager carrying an Abercrombie & Fitch shopping bag.

YOUNG ADULTS

This age group is actually composed of two classifications: those still in college, and those in the early stages of a career. Both have significant needs for fashion merchandise; however, the former group is more focused on relaxed clothing and accessories for classes and special attire for social occasions. The latter group spends on both career dress and after-hours wardrobes. As a whole, they spend more on fashion merchandise than their teenage counterparts since they are usually in better financial situations. They usually shop in specialty shops where they can find merchandise assortments tailored to their needs and can get in and out faster than they can in department stores. Stores such as Ann Taylor, Banana Republic, Limited, Express, Victoria's Secret, and Gap pay close attention to the needs of this group. Young adults also do a lot of purchasing online.

figure 4.4
A young shopper with an Abercrombie shopping bag. This is a company that specializes in apparel for the young adult.

Young Middle-Aged

This group includes those with the highest incomes. Many are top-level corporate executives, business owners, or professionals. Their incomes and lifestyles make them the prime target for the fashion retailers. They patronize prestigious specialty and department stores and make significant purchases from fashion catalogs and online because their time for in-store shopping is often limited. Well-tailored quality designer brands such as Calvin Klein, Ralph Lauren, and DKNY are directed at this audience, where price is a less important factor in their selections. Companies such as Saks Fifth Avenue, Bloomingdale's, Neiman Marcus, Bergdorf Goodman, and a host of upscale fashion boutiques cater to young middle-aged patrons and their fashion needs.

Older Middle-Aged

The people in this group are often of two types. One is still career oriented and requires fashions that are important to their everyday professional lives. The people are often in the market for quality merchandise at upper-level price points. Since their careers often involve social obligations as well, they buy fashionable occasional clothing and accessories. The other segment of this group has retired and spends more time in leisure activities such as travel and recreation. These people still want fashion items but often prefer sportswear because they spend their time playing tennis or golf. Consequently, manufacturers of traditional sportswear offer collections tailored to these interests. Ralph Lauren, for example, features a line of golf clothing that is available at pro shops and department stores.

The retired segment has more time to spend shopping, so the people often prefer to make their purchases in department stores and sometimes on the Internet.

Elderly

The elderly market is not typically as important for fashion retailers. The elderly are usually more concerned with health and other personal problems than they are about fashion. Their purchases are usually for functional merchandise, often lower priced and more conservative in nature. There are, however, a growing number of people in this classification who spend more time on vacations, and cruises are very popular. For those occasions they buy evening wear. Collectively, they are considered to be "difficult" shoppers because many live on fixed incomes and cannot be moved from their preconceived ideas about "proper" fashion.

Table 4.2 summarizes the six age classifications as studied by the U.S. Department of Commerce, with their age ranges, their fashion needs, and the typical retailers they patronize.

Occupations

Today's consumer marketplace is quite different from that of the past. Women, for instance, have made the transition from homemakers to business executives and professionals and have joined the ranks of the male members of society as viable players in the workplace. More and more have become CEOs of Fortune 500 companies. As a combined group, they are an extremely important segment of the population for fashion retailers. However, a major portion of those employed work in blue-collar jobs. While female office workers and non-office workers both have clothing needs, their requirements are quite different. The former segment is interested in a wide assortment

Table 4.2

AGE GROUP SEGMENTS

Classification	Age Range	Fashion Needs	Retail Patronage
Children	Under 13	Younger portion opts for "character" clothing; older group prefers dress of television stars	GapKids, BabyGap
Teenagers	13–19	Trendy merchandise	Express, Wet Seal, Abercrombie & Fitch; online
Young Adults	20–34	Sportswear, career dress, leisure apparel	Ann Taylor, Banana Republic, Gap; online
Young middle-aged	35–49	Upscale fashion apparel and accessories, designer labels	Neiman Marcus, Saks Fifth Avenue, fashion designer boutiques; catalogs and online
Older middle-aged	50–64	Still working: career clothing, after-hours apparel. Retired: sportswear	Department stores such as Macy's and Bloomingdale's; catalogs
Elderly	65 and over	Functional clothing and accessories	Discounters such as Target and Walmart; catalogs

of suits, accessories, and other fashion merchandise. The latter's needs are more basic and functional, and except for special occasions, they have little interest in fashion merchandise.

The apparel and accessories requirements of professionals and business executives also change. In the late 1990s two trends in the business world changed how office workers dressed. The first trend was **Casual Friday** that became popular in the offices of attorneys, investment bankers, and other high-level places of employment. This phenomenon, which allowed men to wear open-collared shirts, sports coats, and contrasting slacks, caused a downturn in sales for merchants who stocked suits and more traditional workplace clothing. They had to change their merchandise assortments to deal with the new casual mode of dress. In fact, in many places, the Casual Friday approach to dress carried over into other days of the week, causing even more concern for those who sold suits, business shirts, oxfords, ties, and other more formal wear. The women's wear market was equally affected, since women wore pantsuits in place of dresses. At the start of the 21st century, many companies returned to the traditional formal mode of dress and still subscribe to it today. This departure from the casual look brought with it a larger market for formal dress. Suits for men began to reclaim their share of the retailer's inventory, and more dresses were sold.

The second trend was the work-at-home phenomenon, which reduced the need for all kinds of career clothing. With approximately 50 million people telecommuting, jeans and T-shirts became the order of the day. Even sleepwear was being bought in greater quantities by those who didn't have to interact personally with co-workers and clients. Again, fashion retailers had to rethink their merchandise mixes to accommodate this ever-growing group of consumers. These recent trends show that retailers must continuously evaluate the business and professional marketplace to ascertain what the components of acceptable dress will be. Figure 4.5 shows a financial planner in a traditional suit.

Today, there is no longer one standard of proper dress for people who are gainfully employed. Retailers must do regular needs assessment to determine that they maintain the proper breadth and depth of apparel and accessories that their targeted markets

figure 4.5
The suit is a sign of professionalism and is a must for those in such fields as law, investments, and so forth.

desire. They must adjust their inventories accordingly to ensure that they can profit from the trends rather than lose money on outdated merchandise.

Income

A person's income plays the most significant role in determining if a purchase can be made. Although shoppers might like to buy Armani creations, their ability to pay for them is the ultimate factor in determining if they will do so. Consumers must first pay for the necessities of life (as outlined in the section on "Maslow's Hierarchy of Needs"). Other parts of their disposable income must be used for other important purchases; eventually, they determine what portion of their income is **discretionary income** that is available for more luxury items such as precious jewelry and designer apparel.

Fashion merchants must evaluate the various income levels of people in their trading area and make certain that they stock merchandise at price points that are commensurate with them.

Education

The manner in which people dress is often based upon their educational level. Those with advanced degrees in law and business administration, for example, will have a greater need for fashion apparel and accessories than those with less formal educational achievements. Attorneys, investment bankers, security traders, and those in similar professions are expected to dress in more traditional attire in their business environments and in the social engagements that are often extensions of the office place. The specialty retailer Brooks Brothers is a perfect example of a company that caters to this clientele; others include specialized department stores such as Saks Fifth Avenue and Neiman Marcus.

Social Class Groupings

One of the concepts most utilized by fashion retailers in the determination of appropriate merchandise mixes and price points is the one involving American **social**

class, by which groups of people are segregated into homogeneous categories according to income, occupation, background, educational levels, and other factors. Studies show that the different groups have different shopping preferences and merchandise needs.

Traditionally, the most popular approach to social class groupings is to divide the population into three distinct classes with two subdivisions within each one.

Upper Class

The most socially prominent group in the three classes is the upper class. This wealthiest segment accounts for approximately 3 percent of the population. It includes in its numbers both wealthy families that have inherited their wealth from past generations and the "nouveau riche," who have come into their own wealth as a result of their own successes.

UPPER-UPPER CLASS

This segment represents about 1 percent of the population. It has among its constituents such family dynasties as the Rockefellers and the Vanderbilts, who are considered to be the socially elite in the United States. Members of this segment make purchases that are often understated and without thought to cost. Their main requirement is quality. In terms of fashion, they prefer understated designs for casual wear and couturier designs for the many social functions that they attend. Some people in this class, in fact, have been known to be the catalysts in bringing new designers to the forefront of the fashion world.

This class patronizes such prestigious specialized department stores as Bergdorf Goodman, Neiman Marcus, and Saks Fifth Avenue and boutiques for both men and women that include Calvin Klein, Ralph Lauren, Yves Saint Laurent, Gucci, Ferragamo, Dolce & Gabbana, and Fendi. They frequent such famous American fashion streets as Worth Avenue, in Palm Beach, FL; Madison and Fifth Avenues, in New York City; Rodeo Drive, in Beverly Hills, CA; Oak Street in Chicago; and overseas venues that include Avenue Foch, Paris; and Rue d'Antibes, Cannes. Fabulous jewelry from such world-renowned companies as Harry Winston, Van Cleef & Arpels, and Tiffany & Co. are also part of their fashion purchases.

LOWER-UPPER CLASS

The remainder of this upper class strata accounts for 2 percent of the population. These are the new rich Americans. Unlike their counterparts of the upper-upper class, these people are business executives in major corporations, owners of companies, professionals, and entertainers who have amassed their own fortunes without inheriting them. In terms of spending, price is not a major factor. They are conspicuous spenders and shop at the finest boutiques and specialty stores around the globe. Fashion purchases are often for products that will make them stand out in a crowd.

Middle Class

Comprising approximately 42 percent of the population, the middle class is the second largest segment. Unlike the upper class, where the two subdivisions have spending similarities, the upper- and lower-middle class have distinctly different habits.

UPPER-MIDDLE CLASS

The smaller of the middle-class segments accounts for approximately 12 percent of the population. These people are concerned with prestige and status and seem to want to make the transition to the lower-upper class. They are professionals and owners of businesses and spend their leisure time trying to emulate those in the classes above them.

Although many in this class are high earners, their wealth is sometimes less than they need to enable them to purchase as freely as they would like. To satisfy their fashion needs with designer clothing and other prestigious merchandise, this group regularly visits well-known fashion department and specialty stores at times when markdowns enable them to purchase upscale, high fashion goods at reduced prices. Off-price shops such as Loehmann's and Marshalls, closeout centers such as Nordstrom Rack and Saks OFF 5TH, and designer outlets of companies such as Ralph Lauren and Anne Klein are regular haunts for this class. Shopping in these places allows them to buy the same fashion labels that are found in the traditional stores but to spend less money. Since recognition, by way of their fashionable wardrobes, is important to this class, they are the best customers for quality merchandise at bargain prices.

LOWER-MIDDLE CLASS

Significantly larger than the upper level of this class, this segment accounts for 30 percent of the population. Members of this class are primarily conscientious workers with conservative values who have a strong desire for their children to earn college degrees.

Unlike members of the upper-middle class, they place less importance on "showy" fashion merchandise and consider price to be a very important factor in making purchases. Whereas the higher classes shop early in the season for fashionable clothes, this group makes its selections as the needs arise, and therefore shops frequently, though rarely spending large sums of money at one time.

People in the lower-middle class typically buy their fashion merchandise from department stores that specialize in popular-priced merchandise, from discounters such as Target and Walmart, and from off-pricers such as Burlington Coat Factory and Marshalls. They are not terribly interested in quality or conservative styles but tend to be attracted by the latest styles and colors. Fashion designer labels are not necessarily important to this group except in cases where they are deeply discounted by off-price merchants.

Lower Class or Working Class

This is the largest class of Americans, at 55 percent of the population. At times when the economy falters, as was the case in 2011, this group has a rough time paying for the necessities of life, let alone fashion merchandise.

UPPER-LOWER CLASS

At 35 percent, this is the largest subsegment of the population. Members of this group are generally poorly educated and hold blue-collar jobs that give them insufficient amounts to spend on fashion merchandise. When they do have fashion needs, they generally buy very inexpensive apparel and accessories. Price is an extremely important factor, so they generally limit their purchases to discount operations, off-price shops, and specialty stores that merchandise the lowest priced lines.

LOWER-LOWER CLASS

With little or no formal education, the lower-lower class accounts for 20 percent of the population. Many in this group are welfare and food stamp recipients and have barely enough to satisfy their needs for survival. Fashion merchandise is generally out of the question, except for the occasional celebration. When they do shop for this type of merchandise, they often head for the second-hand shops, which are rapidly growing.

Since fashion merchandise is available at just about any price point, it is necessary for merchants to know the social classes of their markets. In this way, they can satisfy the needs of their customers and potential shoppers by providing them with the types of retail operations they find suitable to their social stations and the clothing and accessories they desire.

Family Life Cycle

People who are at a specific stage in their family life cycle generally have the same needs as others at the same stage of life. By studying these various segments or stages, fashion retailers can assess the needs of particular groups in their trading areas. For example, if a geographic area is dominated by empty nesters, it is safe to assume that their needs and desires would be similar. However, there are also differences within each group in terms of income, occupations, educational levels, and lifestyles that affect their purchasing potential.

Classifications within the family life cycle have changed in recent years. At one point, retailers that assessed these groups for their planning strategies concentrated on more traditional classifications. Today, however, nonconventional segments have been added to the list and include such categories as **multiple-member/shared households** and single parents.

CHILDLESS SINGLES UNDER 45

This is a very diverse segment of the population. Those in their twenties, for example, are relative newcomers to their careers and generally have lower incomes than their older counterparts. Collectively, however, they represent an excellent market for many retailers. With little responsibility other than to themselves, many in the group have a great deal of discretionary income. Once they have satisfied the needs of rent and utilities, the bulk of their salaries is often spent on fashion merchandise and cosmetics. Often intent on meeting others in similar situations, they have memberships in fitness centers, frequently dine in restaurants, and engage in travel to unique destinations. Each of these activities gives them reason to purchase active sportswear, apparel and accessories, and a host of cosmetics. Those at the upper end of the income scale in this classification are usually devotees of designer labels such as Prada, Dolce & Gabbana, Ralph Lauren, Calvin Klein, and Donna Karan. Those at the midpoint of this segment in terms of earning power opt for less-costly merchandise and do their shopping at companies such as Banana Republic and Ann Taylor, where the latest fashions are readily available. At the lowest level of this group, Gap is a familiar haunt where they can have their fashion needs satisfied.

Childless Singles 45 and Over

In today's society, more and more people are choosing to remain single. As is the case with their younger counterparts, they often enjoy significant incomes that afford them the opportunity to live exciting lifestyles that warrant a great deal of fashion apparel and accessories. Many are in their own businesses, have medical and dental practices, or are employed as attorneys, investment bankers, or technology managers. They too patronize the merchants that offer the latest in fashion.

Although many live alone, others participate in lifestyles that are akin to marriages but without the licenses. In these cases, because they share expenses, they often have greater discretionary spending power.

Single Parents

With a divorce rate that seems to be steadily increasing and the number of unwed mothers also spiraling upward, this has become an important segment of the population for retailers to address when planning their merchandise assortments. Often short on cash, single parents typically do not have sufficient amounts of disposable income to purchase a great deal of fashion merchandise. They have to be able to support themselves and their offspring. Women are not alone in this category, although the majority of them have the children from their former marriages live with them. Men, although not typically the everyday rearers of these children, do have some financial responsibility in their upbringing.

Given their financial stress, when this group does buy fashion merchandise, it is more likely to buy from discounters such as Target, Walmart, and Kmart and off-price merchants such as Stein Mart and Marshalls.

Multiple-Member/Shared Households

The costs associated with housing and other necessary expenses have contributed to the need for people without marital connections to live together. In major cities across America, rents keep rising to previously unseen levels. This phenomenon has given birth to this new family lifestyle category, multiple-member/shared households.

Those who are part of this group include same-sex relationships, opposite-sex relationships with the possibility of marriage, same-sex marriage, opposite-sex relationships without the intention of marriage, and two or more sets of single parents with children who live with them.

The diversity of people involved in this group results in purchasing characteristics that differ widely. Singles who plan to marry each other, on the one hand, are among those who often share dual incomes that enable them to make more than just the basic purchases. Many of these couples have no intention of having children, making them excellent customers for fashion merchants. Companies such as Saks Fifth Avenue and Bloomingdale's and designer boutiques are their main purchasing outlets. On the other hand, single parents sharing a household with one or more children living with them often find it difficult to make ends meet. They often live from paycheck to paycheck and do not have the luxury of buying merchandise other than the basics. When they do purchase fashion items, it is often from discounters and off-price merchants.

SINGLE-EARNER COUPLES WITH CHILDREN

Because of the rising living expenses of raising children, this classification has seen a radical decline in the past 20 years. Of course, some in this category do retain the single-earner status and maintain a standard of life that allows them to satisfy their fashion needs. Attorneys, investment bankers, health professionals, and business owners, for example, are part of the upper-middle class and earn enough to make the luxury purchases they desire.

Those in this classification with limited funds buy their fashion merchandise from discounters such as Target and Walmart; the more affluent members of the group head for the brick-and-mortar operations such as Bloomingdale's and Nordstrom, fashion boutiques, and catalog resources or online sites that specialize in fashion apparel and accessories.

DUAL-EARNER MARRIED COUPLES WITH CHILDREN

With two employed parents, members of this group are financially better off than their single-earner counterparts. Those in this group who have very young children generally require preschool programs or nannies to tend to their children while they are at work. This expense can be considerable and can affect the spending capabilities of these families. At the other end of the spectrum, those with children in college also find their expenses spiraling upward, requiring them to be cautious about spending.

Those who have substantial dual incomes are more likely to shop in the major department and specialty store organizations, while the less financially affluent are more likely to head to Gap and Old Navy, where value fashion shopping is possible.

Once the children have moved out of the house and expenses for college have been satisfied, the sky is often the limit for these families. At this point, especially if both partners are still employed, cost is no longer a factor in terms of fashion purchases.

CHILDLESS MARRIED COUPLES

This classification is composed of couples at any age. They may be newlyweds who do not intend to raise a family (rising trend), middle-aged people, or the elderly. In any case, collectively, they are financially better off than their counterparts who have children. While the taste levels of those in this group vary considerably, they are generally able to buy whatever pleases them. Fashion purchases are generally made at the traditional full-line or specialized department stores and upscale specialty brick-and-mortar operations.

EMPTY NESTERS

Those who have raised families but now live alone, known as empty nesters, are in a position to buy what they want without the need to be cautious. With expenses greatly minimized, they often spend on fashion items that they once considered too extravagant to consider. Many are still working and are at higher levels of income than at any time in their lives. With the ability to travel and join country clubs, they are often in the market to purchase fashion apparel and accessories to suit their new lifestyles. Where they once maintained wardrobes that were business oriented, they now adopt a freer approach to shopping. Designer labels are often their choices, as are the stores that offer them in abundance such as boutiques and specialty shops.

While family life cycle classifications remain constant, the people within them generally move from one to the other, depending upon their times in life. Singles might marry, dual-earners might retire, married couples might divorce, and so forth, making their needs change. This is particularly true when it comes to fashion merchandise. The places in which they make their purchases might change from the traditional department stores to discount operations where value rather than selection might prevail. Fashion retailers must always address these different classifications and determine which family life cycles are most dominant in their trading areas.

While there are numerous theories and concepts that businesses have accepted in the study of consumer behavior and related topics, some companies opt to conduct their own research to determine customer reaction to their products.

THE MULTICULTURAL CONSUMER: A GROWING MARKET SEGMENT

Markets that were untapped by the vast majority of retailers ten years ago are now being carefully scrutinized to determine their importance to a vast array of fashion merchants. By underutilizing **ethnic market segments**, namely African Americans, Hispanics, and Asian Americans, retailers have left approximately $3 trillion on the table according to researchers at the Selig Center. Estimates suggest that these three ethnic groups combined will account for more than $3 trillion by the end of 2015.

While the three leading ethnicities are measured by the traditional methodologies used to assess the general population such as the aforementioned consumer behavior, Maslow's Hierarchy of Needs, and so forth, other factors must be researched to gain the full impact of them as shoppers.

Demographic Analysis

The projections and findings of the last Census Bureau report features population numbers, purchasing power, and income levels, all of which are important for retailers to consider in their merchandise planning.

Population

The most recent Census Bureau projections conclude that the white population will no longer make up a majority of Americans by 2043. America continues to grow more diverse due to the higher birth rates among minorities, with Hispanics leading the way. By 2060, the multiracial population is expected to rise from the present 7.5 million to 26.7 million. The population is projected to increase from 315 million today, to 400 million in 2051, when whites will drop to 43 percent of the U.S. population.

The implications of the minority increase are significant for fashion retailers.

Purchasing Power

The consumer purchasing power of the U.S. multicultural market was $1.3 trillion in 2013. Leading the way were Hispanics with $560 billion, followed by African Americans who spent $478 billion, and Asian Americans with $262 billion.

Income

The Bureau of Labor Statistics' most recent study published in July 2013 reported the following weekly salaries for whites and the three major ethnic minorities. They were:

- $799 for whites
- $634 for African Americans
- $572 for Hispanics
- $973 for Asian Americans

It is imperative for fashion retailers to not only research the overall minority statistics in terms of population, purchasing power, and income, but to carefully study their own trading areas. For example, Los Angeles and Miami are the major Hispanic markets, Atlanta and Chicago are the prime African American markets, and San Francisco the major Asian-American market. General figures are insufficient as tools for all retailers.

REACHING THE MULTICULTURAL SHOPPER

In order to attract the largest potential multicultural market, it is essential that the retailer's effort will include a number of approaches. They include **target research**, studying new shopping technologies, sourcing and featuring Hispanic merchandise throughout selling floors, using bilingual signage, using ads that "speak" Spanish, and culturally relevant campaigns. The *Happening Now* feature emphasizes Macy's quest for the Latina market.

HAPPENING NOW

HISPANIC STYLISTS HELP TO ATTRACT LATINA CUSTOMER

Recognizing that the Latina customer base is continuously growing, and that their inventory does not properly address this growth, Macy's is making a huge effort to target Latinas. One of the initial responses to correcting the problem is to add a complete line of merchandise that bears the name of Thalia Sodi. The collection will feature Thalia dresses, tops, pants, shoes, and jewelry that will be "rolled out" to 300 stores. Such a significant launch will require many different techniques to make it a success, and a great deal of lead time to make it happen. Happening now is putting in place all of the advertising, promotion, merchandise design, publicity, and so forth so that the launch will be ready for spring 2015.

Since Sodi is not a designer, she will have input into the designs with her ideas and own fashion sense. The collection will be created by Macy's private brand team, and geared to the 30-something age group. Recognizing that the Latina segment is the fastest growing in the United States, they want to make certain that they will capture their fair share of the market.

According to Jeff Gennette, Macy's then-chief merchandising officer, now president, in a conversation with *WWD*, one of the reasons for this particular "designer" selection is Thalia's passion for and ability to speak directly to this market segment, as her communication skills indicate. "She really gets this customer," according to Gennette.

Target Research

Many retailers in their pursuit of applying a multicultural strategy have not succeeded because they often do not use target research in their studies. This thorough research encompasses language usage, ethnic traditions, political leanings, geographical concentration, and numerous other variations. Misunderstanding by the targeted audience will often fail to capture them as a viable audience.

Engaging Shoppers

Expand target research to involve the current and prospective customers. Question them regarding their personal family lives, goals, and careers (both now and future ambitions). One of the important findings for fashion and other retailers is that Hispanics are among the biggest users of smartphones and social media sites such as Facebook and Twitter. Using these accounts while they are on the go makes them excellent targets for merchants. Understanding this, it is imperative that mobile ads feature shorter messages to be effective.

Using Bilingual Signage

In the major Hispanic markets, companies like Target use bilingual signs that quickly capture the attention of those who do not read English. While many Latinos are bilingual, a large percentage of Mexican, Cuban, Puerto Rican, and other Hispanics read only their native language. In a recent survey by Walmart, potential growth will come from the Hispanic market and by studying their preferences and other profile factors, they will begin to spend more on targeting them as customers.

Sourcing Merchandise with Minority Appeal

In markets with significant African Americans, Hispanics, and Asian Americans, paying attention to the merchandise mix is extremely important. Today, the fashion producer population features a number of designers from each of the ethnicities. Their offerings run the gamut from couture to popular-priced with many featuring both ends of the spectrum beginning with upscale collections to those designs that they have made for collaborations with major retailers such as Kohl's, Target, and Kmart. The latter arrangement brings them significant recognition from the moderate income population.

Some of the multicultural designers are well known with established companies and others who are beginning to make themselves players in the fashion arena. A very small sampling features designers old and new. They are Sean "Puff Daddy" Combs, Kimora Lee Simmons, Tracy Reese, Stephen Burrows, Azede Jean-Pierre, B. Michael, Patrick Robinson, Phillip Lim, Eunice Lee, Narciso Rodriguez, Carolina Herrera, and Isabel Toledo.

Designer collaborations with major retailers include Kohl's and Jennifer Lopez, Daisy Fuentes, and Derek Lam; Kmart with Sofia Vergara and Selena Gomez; and Target with Phillip Lim.

Through significant advertising and promotional endeavors both partners in the arrangement have achieved great success.

Bilingual Staffing

With numerous retailers experiencing more and more patriotism from Hispanic and Asian-American consumers who are not fluent in English, the best approach is to make those who speak the foreign languages on both the selling floor and the telephone available. It is also important for executives to speak Spanish so they might be able to settle customer disputes.

Two of the largest Spanish-speaking chains are Kohl's and Walmart where shoppers can communicate with staff in Spanish. In these companies the combination of Spanish signage, Hispanic displays, conversation, and promotion gives them an advantage in trying to improve their bottom lines.

MAXIMIZING THE MULTICULTURAL EFFORT

The following efforts are offered by multicultural specialists for fashion retailers to maximize their "reach" strategies. These are by no means the only ones being attempted.

- The establishing of **focus groups** using different ethnicities will help the retailer learn if these consumers' needs are being met.
- By viewing Spanish-using social media and speaking networks such as Telemundo and Univision to capture the essence of what merchandise is being marketed to minorities.
- Using social media and mobile devices, which are largely used by Hispanics, will bring the store's merchandise to the minority population.
- While retailers often appeal to African Americans and Hispanics, they sometimes fail to address the importance of the Asian-American market segment. This group's population, according to the most recent U.S. Census Bureau, has grown faster than any other.

Chapter Highlights

1. Very often, purchasing behavior is based upon different motives. They are either rational, where such factors as price, care, practicality, and so forth are important, or emotional, where factors such as prestige and status come into play.

2. The patronage motive helps a consumer make the decision about where to shop.

3. Maslow's Hierarchy of Needs is a theory that is based upon the order in which humans fulfill their needs.

4. The self-concept theory describes how the consumers perceive themselves.

5. Lifestyle profiling enables fashion retailers to take closer looks at their targeted markets. One of the major researchers in this field is SRIC-BI, a company that has been the pioneer in such studies with its widely used VALS system.

6. Demographics is the study of the population in terms of age groups, geographic concentration, occupations, and income.

7. The population of the United States is categorized into social classes. Each represents a portion of the population and suggests how those in the various groups are likely to spend their discretionary income.

8. The family life cycle offers retailers information regarding how people in the same group are likely to shop for fashion merchandise. The segments range from childless singles under age 45 to the empty nesters, with a host of other classifications in between.

9. Many major companies undertake their own research to study how their potential customers are likely to react to their merchandise offerings.

10. Small fashion retailers, while unable to enter into their own research because of the often prohibitive costs involved, can turn to the Internet and avail themselves of a great deal of material on consumer behavior.

Terms of the Trade

baby boomers	ideal self
Casual Friday	lifestyle profiling
decision making	Maslow's Hierarchy of Needs
demographics	multicultural consumers
discretionary income	multiple-member/shared households
emotional motives	other self
ethnic market segments	patronage motives
family life cycle	rational motives
focus groups	real self
generation X	self-concept theory
generation Y	social class
ideal other	target research

For Discussion

1. In what way do rational motives differ from emotional motives?

2. Why are patronage motives important for fashion retailers to consider?

3. In Maslow's Hierarchy of Needs, at what stage does the fashion retailer begin to surface as fulfilling a need?

4. According to the self-concept theory, at what step does the individual want to make a better impression?

5. What does the VALS system try to predict for retailers, and how does it go about doing it?

6. Define the term demographics, and tell how their study enables retailers to more carefully approach their potential consumer markets.

7. Which demographic age segment is most likely to be attracted to trendy fashion merchandise?

8. For what situations might the elderly still require the purchase of fashion apparel and accessories?

9. How does the upper-upper class differ from the lower-upper class in terms of purchases?

10. Describe the upper-middle class in regard to its fashion purchases.

11. Why do childless singles under 45 represent an excellent market for fashion merchandise?

12. How are some of the households composed in the multiple-member/shared household family life cycle?

13. Do the family life cycle segments remain constant? Explain.

14. Why do some companies, such as Dupont, conduct their own consumer research projects?

15. How do the youngsters in the mature boomlet stage influence fashion purchasing?

16. When is it expected for the multicultural population to exceed the white population?

17. How should fashion retailers engage minority populations?

18. Which minority population group is the greatest user of social media?

19. According to the last Census Bureau findings, which minority population has shown the fastest growth?

20. Which major chains are increasing their product mix with multicultural designers?

Case Problem

Five years ago, Sue Gallop and Muriel Litt entered into a partnership agreement for the purpose of purchasing a small, established specialty boutique. The store, located in an affluent Midwestern suburb, had been owned and operated for eight years by Margie Paxton. Its success was immediate, and Margie enjoyed the rewards of her business for all of the years that she owned it.

Her concept was to offer high fashion, quality merchandise with an equal amount of designer clothing and custom-made models. Her clientele, initially drawn from friends and acquaintances, ultimately expanded to make hers one of the area's most distinguished boutiques.

When Sue and Muriel purchased the store from Margie, they put some of their own touches on the business, and the venture became more successful than when they bought it. Couturier designs from around the world were added to the merchandise mix, and these items became an important part of the store's collection.

As the sales volume began to grow, so did the two partners' desire for expansion. They thought of adding a wing to their existing location but scrapped the idea, feeling it would take away from the intimacy that helped make the store such a winner. The other choice was to open another unit.

After a great deal of searching, they came upon a location that seemed perfect. It was situated 50 miles from their first shop on a busy main street in a community that resembled their other location. The size of the vacant store was appropriate for their needs, as was the rent. A drive through the surrounding area drew their attention to the same types of houses that were in their first trading area. Their immediate response was that this was an ideal situation for a new venture.

Questions

1. Should the fact that the type of housing in the neighborhood near the new venture was the same as the housing near the first be sufficient for Sue and Muriel to go ahead with the additional store? Why?

2. What demographics should they consider before they expand their operation to the new location?

3. What other types of consumer information should they seek before they make an ultimate decision?

Exercises and Projects

1. Select five fashion advertisements of retailers in newspapers and magazines and evaluate each in terms of their motives. Remove each ad from the periodicals and use it for an oral presentation to the class. The two assessments should include Rational or Emotional Motives and Key-Word Motive Clues.

2. Visit five major chains or department stores to assess the tools they are using to attract multicultural shoppers such as signage, etc. If possible, after conferring with management, photograph some of the props they use to capture the attention of these consumers.

chapter five

RETAIL RESEARCH DIRECTIONS IN TODAY'S RETAIL ENVIRONMENT

After reading this chapter, you should be able to:

- Identify the areas of research used by fashion retailers to solve their problems.

- Detail the various steps used in the research procedure.

- Differentiate between the observation and questionnaire techniques for gathering data.

- Explain how primary and secondary data are distinguishable from each other.

- Examine the role that the Internet plays in retail research.

- Assess why focus groups have become an important research tool for merchants to use in making merchandising decisions.

- Describe how retailers develop questionnaires to help assess their potential markets.

In the past, fashion merchants were more likely to base their decisions on intuition than the scientific approaches used today. They often purchased what they believed best suited the needs of their customers in terms of style, quality, function, and price. They offered the services they felt were appropriate to their companies and hoped that consumers would patronize them. For many merchants, these methods worked well. They established successful businesses and enjoyed the fruits of their labor. Others were less fortunate and were forced to close their doors because they were unable to attract enough shoppers to make their businesses profitable.

Were the successful merchants just luckier than the unsuccessful ones? While unseasoned people may talk about success in terms of luck, educated retailers speak in terms of being prepared to tackle problems, such as focusing on the right location, designing the appropriate environment, selecting the merchandise assortment that suits the market's needs, and providing the services required by the clientele. They know that success comes from expertise, not luck!

Those who specialize in fashion retailing have more concerns than their counterparts in other retail operations. Not only must they face the various problems associated with retailing in general, but they must also deal with the sudden changes in fashion, color, seasons, weather conditions, and so forth. The concept of "survival of the fittest" surely applies to the fashion retailer.

To meet the challenges of each day's problems, most of the major fashion operations, be they the brick-and-mortar giants, off-site ventures, or the multi-channel organizations, prepare themselves by studying the marketplace. They must learn as much as possible about consumer behavior, the demographics of trading areas, potential customers' lifestyles (discussed in Chapter 4), the types of services that will make their clientele want to return, and what consumers want in terms of price, style, and quality.

Many fashion retailers are able to address these and other problems and will continue to do so through a number of **retailing research** methods employed by in-house research teams and/or external agencies.

This chapter addresses research theories and techniques that bring the right information to the world of retailing.

THE NATURE OF RETAILING RESEARCH

Retailers must make a variety of decisions concerning store location, merchandising, advertising and promotion, customer services, human resources, sales methods, and competition. They must study each area so that they will be able to function in the most profitable manner. The following sections list the types of questions retailers should consider about these areas; some of them relate exclusively to brick-and-mortar establishments and others relate more to off-site or on-site ventures.

Store Location

1. What is the size of the trading area?

2. What are the demographics of the trading area? Specifically, what are the inhabitants' ages, occupations, education levels, and income?

3. What are the competing stores, and can the trading areas support another profitable store?

4. Is the particular type of retail environment appropriate for the intended business?

5. Do the available parking facilities provide a sufficient number of spaces?

6. Is there a public transportation network that will bring shoppers who do not have their own transportation?

7. Are there competing shopping centers that are more conducive to the consumers' needs?

8. Do compatible stores surround the specific site under consideration?

The Consumer

1. Will the consumers' needs be satisfied with the company's merchandise assortment? Having made a purchase at Chanel, the consumer in Figure 5.1 was satisfied.

2. Does the consumer in the proposed trading area have the finances to purchase at the retailer's price points?

3. Will the store's hours of operation fit in with the time the consumer wants to shop?

4. Is the **targeted market** psychographically segmented to fit the company's merchandising philosophy?

5. Are the consumer's shopping habits in line with the merchant's policies?

6. Are those within a particular sociological group matched to the store's image?

7. Will the targeted market order from the company's website?

8. Is the catalog's format appropriate for the intended consumer?

figure 5.1
Shopper after purchase was made. If consumer was completely satisfied with the merchandise and customer service, loyal patronage might be the result.

Merchandising

1. Does the merchandise mix feature the right brand assortment? Figure 5.2 shows an assortment of shoes featuring different brands.

2. Does the store have an assortment of private-label merchandise that will help meet the challenges of competing discounters and off-price organizations?

3. Is the price structure appropriate for the targeted market?

4. At what time during the seasonal periods should new fashion merchandise be introduced to satisfy the shoppers' needs?

figure 5.2
Nordstrom shoe salon with a good merchandise mix. The company is famous for its shoe collection, which was the initial Nordstrom offering.

5. How many times in a year must the inventory turn over for the company to be profitable?

6. Should markdowns be handled as the need arises, or should they be taken at more traditional times such as after Christmas?

7. Is an automatic markdown system an appropriate vehicle for the company?

8. Would more frequent markdowns help turn the inventory at a faster rate?

9. Should the number of merchandise resources be restricted to just a few or should numerous ones be utilized?

Advertising and Promotion

1. Which of the available media should be used to advertise the company's merchandise, image, and special events?

2. What proportion of the promotional budget should be spent on newspaper advertising?

3. Should advertising be purely promotional, or should a percentage be set aside for institutional purposes?

4. How often should catalogs be sent to the customers?

5. What format should be used for special promotions on the company's website?

6. What types of special events should the company utilize to attract customer attention?

7. Should visual merchandising be handled by a professional in-house team, store managers who follow the preplanned approaches designed by a visual team, or by freelance experts?

8. Would the store be better served with the use of a traditional format that could be easily changed for the seasons, or would an "environmental" concept be better?

Customer Services

1. Would a staff of personal shoppers increase sales?

2. Should gift-wrapping be free, or should a fee be charged for each package?

3. Should there be a shipping charge for Internet purchases?

4. Would a child-care center be beneficial to overall sales?

5. Would the use of foreign language-speaking sales associates help to increase sales?

6. What types of eating facilities would be appropriate?

7. Should there be a charge for alterations?

8. Should expanded shopping hours be instituted once a week to accommodate working men and women?

Human Resources

1. Which sources of personnel provide the best employees?

2. What type of motivational techniques will reduce employee turnover?

3. What training methodologies are most appropriate to teach new employees about company policies?

4. What role should the human resources department play in the selection of employees?

5. Which benefits and services will motivate employees to stay with the company?

Sales Methods

1. Is self-service a viable alternative to personal selling?

2. Should employees be assigned to specific merchandise classifications, or should they be placed in the busiest areas as the needs arise?

3. Should computer stations be used in place of sales associates in some areas?

Competition

1. Should the company institute a system whereby it can assess competitors' inventories?

2. Should the number of competitors in a trading area be evaluated before any final location decisions are made?

While these are by no means the only questions that confront both on-site and off-site retailers, retailers should address them before making major decisions.

THE RESEARCH PROCESS

In cases where retailers need to make significant decisions concerning any of the aforementioned areas, they may engage in some type of formal research. Whether the research is conducted by in-house staff, as is the case of the industry's giants, by an independent organization, or by an outside consultant that works with the company's own research team, the methodology is the same.

The stages and tools that researchers use for retail problems are virtually the same as those used for other business situations.

Identifying the Problem

The first stage is to identify the problem or area of concern. It might be about determining the consumers' level of acceptance of private-label merchandise and whether or not the company should change its in-stock percentage of these items. Another area may center around restructuring price points and the potential problems associated with such change. Still another area could be the impact of separating the company's brick-and-mortar merchandising operations from those used for their off-site ventures such as catalogs and e-commerce.

Whatever the situation, the problems must be identified before further action may take place.

Defining the Problem

After the problem is identified generally, it must be defined specifically. For example, if the retailer wanted to concentrate on the price point problem stated in the preceding section, the researchers would need to know if the new restructuring is in the entire store or in a specific department. In the private-label dilemma, the researchers need to know if the retailer is focusing on every department or just menswear.

Narrowing the stated problems that have been identified is a necessity so that researchers will be better able to solve the problem. For example, the three problems identified in the previous section could be more specifically stated as follows:

1. Will private labeling be accepted in the shoe department?

2. Would the store benefit from **trading up** in the dress department, eliminating the lower price points and adding higher ones?

3. Should the merchandising for off-site divisions include children's wear?

Once the problem is narrowly defined, the research team can continue to the next phase of the study.

Gathering Data

After specifying the problem, the process moves to the stage of collecting data. This is an extremely important area of the study, because the divisions are based on this information.

The data comes from two sources, secondary and primary.

Secondary Data

Data that is already available to the researcher is classified as **secondary data**. It may come from such sources as the company's own records, studies that were conducted by governmental agencies and **trade associations**, private research organizations, and periodicals.

COMPANY RECORDS

A great deal of information is continuously generated by the company's computer, which keeps track of records such as sales figures for every department and merchandise classification, customer returns, vendor analysis, employee turnover rates, and sales associates' commissions. Each of these is important when studying retail problems.

GOVERNMENTAL AGENCIES

Various government agencies provide general information that could help retailers researching a problem. At the federal level, for example, the Census Bureau undertakes periodic studies of the general population, housing, and businesses, all of which provide valuable information for the merchant who is considering expanding the company. The Department of Commerce generates a great deal of timely information on business conditions that is appropriate for retailer use. The monthly Catalog of U.S. Governmental Publications produces a host of materials, free-of-charge, on topics including regular reports on new home construction, employment figures, and cost-of-living adjustments.

By logging onto these governmental agencies' websites or by utilizing a search engine such as www.google.com, researchers can access a wealth of pertinent information. State and local governments provide a great deal of secondary information that researchers can use to find out about business conditions in the retailer's more immediate trading area.

TRADE ASSOCIATIONS

There are many trade associations that deal with various specific aspects of retailing, such as the **National Retail Federation** (NRF) (www.nrf.com), the retail world's largest association, which provides a wealth of information on every conceivable area that affects retailers and their operational needs. In addition to offering a forum that retailers from around the globe attend to learn about the latest industry innovations, the NRF regularly conducts studies that are important to the retail community. NRF members may obtain copies of its research that may help them with their own problems.

PRIVATE RESEARCH ORGANIZATIONS

There are numerous research organizations that engage in original studies, two of which are Gallup & Robinson (www.gallup-robinson.com) and the Olinger Group (www.olingergroup.com). Their websites offer a great deal of information on their research services. Nielsen, another major research firm, specializes in broadcast surveys. By examining its rankings of TV programs in terms of viewership, major fashion retailers are able to assess which programs they should advertise on.

PERIODICALS

Numerous trade papers and magazines regularly engage in research projects that retailers find useful. Fairchild Publications is a leader in fashion news with its *Women's Wear Daily* publications. Almost every issue of this publication provides meaningful information regarding the state of the fashion industry.

Stores magazine, published by the NRF, presents studies that can assist retailers with their decision making; *Visual Merchandising and Store Design*, a monthly periodical published by ST Media Group, is especially important for fashion retailers because its pages cover every detail of store design and display; and *Chain Store Age* offers the latest developments in that area of merchandising.

In addition to these periodicals that are expressly directed at the retail arena, others, such as *The Wall Street Journal* and *The New York Times*, often feature articles that may pertain to retailers and their problems.

Primary Data

It's possible that retailers can get enough information from secondary data to make their decisions. If they require more data specific to their particular situation, however, they need **primary data**. Primary data are the data that must be obtained firsthand through original research. The information is gathered from customers, potential customers, employees, vendors, market specialists such as resident buying offices, and the media through **questionnaires**, focus groups, and observations. Though valuable, primary research is often very costly to obtain.

QUESTIONNAIRES

The questionnaire is the method most often used for information gathering. It is more costly than any of the other techniques, but by and large it provides the broadest range of data. Questionnaires may be distributed through the mail, filled out by surveyors as they talk to subjects on the phone, completed by online users, and used with **intercept surveys** (these different types are discussed in the following sections). The type used depends on such factors as the trading area to be examined, the size of the research team available for gathering the information, specific demographics, finances, and the time allocated for the collection of the data. Each does have advantages and disadvantages. When composing the questionnaire, retailers should consider the following:

1. The length of the questionnaire is important. It should be as brief as possible, rarely occupying more than one page. This is particularly true when mailing the questionnaire to respondents. Many potential respondents will discard the questionnaire if it seems to be too long.

2. The language in the questionnaire must be easy to understand. When reading questionnaires received in the mail or posted on the Internet, respondents might misunderstand ambiguous questions or just pass over them, so the questionnaire results are less than perfect. Even in the case of personal or telephone interviews, during which interviewers can clarify a question, interviewer bias might affect the respondent's answers.

3. Questions must be arranged sequentially for a smooth transition from one to another.

4. Every question must be specific. When words such as "generally" or "usually" are used, there is too much room for interpretation. The two words might have different meanings to the respondents and could alter the reliability of the research.

5. Wherever possible, the answers should be in a multiple-choice format. This makes the data easy to tabulate and does not necessitate researcher interpretation. Where using open-ended questions, provide sufficient space for the responses.

MAIL QUESTIONNAIRES

When retailers want to survey a very large market and they think that respondents will require more time to study the questions, they often use the mail questionnaire. This format is sometimes favored by researchers because it eliminates interview bias. Only the respondent will answer the questions. Costs are generally lower than those of the telephone and personal interview formats, because they do not require paid surveyors. Another advantage is that respondents can complete questionnaires at their convenience.

The mail questionnaire has its disadvantages. The rate of response is very low, with a 10 percent response considered excellent. Some retailers offer incentives, such as a nominal amount paid for a completed form or a company discount on a future purchase; this can significantly improve the return rate. Another problem rests with the respondents' ability to comprehend the questions. If questions are difficult to understand, and there are no interviewers to explain them, this might result in an incomplete response. A way to avoid this pitfall is to first distribute the questionnaire to a small group and have observers determine if these respondents had any doubts about the questions' meaning.

TELEPHONE QUESTIONNAIRES

When researchers require an immediate response, the telephone survey is the quickest method. It is also fairly inexpensive, as calls can be made from a central location, thus eliminating the field staff needed to make personal interviews.

Confusing questions can be explained, although this necessitates using professional, unbiased interviewers. Telephone surveys also allow for follow-up questions, an advantage not available with mail questionnaires.

The use of the telephone also has some shortcomings. Interviewees are often reluctant to divulge information of a personal nature over the phone, which can severely limit the number of respondents. Also, with many families composed of dual earners, respondents are either not at home or have less time to participate. Many households employ caller ID to screen their calls. Answering machines also screen calls, and people only return those calls they deem important.

Many researchers use computer-assisted calling systems in place of humans to conduct their surveys. A machine dials a number and a recorded voice describes the research and asks the questions. Some companies are finding that this reduces the cost of interviews, and if the call is unsuccessful, the machine can quickly dial the next number.

ONLINE QUESTIONNAIRES

These are excellent means for conducting primary quantitative research, because today's computer-savvy consumer uses the Internet for a variety of reasons, ranging from business to personal use. Online questionnaires are interactive and less intrusive than other methods. Their benefits include potentially lower costs, rapid information gathering, and respondent completion at their convenience. The rate of return has been found to be greater than that via the mail.

On the downside, the responders to online questionnaires tend to be from the younger generations. Those in the senior category, sometimes an age group that researchers want to study, are often computer illiterate.

Dr. Don A. Dillman, a major contributor to the development of modern mail, telephone, and Internet survey methods, wrote with colleagues Jolene D. Smyth and Leah Melani Christian *Internet, Phone, Mail, and Mixed-Mode Surveys: The Tailored Design Method*, in which he addresses the profound changes that have taken place in recent years. It is possible to find other materials he has written by searching his name on the Internet.

INTERCEPT SURVEYS

Intercept surveys employ trained interviewers who are positioned at preselected public locations. One example of this marketing research method is the **mall intercept**, in which interviewers positioned in a shopping mall approach people and ask them to participate in an intercept survey. The interviewer administers the questionnaire to the participant face-to-face. This method is especially successful in researching problems for the fashion retailers that are the "anchors" in the malls.

The advantages of intercept surveys include the interviewers' ability to mediate the process, ensuring accurate questionnaire completion; control of the number of respondents; the ability of the interviewer to observe the respondents' facial expressions and body language; and the allowance of time for material sampling.

The main disadvantage to this type of survey is that sometimes shoppers are too busy to stop and answer the questions. It is also costly, as the interviewer must be paid. Figure 5.3 is typical of a questionnaire used by fashion retailers. In this case, the targeted group is composed of regular customers who have company charge accounts. The questionnaire is designed to determine the fashion needs of the retailer's existing clientele.

Observations

Although not used as frequently as the other research methodology for data-gathering, the **observation technique** is valuable in specific circumstances. For example those considering prospective locations for their companies must, in addition to studying the typical demographics of the area, determine if there is a sufficient amount of traffic in

figure 5.3
A typical fashion retailer questionnaire.

Dear Charge Account Customer:

In our attempt to bring you the timeliest, fashion-forward apparel and accessories, we have always scouted the domestic and international designer markets. Because we believe that many of you appreciate a fashion collection that includes merchandise exclusive to our company, we are developing a new, private label that is designed with you in mind. We will continue to feature all of your designer favorites and those on the cutting edge of fashion along with the new private-label brand. Since we value your judgment and opinions, we would like you to participate in a survey so that our new concept will reflect your fashion needs.

Please complete the following form and return it in the provided self-addressed envelope. If you prefer, you may complete the form on our website, **www.emery's.com**. In either case, if we receive your response within ten days from today, we will show our appreciation by sending you a 20-percent discount certificate that can be used on your next purchase.

We want to assure you that your answers will be kept anonymous.

1. What percentage of your fashion needs are purchased from our company? _____

2. In which department(s) do you buy most of your fashion items? _____

3. What prices, in the following merchandise classifications, are indicative of your fashion purchases?
   Dresses _____ , Sportswear _____ , Suits _____ ,
   Coats _____ , Shoes _____ , Accessories _____ .

4. Which designer names do you consider to be your favorites? _____
   _____

5. In which product classifications would you favor private labels? _____

6. Would you like the private-label items to be featured along with the regular designer items in the same department, catalog, or Web site page? _____ yes _____ no

7. Could you suggest a name or names for the private label(s)? _____
   _____

8. Are you employed outside of the home? _____ men _____ women

9. What is your approximate family income? Under $25,000 _____
   $25,000–$34,999 _____
   $35,000–$44,999 _____
   $45,000–$54,999 _____
   $55,000–$64,999 _____
   $65,000–$74,999 _____
   Over $75,000 _____

10. How would you describe your family status? _____ single; _____ newly married; _____ married with small children; _____ married with grown children (home); _____ empty nester (still working); _____ empty nester (retired); _____ divorced

a particular locale to warrant opening a brick-and-mortar operation there. A **traffic count** is undertaken to study not only the amount of vehicular traffic passing the proposed site but also the types of vehicles and the number of passengers aboard each vehicle. Through these recorded observations, it is possible to draw conclusions about the numbers of passersby and their genders, approximate ages, appearance, and so forth, all of which may be meaningful to the location decision.

Another type of observation is the **fashion count**. Some fashion retailers use this method to record the specific styles worn by a particular group to help determine if their fashion projections are in line with customer preferences. This theory is based upon the premise that if people are wearing certain styles, they will buy more of them. Thus, if a large percentage of women in the study are observed wearing leather boots with high heels, this is a signal to the retailer to purchase more boots.

The fashion count is particularly important in times of radical fashion change. When evidence from the past five years, for example, indicates that women are happy with longer-length skirts but the industry promotes micro-minis, the buyers may be uncertain of how to replenish their inventories. While fashion-forward retailers must always embrace the latest styles, they must also be aware of the dangers inherent in overstocking what the industry is trying to promote. Too many times merchants have had to take enormous markdowns when they discover that their customers do not always follow the fashion market's dictates. By taking fashion counts in such situations, retailers can assess the pulse of the consumer market and follow a safer route.

Some of the advantages of both traffic and fashion counts are their low costs, the ease in which they are organized, and the little time it takes to gather the data. It is very important that the recorded information be accurate.

Traffic counters most often record such information as the types of vehicles that pass the location, the times they pass, and general descriptions of the occupants. The forms they use enable them to quickly note what they have seen.

Fashion counters usually record three or four different style elements worn by a preselected group. They are sent out in teams, with prepared forms in hand, to places where people they wish to count congregate. If high fashion evening wear is being investigated, for example, they go to the opening night of the Metropolitan Opera at Lincoln Center in New York City. If swimwear is the style, the counters go to the resort beaches during the winter season so that buyers can make proper purchases for the summer season. Whatever the situation, they must target the right place if the results of the count are to be meaningful.

Focus Groups

Focus group research has become the most common form of all qualitative research methods, providing in-depth information regarding a particular problem or issue by using group dynamics. By using panels of four to eight, the way the respondents interact with each other provides more robust information than individual responses. In Figure 5.4 four women in a focus group interact with each other. In focus group research, the group is guided by a moderator who openly discusses attitudes and ideas about a particular issue. A focus group assembled for a fashion merchant might discuss the fashion assortments carried by the company, the pros and cons of personal shoppers, types of customer service, and so forth. The selected panel may come from any number of sources, such as regular customers, charge customers, or those selected at random who know the company but do not shop there.

figure 5.4
These women are in a focus group giving their opinions. It is these groups that supply the information about merchandise, pricing, and customer services, that gives the retailer the right path to follow for success.

These groups are used on a regular basis such as once a month, or are gathered for only one session. The panel is generally given an incentive to participate, such as cash payments or discounts for future purchases.

Extremely important to the success of focus group research is the selection of the moderator. Moderators should have a background in industrial psychology and the ability to communicate with the participants. Their role is essential to the process, because they guide the conversation and elicit interaction among the group to generate information that will be analyzed. Group dynamics are assessed as participants engage in a discussion with each other.

In some setups, the retailer can anonymously observe the focus groups from a viewing room, and forward any additional questions to the moderator during the sessions.

The benefits of focus group research include gaining insights into people's shared perceptions, observing the ways individuals are influenced by others in a group environment, providing direct involvement for the client, and observing participants' facial expressions and body language.

While all of these research techniques are still in use, there are many new technologies that are being applied to these proven methodologies instead of completely new ones. In the following *Happening Now*, a discussion of some of these are presented.

Selecting a Sample

When a market is being studied, it is neither necessary nor practical to survey everyone in the market. A **research sample**, or representative group of the body of people to be surveyed, must be selected. Research samples can be drawn from the customer base, such as the company's charge account clientele, or a potential group of shoppers. In either case a small number of them will be sufficient to help with decision making.

The same principle is used to predict the winners of elections. In a presidential election, for example, it is necessary to survey only about 1,000 people to accurately

HAPPENING NOW

THE NECESSITIES OF RETAIL RESEARCH

In an examination of the market research sector for retailing and other businesses, companies are starting to use a variety of techniques to gather information in a somewhat different manner than in the past. While questionnaire surveys, observations, and focus groups are still the norm, many have been adapted to make them realistic trends.

Some of the recent innovations have been summarized by www.mymarketresearchmethods. com and are useful to discuss the new methodology, one of which makes significant use of smart phones and tablets. Poll Everywhere, a research company, has developed a system that enables respondents to answer questions via text messaging. This is a time saver since the responses are often immediate.

One of the problems with focus groups is that the leader of the group has to engage them in conversation. In order to overcome this, companies have developed hand-held remote control devices that are used for participants to respond to questions that have been shown in PowerPoint presentations, thus allowing for anonymity among those being surveyed.

Another recent innovation is "online collaboration tools." Skyping and instant messaging enable the researcher to gather information in a less costly manner than with the use of assembled audiences and to broaden their audiences to larger geographical venues. In Figure 5.5 a businessman is Skyping with a client to offer new products.

This is just the beginning of the new research practices that are *Happening Now*, with many more on the research horizon.

figure 5.5
Skyping enables researchers to gather information in a low cost manner. It is a quick way to interact with customers to conduct research.

---

predict the outcome. If a retailer wishes to evaluate the size of a television audience for the purpose of selecting a program on which to place commercial spots, taking a sample of 1,200 families would have the same results as polling the entire population of the country. Careful sample selection is imperative if results are to be on target.

Collecting and Tabulating the Data

Once a retailer has made the decision to undertake the project and constructed all of the forms, the data must be collected. If the questionnaire is the instrument of choice, the methodology for data collection, such as the mail, telephone, websites, or interception, should be decided. In some instances, more than one technique might be used. In the cases of the telephone questionnaire or intercept survey methods, which use information gatherers, they must receive sufficient training so that bias will not enter into the questioning technique and everyone understands the nature of the project.

If the observation method is used, the locations where the counts are to be taken should be carefully selected. The observers must be chosen and trained in terms of what they are to record so that they will properly carry out the survey and record accurate results. Focus groups and their moderators must also be carefully chosen to guarantee that the derived information is exactly what the company is seeking.

When professional data gatherers are used, they do not require as much training. However, when novices such as college students are used, it is important that they are thoroughly trained in the manner in which to approach the consumer, either on the telephone or in person; the handling of unwilling participants; the recording procedures; and so forth so that they will obtain accurate data.

After the data have been collected, they are compiled and processed. Computers can easily and quickly tabulate the data and make it ready for the marketing research experts to prepare their findings.

Data Analysis and Report Preparation

The researchers compile and summarize the data collected for the project in a variety of formats. They construct charts, graphs, and other instruments used in research to show their findings and recommendations. Each project requires a different amount of time and effort for data analysis and report preparation. The information gathered from a focus group is simple to analyze, compared with that from major surveys that require hundreds of responses from questionnaires.

Whatever the size of the report, the researcher always presents the findings in a written report that summarizes all of the stages of the research process, the methodology used in the collection of the data, analysis of the data, recommendations, and an appendix that includes the data and their secondary and primary sources. In Figure 5.6, the researcher writes the report using important graphs to accompany the document.

Making the Decision

The information generated from the study and the recommendations of the research team are prepared for company management to examine and evaluate. The researchers, whether they are in-house or from a private agency, do not have the authority to decide what direction the company should take regarding the problem. The management team has the ultimate decision-making power and must carefully examine everything that has been presented to it before taking any steps.

figure 5.6
Analysis of the collected data is summarized and written in report form. This information is presented to management to help them make the proper decisions regarding the problem.

Chapter Highlights

1. While many nonprofessionals believe that the success of a retail operation is just luck, those with experience understand it is consumer research that plays the most important role.

2. Fashion retailing offers more challenges to operators than any other retail classification.

3. Retail research spans a wide number of areas including store location, consumer assessment, merchandising, advertising and promotion, customer services, human resources, sales methods, and competition.

4. The research process is a multistepped plan that ultimately brings potential solutions to retailer problems.

5. Initially in the research process, the problem must be identified; it must then be clearly defined so that the research team will be able to offer suggestions regarding solving the problem.

6. Secondary data includes data that is already available to the researcher via such sources as company records, governmental agencies, trade associations, private research organizations, and periodicals.

7. If there isn't a sufficient amount of information culled from secondary sources, primary research is necessary to solve the problem.

8. Primary research involves the use of such tools as questionnaires, observations, and focus groups.

9. Intercept surveys involve the use of interviewers who are positioned in strategic locations for the purpose of conducting interviews with consumers.

10. Questionnaires can be delivered via the mail, by telephone, online, or through personal interviews.

11. Fashion counts are used to record the styles that people are wearing so that the information may be used for future merchandising plans.

12. The focus group has become one of the more important tools for consumer research, because it is comparatively inexpensive to use and the information is immediately obtained.

13. A research sample is a representative group of the body of the people to be surveyed.

14. Once the data has been collected, tabulated, and analyzed, a final report is written by the research team in which suggestions to solve the problem are offered to management.

Terms of the Trade

fashion count	retailing research
intercept surveys	secondary data
mall intercept	targeted market
National Retail Federation (NRF)	trade associations
observation technique	trading area
primary data	trading up
questionnaire	traffic count
research sample	

For Discussion

1. Why is it necessary for retailers to conduct research studies for their companies?

2. What must the retailer learn about the consumer to maximize potential profitability?

3. What are some of the areas of concern for brick-and-mortar retailers to assess before choosing a location?

4. Can advertising and promotion research provide information to the retailer that will make its promotional investments more likely to result in greater sales volume? Explain.

5. Describe some of the retailer's concerns regarding human resources that require research.

6. What is the first stage of the research process?

7. How do the first and second stages of the research procedure differ from each other?

8. Why is it necessary to conduct secondary research first?

9. From what sources are secondary data obtained?

10. How can trade associations help the retailer save money on a research project?

11. What does the term "primary data" mean?

12. List three techniques used to gather primary data and explain how they differ from each other.

13. What does the term "intercept survey" mean, and why does it sometimes offer more reliable information than mail questionnaires?

14. What are some of the benefits of using online questionnaires?

15. How does a fashion count help a retailer with merchandising problems?

16. Why do some merchants use traffic counts when researching prospective locations?

17. What is a focus group?

18. How can a retailer conduct primary research that is reliable without surveying every individual in the group?

19. Once the data is tabulated and analyzed, what is the final stage of the research project?

Case Problem

Cameo Fashions is a small retail organization. It has been in business for 12 years and has been able to expand its operation to five units. Each year, sales have increased, and the company has become extremely profitable.

The company's merchandising philosophy has been fashion forward, providing the latest styling for its customers at price points that would be considered moderate. Dresses, for example, range from approximately $90 to $225, sportswear from $35 to $150, and accessories from $25 to $125. Cameo offers a host of services and enjoys a very loyal customer base. During the last year, the Cameo partners, John, Marc, and David, have become aware of a situation that might be meaningful to their organization. Real estate value has soared, and many homes have started to sell for prices never before witnessed in their trading areas. Along with the higher-priced homes has come an influx of more affluent families. Another factor with implications for the company is the construction of three new luxury developments in locations close to three of Cameo's stores.

After a great deal of discussion, the partners remain divided on how to approach the area's wealthier population. John believes trading up to higher price points would be the best approach. Marc suggests that they have been successful for all these years and should not look for trouble. David believes that a broad price range would be most practical and would accommodate the old and new customers.

Questions

1. Should the partners follow any of their own beliefs?
2. How should they approach the situation in a more scientific manner?

Exercises and Projects

1. As a class, decide upon a topic that would best be researched through the use of the observation technique. It might be a fashion or traffic count. Once the subject has been selected, develop a form that could be used to make the count. After selecting the appropriate place for the research to be conducted, divide into teams and go into the field to collect the data. Sort the data into categories, and prepare a report to show the findings of the study.

2. Contact a fashion retailer in the area to discuss the possibility of doing a research project for the company. It might focus on the company's merchandise assortment, customer services, or anything of interest to the retailer. After gaining the retailer's approval to conduct the study on the store's premises, follow the stages of the research process as outlined in this chapter. Once secondary sources have been studied, develop a questionnaire that should be used at the store's entrance. After collecting and analyzing the data complete a written report and present it to the company.

chapter six

ETHICAL PRACTICES AND SOCIAL RESPONSIBILITY BY RETAILERS

After reading this chapter, you should be able to:

- Define business ethics and explain how it affects a company's operation.

- Describe the typical ethical dilemmas that businesses face.

- Differentiate among the numerous areas of ethical concerns for business organizations.

- Establish the stages for the proper handling of ethical problems.

- Analyze the research that underscores the complexity of business ethics.

- Determine why questionable pricing strategies might adversely affect the running of a retail operation.

- Summarize the key points in a company's code of ethics and how they are written to meet the needs of business organizations.

- Establish the need to include social responsibility in the retailer's overall marketing plan and describe the ways in which fashion retailers are becoming more socially responsible.

- List the many ways in which fashion retailers do their share to aid charitable and other causes.

Is it ethical to conduct personal business while on the job, call in and claim you're sick when it is just an excuse to take a day off, habitually arrive late for work and leave before the workday ends, lie to customers about the advantages of the merchandise you are trying to sell, or to surf the Internet during company time? Those in management as well as the rank and file employees are tempted by these types of **ethical dilemmas**.

Although **ethics** debacles in the recent past such as the cases involving top executives at Adelphia Communications, Arthur Andersen, Enron, ImClone Systems, and Worldcom are not directly related to the fashion-retailing industry, the implications from their misdeeds are numerous and could someday surface in the retailing arena and affect those who work in it. At the time of this writing, Macy's and J. C. Penney are embattled in a suit concerning their ethics with the Martha Stewart debacle, which may result in a scenario that could affect future employees.

There seems to be a feeling in the business community that the stories behind the scandalous headlines are only the tip of the iceberg and that other companies will be called upon to defend some of their questionable practices. Fashion retailers, in addition to making certain that their in-house activities are ethically based, need to ensure that their business relationships with outside companies do not compromise their own standards. It is a common yet inappropriate phenomenon that some vendors offer personal gifts and monetary rewards, tickets to out-of-area sporting events and rock concerts, and fully paid vacations to their most valued buyers.

It is crucial to the retailer's success that it conducts its business in a manner that is above reproach, and that it establishes **codes of ethics** for employees to follow that take any guesswork out of the decision-making processes. Once in place, these codes must be understood by everyone in the company—from those in the uppermost levels of management to those who perform more menial jobs as well as those outside organizations that the company does business with. For retailers specifically, vendors who supply their merchandise must understand their governing ethical rules and regulations; and the market specialists, such as resident buying offices who act as advisory consultants, must also be aware of their clients' ethical dos and don'ts.

Whether it is in the advertising campaigns that are targeted to the consumer, the methods used in recruitment, the veracity of the sales associates in their interactions with shoppers, or the actions of members of management as they interface with their subordinates, every action must reflect an awareness of right from wrong.

Retailers also participate in their community's social programs; this not only helps numerous causes, but also plays a significant role in helping the retailer to build positive images with their consumers.

When companies practice ethics in a manner that upgrades their standards, and take part in programs that foster **social responsibility**, it is likely that they will be better-run organizations.

THE IMPORTANCE OF BUSINESS ETHICS

The realm of ethics in the retail environment has many facets. There are ethical concerns that are different for companies of different sizes, dilemmas that retailers must confront almost every day, developing a code of ethics, and so forth. Before a retailer can write an effective company code of ethics it must first understand what the word ethics means, become familiar with research that concentrates on ethics, focus in on pertinent ethical concerns and dilemmas, and examine existing codes of ethics used by similar companies. The following sections discuss these different areas.

Defining Business Ethics

It is essential to understand what the word "ethics" means. As defined in Webster's Dictionary, ethics are, "moral principles, rules of conduct." It requires that people learn right from wrong. Of course, people do not always agree on what is right or wrong and they use their own interpretations of a situation. For example, if Johnny is asked to tell a lie to cover for his boss, is he merely following orders from his superior, or is he engaging in an unethical practice? Some ethicists believe that ethical decision-making is duty based and that it should be universally applied. Others, however, theorize that ethical decision-making is situational ethics and depends upon what is happening at that time.

Using these concepts as a starting point, the term **business ethics**, according to some theorists, refers to learning to know what is right or wrong in the workplace, and doing what's right in terms of how the decisions affect a company, its products, services, clients, and stakeholders. Of course, this is only one understanding of the term; there is no universal agreement on the subject, as is obvious by the arguments offered by those in the media's headline stories regarding the multitude of questionable practices in today's world of business.

To understand the complexity of business ethics and solve the problems inherent within it, companies should address the following areas:

- Ethical issues must be recognized.
- Analytical skills must be developed to address the problems.
- A sense of moral obligation and personal responsibility must be elicited before a solution to the problem can be rendered.
- Disagreement among the parties must be tolerated.
- There must be an opportunity to apply ethical decision-making skills to solving the problem.

Research Findings Regarding Ethics

Many studies have been conducted recently to evaluate the effect of the scandals plaguing just about every business arena. By paying close attention to these findings, companies of every size and stature can understand the adverse images that have been cast upon the business community and why they may either need to establish a code of ethics in their organizations or rethink those codes that are already in place.

Key findings in a study by Walker Information show the following trends:

- Only 49 percent of U.S. employees believe that their senior leaders are people of high personal integrity.
- Regarding ethical/compliance issues, 55 percent of U.S. employees say there is little pressure to cut corners.
- Nearly half of U.S. workers (48 percent) are comfortable reporting ethical violations. Yet a widening majority (65 percent) who know about a violation do not report it for reasons that include lacking enough facts and lacking faith in their employers' response and reporting systems.
- From a checklist of ethical violations, 54 percent of U.S. employees cite at least one occurring in the past two years at work, with lying to supervisors and poor treatment of employees at the top of the list.
- Industries with the worst ethics ratings are transportation, retail, government, and manufacturing.
- Industries with the best ethics rating are financial services, technology systems, and insurance.
- Integrity at work relates to employee loyalty. Nationally, 40 percent of employees who say their senior leaders have high personal integrity are also truly loyal to their organization. That number drops to only 6 percent when employees do not believe their senior leaders have integrity.

The implications of the study are quite clear for retailing, in that it is among the industries with the worst ethics ratings. Because manufacturing is also on the worst ethics list, and many retailers are involved in manufacturing through their private-label collections, it is imperative for retailers to take a clear look at their practices and make certain that they are ethical.

Areas of Ethical Concern

Retailers are involved in a wide range of activities to achieve their goals. These include purchasing merchandise, developing advertising campaigns, recruiting and evaluating employees, preventing losses, dealing with **conflicts of interest**, and choosing vendors. Inherent in each of these activities are practices that govern the people who carry out these responsibilities. The following sections explore these and other individual specialties that comprise the retail operation in terms of their potential for compromised ethics. One of these other areas of concern is the fair treatment of shoppers. They are the lifeblood of the store and must be treated fairly without regard to the impressions they convey. As told in the *Happening Now* feature, an ethical concern of one segment of the population has been making headlines and has yet to be resolved. As of this writing the adverse publicity that a major retailer is receiving is an ethical concern that could seriously affect future business.

HOW ADVERSITY IS HANDLED BY RETAILERS

In October 2013, two African Americans were questioned by officers of the New York City Police Department after making expensive purchases at the Barneys' flagship store, setting off a period of turmoil that was said to be racially motivated by some of the company's employees. Picket signs surrounded the entrance to the store on Madison Avenue decrying "No Justice, No Shopping" and "Boycott Barneys." At the time of this writing, a few months later, the dispute still has not been resolved and the management's defense was that it was not store policy to discriminate against African Americans or to practice "profiling."

The company held a press conference led by the C.E.O. of Barneys in which he stated, "Our preliminary investigation concluded that, in both of these instances (there were two), no one from Barneys New York raised an issue with the purchasers, brought them to the attention of internal security or reached out to authorities."

Joining the list of the accused was Macy's. At a forum convened by the Committee of Civil Rights, they were also singled out as a store that engages in racial profiling. At the forum two letters were read that came from absent executives of the retail organizations. Both

denied the actions that were charged, and Barneys' statement said that the company has a 90-year policy of "zero tolerance" for any form of discrimination.

In subsequent revelations, the Barneys customer said she was told by the New York City Police Department officer that someone at the store had raised concerns over the sale. The Macy's purchaser reported that she had a similar experience after buying an expensive handbag.

At the time of this writing, in mid-2014, neither incident has been resolved.

Buyer Conflicts of Interest

In pursuit of the best merchandise to fit their company's product mix, buyers regularly visit many vendors to screen their lines.

While the majority of buyers approach their purchasing needs in a scientific manner, using computer-generated past sales records, meeting with market representatives such as resident buyers, and examining the appropriate trade publications for editorial direction, some buyers write their orders based on personal rewards.

The vast majority of merchants have developed company positions regarding potential conflicts of interest and how those in their employ must handle them. Stein Mart, an off-price fashion retail chain with stores across the United States, for example, makes it quite clear to its staff that those conducting business on behalf of the company shall do so in an honest and ethical manner. Those in positions of authority who interface with vendors and suppliers "may not accept cash payments, loans, gifts greater than nominal value ($50), services or non-local entertainment." Not only are employees made aware of this edict but also the vendors with whom they have business relationships are told of it. To make certain that everyone with the potential for unethical conflicts of interest can be aware of this policy, Stein Mart makes it available in written form at its premises and online at www.steinmart.com/contact-us.stml.

Conflicts of interest are not only in the realm of buying. The potential for concern crosses into every part of the retail operation.

Vendor Standards

When glaring headlines a few years ago blasted such unethical manufacturing practices as those of Kathie Lee Gifford's company, with its employment of minors to make its products sold in Walmart, many major retailers rushed to develop initiatives that would prevent such adverse press coverage. Today, after the horrendous Bangladesh incident where a vast number of employees lost their lives due to unethical factory practices, the fashion industry is still making changes to prevent this from ever happening again and to protect its own image. Since many fashion retailers have their own factories in Bangladesh, they are trying to improve their own images by making changes. By participating in questionable practices, retailers run the risk of losing business and causing shoppers to be wary of purchasing from them. Figure 6.1 shows the Kathie Lee Gifford brand.

In today's fashion-retailing sector, more merchants are developing their own brands and labels. Since the cost of production is considerably lower in many global markets, most production takes place overseas. Unlike the strict legislation in the United States that clearly states the rules and regulations governing manufacturing in this country, many offshore production companies do not have such guidelines to follow. Since many American retailers have working relationships with these producers through joint ventures, they have direct responsibility to make certain that overseas producers follow the standards required by American law as well as the company's standards. Even where the production is accomplished domestically, these standards are not always met.

The Target Corporation has established a corporate compliance program that focuses on enforcement of its **vendor standards**. Some of the important features of the program involve an inspection program, during which random visits are made to vendor and subcontractor manufacturing facilities. Since many of Target's vendors are based offshore, a full-time overseas-based staff regularly checks for compliance to the company's program. If and when violations are discovered, the penalties range from administrative probation to severance of the relationship. Assisting in this endeavor to maintain the highest ethical standards are the company's buyers and other personnel who visit vendor factories. They undertake a vendor compliance evaluation that is used as a screening tool to determine if a full inspection of a facility is warranted.

More retailers are requiring domestic vendors to sign contracts that mandate them to guarantee that all goods are produced in compliance with such laws as the Fair Labor Standards Act of 1938, legislation that governs how employers pay and treat their employees. Even though non-U.S. markets generally do not have such stringent standards, most American retailers have established basic minimum requirements to cover their offshore vendor relationships.

figure 6.1
Kathie Lee Gifford said she was unaware of underage workers at the factory with which she was associated. This underage action put American companies on alert to carefully check the employee safety standards that they employ in the production of their goods in offshore factories.

In the absence of any vendor standards, companies run the risk of having their images tarnished when substandard working conditions are made public.

Questionable Pricing Strategies

Most everyone loves a bargain, and retailers are often ready to legitimately offer them to shoppers. In both on-site and off-site operations, there are times when promotional pricing is used to motivate consumers to buy. In some of these situations, retailers resort to practices that are not only unethical but illegal. In the case of home shopping networks, for example, the thrust is always on the bargain that is available to viewers if they act in a timely fashion.

Often, merchants who engage in promotional pricing do so with practices that are questionable. Typically, the offerings speak of the "regular" prices, but the information regarding when they were offered at these regular prices—and in the case of the cable home shopping shows, where these products were offered at the higher listed prices—is not mentioned.

Such pricing strategies might be conceived as misrepresentations and can cause distrust among potential shoppers. While the temptation to use this strategy is great, it can invariably discourage consumers from patronizing that retail operation.

Advertising Misrepresentation

The larger fashion retailers use regular advertising as a means of attracting shoppers to their stores, websites, catalogs, and mobile promotions. Occasionally, these merchants tempt shoppers to their selling channels by advertising well-known products at prices that are well below their usual selling prices. These ads sometimes feature merchandise that is in short supply, and when shoppers come to the store or off-site tool to buy it, they are told that the item is out of stock, and efforts are made to sell them another product that will bring a better markup to the company. The technique is known as **bait and switch**, and it is not only unethical but illegal in many states.

Another questionable practice concerns placing conditions in **fine print** at the bottom of an advertisement. For example, if an ad features a storewide sale the fine print lists the exceptions to the sale. The unaware shoppers are motivated by the price reductions to come to the store only to discover the fine print has excluded their favorite brands from the sale. This poor communication practice, while legal, does compromise company ethics.

Recruitment and Advancement Irregularity

Charges of discrimination in the workplace are frequently the topics of newspaper articles. Minority groups continue to level charges against businesses that practice discrimination in hiring and promotion. Not only is this illegal but it also presents the perpetrators in an extremely poor light that can seriously affect their image. Bad press causes irreparable harm, and cannot easily be fixed by even the best public relations firm. Retailers should emphasize hiring the best-qualified candidates for positions, and offer promotions to those who qualify, regardless of their race or religious beliefs. With the use of sensitivity training sessions and focus groups, discriminatory hiring and advancement practices can be eliminated.

The National Association for the Advancement of Colored People (NAACP) has played a vital role in uncovering such egregious actions and has called for boycotts of these companies that practice discrimination. This poor publicity is detrimental to the profitability of retailers and other businesses that engage in such practices.

Internal Theft Justification

As will be discussed Chapter 11, "Merchandising Distribution and Loss Prevention," employees are stealing from their employers at record rates. These culprits are employed in every level of the organization, ranging from the upper levels of management to those who work in the stockrooms. While lower-level employees are often looked upon as the group that steals the most, it is often members of management, with their easy access to merchandise controls and an understanding of the company systems, who are the perpetrators.

Some, when caught, offer the excuse that they are underpaid and steal only as a means of getting what they believe they deserve. This is an unacceptable answer, and criminals must be punished for their crimes or the situation will become even more severe.

Through seminars at the time they are hired, employees should be told the company's position on internal theft and how those who steal from the company will be prosecuted.

Ethical Dilemmas

The fact that a code or system of ethics exists (a subject that will be fully explored later in the chapter) does not guarantee that potential and current employees will understand and follow it the same way. People are influenced by their religious upbringing, moral attitudes, responses to peer pressure, and other things to have different reactions to the same situations.

Typically, the following ethical dilemmas are faced on a daily basis by those engaged in retailing as well as other professional endeavors.

- *Exaggerating credentials on resumes.* To increase their chances of getting job interviews or to get an edge over others applying for the same positions, many job seekers exaggerate their skills and talents. This practice is the first indication that the candidate may also cheat on the job. Pure and simple, it is unethical to lie, and the potential for getting caught is significant.
- *Using the Internet and social networks during working hours.* Employee salaries are based upon the hours they spend performing professional duties. Buyers, for example, among other responsibilities, are paid to plan their purchasing needs for each season. In doing so, they are constantly working on their computers to check past sales records, analyze the performance of specific items, verify markdowns, and so forth. Their computers also give them access to the Internet, where more than just business information is available. Is it ethical for them to log onto particular websites or surf the 'net for their own pleasure during work time? Some buyers maintain that if they finish their professional obligations it is all right to use the computer for their own needs. Personal use of the computer to access the Internet unless clearly spelled out by employment manuals or supervisory personnel, isn't ethical. Buyers can always find work-related ways to occupy their time, such as going onto the selling floor and making visual observations of the shoppers, meeting with sales associates to learn what is in stock, and so forth. Employees who use every minute of the day to help the company reach its goals will more than likely benefit as well.
- *Bypassing the immediate supervisor.* In most large retail operations, there are tables of organization that indicate lines of authority (see Chapter 3, "Organizational Structures"). These routes spell out the appropriate staff members to address for a

variety of reasons. In cases requiring dispute resolution, it is standard practice for subordinates to speak to their immediate supervisor. If there is a dispute between the supervisor and the subordinate, the person at the lower level may be tempted to bypass the superior employee and go to the next in line to solve the problem. This is generally not permissible. Disputes must be settled according to the dictates of the table of organization; and not abiding by the rule can adversely affect the lower-level employee. While the lower-level employees may feel frustrated, any "end-runs" are considered to be unethical.

- *Becoming romantically involved with the manager.* Many business environments bring two people together on such a regular basis that it is possible for romantic entanglements to occur. Is it ethical for these relationships to continue? Will questions be raised among the other employees, especially if the involvement is between a manager and subordinate? The question of ethics in this case is a difficult one. On the one hand, two people, if properly performing their duties and responsibilities on the job, are certainly entitled to engage in personal relationships after the workday has ended. On the other hand, people in the same department might notice the manager conveying a degree of favoritism to the subordinate, which could lower morale for the other workers at the same level. Even if the manager is careful not to offer special treatment, the perception that it is there often exacerbates the situation. Romantic involvement is not unethical unless the company forbids it or it interferes with the functioning of the workplace. In Figure 6.2 it seems as though the female employee is offended by her manager's obvious advances.

- *Feigning illness to take a day off.* Although this is regularly practiced by people in every type of business and at every level of employment without question, this is unethical. Employees needing some personal time should contact those in charge and explain the circumstances surrounding the need. In this way, they will most likely gain the confidence of those in charge and will probably be considered more valuable, ethical employees.

- *Becoming a party to another's lie.* On some occasions, situations arise that cause one employee to lie for another. For example, a manager might ask a salesperson to lie to upper management and say that he was on the selling floor when in fact he was away doing personal business. This type of situation puts the salesperson in a precarious position. Becoming a party to such actions might result in the manager making regular demands for lying. On the one hand, if the salesperson doesn't acquiesce to the wishes of the manager, the manager could give him or her unfair evaluations. On the other hand, lying is not only unethical but also immoral. The salesperson asked to back the falsehood must make such decisions about whether or not to tell the truth.

- *Unfairly evaluating employee performance.* Supervisory personnel must objectively evaluate employee performance. Standards and procedures are usually established to provide guidelines for employee evaluations. Sometimes, however, personal biases are reflected in these ratings. There is no room for such wavering from the truth, and anything less than the truth is unacceptable. Too often, disgruntled employees who feel they have been unfairly treated in these reports file discrimination charges. The ramifications of such

figure 6.2
Sexual harassment is not an acceptable practice in business. Not only is it illegal, but it raises many questions about proper manager–employee relationships.

behavior are many and include the potential for costly lawsuits, adverse publicity for the company, and other negative results. There is no place in business for ethical misdeeds of this nature. Figure 6.3 features a supervisor reviewing documents regarding an employee's performance.

- *Misrepresenting product information.* Sales associates are often called upon to help customers evaluate the merchandise before they decide to buy. Misrepresenting the facts, or coloring responses that are not exactly truthful is unethical. For example, telling a customer that a garment is washable when it isn't will surely result in the shopper returning the merchandise and losing confidence in the store. Such actions also require that the merchandise be returned to the vendor, who might be wary of accepting the return, and the store will have to incur the expenses for the delivery charges.

- *Falsifying expense accounts.* In fashion retailing, buyers and merchandisers spend considerable time in domestic and international markets trying to find excellent merchandise. In these travels, expense accounts are used to cover the costs of the trips. **Expense account falsification** has become a significant problem for retail organizations. Taking a spouse on such a trip and charging his or her expenses to the business is an example of an infringement. Not only are such practices unethical but they also tend to cost the company. It is never acceptable to be a party to padding of expense accounts or to using them for purposes other than those directly related to the business.

- *Blaming others for personal mistakes.* People rarely want to accept the blame for misdeeds and tend to pass it on to others. For example, a buyer who mismarks the merchandise and prices it below the intended price, passes the blame to his or her assistant when discovered. Blaming others for one's own mistakes is unethical and can cause severe downturns in employee morale. Few of the accused will readily accept that they are the ones responsible for the errors, and this could result in ugly confrontations. Those who err should be ready to take the blame and suffer the consequences.

figure 6.3
Employee evaluations must be objective as stated in many codes of ethics. In this way, employees gain confidence that they are being fairly treated.

• *Betraying the confidence of others.* Sometimes employees share their personal problems with others and ask that they hold the details in strict confidence. Since there is no guarantee that the secret will be kept, those who confide in others run the risk of exposure. Although it is unethical to do this, it is not illegal. However, employees who betray their co-workers' trust could cause the working environment to become less pleasant, diminish morale, and create fights, all of which could affect the running of the operation.

People view these types of dilemmas as ethical or unethical based upon their own experiences and beliefs. Management should carefully discuss the potential for ethical problems with new employees and hold seminars to refresh the memories of current employees. This will take many problems out of the work environment.

Codes of Ethics

Companies of all sizes are developing codes of ethics and codes of conduct that address their expectations of employees and other companies that interface with them. It is commonplace to state basic ground rules and acceptable practices to prevent poor judgment. When employees adhere to specific ethical practices, as outlined in these codes, they can carry out their jobs without having their decisions second-guessed. One of the major fashion retailers in the world is The Gap Stores, Inc.; its code was originally initiated in 1998 and has been regularly updated. Gap stresses a "Zero Means Zero" policy. The code clearly states that:

> We're an equal opportunity employer. All employment decisions are made without regard to race, color, age, gender, gender identity, sexual orientation, religion, marital status, pregnancy, national origin/ancestry, citizenship, physical/mental disabilities, military status or any other basis prohibited by law. Every employee is responsible for helping prevent discrimination and harassment in the workplace.
>
> Zero Means Zero
>
> At Gap Inc., we work hard to make sure that we treat our customers—and each other—with integrity and respect, regardless of appearance, skin color, gender, or any other such distinction. We have zero tolerance for discrimination of any kind.

Attempting to avoid any potential for a wide variety of problems, the code specifically addresses a host of issues such as complaint procedures, accommodations for disabilities, workplace violence, labor laws, alcohol and drug use, international trade regulations, bribes and improper payments, fair dealing, health and safety, confidentiality, **insider trading**, conflicts of interest, and gifts and entertainment.

Many professionals have expressed their opinions on the need for codes of ethics.

Stuart Altmann, the chair of the ethics committee for the Animal Behavior Society, states, "The need for special ethical principles in a scientific society is the same as the need for ethical principles in society as a whole. They are mutually beneficial. They help make our relationships mutually pleasant and productive. A professional society is a voluntary, cooperative organization, and those who must conform to its rules are also those who benefit from the conformity of others. Each has a stake in maintaining general compliance."

Writing a Code of Ethics

The need for establishing codes of ethics involves many factors. The most important reasons have been presented by the Life Skills Coaches Association of British Columbia. They are as follows:

- To define accepted/acceptable behaviors.
- To promote high standards of practice.
- To provide a benchmark for members to use for self-evaluation.
- To establish a framework for professional behavior and responsibilities.
- To be a vehicle for occupational identity.
- To be a mark of occupational maturity.

Understanding the need for a code of ethics only begins to address the problem. Individual companies, whether they are retail organizations or other types must first assess their own needs. Once companies have established their codes, they must be written down and made available to all employees.

Typically the development of a code should consider the following elements:

1. Stating the purposes of the code. This may be to provide an acceptable behavior policy, how employees properly interface with those above or below them in their tables of organization, or other reasons.

2. Creating a set of documents that serves the purposes of the company.

3. Developing a code that is specifically tailored to the needs and values of the organization.

4. Preparing a list of the organization's rules and regulations so that there will be no doubt in the employees' minds of what is expected of them.

5. Clearly stating the penalties of violating the principles set forth in the code.

6. Detailing the manner by which violations of the code of ethics will be punished.

7. Organizing a company committee that will develop the code of ethics. It is best to involve both upper management and people at all levels of employment so that their thoughts could be considered. Limiting this development stage to only the upper-level decision makers will often cause a problem in morale.

8. Describing the manner in which the code of ethics will be implemented. Making certain that employees inside of the business as well as employees of companies that interface with the company are aware of the code is extremely important if it is to work. In the case of fashion retailers, who work closely with vendors, and market consultants, who often coordinate purchase plans, it is imperative that they know the company's code so that no unethical problems arise.

9. Preparing a formal document that will encompass every aspect of the code.

10. Providing for a periodic review system that will allow for revisions and updates so that the individual aspects of the document will always be current.

SOCIAL RESPONSIBILITY

The print, broadcast, mobile and social media have made most people aware of the different types of social programs that retailers, as well as other business institutions, are underwriting.

Showing social responsibility rewards merchants in a number of ways. Not only do retailers provide funding for those in need but retailers improve their images as members of the business community. Each year, more fashion retailers are joining the bandwagon and setting aside funds earmarked for such purposes. However, retailers must be careful not to give the impression that they are only contributing funds to improve their image in the public eye. This will make them seem self-serving and might adversely affect their commitments. The public must be made to believe that the company's involvement is sincere.

Professional public relations people can help bring attention to a company's endeavors in a manner that will not cause suspicion.

Major fashion department store groups such as Saks, Inc. and Macy's, Inc. and chains such as The Gap Stores, Inc. have ongoing sponsorships with major charitable and community organizations as well as special commitments that address the needs that arise from circumstances in specific locations.

Some of the programs that the fashion-retailing community are involved in include AIDS research, cerebral palsy, United Way, the Susan G. Komen Foundation, pediatric AIDS, Make-A-Wish, Habitat for Humanity, and the Juvenile Diabetes Research Foundation (JDRF). Figure 6.4 features a fundraiser for JDRF sponsored in part by FAO Schwarz for the movie *Stuart Little 2*.

These and other fashion retailers do more than make financial contributions. Company employees also engage in **volunteerism** donating their time to a variety of causes such as mentoring programs, playgrounds maintenance, food and clothing drives, environmental projects, tutoring inner city youth, nurturing children, donating blood, and painting projects.

A relatively new approach to doing good for consumers and the environment involves an **eco-friendly** movement, "Sustainable Fashion," which involves the production and distribution of a wealth of **sustainable fashion** products.

Sustainable Fashion Products

In an ever-growing market, sustainable fashion products are starting to be seen in traditional retail stores, websites, and catalogs and not just those that were once considered oddballs in the industry. Department stores such as Bloomingdale's, Macy's, and Nordstrom are adding more and more of these products to their merchandise mixes. In order to discuss and understand sustainable fashion there are several definitions of the topic. The website www.triplepundit.com offers one definition: "Sustainable fashion, also called ethical fashion, combines social responsibility and environmental stewardship with the creation of positive impact. For example, workers are paid living wages and have a safe and healthy working environment. Sustainable fashion operates on the triple bottom line in which profits, social impact, and environmental impact are given equal consideration."

figure 6.4
The stars come out to help with the Juvenile Diabetes Research Foundation funding. Stuart Little for FAO Schwarz is an example of "celebrity" involvement in social responsibility.

Many major chains are also adding sustainable fashion to their inventories. Even H & M whose claim to fame has been fashion with little regard to eco-friendliness has joined the bandwagon. With its "Conscious Collection," all designs are made out of recycled fibers. The company's clout, with more than 2,500 stores worldwide, has pressured manufacturers to produce fabrics that use fewer chemicals and natural resources.

Early on, two eco-friendly retailers were proponents of sustainability. Recreational Equipment, Inc. (REI) and Patagonia, Inc., continue to lead the pack with REI providing eco-sensitive labels on all of its clothing that are made from recyclable materials and Patagonia (featured in Figure 6.5) offering an organic cotton line and a recycling program that takes worn out Patagonia products and makes them into new items.

Other "name" retailers that offer eco-friendliness are Timberland, American Apparel, Nike, and Walmart.

Eco-Friendly Fashion Retailing Online Sites

The trend for sustainable fashion has now significantly grown for new merchants to sell by way of eco-friendly fashion sites. They are not only from the United States but also from the U.K., Australia, and other global fashion centers.

They include ASOS Green Room, BeGood, Beklina, EKOLUV, Ethica, Helpsy, Kaight, and Modavanti. Each may be found by using a search engine such as Google where full descriptions of their offerings are available.

Some of the reasons for this growth include:

- The sites are easy to find by entering key words on a search engine.
- The costs of starting such business are less than that of beginning a brick-and-mortar operation.
- Global markets can be easily accessed.
- Discovery of products takes less time than visits to stores.

figure 6.5
Patagonia is still one of the most important sellers of eco-friendly fashion. Using this approach long before it was "fashionable" has given it the edge on recent retailers who are now embracing eco-friendliness.

Sustainable Fashion Associations With Retail Membership

Two of the associations with retail involvement are the following:

- **The Sustainable Fashion Coalition** was formed by Patagonia and Walmart and now includes American department stores such as Nordstrom and foreign entities such as the U.K.'s Marks & Spencer. Today it has more than 30 members including Levi Strauss, New Balance, Gap, H&M, Zara, JCPenney, Kohl's, L.L. Bean, REI, Ann Taylor, Loft, and Target.
- Retail Industry Leaders Association is an organization that deals with sustainability. Among the fashion retail membership is Crate & Barrel, Old Navy, American Eagle Outfitters, Gap, Belk, J. Crew, Target, Bed Bath & Beyond, REI, Sears, Kmart, and JCPenney.

To keep their membership informed, the association sends a bimonthly newspaper to them regarding sustainability and features large seminars in places like Orlando to provide a mixing place for members.

Evaluation of Sustainable Fashion

Oftentimes the words "**green**" and "eco-friendly" are inappropriately used to motivate shoppers to purchase. While these terms are important indicators of sustainability, their use is sometimes stretched to make them realistic for many fashion items.

In 2009 the Green Good Housekeeping Seal was introduced "to help consumers sift through the confusing clutter of 'green' claims of hundreds of products on store shelves today." Through the Good Housekeeping Research Institute (GHRI), a wide range of products, including apparel, are reviewed and verified according to their environmental impact. Some of the factors studied are claims regarding the reduction of water used in the manufacturing process, energy efficiency in production and product use, ingredients and product safety, and packaging reduction. Evaluation is undertaken by scientists and engineers at GHRI before certification is awarded to, and before the Good Housekeeping Seal may be affixed to, the products.

In seeking the Seal, an extensive application addressing a whole range of environmental criteria must be completed. The worthiness of Good Housekeeping's Seal is internationally recognized as an honest and unbiased designation. It is one of the more important product attachments that are regularly sought after by producers and consumers alike.

Chapter Highlights

1. The rash of unethical occurrences in business has caused retailers to make certain that their codes of ethics address a variety of issues to prevent improper actions by their employees.

2. In understanding the complexity of ethics, it is essential that the issues be recognized and that skills be developed to address the problems.

3. Research indicates that retailing is among the industries with the worst ethics ratings.

4. There are often buyer conflicts of interest in regard to their relationships with vendors.

5. In the absence of any vendor standards, companies run the risk of having their images tarnished when substandard working conditions are made public.

6. Advertising misrepresentation causes a great deal of trouble for retailers in terms of their public image.

7. Ethical dilemmas run the gamut from exaggerating credentials on resumés to feigning illness to take a day off from work.

8. Falsifying expense accounts is a major problem for retailers. Oftentimes, management personnel such as buyers and merchandisers "pad" their expense accounts when away on business trips. The end result is a decrease in profits.

9. Codes of ethics are essential for companies of all sizes so that employees will be able to carry out their duties and responsibilities without being second-guessed.

10. A written code of ethics should define acceptable behaviors and promote high standards of practice.

11. Retailers of all sizes participate in social causes as a means of helping those in need and at the same time, raise their image.

12. Social responsibility comes in the form of dollar expenditures for charitable and worthy causes as well as from volunteerism on the part of company employees.

13. Major department stores and chains have ongoing programs with charitable and community organizations to help address their needs.

14. There are numerous online sites that feature sustainable fashion products which may be easily located with the use of a search engine.

15. Sustainable fashion is most notably evaluated by the Good Housekeeping Seal.

Terms of the Trade

bait and switch	fine print
business ethics	green
codes of ethics	insider trading
conflicts of interest	social responsibility
eco-friendly	sustainable fashion
ethical dilemmas	Sustainable Fashion Coalition
ethics	vendor standards
expense account falsification	volunteerism

For Discussion

1. Which fashion guru, by her actions, has caused significant potential harm for her retailing affiliate?

2. Why should retailers develop codes of ethics for their employees and the industry partners with whom they interface?

3. How would you define the term "business ethics"?

4. What is meant by the term "situational decision-making" as it applies to ethics?

5. Which four industries are reported to have the worst ethics ratings?

6. Why do many fashion retailers disallow vendors to give buyers gifts worth more than $50?

7. Describe one questionable pricing strategy used in retail advertising that often causes ethical concerns for consumers.

8. What are some of the unethical and illegal practices that some employees use when caught stealing?

9. Why is the exaggeration of credentials a telltale factor for a person applying for a position with a retailer?

10. Is it ethical for workers to use the Internet for personal reasons during the workday at the office?

11. Is it ethical for employees to take sick days when they aren't really ill?

12. Might workers lie for their supervisor if they are asked to do so? Why?

13. How can falsifying expense accounts harm the company?

14. What is the basic premise that any code of ethics begins with?

15. Why should retailers become socially responsible?

16. What types of organizations do major retail organizations support in their social responsibility programs?

17. In addition to providing monetary contributions to charities and other needy causes, what other actions do retailers take in their endeavors to become socially responsible?

18. What benefit do fashion retailers get from being socially responsible?

19. What major organization gives impartial ratings for sustainable fashion?

Case Problem

Questions

1. Do you think her use of the Internet for personal reasons is appropriate? Why?
2. How should the company make it clear that such practices are unacceptable?
3. Is there any time when such personal use could be considered proper?

Joy Green has been employed as a buyer for the Male Ego, a specialty chain of 50 units, for more than five years. Starting as an executive trainee 10 years ago, she was promoted to her present position because of excellent performance. She has always conducted herself in a manner that is both professionally and ethically principled. Her buying expertise has made her department one of the most profitable ones in the company.

Joy's performance has been exemplary in that she bases her purchases on last year's sales figures, adjusting the vendor base according to the sales of each one. She carefully researches the wholesale market and chooses vendors that she believes will deliver the most appropriate merchandise for her department. She is not prone to take gifts of any nature, except perhaps the business lunch offered by the vendors with whom she is working at the time of purchase planning. She is, in fact, considered by her supervisor, the divisional menswear manager, the most ethical person in the company's roster of buyers.

Bearing all of these positives in mind, a question of ethics has surfaced regarding one of her actions during the workday. The unidentifiable complainant accuses her of using the Internet for personal reasons during the workday. The complaint states that her time spent on the job is not being exclusively used to perform job-related activities such as purchase planning, model stock development, and so forth. She has been reprimanded for her actions and told if the practice continues, she is likely to be sacked.

Exercises and Projects

1. The concept of ethical practices is widely discussed on numerous websites. Each provides a wealth of information on the subject. Select five websites that have specific references to business ethics, and use the information to complete a two-column chart with one header indicating *Website* and the other *Ethical Considerations*.

2. Contact a major retail operation either by telephone, fax, or email and request an interview with a member of the human resources department to learn about the company's code of ethics. Write a two-page, typewritten paper outlining its code.

chapter seven

ON-SITE AND OFF-SITE LOCATIONS

After reading this chapter, you should be able to:

- Determine how a retailer analyzes a potential location before determining its viability for a successful operation.

- Assess the importance of population, area characteristics, and competition to brick-and-mortar locations.

- Describe the various types of shopping districts for fashion retailer use.

- Analyze site selection in terms of competition, neighboring stores, and travel convenience for potential customers.

- Identify current trends in store location.

When seasoned retailers are asked which three factors they consider most important to the success of a new brick-and-mortar venture, they generally answer, "location, location, location!" This does not undermine the importance of the many other factors to be considered before embarking upon a new venture but underscores the vast significance played by location in terms of success. All too often, inexperienced would-be merchants elect to forego a choice location in favor of a lesser one simply because they consider the costs of leasing a prime site to be too high, but they are willing to spend considerable sums on store design, fixturing, visual merchandising props, and so forth. There is nothing as disheartening as a store that is elegantly designed located in a place where consumers rarely venture. While it is occasionally true that a merchant finds good fortune in an **off the beaten path** location, this tends to be the exception rather than the rule.

The choices for store location are more varied than ever before. While once the **downtown central districts**, or the huge **regional malls** were considered to be the most viable retail locations, today merchants are discovering a host of new environments in which to begin or expand their businesses. Fashion merchants are choosing places previously considered to be inappropriate for their needs and have achieved unparalleled success in them, such as abandoned factories and warehouses, reclaimed historical landmarks, superhighway arteries, and "**power centers**." It is a combination of location analysis and creative thought that has given the retailers such new homes for their businesses.

While the emphasis of this chapter is on brick-and-mortar locations, it is also essential for off-site merchants to consider such factors as proximity to shipping terminals, space potential for expansion, and so forth, before making a choice.

CHOOSING THE BRICK-AND-MORTAR LOCATION

Selecting the most suitable location involves a three-pronged approach. First is the choice of a trading area that best serves the needs of the particular company, second is the exploration of the available shopping districts within the desired trading area, and third is the choice of the exact site on which the store will stand. The following sections explore each prong and show its importance to success.

Analysis of the Trading Area

How far a customer will travel to a particular store depends upon that store's drawing power and the customer's need for the specific merchandise it offers. When people are looking to buy a newspaper or a container of milk, they will go to the closest possible place. If, however, the shopper wants to buy an expensive dress, she will often travel great distances. The places from which retailers can expect their customers are called trading areas. Some companies enjoy unusually large trading areas because of the nature of the products they offer and their exclusivity. L.L. Bean, for example, the world's largest purveyor of outdoor clothing and equipment, is based in Freeport, Maine, where it occupies more than a full square block. The destination is so popular that shoppers come from many surrounding states and Canada, making Bean's trading area unusually large. As a result of its unusual success as a **destination location**, the surrounding area has developed into a thriving off-price designer center that features such marquee labels as Ralph Lauren, Cole Haan, and Burberry. Mall of America, in Bloomington, Minnesota, is America's largest shopping venue; it also has an unusually large trading area. Shoppers travel hundreds of miles to visit the unique center to shop and to enjoy the multitude of unique attractions. Most regional malls have much narrower trading areas. Throughout the United States, there is a major mall approximately every 10 miles. Since the malls are virtually all the same, it is unlikely that a shopper will travel past one to go to another that is farther away. Occasionally, some cities have malls that are even closer to each other than the standard 10 miles. In Chicago, on Michigan Avenue, for example, there are three major **vertical malls** in less than 1 mile. With the limited amount of space in these high-rise ventures, there is little room to house all of the merchants who want a presence in them. Thus, there is a need for several of these entries.

Town Centers, which are essentially outdoor shopping centers, are the new craze in store location. Besides offering many distinctive fashion emporiums, they also feature a wealth of restaurants that help keep the shoppers there for more time to shop.

To determine the extent of the trading area and if it is appropriate to support a potential business, retailers need to consider factors such as population, area characteristics, and competition.

Population

The size of the population alone is not sufficiently indicative of the type of people who inhabit a trading area. Income levels, ages, occupations, living conditions, and so forth should be considered in the overall assessment. This information is available from sources such as the Census Bureau. Since the general population census is taken every 10 years, major retailers undertake their own studies that are more timely and also better tailored to their specific needs.

The demographics important to fashion merchants include the following:

- Income level of the population plays a significant role in the evaluation of an area. For fashion retailers, this is probably the most important of the considerations. While fashion merchandise is available at numerous price points, it would be unwise to begin an operation in a socially and economically deprived area. Although retailers of food and other necessities are found in disadvantaged communities, those who sell fashion would not consider those lucrative areas. However, people with modest incomes do buy fashionable items. Since the fashion industry makes goods available at a variety of price points, the retailer must determine if the income level in a specific geographic area is appropriate for its particular brick-and-mortar operation.

- Different age groups have different fashion needs. Young professionals generally choose merchandise that offers status without considering price. Senior citizens, however, are generally very careful shoppers, primarily considering price and value. Similarly, each age group has specific needs and buying preferences. Since the wants and needs of all the groups are different, the merchant must study the population to determine if the predominant age group in the trading area is the one the retailer can accommodate.

- Occupation is an important consideration in the fashion needs of consumers. Career women, a population segment that is at an all-time high, are major purchasers of fashion goods. They need clothing and accessories for their professional lives and their social lives. A shop that serves the needs of this population would be best located in the major city where these women work—and often live. Such a venture in a suburban location that is predominantly inhabited by families with infants and toddlers often fails.

- Marital status and gender of the trading area are worth considering. In some places, unmarried people dominate. This is particularly true in the Upper East Side and West Side of New York City, where a significant number of singles live. Since unmarried people have different spending patterns from married people, retailers should be aware of the marital status of potential customers. Singles, for example, are big spenders on clothing that could attract a potential partner. In some locales, there is a definite majority of older women, signaling a greater need for fashion retailers who specialize in clothing and accessories for the more mature female population.

- Household permanency can be a determining factor. For example, resort areas provide shopkeepers with people who are in the trading area for a short time. This can be a plus for the retailer, since people on vacation tend to spend more freely than when they are at home. In some vacation destinations such as ski areas, however, the retailer must determine if the business seen in a few months is sufficiently profitable to make it worth locating there. Seasonal ventures are often profitable, but retailers must carefully consider the pros and cons when embarking upon such an endeavor.

- Religious affiliation should be considered to make certain that there is nothing in the retailer's method of operation that would be offensive to the majority of the trading area in the form of the style of fashions sold or hours of store operation. For example, Orthodox Jews do not shop on the Sabbath, which could mean a considerable loss of business to merchants who view Saturday as their most important day of operation. Although this problem might be a minor one, it should be carefully addressed before any investment is made.

- **Population shifts** are common and should be explored. While an area might presently house an appropriate number of potential customers, the figure alone will not reveal whether the population is increasing or declining or if the characteristics of the population are stable. If there is a population explosion in a trading area, there might be a different type of consumer group moving in. In the Lincoln Park area of Chicago, for example, upper-middle class young marrieds have replaced the lower-middle class population. Upscale shops now reign in what was once reserved for merchants who offered low price points. And downtown metropolitan areas in other cities, once havens for the poor, have become places where the upper-middle class now resides. These people once lived in the suburbs but are now moving back to the cities and bringing with them the need for upscale merchandise. Of course, the reverse could be true, with lower socioeconomic groups replacing the more affluent ones.

If merchants do not pay close attention to these and other population characteristics, their businesses might not succeed.

Area Characteristics

Fashion brick-and-mortar operations need to study the particular area under consideration to determine if it offers certain advantages or disadvantages. Characteristics worth studying include the following:

- New York City, London, and Paris are considered to be prime trading areas for fashion merchants not only for their regular inhabitants but for the multitude of tourists attracted to these cities throughout the year. They offer excitement, entertainment, and culture. People visit New York City for its theater and museums, Paris for its art and beauty, and London for its historical richness. Although people don't go to these cities just to shop, tourists tend to buy more when traveling than they ever would at home.
- The accessibility of the trading area is of vital importance to the retailer. In places where public transportation is insufficient, the area should have adequate parking and an excellent network of roads to bring in the shoppers. In downtown Chicago, where street parking is almost impossible to find, the vertical malls such as the Water Tower have multilevel, underground parking facilities.
- Local legislation must be investigated to determine if the retailer will face prescribed obstacles that would prevent business from operating freely. For example, some communities forbid Sunday openings, a day considered by many retailers necessary for conducting their business. Some areas have local sales taxes that deter people from patronizing the area when they can go to tax-free shopping venues close by.
- The number of competitors in the area should be assessed to make certain that there is room for similar businesses. Competition is a positive factor, since it indicates that the trading area is appropriate for a similar type of company. However, oversaturation of a location with too many similar stores can be a problem, spelling trouble in terms of price wars and the ability to enter the market. Lack of competition, though, could indicate that other companies did not have much faith in the area and chose not to open there.
- Promotion for most fashion retailers is a must. Relying upon word of mouth to gain a share of the market is not sufficient for most retailers. Fashion retailers therefore generally use the advertising media, so they should determine whether the trading area has a sufficient number of newspapers and other media with which

to promote their business. Today the use of social media and the Internet has become an important advertising tool since its reach is significant.

- The availability of human resources is of paramount importance to the success of the fashion retailer. Companies such as Nordstrom and Neiman Marcus, merchants of the highest level of fashion retailing, carefully explore areas not only for good customer bases but for qualified personnel to carry out their businesses. With the enormous amount of competition in the fashion retail industry, merchants are recognizing the importance of customer service in attracting shoppers, and they need good employees to supply it.

CLASSIFICATION OF SHOPPING DISTRICTS

If the proposed trading area meets the prospective retailer's criteria, the next decision it needs to make involves selecting the specific type of district in which to open the store. At one time, merchants were limited as to the types of available districts, and downtown central shopping districts and the regional malls were the most dominant in the field. Today, retailers of fashion merchandise can also choose from town centers, power centers, **mixed-use centers**, outlet and **off-price centers**, downtown vertical malls, **festival marketplaces**, and theme centers. Old suburban malls, such as Roosevelt Field on Long Island, New York, are being refurbished and expanded to meet the competition of new shopping centers; neglected historical sites have been restored and repositioned as exciting shopping districts; and downtown areas once blighted by hard times have been resurrected as vital shopping centers. Not every shopping district is appropriate for every fashion retailer. Careful analysis of each should be undertaken before the choice is finally made.

Downtown Central Districts

The downtown central districts in cities all across the United States have been home to major retailers ever since large-scale retailing began. Just about every giant department store organization has been headquartered in a downtown area. These districts not only provided a customer base from the area residents but they also hosted a daily influx of workers and in some cases throngs of tourists.

Although the downtown areas are currently alive and well in most parts of the United States, there was a period when the inner cities were being abandoned by many middle-class families that headed toward the suburbs. They were replaced by families with lower socioeconomic backgrounds that had different buying power. This in turn transformed the downtown areas from viable business districts to unappealing places. Today, however, the revitalization of downtown shopping districts is at its peak, returning these city areas to the glory days. Cities are spending enormous sums to redevelop the areas and make them more attractive. Following their lead, fashion retailers by the score are remodeling their flagship stores, and other types of stores, such as those by the couturiers, are opening enormous flagships like never before. One only needs to walk along Fifth and Madison Avenues in New York City and Oak Street in Chicago to see the extravagant couturier entries. The benefit of such revitalization has caused many suburbanites to make the cities their homes. Even the small-city counterparts, that were once severely damaged when major regional malls opened less than a mile from their downtown centers, are enjoying a renewed interest from consumers. Many chains are lining these streets, as are fashionable entrepreneurs, to cater to the crowd that prefers this type of shopping to the overcrowded mall scene.

Downtowns are no longer the ghost towns of the 1980s but are now in many cases viable shopping alternatives.

An unusual practice is the one that Target is experimenting with. Instead of the trend for giant outlets, they are researching the idea of opening much smaller units in downtown areas and city locations. In *Happening Now*, Target's newest venture will be discussed.

HAPPENING NOW

TARGET TAKES A NEW DIRECTION

As reported in *The New York Times* Sunday edition of January 17, 2014, Target announced its innovative company experiment, opening new stores that are much smaller than the ones the company has previously operated. A lease was signed that would house the smallest of the Target ventures of just 20,000 square feet in Minneapolis. The new format will be known as TargetExpress. The new entry, the smallest Target has ever opened, would "allow the company to open more locations in dense urban areas like New York." Its initiative comes from the fact that more and more young people are choosing to live in cities rather than suburban areas.

The first TargetExpress is set to open on the ground floor of an apartment building near the University of Minneapolis campus while this text is in preparation. The location was not only selected for the built-in market of students, but also for the proximity of its headquarters making it easy for executives to watch the construction and tweak it whenever necessary.

If the experiment is a success, Target will open a multitude of these stores in urban areas throughout the United States, trying to attract an audience familiar with the larger Target stores in suburban areas where they once lived with their parents.

Inner Cities

There is a trend toward reevaluating inner-city locations by retail developers. The International Council of Shopping Centers has cited several areas in New York City, for example, that have reemerged from being fashion-deprived retail centers to vibrant higher-grade fashion merchandise venues. Just one example of these revitalization programs is the project on Harlem's 125th Street, once a shopping street void of anything fashionable that now features such companies as H&M, a leading global fashion retailer catering to teenagers and young adults who seek trendy merchandise.

Regional Malls

When the population movement to the suburbs reached major proportions in the 1950s, the stores that dotted the main streets of these now-booming towns were inadequate to serve the needs of the inhabitants. Some department stores had branches in these areas that brought significant business to their organizations, but there were no major centers such as those in the important downtown central districts. Two of the earliest malls flanked New York City. Green Acres, on the New York City line, and Roosevelt Field, a little further east on Long Island, opened their doors in the mid-1950s as prototypes of what was on the horizon in retailing. With these two successes, the regional mall was off and running. Roosevelt Field would eventually expand into the fifth-largest mall in the United States, with companies such as Macy's, Bloomingdale's, and Nordstrom as anchors. Initially, Roosevelt Field was an outdoor mall, eventually enclosing its environs to compete with the first enclosed mall to be built that way, Walt Whitman in Huntington, Long Island, which was only a few miles away. Featuring climate control, these malls became the norm for regional malls. Later on, many regional centers would again adopt an outdoor design, such as Jacksonville's Town Center in Florida.

The **controlled shopping centers** were the first type of regional mall. That is, competition within the mall was controlled to enhance the probability that each store would realize a profit. Without the control concept, stores might be rented on a first-come, first-served basis, resulting in too many shoe stores, for example, and an insufficient number of dress shops. The draw of the mall then was the anchor stores, as it is today. Early on, there were usually two, one at either end of the facility. The **mall anchors** were the well-known department store branches with immediate name recognition. Since the department stores were, and still are, retailing's major advertisers, they attracted large numbers of consumers to the shopping area. Not only were the anchors successful, but the other stores in the mall were successful too because of the crowds in the malls which came to visit the anchors.

Today, regional malls bear little resemblance to their predecessors. They are often built as multilevel environments with as many as six anchors, movie theaters, and food courts to attract large crowds. People who patronize these centers may spend a full day there, enjoying themselves with shopping, eating, and entertainment.

Aside from the sufficient parking and easy access through highway arteries, the mall's success is due to a number of factors. It has become a place to spend time in addition to shopping. Many of these facilities are used by **mall walkers** who enjoy the controlled climate for their workouts.

Some of these shopping arenas are outdoor ventures such as Old Orchard in suburban Chicago, the Falls in Miami, the Esplanade in Palm Beach, Town Center in Jacksonville, and Bal Harbour Shops, in Miami Beach. Retailers also enjoy many organized promotional activities undertaken by regional malls management, such as visits from Santa Claus and the Easter Bunny, automobile shows, fashion shows, art and antique events, and the like. Expenses for these events are either paid by the developer or shared by the mall's tenants. The individual retailer gets the benefit of the resulting large crowds without having to foot the promotional bill alone.

Today, every major city boasts one or more regional malls. The new ones have vastly improved on the old, and the older malls are modernizing to remain profitable for their tenants. All across the country, mall facelifts are commonplace, with new floors added for additional stores. Revitalization is necessary to serve the needs of the existing market, and land has become too scarce and costly to develop new malls on. Figure 7.1 features the typical shopping mall.

Although the United States is by far the leader in the regional mall game, other countries are now playing and, in some instances, outdistancing the United States with some of their entries. Canada, for example, boasts one of the world's largest malls, in Edmonton. Not only does it house more than 800 stores selling a variety of merchandise, but it features a giant pool complete with waves, rides and attractions, and a full-size ice-skating rink. Not to be outdone by any other country, the United States Mall of America is also a megamall and the largest in the United States, with a wealth of stores and attractions. The success of this **megamall** has a $1.2 billion economic impact on the state of Minnesota annually.

figure 7.1
Cherry Hill Mall in Cherry Hill, New Jersey is enclosed, enabling shoppers to visit no matter the inclemency of the weather.

Vertical Malls

As land became less available in the downtown central districts and the areas became more populated with household tenants, workers, and visitors, retailers found it impossible to find space in which to open their businesses. To accommodate many of these ventures and to make the prime locations better revenue producers, retailers began to think about high-rise, or vertical malls to house scores of tenants in buildings that would otherwise be occupied by just one major company. Some buildings were erected from the ground up on the sites of old existing structures, and others were constructed by revamping vacant buildings. In Chicago, which has become the home of the vertical mall concept, one of the most profitable entries began as a new complex called Water Tower Place. Much like the sprawling suburban malls, it has two anchors, Macy's and Lord & Taylor, and a host of upscale fashion specialty retailers. Its customer base comes from a mix of people who work in the area, those who live close to the center, and tourists, many of whom stay in the Ritz Carlton Hotel that towers above the shopping center. Based on this success, two more vertical towers were erected close by. One houses Bloomingdale's and numerous fashion boutiques, and the other Saks Fifth Avenue and a wealth of fashion emporiums.

Mixed-Use Centers

One of the newest major shopping districts to be built is the mixed-use center. As the name implies, its composition is not strictly retail oriented, but incorporates office space, hotels and entertainment outlets along with the stores. The concept provides a diverse market mix that consists of office workers, tourists, and entertainment seekers who not only utilize the shopping facilities but the other attractions as well. These centers are built all over the country and are achieving enormous success. One of the first mixed-use centers that led to the current trend in shopping districts is the Fashion Centre at Pentagon City outside of Washington, D.C. Flanked by two existing upscale regional malls that housed the likes of Nordstrom, Neiman Marcus, and Saks Fifth Avenue, the developers believed that the massive Pentagon building, more than four million square feet and the site of thousands of workers and visitors, would provide a captive audience. In addition to such anchors as Macy's and Nordstrom, and fashion specialists such as Ann Taylor, Victoria's Secret, and Coach, the location includes a high-rise office building, a Ritz Carlton Hotel, and a high-rise residential office building. Adding to the convenience of shopping there is the fact that the Fashion Centre is situated on the Metrorail, one stop away from the Pentagon, and a few stops from Washington, D.C.

Power Centers

Usually composed of 20 or more stores, the power center is a complex that utilizes high-volume, high-profile outlets to draw customers. Most of these centers have at their core **big box retailers** such as off-price merchants Best Buy, and fashion operations such as Marshalls and T.J. Maxx. The power centers occupy anywhere from 250,000 to 500,000 square feet and are located on major arteries or highways. Today, more and more discounters and off-pricers are dominating these centers.

Off-Price and Outlet Centers

Off-price fever has reached just about every corner of the United States. So successful is the concept that manufacturers and designers of fashion goods as well as the traditional fashion retailers are opening more outlets to dispose of their slow sellers and leftover merchandise. The vast majority of the items sold are fashion-oriented clothing and accessories for men, women, and children at every price point.

One of the largest of these **outlet centers** is the Mills. Beginning with Potomac Mills in Woodbridge, northern Virginia, the company has gone on to open these giant centers in locations throughout the United States such as Franklin Mills in Philadelphia, Pennsylvania; Opry Mills in Nashville, Tennessee; Gurnee Mills outside of Chicago, Illinois; and Sawgrass Mills, the largest of the group, in Fort Lauderdale, Florida. With more than two million square feet under one roof, the ever-expanding Sawgrass Mills features enormous spaces for outlets of Saks Fifth Avenue, OFF 5TH; Last Call, Neiman Marcus; and manufacturer and designer outlets of DKNY, Ralph Lauren, Calvin Klein, Barneys, and others. Along with the retail outlets that draw thousands of shoppers every day, prominent restaurants such as the Cheesecake Factory and a multitude of entertainment centers make this arena a regular destination for those who live in the regional market as well as tourists from all over the world.

Outdoor centers also continue to be successful ventures for the merchants who locate within them. They are found in every part of the country such as Freeport and Kittery, Maine; Secaucus and Flemington, New Jersey; North Hampton, New Hampshire; Orlando, Florida; Niagara Falls, New York; and Central Valley, New York. Marquee labels such as Calvin Klein, Burberry, Anne Klein, Patagonia, Jones New York, and others dominate these centers.

The major players in the off-price centers and outlet centers are the Simon Property Group (which took over the Mills Corporation and many of the Prime Outlets), Belz Factory Outlet World, and Tanger Factory Outlet Centers, Inc. Collectively, they own hundreds of value centers throughout the United States. Figure 7.2 is an example of an outlet center.

Festival Marketplaces

When Faneuil Hall in Boston was "rediscovered" in the 1970s, a developer with foresight saw it and the immediate surrounding areas as an ideal location for a different

figure 7.2
Tanger Outlet Center is one of the busiest in the United States, and features merchandise for the value shopper.

type of shopping environment. Situated adjacent to Boston's waterfront—which was run down—a revitalization program was initiated that resulted in the now-famous Quincy Market. It would soon become the prototype for other festival marketplaces.

It wasn't long before other downtrodden or underutilized facilities and locations would be transformed into centers that tourists and residents could enjoy. In New York City, the South Street Seaport was born in a place that formerly housed the wholesale Fulton Fish Market. Amid cobblestone streets and numerous restaurants, a wealth of merchants set up shop to make this an outstanding tourist attraction. The old St. Louis Union Station was refurbished as another festival marketplace, as was the waterfront of Baltimore, which became Harborplace, and St. Johns River waterfront in downtown Jacksonville, Florida, which became The Jacksonville Landing.

Different from the traditional mall and downtown central district settings, the festival marketplaces are unique environments where shopping and entertainment co-exist.

Fashion "Streets"

In affluent areas of the United States and abroad, fashion boutique flagships of renowned international designers are opening on specific streets. Rodeo Drive in Beverly Hills, California; Fifth and Madison Avenues in New York City, New York; Worth Avenue in Palm Beach, Florida; Rue d'Antibes in Cannes, France; and Rue de Rivoli in Paris, France are home to such famous couturiers as Armani, Chanel, Yves Saint Laurent, Ferré, Gucci, and Givenchy as well as the designer collections of Ralph Lauren and Donna Karan.

While the vast majority of the population shops in malls and downtown central districts, those who desire and could afford the extravagances of these extraordinary creative geniuses prefer the lesser-congested environs of these shopping venues. Together with visitors from all over the globe, those who populate the prestigious areas that surround these **fashion streets** are the mainstays of the boutiques' clientele.

Of course, the number of these locales is extremely limited, because their targeted customers are composed of the two segments of the upper class who have significant wealth.

Transportation Terminals

People who travel are finding that they often spend a significant amount of time in airports and train terminals. With stopovers or plane changes becoming increasingly more prevalent because of weather delays, the waits can be anywhere from an hour to several hours. Check-in times have also gotten earlier because of time allowed for security screening, which means that waiting an hour or two is the rule rather than the exception. Even long-distance train travel has become fraught with delays, leaving the traveler with time to spare.

These conditions have prompted retailers to take advantage of the situations by opening shops that appeal to the traveling masses. Airports, once the home of duty-free shops, restaurants, bars, and newsstands, have been joined by the likes of Gap, Victoria's Secret, and other fashion-oriented stores. The trend for the development of these **transportation terminal centers** is increasing in the United States, but it pales by comparison to those found overseas. Heathrow Airport in London is a shopper's paradise. Companies such as the globally renowned Harrods have a branch inside the terminal, as do the boutiques of many upscale designers. In France's Nice Airport, Hermès, Chanel, and Versace offer an assortment of their products to the waiting travelers.

Trying to play catch-up, some of America's retailers have entered these locations in large numbers. In many of the major domestic airports, Brooks Brothers have a dominant presence. Airports with major collections of stores include LaGuardia Airport in New York City, Ronald Reagan National Airport in Washington, D.C., and O'Hare Airport in Chicago. For train travelers, New York City's Grand Central Station, and Washington, D.C.'s Union Station offer a large number of shops that specialize in fashion merchandise. Figure 7.3 features a new service at Heathrow Airport for shoppers.

Freestanding Stores

In today's retail landscape, a single **freestanding store** is a rare occurrence. Unless the retailer has significant clout and offers something that is unique, it is unlikely that a sufficient number of customers will come to patronize that store only. There are, however, a small group of these merchants whose presence warrants such locations: the warehouse clubs such as Sam's, Costco, and BJ's. Their emphasis on value makes them destinations for masses of shoppers. While at first glimpse their merchandise assortment is composed mostly of food items, products for the home, electronics, and pharmaceuticals, a wealth of fashion items such as Polo, Perry Ellis, and Calvin Klein round out the product mix at prices that are far below what they cost at traditional retail outlets.

Unless the drawing power is sufficient to attract such crowds, setting up shops as freestanding stores isn't a good business decision.

Neighborhood Clusters

Rather than utilizing the controlled nature of such centers as malls, these locations are unplanned in every sense of the word. Merchants such as pharmacies, beauty salons, food stores, and butcher shops generally dominate these locations. In some cases, small boutiques and specialty stores are interspersed among these nonfashion operations.

figure 7.3
London's Heathrow Airport features personal shoppers, who help passengers make merchandise selections while waiting to board their flights. With significant layovers between flights, retailers can take advantage of these consumers who have time to spare.

Occasionally, there are clusters that are predominantly fashion oriented and feature a host of women's shops, men's haberdasheries, shoe stores, jewelers, and accessories operations.

The success of the **neighborhood cluster** is that it offers small retailers that are unable to afford the enormous expense associated with downtown or mall locations an opportunity to serve a small trading area. Frequently the people who patronize the neighborhood clusters do so on a regular basis, often visiting daily.

Strip Centers

Akin to the composition of stores found in neighborhood clusters are those that are located in **strip centers**, configurations that usually feature a row of stores flanked by parking lots. Unlike the neighborhood clusters, where the buildings that house the stores are generally individually owned, the strip center is owned and managed by a single real estate developer. With this single ownership, the leasing of stores is more controlled, as in the case of malls, giving the lessees less competition. In the neighborhood cluster, with so many different landlords, there is the potential to have several similar shops in the one general location.

Flea Markets

These bargain arenas are primarily the destinations of value-hunting consumers. In parking lots of drive-in movies and racetracks and in abandoned indoor facilities, there is aisle after aisle of vendors selling everything from electronics to fashion items. The fashion merchandise is often leftovers from previous seasons, manufacturer overruns, or seconds. The majority of **flea markets** are part-time businesses open primarily on the weekends.

SITE SELECTION

Once the retailer has decided which shopping district is best suited to serve its needs, the next step is to select the specific site within it that will offer the best chance for success. Even within an enormous mall, one site might be more beneficial to a specific retailer's needs than any other. This decision also requires a good deal of research. Governmental agencies, trade associations, and primary research can provide information to help with the ultimate choice.

Competition

It is important to assess the competition when selecting a general trading area, and it is important to assess the competition when selecting a specific site. Setting up a business that is near others that are similar may lead to failure. If a new retailer offers a unique product mix, it will be possible to lure customers away from the stores they already patronize. In a proper mix of tenants, the new business has a chance for survival.

Neighboring Tenants

A location between two established stores for **neighboring tenants** is advantageous to the new retailer as long as they are not direct competitors.

In malls and downtown central districts, department stores attract the largest number of shoppers. If the new merchant can secure a location that is adjacent to such major retailers, the traffic that they generate could bring a wealth of shoppers to its premises.

Another advantageous location is near stores with complementary merchandise. If, for example, a new children's shop locates between a women's clothing store and a shoe store, the new venture will likely attract their shoppers.

Price points are another factor. It's not a good idea to open a fashion-forward upscale shoe boutique next to a value-oriented operation such as a discounter or off-price store because each attracts a different type of market.

High-traffic areas such as food courts and movie theaters bring steady pedestrian traffic to retailers in those locations.

The ideal location is not always available. Choice sites in malls are generally taken. Similarly, downtown areas rarely have locations open near the major retailers. In these cases merchants should look to new centers that will provide them the opportunity of getting in on the ground floor so they can start on a positive note and refine their merchandising plans.

Transportation Accessibility

In downtown central shopping districts, parking space is often difficult to find so it is essential to assess the modes of transportation that bring the shoppers to the store. If subway lines and buses exist, merchants should check the proximity of their stops to the site they are considering. Being close to the subway station or bus stop will ensure that a steady stream of people will pass by who might become customers.

If there are a sufficient number of parking facilities close to the considered site shoppers will be able to come to it. Locations near parking garages are also good, as more shoppers will see the store on their way to and from the garages.

Pedestrian Traffic

A visit to any major city's central shopping districts such as those found in Chicago, New York City, or San Francisco immediately reveals the throngs of passersby. Whether they are residents of the area, commuters, or tourists, many are interested in shopping. The more pedestrians, the more the likelihood of reaching sales goals. Even in the regional malls, where there is usually an abundance of pedestrian traffic, all spaces are not equal. Most people frequent the main halls or arteries, with fewer passing through the secondary spurs. It is therefore essential to scout the potential site to make sure the location is in the path of passersby.

Entertainment and Dining Facilities

In major shopping centers, such as regional malls, there are increasing numbers of dining facilities and entertainment attractions. Retailers benefit from these attractions because they not only bring people to the malls but they also make the shopping experience last longer. People with small children, for example, will often use an amusement area to entertain the children and extend the shopping day. Food courts help to satisfy hungry patrons and keep them at the center for longer periods. Figure 7.4 features a mall's food court.

Megamalls such as Mall of America, for example, are excellent examples of the power of these facilities. Studies show that the time a shopper spends in such places is significantly longer than in those centers without entertainment and dining facilities.

figure 7.4
A child eating in a mall's food court. The food court often serves the purpose of extending the family's shopping time in the mall.

OCCUPANCY CONSIDERATIONS

Once a retailer decides on a particular trading area, it is important to consider the arrangements necessary to secure a space. In major shopping centers such as malls or festival marketplaces, retailers must obtain leases. In a downtown central district or neighborhood cluster, retailers may be able to buy spaces. If the retailer can choose an option, it is important to consider the pros and cons of both.

Leasing

The developers of the property have the ultimate say in the terms offered to the potential tenants. When the tenants are household names such as Macy's, Bloomingdale's, and Saks Fifth Avenue, and will be the mall's anchors, the developer is more apt to provide certain leasing advantages. These major retailers attract the crowds to the malls through their extensive advertising and name recognition, and without their presence, the success of the mall would be limited.

Leasing arrangements include the **fixed lease**, where the tenant pays a set amount for the space, and the **graduated lease**, where escalating rent clauses are built in, and the retailer's expense for the space increases over the life of the lease. Sometimes the cost of leasing space is based upon a set amount plus a percent of the sales that the retailer generates.

The property developer also sets rules to which the tenant must agree. Hours of operation are generally spelled out in mall locations so that there are not different operating hours for different stores. There might be a periodic fee for general advertising, and each merchant must share in the expense of advertising the location. Occasionally, developers stipulate that merchants are required to pay maintenance fees to cover the costs of repairs. The retailer should go over the total lease agreement before signing the lease so there are no surprises that could hamper the merchant's potential for success.

Ownership

Some retailers opt for ownership if it is possible. In particular, many of the major discounters such as Costco and Sam's Club purchase tracts of land where they set up shop. By owning a piece of property, the retailer is not at the mercy of the developer or landlord. Oftentimes, when businesses are successful, as the lease is nearing the end of the term, the owner of the property will ask for exorbitant rental increases. The retailer faces the option of signing the new agreement or moving to another location. Sometimes the demands are so great that they cut into the merchant's profits and turn a success into a failure. Ownership avoids such penalties. There are also no occupancy rules. When retailers own their premises, they decide the days and hours of operation and any other conditions that affect their business.

CHOOSING THE OFF-SITE LOCATION

Although the "rules" are less applicable to off-site locations that warehouse goods to be shipped directly to the consumer through their catalogs and websites, there are, however, some considerations that must be addressed before the locations are selected.

Some of these include the following.

- *The proximity of shipping terminals.* This is essential because the merchandise must be shipped as quickly as possible to reach the stores for stock replenishment, and catalog and website orders that go to the customers. They are especially important for global shipping. The closer to these terminals, the better. Often, time is of the essence for the overseas purchasers. Figure 7.5 features a shipping container terminal.
- *Space availability for expansion.* When a warehouse is opened, there is no telling if the space availability will satisfy the needs of the retailer in the future. A move to a larger location might not have the benefits of the existing one, and the costs for relocation will usually be more costly than the expansion of the one that is currently used.

figure 7.5
This Hong Kong shipping terminal is close to manufacturers' warehouses, which facilitates the shipping process and usually saves the shipper some of the costs of moving merchandise.

- *Ease of access for employees.* Making it to off-site locations in a timely manner is essential to the proper functioning of the company. Easily traveled roads for those with their own automobiles, and public transportation for the rest, is a must.
- *Cost of rent.* For those renting, the costs must be sufficiently affordable so that the costs of the warehousing will not increase the costs of the merchandise stored. In cases of purchasing the facility, it should be determined if the rental could be for a certain period with the understanding that a later outright purchase is possible.
- *Taxes and other expenses.* Different locations have different tax implications. Often deals can be made to receive tax abatements. Other expenses such as energy rates, etc. vary from locale to locale and must be determined before agreeing to the rental.

Chapter Highlights

1. Initially, the trading area must be assessed before any plans to open a store can begin.

2. Population studies must be undertaken in terms of income levels, age groups, occupations, marital status, degree of stability, religious affiliation, and population shifts so that the merchant will know if the appropriate consumers are present to make the store a success.

3. Many areas have the benefits of unique attractions such as amusement centers that help to bring shoppers in.

4. With so many different types of shopping districts available to retailers, they should perform careful analysis of each before making a final decision.

5. The downtown central districts are home to the major department store flagships, making them extremely desirable places for other retailers.

6. Regional malls have been the mainstays for suburban shopping since the 1950s and have continued to expand to meet the needs of the ever-growing populations in those areas.

7. In downtown areas where retail space is at a premium, vertical malls have been erected to provide additional selling space.

8. Off-price centers have developed in every part of the United States as places where bargain-hunting shoppers can satisfy their purchasing needs.

9. Festival marketplaces have been developed in areas that were once downtrodden, such as historical landmarks, city waterfronts, and old railroad terminals.

10. Fashion streets are important venues for designer flagships and include such locales as Madison Avenue in New York City, Worth Avenue in Palm Beach, and Rodeo Drive in Beverly Hills.

11. Freestanding stores can only be successful if the retailer is a high-profile operation that will draw consumers without the aid of other retailers.

12. Specific site selection is based upon such factors as neighboring tenants, competition, transportation accessibility, pedestrian traffic, and entertainment facilities.

13. There are two types of occupancy considerations: leasing and outright ownership.

14. Town Centers are outdoor shopping venues that are providing significant success for retailers.

15. Off-site facilities such as warehouses must be carefully assessed before the terms of the rental contract are agreed upon.

Terms of the Trade

big box retailers	mixed-use centers
controlled shopping center	neighborhood clusters
destination location	neighboring tenants
downtown central district	off the beaten path
fashion streets	off-price center
festival marketplace	outlet center
fixed leases	population shifts
flea markets	power center
freestanding stores	regional malls
graduated leases	strip centers
mall anchors	town centers
mall walkers	transportation terminal centers
megamalls	vertical malls

For Discussion

1. What are the places to which stores expect to draw their shoppers called?

2. In addition to the size of the population, what other population characteristics should be considered before any location decision is made?

3. Should fashion merchants consider the occupations of those in the trading area before deciding upon a particular location? Why?

4. Can religious affiliation in any way help determine the retailer's choice of location?

5. Why are New York City, London, and Paris such excellent places for fashion retailers to open stores?

6. Who are the major tenants in a downtown central shopping district?

7. When did the regional mall concept first appear, and in what types of locations did the malls initially operate?

8. What is meant by the term "controlled" shopping center?

9. Why is it necessary for some downtown shopping districts to erect vertical malls?

10. What is a mixed-use center?

11. Who are the typical tenants of a power center?

12. How does a festival marketplace differ from the traditional mall?

13. Why have transportation terminals become viable places for retailers to open stores?

14. What is a fashion street?

15. How does a neighborhood cluster differ from a strip center?

16. Why is it beneficial for a retailer to open a store in a location that is flanked by two established stores?

17. Should a retailer consider opening a store that is next door to a competitor?

18. What are the two major types of leases that are available to retailers?

Case Problem

Questions

1. If you were the person making the decision, which route would you take?

2. What factors did you consider in making your choice?

The Sophisticated Woman is a major fashion retailer with approximately 800 stores in the United States. Its success story is unparalleled in retailing in that it opened its first unit 20 years ago and has become one of the most profitable fashion retail specialty chains in the country. The proper merchandise mix and appropriate location choices have given the chain this enviable position. Whenever a prime location in a suburban or vertical mall has become available, the company has opened a unit.

Currently The Sophisticated Woman is facing a location dilemma. One of its most successful units is in a suburban fashion mall in southern Florida. The mall is anchored by two of Florida's leading department stores as well as department store branches of two that are based in New York City, which draw a considerable amount of traffic to themselves and the other specialty stores in that shopping district. So successful has business been that when the adjoining space became available, The Sophisticated Woman expanded its store and remodeled it into a very profitable shopping environment.

The Sophisticated Woman is always on the lookout for locations that would be as appropriate. Generally, the primary consideration is the distance of one unit to the other, with approximately 4 to 5 miles considered ideal. The problem that must be addressed concerns the projected development of a major mall that will be built just two blocks from the Florida mall in which the successful store is located. The new mall will be anchored by three major department stores and will be built as a multilevel structure that promises to be the most beautiful in the South.

Mr. Drummond, vice president in charge of site selection, believes that the company should close the existing store and move to the newer location. Ms. Connors, a senior executive in charge of merchandising, is of the opinion that the company should remain in the present location because of its profitability and forego the chance to open in the newer environment. Another route proposed by members of the senior management team is to maintain the old unit and open another in the new mall.

With space going quickly in the new facility, The Sophisticated Woman must come to a decision if it wants to open in the new mall.

Exercises and Projects

1. Either through in-person investigation or the Internet, research one off-price mall, power center, mixed-use center, or vertical mall. In an oral report, present why you believe the chosen facility lives up to its shopping center designation. In addition, describe any of the additional draws or attractions that make this area a viable shopping district.

2. Analyze the trading area of the largest city close to where you live in terms of its demographics and characteristics. Prepare a written report highlighting those aspects of store location that make it appropriate as a trading area.

chapter eight

DESIGNING AND FIXTURING BRICK-AND-MORTAR PREMISES

After reading this chapter, you should be able to:

- Identify the various design concepts that fashion retailers use in their stores.

- Describe the types of storefronts and window structures available to merchants.

- Differentiate between interior layout designs for single and multilevel stores.

- Classify the different fashion departments and designs.

- Establish why major retailers in their flagships and branch stores are using in-house shops.

- Detail the layout of a store and why different departments are located in particular areas.

- Describe the different types of fixturing that fashion retailers employ in their brick-and-mortar operations.

- Detail the wall and flooring surfaces used in today's retail environments.

- Explain the types of sustainable materials used in fixturing.

- List the reasons for the use of sustainable fixtures.

Fashion retailers are increasingly changing the look of their stores from the traditional appearance that was once typical of brick-and-mortar design. The lack of originality in store design made stores look so much alike that consumers often couldn't identify which store they were in once they were inside.

In today's highly competitive fashion retail arena, unique interiors are the rule rather than the exception. Retailers are finally using the fervor in selecting their store designs that they employ in selecting their merchandise designs. They are realizing that their physical surroundings should differentiate them from their competitors the way their merchandise assortments do.

Ralph Lauren's flagship, on fashionable Madison Avenue in New York City, is housed in a former mansion, once the Rhinelander, instead of the typical brick-and-mortar structure. As shoppers enter the door, they are immediately surrounded by majestic antique fixtures, an elegant, late nineteenth century staircase, and paintings that help to make this setting more like a manor than a store. The Lauren collection is skillfully arranged in spaces that once served as the dining room, living room, and bedrooms so that the clothing takes on an aura of elegance. At the other extreme is the contemporary design in H&M stores, Uniqlo, and Massimo Dutti, all from global origins that cater to the young set around the world. An abundance of glass and chrome make up these environments that are devoid of frills and sets the scene perfectly for the trendy merchandise offered for sale. Such **minimalist interior design** is a trend that lessens the impact of the store but concentrates on the merchandise.

Once fashion retailers come up with a design for their environments, it does not have to be set in stone. Occasionally, fashion merchants radically change their fashion concepts, and the new vision should be reflected in their environmental settings as well. Brick-and-mortar "makeovers" are being used by retailers to make their premises more up-to-date. They use new flooring, fixtures, lighting, etc. to achieve this goal. A case in point is Banana Republic. Its store interiors and fixturing once were "safari oriented," using a wealth of bamboo, raffia, netting, and other outback materials to enhance its khaki clothing image. Today's Banana Republic stores are a far cry from that design concept. As it changed its merchandise focus to a more contemporary look with broader appeal, it also changed its store environments to a sleek contemporary interior replete with glass, beautiful woods, and leather accents.

The budgets for brick-and-mortar design and fixturing have exploded in recent years. No longer are run-of-the-mill architects the order of the day in store design. Retailers are willing to pay specialists who can translate an empty space into a store that not only truly enhances their merchandise but also stands out from the competition. Even the discount retailers and off-pricers have moved in the direction of better design and not just the lackluster arrangements once dominant in these types of stores.

The vast number of environmental design specialists' websites highlight their diversity. The Internet has made it easier to locate and identify the wealth of different directions and alternatives in store design that retailers can pursue. A quick perusal will offer a wealth of these new design approaches.

PLANNING THE CONCEPT

Before fashion retailers make any decisions concerning what shape the store's exterior and interior will take, they must first examine their objectives, image, and choice of location. If, for example, the operation is one that specializes in off-price fashion merchandise, uses the **self-selection** method of selling, and is located in an outlet power center, the design needs will be entirely different from those of the company that specializes in high fashion, stocks designer labels, emphasizes service as its forte and is organized around **collection areas**, where certain lines of merchandise are separated out to give the brand greater impact. A look at Marshalls and Bergdorf Goodman immediately reveals that their needs are at the opposite ends of the design spectrum.

Whether retailers are small ventures or giant retail operations, they must establish a budget that includes how much they can spend on construction, fixturing, lighting, floor and wall decoration, heating and ventilation, and so forth before initiating their plans. Once they have finalized their financial considerations, it is time to begin the brick-and-mortar design.

It should be noted that "sustainability" in fixturing has become an important factor in fixture choices. Not only does it help with environmental concerns but also as a way to improve store image.

The best approach is to employ an architectural firm that specializes in fashion retailing store design. The Internet makes it easy to find a host of different firms. By studying their websites, retailers can determine which company will best serve their design needs. The Retail Design Institute, a professional organization for retail planning and design, is an excellent resource. Its website, www.retaildesigninstitute.org, has a directory that lists a wealth of design firms in specific geographic areas. Another approach is to examine the pages of *VMSD* magazine, which has an annual listing of the top-50 design firms along with the clients they have served.

Although many of the world's leading fashion retailers have in-house store designers, the vast majority of them also utilize outside design groups. The collaborative efforts of the two make the ultimate design the one that best serves the store's needs. And although small retailers are often limited in terms of their design-planning budgets, it is worth it to spend the money for expert advice so as to avoid costly mistakes.

Once retailers have selected a professional firm, they need to meet with the designers to discuss such areas as store image, target customers, merchandise mixes, services, and location so that the design will be appropriate for the store's operation. Some firms concentrate on design and leave the preliminary considerations to the retailer. Others totally involve themselves in the preplanning procedures and investigation as well as the actual design alternatives.

Some types of locations, as discussed in Chapter 7, "On-Site and Off-Site Locations" may place limitations on certain aspects of the design such as storefronts, entrances, and window structures. In the major regional shopping centers, for example, the developers often establish a set of design rules to which the tenants must conform. Freestanding stores, however, are generally free from such restrictions other than those that might be imposed by governmental regulations.

Designing the Exterior

The exterior of a store is important for a number of reasons. First, it gives passersby a quick impression of the store and the type of merchandise sold inside. Second, it allows window configurations that feature the items that the merchant wishes to attract the shopper's attention. And finally, if it is part of a chain that uses a recognizable façade, it signals that this unit offers the chain's merchandise.

Today's retail exteriors run the gamut from the traditional types favored by department store flagships to the unique designs of trendy designers.

Store Fronts and Window Structures

A walk through any downtown central shopping district, regional mall, festival marketplace, or other shopping venue immediately reveals a host of different types of display windows and store entrances. Each is designed to match the allocated space with the store's merchandising mix, and the retailer's concept of how to best attract shoppers.

Typically, these fronts feature the traditional designs that include **parallel-to-sidewalk windows**, windowless formats, arcades, and **open windows**, which are described in the following sections.

Parallel-to-Sidewalk Windows

The ideal arrangement for making the greatest impact on the shopper is the parallel-to-sidewalk configuration. The design, typical of the giant downtown central district's department store flagship, requires a large frontage. The main entrance to the store is flanked by as many as four large windows that are approximately 12 to 15 feet wide and about 8 or 10 feet deep. They offer a stage setting concept in which the merchandiser may install spectacular displays such as the famous Christmas windows that draw shoppers to Lord & Taylor, Macy's, and Saks Fifth Avenue. These and other retail giants such as Bloomingdale's and Nordstrom spend considerable sums throughout the year designing displays that bring their fashion images to the passersby. Figure 8.1 features a Macy's storefront.

Although this type of window structure can generate more excitement than any other, it is very expensive. Only those merchants that either own their own retail spaces, or have lifelong leases can avail themselves of this extravagant display space.

Windowless Store Fronts

In the major regional malls throughout the country, many fashion merchants subscribe to the **windowless storefront**, where display windows are replaced by large glass walls

figure 8.1
Macy's window trimmers preparing for the holiday windows. It is essential that windows are changed periodically to take advantage of the current selling season.

that separate the interior from the exterior. With space so costly and limited in these giant selling environments, the vast majority of it must be utilized for selling. The entrance is often a large glass front through which shoppers may see the entire store or a portion of it. Instead of using formal display installations, the store's merchandise on the selling floor serves as the display. In many malls, the trend is to eliminate stationary glass structures or windows entirely and install sliding glass panels that are pushed out of sight when the store is open for business.

Although these stores relinquish the valuable formal display windows, they gain more accessibility from the mall's corridors and more selling space.

Arcade Fronts

Stores that have little frontage but need formal window space to feature their merchandise sometimes build **arcade windows**. In this arrangement, the store's entrance is recessed 10 to 15 feet from the building line and a large, rectangular window is constructed on either side of the entrance. This enables the merchant to feature merchandise that might tempt shoppers to come inside. One of the disadvantages of this arrangement is that it reduces the amount of selling space.

Open Windows

Retailers that do not want to relinquish their space to arcades or parallel-to-sidewalk structures but still need to have some way to display merchandise opt for the open window. The open windows typically have panes of glass on either side of the store's entrance that feature small "stages" on which the merchandise is featured. With no backing to these stages, the passersby can see into the store. The only disadvantage of the open window is that the shoppers can handle the merchandise in the display and make it untidy.

Miscellaneous Windows and Fronts

While the aforementioned models serve the needs of most retailers, design uniqueness can give a retailer an edge in the pursuit of success. In today's retailing arena merchants are often opting for unusual, eye-catching windows and fronts that sometimes act as "**silent sellers**" and motivate the passersby to enter the premises. In every part of the country, fashion retailers in particular are putting their best feet forward to capture the market in what has become an extremely competitive industry. Figure 8.2 features a unique rounded corner window.

Designing the Interior Space

Once the decision has been made for a particular storefront and window structure, the remaining space must be apportioned for the store's operation. The largest and most important areas are those that sell the store's merchandise. Although as much as 90 percent of the space is allocated for customers to make their selections, there must be some set aside for nonselling functions such as receiving, storage, merchandise alterations, **visual merchandising**, promotion, buying, merchandising, and store management.

The way space is apportioned depends upon the status of the store. If it is a company flagship, more space is needed to perform the nonselling tasks. If the stores are units of a chain or branches of a department store, the space is apportioned primarily to sell merchandise because most of the nonselling operations are based in the flagships or central headquarters.

The following sections address the types of selling and **nonselling departments**.

Locating the Selling Departments

There are many factors to consider in where to locate the selling departments. Among them are the size of the store, the number of levels it occupies, the merchandise assortment, entrances, and the means for moving the shoppers from floor to floor.

figure 8.2
This giant photo in a rounded window on Regent Street in London enables shoppers to view from converging streets.

SINGLE-LEVEL STORES

Most fashion-oriented stores that occupy one level are usually specialty stores or boutiques. Since the merchandise assortment and selling space are limited, the choice of how to arrange the departments is simpler than in the multilevel type. In fact, the merchandising classification is often so narrow that merchandise is freely placed throughout the selling floor with little attention as to its type. Stores such as Gap, for example, which restrict their assortment to casualwear such as jeans, shirts, sweaters, and other sportswear and are generally one-floor operations, do not separate their merchandise into departments. The newest items are usually placed near the store's entrance until the supply dwindles and they are replaced by the next new items. This alerts passersby and those who enter the store of the latest merchandise.

Stores such as Talbots, Ann Taylor, and The Limited, which stock more diverse assortments, have a greater task in merchandise location. These stores generally separate goods into distinct departments. They often place a few pieces from each department at the store's entrance to show prospective customers the breadth of the store's offerings. These spaces are regularly updated to allow the most recent merchandise to hold center stage for a period of time. The remainder of the goods are arranged in such departments as casual dresses, eveningwear, accessories, and shoes. The departments closest to the store's entrance are usually those that the store is expecting to generate the greatest sales volume.

The lower-volume departments are near the back of the store, and the selling locations farthest from the entrance are often reserved for the most expensive items.

There are no hard and fast rules in the location game; the company's management team decides what works best for each site.

MULTILEVEL STORES

Some specialty chains such as Banana Republic and Ann Taylor have expanded their inventories and have opened larger units that occupy two or more levels. Banana Republic now features shoes and some home furnishings in these larger stores. Stores expand into **multilevel stores** because they have more extensive inventory, but they also do so because in many locations, obtaining a large selling space on one floor has become too expensive to lease. Such is the case of Banana Republic on Chicago's North Michigan Avenue, where it has three floors to house its collection. In other North Michigan Avenue venues such as the vertical malls, specialty stores frequently occupy several levels. On Madison Avenue in New York City, where fashion retailers vie for space, The Limited occupies four floors.

Although the multilevel arrangement might be new to specialty store retailing, it is typical of department store flagships and branches. Not only do these stores have to grapple with as many as ten floors but they also have to deal with selling space allocation for a vast number of departments.

There are several "rules" that the retailers of multilevel operations tend to follow. The rules include the following:

1. The main, or first floor, is usually reserved for merchandise that is either bought on impulse, is at the store's lower price points, is high margin, or would sell less than expected if it were placed anywhere else in the store. Cosmetics, a money-making fashion enhancement, occupy a wide area on most main floors. Many women purchase their cosmetics and fragrances without planning to buy them. When they

pass through the main floor, women are often motivated by an attractive display, an exciting demonstration, or being sprayed with a fragrance by a company representative. Figure 8.3 features a large fragrance department on a main floor.

Since the main floor is the most heavily traveled, it is the only place where cosmetics and fragrance sales are sure to be profitable. Similarly, fashion accessories are located on the main level because they too are often bought by customers attracted as they pass by. A traditional mainstay for the first floor has been menswear. While women usually spend more time looking for clothes, men often demand that they find what they need with a minimum amount of effort in the least amount of time. When the men's department is on the main floor, men do not get caught up in crowds and do not have to wander through the store; they are more likely to patronize stores with this layout. This is starting to change, however. In today's retail environments, first floor space is sought by many of the fashion department's buyers and merchandisers, so the men's offerings are being placed on more than one floor. The main floor might feature only shirts, ties, shoes, and other haberdashery items, with suits, sports jackets, dress trousers and the like relegated to another location usually one flight up. Of course, some department stores opt for other menswear placement. Macy's, for example, in its Chicago Loop store, locates its men's collection on one of the top floors in the stores. Some multilevel operations feature **satellite departments** on the first floor, with the remainder of the items elsewhere in the store. In this way, more departments can get a share of the high-traffic space on the main floor. Bloomingdale's flagship in New York City uses the satellite configuration for menswear.

2. The store's most profitable departments should be given location priority. They should be within the customers' view when they enter the selling floor and should be close to the store's elevators and escalators.

3. Higher-priced fashion merchandise such as designer collections are considered to be specialty goods, so shoppers are willing to seek them out in less traveled parts of the store. This is often the store's costliest merchandise too and is best kept away from the heavy traffic areas and out of the reach of would-be shoplifters.

figure 8.3
This perfume department is located on the main floor of Galeries Lafayette in Paris. The sales potentials are significant due to the heavy flow of foot traffic.

4. Compatible departments should be next to each other. Fine shoe departments are often next to the store's better apparel department so that shoppers buying a dress or business suit can find a pair of coordinated shoes. Not only does this make the task of shopping easier for the customer but the store makes a larger sale when selling multiple items.

5. Since most department stores generate more business from fashion merchandise than hard goods, the former should always take preference over the latter.

Some less traditional retailers break these rules. Saks Fifth Avenue in its New York City flagship locate the men's clothing department on their top floor because they think that such a location, with easy access to elevators, makes shopping a quieter experience, away from the throngs that move through the main and lower selling floors.

Locating the Nonselling Departments

Administrative and sales-support departments should be located in places that are least desirable for selling. As a general rule, single-level stores place their nonselling departments in the rear of the store, and multilevel units utilize the upper floors or rear portions of a few floors for these departments.

In present-day retailing many fashion merchants are reducing the size of their inventories and are eliminating extra inventory and stockrooms. Many merchants are avoiding the deep "**reserves of merchandise**" and are replacing the sold goods with new styles. This allows a steady flow of fresh merchandise to make its way to the selling floor. Departments that sell shoes, however, still utilize stockrooms for their goods, and such space must be provided for in the store's layout. Stockrooms are usually located within the selling departments to make the goods readily available to the sales staff.

Receiving and marking departments also tend to be smaller than those found in yesterday's operations. By having the merchandise pretagged by the vendors according to the retailer's instructions, or shipped to centralized warehouses where it can be checked and ticketed and then sent to the stores, a great deal of in-store space once used for such practices may be used as selling space. The receiving departments are usually confined to out-of-the-way areas that are less conducive to selling. Many major retailers once used significant portions of their basements for storage and receiving, but the practice has generally been eliminated since basement floors have become primary selling environments. Stores such as Macy's, with its famous "Cellar," have led the way for other merchants to move the receiving area elsewhere.

Many stores are locating their administrative offices on the highest floors or in buildings that are adjacent to the store. Others use a separate floor to house their administrative staff. The Macy's New York City flagship, for example, uses several floors high above the selling spaces for the offices of buyers, merchandisers, advertising and promotion executives, publicity personnel, human resource managers, computer experts, and other management people.

FASHION DEPARTMENT CLASSIFICATIONS AND DESIGNS

Once the general space allocations have been addressed and department sizes and places have been delineated, it is time to design the environment for each. In the case of the smaller fashion-oriented chain units, there is usually one design theme that follows throughout the store. The same holds true for individual specialty stores and boutiques. Only where specific areas need further definition do selling areas have distinctive decors. In department stores, with their host of merchandise departments and different market segments, interior design distinction is a must. The department that caters to juniors will certainly be better served if it is different from the one that specializes in large-size apparel. Different price points, consumer markets, fashion directions, and so forth warrant individualized environments.

Traditionally, fashion retailers have segmented and classified their departments according to standard designations such as juniors, budget dresses, fashion accessories, and evening wear. While some merchants still departmentalize according to these conventional rules, today's major fashion operations use different approaches, creating exciting and distinctive names to describe their fashion departments and their more diverse merchandise mix. Some fashion merchants are offering the highest-priced designer fashion collections and are featuring separate areas for each of them. Still other fashion merchants are erecting **in-house separate shops** for specific marquee label offerings. Whatever the approach, it is imperative that the design team understands the merchandising concept for each department and creates an environment that makes each one unique and conducive to shopping.

Traditional Fashion Departments

Within most stores, the traditional fashion departments generate a great percentage of the volume. Whether they are named "Moderate Sportswear," "Lingerie," "Hosiery," "Coats and Suits," or classified with more updated nomenclature such as the "Action Shop," "Junior Innovations," "After Five," and "The Contemporary Woman," they must be designed to reflect the image for which they were conceived. Merchandise in these departments is usually plentiful, racks and counters are often close to each other, and the environment generally follows the basic design concepts of the store. Fixturing is generally functional.

Designer Salons

Most fashion-oriented department stores such as Saks Fifth Avenue, Bloomingdale's, Nordstrom, and Neiman Marcus differentiate their fashion couture and prêt-à-porter (ready-to-wear) collections from the standard fashion fare by installing separate departments for these offerings. Since the fashions comprise the store's highest price points, their merchandising requires a different approach than anything else the store has to offer.

Individual **designer salons** are generally the choice so that each collection can receive the shopper's individual attention. Internationally renowned names grace these small salons, or boutiques, as they are often called, with each featuring the most elegant décor and appointments.

Designers such as Donna Karan, Gianni Versace, Christian Lacroix, Chanel, and Yves Saint Laurent are marketed in this manner.

In-House Separate Shops

A trend has developed that separates specific collections of merchandise from everything else in the store by installing individual "stores" within it premises. In the designer salons, which are small and are not often totally separate from each other, the same sales associate may service customers in more than one salon. These in-house separate shops, however, often are enclosed environments where individual staff, sometimes provided by the vendors, only service these areas. One of the reasons for this approach is the insistence of the manufacturer or designer. Ralph Lauren, for example, was an innovator in this area. He made it a rule for stores that carry his menswear collection to build a separate facility specifically for the Lauren line. In Bloomingdale's New York City flagship, the Ralph Lauren men's collection is housed in such a setting. To make the shop different from the others in the store, the merchandise fixtures are often antiques or antique-inspired pieces that have become the hallmark for displaying Lauren merchandise.

DECORATIVE AND FUNCTIONAL SURFACE MATERIALS

Having determined the location of the various departments and the different arrangements that the store will feature, the retailer must select the materials used in the design. Floors and walls must be decorative as well as functional. An attractive floor tile might have considerable floor appeal but might not be sufficiently durable to meet the challenges of heavy traffic. Similarly, an industrial carpet may be durable but its drab colors do not complement the merchandise. The perfect marriage of the two must be assured to derive the maximum benefits.

When professional interior designers are contracted for this task, they already have the expertise to select the best materials for the installation. When inexperienced merchants are planning their first retail ventures and are working with a limited budget, they rarely have the background to make the best design decisions on their own. In these situations, merchants must educate themselves regarding the availability of decorative and functional materials to avoid making poor choices. By carefully examining *VMSD* magazine's annual buying guide, professionals and novices alike can explore the various offerings from manufacturers and distributors.

Flooring

There are many types of flooring materials used in retail environments. While big box retailers and supermarkets usually choose cost-effective products that can handle the crowds, fashion retailers have different needs. Appearance and comfort and ease of care are among the considerations they need to address.

Little else provides the feeling of luxury like carpet. Today's fashion merchants often opt for commercial grade carpeting that easily withstands a lot of traffic while at the same time provides the aesthetic appeal they are seeking to enhance their interior designs. In the past, the commercial varieties were often nondescript, leaving many merchants to take the chance with more attractive but less functional designs and replace them when they showed wear. Now, however, the choice of commercial carpet has significantly grown. A wealth of attractive patterns and fibers are now available that will fit any retailer's need for attractiveness and functionality. Coupled with the fact that it is comparatively simple and inexpensive to install, carpet is often the choice for any fashion salon.

The opposite end of the flooring spectrum includes hardwood. In addition to being attractive it is especially functional. Figure 8.4 features a wooden floor in a store.

Covered with laminates such as polyurethane, wood flooring can last for a long time. When it does begin to show signs of wear, it can be refinished and brought back to its original appearance. The artistry of competent installers guarantees a vast array of interesting patterns that range from the standard diagonal designs to herringbone and parquet motifs. Used either alone or in combination with rugs, wood has become the choice of many merchants. The variety of rugs available includes patterns in kilos, dhurries, Persians and contemporaries that enhance any underflooring and retail setting. Each has a personality of its own and immediately transforms a mundane floor into one that adds to the image and style of the retail environment. Like their wall-to-wall counterparts, rugs can be cleaned and refurbished to making them practical choices for fashion retailers.

When a retailer wants an impressive and elegant environment, designers often select marble. It comes in a variety of patterns and colorations. Aside from the sometime prohibitive costs of the product, it is also very expensive to install. However, many upscale environments use marble for their floors, often in conjunction with other materials such as wall-to-wall carpet and wood, and it is often covered in areas by rugs. Marble is easy to clean, but when it is used without any rugs, it can be extremely hard on the feet of the sales associates who spend full days on the selling floor.

Ceramic tile is an excellent choice for a permanent floor installation and is extensively used in fashion environments. Ranging from traditional to contemporary patterns, it can serve any retailer's needs. In addition to those standard offerings, a new breed of tile is available on which designers can digitally master any pattern. In this way, a designer can perfectly augment the store's fixturing and come up with a unique exclusive pattern not seen in any other venue.

While the word "concrete" immediately signals a rather mundane, lackluster flooring, it has become the choice of many retailers. Once poured, it can be painted in a variety of patterns and finished to protect it from foot traffic. While it is a hard surface that will sometimes cause discomfort to the feet, it is relatively inexpensive to install and can serve the purpose of the retailer who wishes to minimize flooring expense.

Poured aggregate or terrazzo emulates marble and provides a lasting floor for retail environments. It is less costly than marble but provides a look that many merchants opt for. Just like any other hard surface, rugs can cover some of its areas and provide a softness to the setting.

Rounding out the flooring choices are vinyl tiles in a variety of patterns, real brick or brick veneers, cork, rubber, laminates, and bamboo, a wood that will be discussed later in the chapter as a "sustainable" product, so important to the protection of the environment.

Walls

Among the wall coverings are paint, wallpaper, fabric, wood, mirror, bamboo, foils, marble, plastic panels, leather, and metallics. Each offers the designer an opportunity to enhance other fixtures in the store, and provides uniqueness to the fashion environment. The most commonly used is paint. Available in an almost unlimited array of colors and textures, it can provide almost instantaneous results at minimal expense. For those fashion settings that require more than just basic painted walls, experienced painters specializing in **"faux finishes"** can accomplish a wealth of different patterns and

figure 8.4
This store in Beijing has a wooden floor with a parquet insert in it to give it a more dramatic look. Such small things can often appeal to the discriminating shopper who sometimes judges any environmental enhancement as a shopping plus.

dimensional surfaces. They can create motifs that rival real marble, for example. Of course this is considerably more costly than the typical paint job. The major advantage to painting walls and the reason why so many fashion retailers do so is that it is easy to quickly apply different paint to enhance a particular merchandise season or collection.

It should be noted that today paints are more environmentally friendly and will be discussed later as a "sustainable" and "eco-friendly" product.

A look at the wallpaper from companies such as Schumacher and Waverly immediately reveals a wealth of different patterns that could provide the exact feeling needed for a particular fashion environment. They can create motifs that rival real stone, for example. Available in traditional to contemporary designs in a host of textures, it is possible to install almost any environmental concept. In addition to the typical rolls of wallpaper there are numerous wallpaper murals than can quickly produce eye-appealing scenery that rivals hand-painted installations at comparatively low cost.

Foil is yet another choice for the designer. It is a paper-backed product that comes in a roll and is installed in the same manner as wallpaper. While more costly than most wallpapers, it provides a long-lasting metallic surface.

For the feeling of warmth and luxury, many designers opt for fabrics. An enormous variety of patterns and textures in moirés, brocades, velvets, velveteen, satins, denim, felt, damask and shantung can enhance any fashion environment. Each provides a distinct look that immediately transforms the bare walls into arenas of excitement.

Designers creating more permanent space can use different types of wood planks and panels that range in style from the highly finished variety to the more rustic types that can be stained. Wood requires little maintenance and damaged walls can be covered to hide the blemishes. Even curved walls can be covered, with flexibly crafted varieties of wood.

Mirrors, both clear and veined, are used in more upscale fashion boutiques and specialty stores. Not only does this look elegant but mirrors help to create the illusion of greater space.

Glass covered with acrylic film is an exciting wall covering making its way into upscale fashion emporiums. Tag Heuer's SoHo flagship features such walls in a vivid turquoise color that immediately draws attention. Glass panels with intricate detailing are being used to convey the feeling of opulence. C.D. Peacock features two 7-foot × 3-foot glass panels etched with images of facing peacocks, artistically personalizing the company while giving the impression of old-world elegance.

The same marble and ceramic tile used as flooring may also be used on the walls. They lend an immediate aesthetic quality to the environment. Although the product costs and installations are comparatively expensive, they serve as excellent, long-lasting alternatives to the other available wall coverings.

Other wall coverings seen in fashion boutiques or departments of major retail emporiums are leather, bamboo, and other exotic materials, which can create a unique atmosphere when coupled with an exciting overall design.

FIXTURING

The image of the fashion environment is further enhanced by the choice of fixtures. There are three fixture categories: the first holds the merchandise, the second illuminates it, and the third displays the items used in visual presentations. The variety within each group is enormous, and fixtures must be selected with appearance and function in mind. A beautiful counter that does not hold a sufficient amount of merchandise will be as poor a choice as a lackluster display rack that features designer gowns.

This section explores the first two types of fixtures. The display fixtures will be examined in Chapter 9, "The Importance of Visual Merchandising to Stores."

Merchandise Fixtures

The wealth of merchandise fixtures available today is quite a contrast to what was offered to fashion retailers in the past, when function was the main concern and style played a secondary role. Today designers may select from a variety of types that can help achieve a particular image without sacrificing function. First, though, it is important to consider the retailer's sales methods. Value merchants such as Target that sell a great deal of fashion merchandise emphasize self-selection, so open counters are a must. Fashion boutiques and salons show merchandise to customers, so they need closed counters to house the merchandise. This is extremely important when selling precious jewelry, where security is of paramount importance. Most fashion merchants use a combination of fixtures, since they often utilize both self-selection and personalized selling.

In addition to serving the retailer's selling techniques, merchandise fixtures play an important role in visually merchandising fashion collections. When shoppers enter a store or department within a store, their attention should be directed to the merchandise the retailer wants to feature. The appropriate counters, aisle tables, wall cases, and other fixtures help to show the merchandise to the best advantage. The Neiman Marcus store in Willow Bend, Texas, in addition to the conventional fixturing, uses a TV table that features a 4-foot × 4-foot glass tabletop embedded with 12 video screens as a setting for home décor items. It immediately attracts the shopper's attention. In the Tommy Bahama stores, the fixturing instantly gives the shopper the feeling of an island setting and perfectly accents the merchandise.

The Ralph Lauren flagship on New York City's Madison Avenue uses the epitome of unique fixturing. Instead of the mundane cabinetry that often holds merchandise, antique armoires, unusual period tables, iron-encased racks, and other special fixtures contain the Lauren signature merchandise. The shopper is treated to an environment that at once makes the offerings more special.

The fashion retailer should consider fixtures as carefully as the products placed in them. Whether they are the ready-made variety available at commercial vendors who specialize in store fixtures, or the more expensive customized cabinetry, there is a wealth of choices available to fit each store's needs.

There are many fixture suppliers that can meet the requirements of any retail environment. Fashion retailers should consult the pages of trade periodicals such as *VMSD* or check the Internet to learn about the vendors and their specialization.

Lighting Fixtures and Sources

One of the most exciting areas of store design is lighting. Once limited to the mundane choices of **fluorescent lighting** for overall illumination and **incandescent lighting** for emphasis, the lighting designer now has a host of different products from which to choose.

As in the case of other design decisions, lighting designers must consider store image, merchandise, and finances. While fluorescents are still the most economical light sources, they are not the appropriate choices for most fashion environments. Even the value retailers, such as Target, who deeply discount their fashion goods; the off-pricers such as Stein Mart and Marshalls; and the designer closeout shops such as those operated by Ralph Lauren, DKNY, Calvin Klein, and Gianni Versace find that fluorescent lighting leaves much to be desired when showing the merchandise at its best. Today's technology has made **energy-efficient lighting** available to even the most cost-conscious merchant. By choosing carefully, it is possible to create a more attractively lit environment at considerably lower costs than in the past.

The choice of the right lighting and design company is essential. There are numerous products and companies that can improve any type of fashion retailing environment. One exciting lighting example is the one in Jil Sander's London flagship. Working with the elements of the historic building housing it, and not using any lighting that would interfere with the architecture, lighting designer Ross Muir recessed a multitude of lights in the existing ceiling beams to give the appearance of the original design. The *VMSD* magazine's annual buyer's guide lists many lighting companies, and retailers can consult it for help in making their choices and can then visit them or check their websites. The incandescent bulb is becoming a thing of the past and is being replaced by varieties such as digital, light-emitting diode (LED), and compact fluorescent (CFL) lamps. The *Happening Now* feature centers on the incandescent's demise and those lamps that will replace them.

HAPPENING NOW

THE DEMISE OF INCANDESCENTS AND THE BULBS THAT REPLACED THEM

Starting January 1 of 2014, the federal government began enforcing restrictions on incandescent light bulbs, beginning with the restriction of the 75 and 100 watt variety, the country's most popular bulbs, and then followed by the ban of the 40 and 60 watt variety. What has been a mainstay for the illumination of retail interiors and windows will no longer be available and will be replaced by LED and CFL bulbs.

The advantages of the new bulbs include CFL's ability to use one-fifth to one-third of the electric power and last 8 to 15 times longer. Plagued with the comments regarding the color quality of the CFL, the use of LED bulbs offers more natural warm light and longer life spans than the incandescent variety. One of the disadvantages of the CFL bulb is the cold, blue light emitted from it. When a fashion retailer chooses lighting for the store's interior and

windows it is essential that the color emitted from it enhances the store's environment and the people's complexions who are trying on the merchandise.

The next generation of bulbs is still on the drawing board. The best hope for efficiency, lifespan and brightness is the digital bulb. They are still available, but at high costs. It is expected that the latest model will be cost-effective and answer the needs of the retailer's environment.

Creative designers sometimes use natural light to dramatically illuminate the retail setting. The use of natural light plays an important role in illuminating the retail premises. Today's retailers are more aware of the savings achieved from natural lighting and also the importance of energy savings.

SUSTAINABILITY: MATERIALS AND FIXTURES

As has been discussed in the "Decorative and Functional Surface Materials" section of this chapter, the key factors that comprise an interior designer's materials and fixture choices are decorativeness and functionality. While these still are the very determinants that play a significant role in designing the store's interior, today with the widespread attention being paid to such terms as "eco-friendliness," "environmentally correct," and "sustainability" in trade papers, magazines, the Internet, and so forth, more and more retailers are addressing these concerns in their store designs.

In Chapter 6 we learned that many merchants are very cautious about the materials they use in their merchandise mix to make certain of their sustainability. Early leaders such as Patagonia and REI have led the way, and today many retailing upstarts are featuring merchandise that is eco-friendly.

The concept has become an important factor in the design and fixturing of retail premises. Not only are interiors and storefronts becoming more environmentally correct, but so too are the choices for the entire building's façade and interior. Figure 8.5 features solar panels for retailers to reduce energy costs.

Sustainable Flooring

In the last few years, bamboo flooring has become a popular choice for commercial usage. It is stronger and denser than most traditional hardwoods, extremely resistant to moisture, and its installation is comparatively inexpensive and easy to maintain.

Bamboo is a common grass which quickly grows and can reach up to 100 feet! When they reach maturity, the stalks are split and flattened before being laminated together with glue under high pressure, resulting in planks. In addition to being durable, with long-lasting stability, it is also sustainable since it regenerates very quickly. This, coupled with its modest cost and aesthetic values, has made bamboo the choice material for interior designers who are interested in the protection of the environment.

Another product that has been around for many years with its primary use as wine bottle stoppers is cork. Today, however, it has taken on a new use as desirable flooring for commercial and home installation.

Cork is a product that is harvested from the *Quercus suber* tree that is generally referred to as a cork oak tree. It is grown in the Mediterranean region and has a potential life span of 250 years. Only the outer part of the tree is cut down making it a valuable renewable resource which re-grows in a very short time.

Some of cork's features are that it is a completely natural product, a comfortable cushioned surface that is naturally fire resistant, reduces noise, is durable, mold resistant, and easily repairable with excellent longevity. It is also completely recyclable making it a material with an unlimited lifespan.

figure 8.5
Workers in Shanghai producing solar panels that are eco-friendly components to reduce energy costs.

Chapter Highlights

1. Environment designs should not be set in stone but should be changed when they become shopworn, or when the company embarks upon a new merchandising philosophy that the old design wouldn't suit.

2. It is important to familiarize oneself with the latest trends when planning exterior and interior designs. Trade journals such as *VMSD* magazine, websites of design

firms, and the website of the Retail Design Institute, which offers a wealth of design consulting firms, are ways to gain information.

3. Exterior designs are important because they are the shopper's introduction to the store. Included in these designs are a number of storefronts and window structures.

4. More stores are leaving less of their overall footage space for windows and are using the windowless storefront concept instead of the more formal configurations.

5. In multilevel stores, the high-volume merchandise is placed on the main level, with impulse products such as cosmetics, shoes, jewelry, and accessories dominant.

6. Nonselling departments are located in out-of-the way places, leaving the prime locations for the selling departments.

7. Major fashion merchants are opting for designer salons and in-house separate shops for their marquee labels to give shoppers a sense of being in smaller, individual private boutiques.

8. The materials that are used on the store's walls and floors are functional as well as decorative. A rash of new types allow environments to take on a more individual appearance.

9. Preparing to purchase merchandise and lighting fixtures is best achieved by looking at designer websites or by examining the pages of such trade periodicals as *VMSD* magazine.

10. More traditional fashion retailers are in the makeover mode to bring them into the era of modern-day retailing.

11. Sustainable materials such as bamboo and cork are becoming more prevalent in store flooring and fixturing.

Terms of the Trade

arcade windows	nonselling departments
collection areas	open windows
designer salons	parallel-to-sidewalk windows
energy-efficient lighting	reserves of merchandise
faux finishes	satellite departments
fluorescent lighting	self-selection
incandescent lighting	silent sellers
in-house separate shops	visual merchandising
minimalist interior design	windowless storefronts
multilevel store	

For Discussion

1. What is the best approach for brick-and-mortar retailers to use in the initial planning of their environments?

2. In addition to using the trade's periodicals to learn about different design firms, what other resource can the merchant use to gain this knowledge?

3. Why is it important for the store's façade to be carefully designed?

4. Which type of window structure is most typical of department store flagships?

5. Why don't most retailers use the parallel-to-sidewalk windows for their brick-and-mortar operations?

6. What is a windowless storefront, and how does it help to attract the attention of the passersby?

7. In retail locations with little width, what type of window structure may the merchant employ that provides ample space to formally display merchandise?

8. In single-level stores, which merchandise is generally located at the rear?

9. Why do most major department stores locate their cosmetics, shoe, and fashion accessories departments near their main entrances?

10. How can retailers assign space to more departments on the main floor without forfeiting the potential for greater sales for each of the departments?

11. Where are the nonselling departments usually located on single-level and multilevel stores?

12. Instead of using only the traditional department approach, how are most major fashion operations defining their designer and couture departments?

13. In addition to providing an attractive impression of the store, what other consideration must the retailer address in the selection of wall and floor surfaces?

14. In what way is concrete being used as an attractive floor surface in brick-and-mortar operations?

15. Why is paint generally the choice for wall coverings?

16. How has Ralph Lauren's New York City flagship approached its choice of store fixtures to make it a unique environment?

17. What resources can merchants investigate before making any decisions regarding their lighting projects?

18. What is meant by the term brick-and-mortar "makeover"?

Case Problem

Collins and Sanders, a full-line department store with several branches, has decided to open another unit. Unlike the other branches, this one will confine its merchandise mix exclusively to fashion merchandise. The reason for the decision is that the company has realized a decrease in the store's hard goods sales. The new store will serve as a prototype for the company and will hopefully be the first of many fashion units to be developed.

As successful merchants for more than 45 years, Collins and Sanders has been through many expansion programs. It has always used the same architectural firm for its stores and has been satisfied with the results. The architects and designers meet with top management for guidance in terms of space requirements for merchandise and to learn about any design preferences. Throughout the years, the company always subscribed to the traditional approaches for its fashion department layouts as well as for the rest of the store, and business generally flourished.

Before approaching the architects, Collins and Sanders held a meeting of its top management team and those responsible for visual merchandising. The meeting resulted

Questions

1. With which group do you agree? Defend your answer with logical reasoning.

2. Discuss the concepts of traditional fashion departments and the newer approaches to fashion department classifications and layouts.

in two different schools of thought for the new store's department designs. Top management believes that the traditional approach always worked for the company and the same approach should be taken.

The visual merchandisers feel that the new store should utilize a more contemporary approach to interior design. They believe that with the new store's emphasis totally on fashion, the company would be better served with the establishment of several different department classifications and layouts.

Exercises and Projects

1. Photograph the windows of a downtown department store or specialty store and those stores in a regional mall or neighborhood cluster. Mount the ten best on a foam board and describe the categories of window structures in which they fall to the class, or prepare a PowerPoint presentation to show each of them.

2. Visit a major fashion-oriented department store to learn about the names of ten of its departments and the merchandise offerings within each of them. Use a chart to record your observations.

3. Using any of the lighting design company websites featured in the chapter or any other that you select from the Internet, prepare a report on why you consider this one to be perfect for designing the lighting of a fashion retailer's premises. Include in your assessment the following:

   - History of the company.
   - Approaches to making the lighting decisions.

chapter nine

THE IMPORTANCE OF VISUAL MERCHANDISING TO STORES

After reading this chapter, you should be able to:

- Define the term "visual merchandising" and explain how it differs from the term "display."

- Identify the three major means by which fashion retailers carry out their visual merchandising plans.

- Compare the approaches used to display merchandise in windows and on the selling floor.

- List and describe the importance of the different elements that make up a retailer's visual presentations.

- Identify the different principles of design that go into the creation of visual presentations.

- Summarize the ways in which the retailer's "trimmers" help to maximize the visual program's success.

When passersby stop and look into the flagship windows of such fashion retail giants as Lord & Taylor, Macy's, Nordstrom, Saks Fifth Avenue, and Neiman Marcus, they are immediately treated to visual presentations that often motivate them to come into the store. So visually attractive are these window displays that even those with limited time stop to admire the offerings. These are often referred to as silent sellers.

Of course, visual merchandising is not limited to the major fashion retailers and their windows but it is used by every type of retail entry that offers apparel, accessories, or home fashions inside and outside their retail environments.

With a significant global presence, major worldwide companies like Zara and Massimo Dutti show their artistic talents as architects of visual presentation. Zara's importance as a fashion merchant with stores all over the globe, and Massimo Dutti's quick expansion to most of the world's fashion centers are making these Intidex companies household names. And contributing to their unusual success is the visual presentation of the brick-and-mortar windows. As one peruses these storefronts most people have a positive reaction and enter the store even though that was not their intention.

Home product stores like Crate & Barrel and Williams-Sonoma are excellent examples of what creative display can do to transform somewhat ordinary products into exciting presentations. These superb visual offerings often stimulate shoppers to make unplanned purchases.

With the highly competitive climate that every retail operation faces today and the "me-too" aspect of the fashion industry, it is sometimes the creative hands of the company's visual team that sets its environment and merchandise presentations apart from the rest with creative displays that will help the store sell its merchandise. In the past, the term "display department" generally described the company's division responsible for installing windows and formal interior "showcases." Today, this nomenclature is all but gone, replaced by "visual merchandising department" since visual presentation tasks have been expanded to include the placement of merchandise on the selling floors, the development of **signage**, and assistance with the design of environments. Those who head these divisions often carry the title of vice president, showing that they have the same importance as other members of the upper management team.

A store's visual presentations are not always developed and installed by in-house teams but can be done by others who either work as **freelancers** (if the store is part of a chain) or are in the chain's central headquarters. Regardless of the arrangement, the visual elements that the visual merchandisers deal with and the design principles they follow are the same.

RESPONSIBILITY FOR THE VISUAL MERCHANDISING FUNCTION

Ideally it is best to have **in-house staff** to provide the creative and developmental concepts of visual merchandising and to carry them out at a moment's notice, if necessary. In reality, however, this luxury is limited to those giant fashion merchants with department stores encompassing enormous square footage in their flagships—and some branches—and the budgets necessary to make them visually appealing.

Other companies, such as chains that have as many as 2,000 individual selling units, generally have little need for in-house visual specialists since the space of the vast majority of the units doesn't warrant such hands-on attention. These organizations often subscribe to a centralized management approach to the visual function, where the actual installments are left to each unit's manager or assistant, who is guided by the directions of the company's central visual team. Small, independent retailers generally opt to use freelancers to install their window displays and offer assistance regarding the proper positioning of merchandise on the selling floor. Figure 9.1 shows a trimmer dressing a mannequin.

The following sections describe these three approaches.

figure 9.1
This is a "trimmer" changing a mannequin. Mannequins are one of the more effective "silent sellers" and should be changed regularly to show the passersby what's new in the store.

In-House Staffing: The Department Store Approach

The major department stores have full-time staffs that develop and execute their visual programs. A visit to any of these stores, especially the flagships, immediately reveals the scope of their involvement. With the advent of a new season or the beginning of a special holiday selling period, these visual teams transform their environments almost overnight from one theme to another.

As sales usually wane soon after the introduction of fall fashions, retailers are ready to get their premises revitalized for their biggest selling season of the year, Christmas. Each year, with as much as six months' lead time, the major merchants across the country go all out, in terms of money and planning, to provide the most unique visual presentations that their staffs can design. The Christmas period traditionally begins with "Black Friday," the day after Thanksgiving and concludes with the day after Christmas.

Headed by a visual merchandising director or vice president, in-house staffs prepare for their assignments with the same vigor and dedication as fashion apparel designers who are preparing for the latest collections. Teams of prop builders, sign makers, painters, carpenters, photographers, and **trimmers** work diligently to make each year's presentation equal to or better than the one that preceded it.

Many of the retail fashion giants use their own teams to present their themes but also contract with outside display designers to construct the props that best enhance the themes. The dominant outside group is Spaeth Design in New York City which year after year has created the designs for Christmas windows at Lord & Taylor, Macy's, and other retail giants.

Centralized Visual Merchandising: The Chain Store Organization Approach

The size of a chain store organization, by definition, ranges from a company with as few as two units to the giants of the industry, with as many as 2,000 or more. While those with fewer stores do not generally utilize a centralized approach to visual merchandising, those with numerous units are generally proponents of this concept.

The smaller chain operations often utilize one or two who go from store to store installing window displays and making interior merchandise changes in counters, showcases, vitrines (glass display pedestals used for small, formal presentations), and other fixtures. Their efforts generally center upon changing the merchandise displays rather than drastically transforming the store to depict different seasons.

Larger chains often subscribe to the practice of **centralized visual merchandising**, which involves a small professional visual team that operates from a company's central headquarters or home office. A staff headed by a visual merchandising director plans each window and interior presentation. After the designs have been executed in "sample" windows and typical interior spaces, they are photographed. The photos are then emailed to the individual units. Some props, signage, materials, and instructions are then forwarded to the stores. So carefully executed are these visual merchandising plans that the store manager or assistant can easily install them.

This route is utilized for a number of reasons. First, it saves the company considerable expense by eliminating the necessity for professional trimmers. Second, the practice guarantees the uniformity of visual presentation throughout the organization. Third, it allows the central office to quickly make changes throughout the company without sending trained professionals to each store. Organizations such as

The Gap Stores, Inc. and Williams-Sonoma rely upon central visual merchandising for their stores.

Freelancing: The Small Store Approach

Small fashion merchants, such as those who operate upscale boutiques or specialty stores, neither have the need for in-store trimmers nor the budgets to afford the expense associated with such practices. They do, however, understand the need for creative, timely visual presentations in their windows and interiors, and many choose freelancers to carry out these responsibilities.

These professional trimmers provide all of the elements necessary to create interesting displays. They either sell the necessary seasonal props, background materials, individualized signage, and other elements to the stores to use at other times or to rent out these fixtures. Together with the merchant's own **mannequins** and merchandise, these design elements create visual presentations that will tempt shoppers to enter the store's premises. For their services, freelancers are paid on a fee basis and usually contract for a period of one year.

Between these professional periodic installations, many fashion entrepreneurs make their own merchandise changes in their display windows. Sometimes they do so because a customer wants a particular item in the window that is in short supply in the store, or because they want to show new items that weren't available at the time of the installation.

Many of these merchants are fashion savvy and hone their display skills through classroom instruction. They master such simple techniques as mannequin dressing or pinning and draping in these courses. By altering the original installations, they are able to make their own changes before the next professional display is installed.

Whatever approach retailers use to achieve visual displays, they need to understand that a window's timeliness and perfection often motivates shoppers to enter the store to take a closer look at what is offered.

THE ENVIRONMENTS OF VISUAL PRESENTATION

Visual merchandisers work on two separate store environments: the windows and the interiors. They design displays in each to capture the attention of shoppers and motivate them to purchase merchandise. The presentations in each area are changed regularly so that the retailer can display new fashion merchandise that corresponds to different seasons, holidays, or other selling events. The following sections describe how visual merchandisers work in these two store environments.

Windows

As was discussed in Chapter 8, "Designing and Fixturing Brick-and-Mortar Premises," retailers have a variety of window structures to display their merchandise. The function of each is the same: to tempt passersby to enter the store and purchase merchandise.

The smaller retail operations have one or two window spaces to display their featured merchandise; the larger fashion merchants, especially in their downtown flagships, have as many as 100, or even more. Regardless of the number of windows a store has, it is imperative that the retailer plan the use of the display space to have a successful visual program.

In the major retail operations, visual merchandisers work closely with the buyers to determine which fashions will be featured and how they can be best presented to the shoppers. Using this information, they then prepare window schedules for six-month periods that indicate the dates of each presentation, the merchandise classification or institutional theme to be featured, the nature of the background materials and props, the length of time each installation will remain, and the exact location of each window or display case. Fashion buyers then work with these schedules when they contract with the vendors to make sure that the merchandise that is to be featured in the displays arrives in time to coincide with its allocated window time. Institutional window presentations, such as those displayed from Thanksgiving to Christmas that do not feature merchandise, are planned by the visual merchandising director or vice president.

The most extravagant window displays are those that adorn the major fashion department store flagships in busy downtown areas where pedestrians continuously pass the windows. Most of the fashion giants such as Nordstrom, Lord & Taylor, Saks Fifth Avenue, and Neiman Marcus in America and Harrods in London spare little expense when they are designing their major window presentations. Usually changed weekly, these displays feature different merchandise classifications, specific designer collections, seasonal themes, or institutional endeavors that concentrate on the store's image, and the planning that goes into them is as painstaking as that of many theatrical productions. Figure 9.2 shows a Lord & Taylor window at Christmas.

Stores in malls usually have less formal window designs. The windows are smaller and sometimes are just enormous glass partitions that separate the people walking by from the store's interior. The square-footage cost of the selling space is often so costly that there is not much space left for the formal visual merchandising presentations. Therefore, retailers devote less expense and attention to this type of window display. They might just use a few mannequins at their entrances, and change the clothes on them, or incorporate some props that are indicative of a theme or season. Some merchants feature small glass-encased shadow boxes in addition to the mannequin presentations. In the *Happening Now* feature, some trends that are being followed by many retailers are explored.

figure 9.2
The greatest portion of the visual merchandising budget is at Christmas. The crowds looking into these windows at Lord & Taylor, an early entry into extravagance at Christmas, sometimes wait in line to view them.

TRENDS THAT SOME RETAILERS ARE USING IN VISUAL MERCHANDISING

At a time when expenses are often spiraling out of control, retailers of all sizes are concentrating on ways to reduce operating expenses while still keeping their images fresh and without sacrificing sales. One of the ways in which many merchants are cutting operating costs is by reducing the costs associated with window displays. If attacked carefully, sales will not be affected, and shoppers will still enter the store's portals to purchase.

The concept that is appealing to more and more visual merchandisers begins with the uncluttered look. Less is more when it comes to attracting the passersby. Too many items in a cluttered window detract from those that are expected to bring shoppers inside the store. It should never be forgotten that the star attraction of the display is the merchandise. The items should be carefully selected to draw the attention of the customers.

Instead of cramming the windows with an overabundance of display **props**, many visual merchandisers are limiting their use and minimizing the "factory-made" variety. Instead, they are turning to found objects such as old picture frames, abandoned tables, and other items that have been discarded and are refinishing them into interesting props. This is not only less expensive, but adds distinction to the window.

If the window displays are not appropriately illuminated, then the aforementioned efforts will be wasted. The trend is to use new generations of lighting that are sustainable.

Mannequins have long been the mainstay of fashion window presentations. Twenty years ago the realistic form was the choice of most retailers, with prices for them often escalating each year. Today mannequins come in a variety of types such as headless, stylized, stark white, futuristic, and so forth. Even the traditional variety is available in different poses and custom-made wigs that show an up-to-the-minute fashion-forward look to add excitement to the window. Some retailers are substituting in-house made mannequins that are inexpensive and unique. The more creative the visual merchandiser, the more effective is this type of mannequin.

Themes are becoming very important in window displays. Instead of haphazardly choosing unrelated items, the merchandise forms a cohesive installation.

These "rules" are gaining more attention from display people and are resulting in significant savings and maintained or improved sales.

Interiors

For many years, retailers allocated more funds for windows than for interior installations because they felt the windows had more drawing power as silent sellers. Today, however, few retailers other than the downtown flagships of major department stores allocate space for formal window structures. Retail space in malls is costly, and many shoppers come directly from the parking lots into stores that are devoid of showcase windows.

Interior visual merchandising is more than a few mannequins dressed in the store's clothes. A great deal of attention is focused on effectively presenting the merchandise so that it beckons the customer. Figure 9.3 features an interior store display.

Gap and Banana Republic have transformed themselves from moderately successful to significantly profitable operations, in part because of their visual merchandising approach. Abundant quantities of merchandise are carefully folded on self-selection counters in color-coordinated stacks. The offering is regularly rotated, with new styles replacing the older ones. Crate & Barrel employs the same philosophy to displaying its household fashions. Color-coordinated stacks of glassware, serving pieces, vases, and other items are featured at the front of the stores' entrances, enticing shoppers to closely inspect, handle, and often purchase the displayed items. The Crate & Barrel merchandisers concentrate on one or two color schemes that make even the most mundane items more appealing.

Another direction for interior visual merchandising is the **environmental visual concept**. Initially started by Banana Republic, which featured bamboo and rattan interior props and fixturing to enhance its then safari-like merchandise (this has now been changed to suit its newer contemporary clothing lines), others have followed suit. Tommy Bahama stores, for example, feature permanent reed and raffia Bahama-like fixturing to enhance its island-type merchandise. This eliminates the need to make seasonal or thematic changes throughout the year.

Most retailers, however, make seasonal interior changes. Each spring, summer, fall, and winter, the selling floors are transformed into new, exciting environments designed to notify shoppers that new merchandise has arrived and is available for sale. Similarly, holiday periods call for elaborate interior displays, and visual merchandisers trim the selling space accordingly to stimulate shopping during these times. Besides Christmas, when the bulk of retail sales are made, Valentine's Day and Mother's Day are periods when retailers highlight women's fashions; Easter is when retailers feature fashions for the entire family; Presidents' Week is the time when retailers have remarkable sales to dispose of the previous season's offerings.

No matter which approach to visual presentation the store features, the creativity of the visual team transforms bare environments into settings that will stimulate shopping. Without their expertise, retailers' sales arenas take on a mundane atmosphere and look like any other store. In these competitive times, retailers cannot afford to let this happen.

figure 9.3
This interior illuminated display attracts shopper attention.

ELEMENTS OF THE VISUAL PRESENTATION

Whether they are designing formal window displays, creating interior environments for a major fashion promotion, or featuring a specific style on a mannequin in a department, visual merchandisers have to properly coordinate many elements, such as merchandise, materials and props, lighting, color, signage, and **graphics** to maximize the visual effects. These elements are discussed in the following sections. Unless otherwise stated, the visual presentations described are not institutional installations, which have different goals that their displays are designed to meet.

The Merchandise

First and foremost in any visual presentation is the merchandise the retailer wants to sell. Too often those responsible for display forget that their goal is to present the merchandise in the best possible way, and they proceed to develop concepts and themes that overpower the fashions. The retailer is trying to sell merchandise, not props and background materials.

The visual planner should first meet with the buyer, or in the case of the small operation, the freelancer should visit the store and speak to the owner, to examine the specific items that are to be included in the display and decide on the proper vehicle for their promotion. If the shopper cannot immediately determine what merchandise the display is selling, the display is ineffective.

Most of the major fashion retailers have forms that the buyers complete when they send merchandise to the visual merchandising department. These forms include such information about the items as material, construction, price, or other details that might play a part in the window or interior presentation. If the actual merchandise isn't available, as is often the case when preseason planning is essential, the buyers can send photographs, drawings, and descriptions as substitutes.

Materials and Props

Once the particular items have been selected and examined, it is time for the visual team to determine how best to show them to shoppers. Some teams have large budgets that allow them to purchase sophisticated and costly props. While these display pieces are often elaborate and functional, they are not always the ones that generate the most excitement. Household objects such as ladders and tables, antiques, and even items pulled from the junk pile can effectively enhance the merchandise. Knowledgeable and creative visual merchandisers know what is best suited for a particular display.

The trade periodical *VMSD* (Visual Merchandising and Store Design) is an excellent up-to-the-minute reference guide for materials and props.

Mannequins

One need only look into the windows of the world's fashion emporiums to see the diversity of mannequins that wear their clothing. Just as apparel designers and merchants take different fashion directions, so do mannequin designers. Figures that feature men's, women's and children's fashions run the gamut from the highly sophisticated models that cost as much as $2,000, to those that are created by the store's visual team. Figure 9.4 features upscale mannequins.

The traditional models are still popular, but stylized versions are readily available to fit the most unique requirement. Table 9.1 features selected mannequin resources.

Those responsible for purchasing mannequins often approach their task with the same enthusiasm and care exercised by the merchandise buyers. They must work within the framework of a budget; consider the image of the company they represent; examine the offerings of the marketplace; evaluate what is available in terms of quality, durability,

figure 9.4
Sophisticated mannequins in a display. These mannequins are primarily used by high-fashion merchants such as Saks Fifth Avenue, as seen here, to display their upscale merchandise.

and flexibility; and make certain that final choices meet the merchant's needs. For example, while athletically built male models might be quite fashionable, putting them in the window or on the selling floor of a conservative men's store would not foster the store's image or properly feature its merchandise.

The best way to purchase mannequins is by making market visits; perusing the pages of such publications as *VMSD*; logging onto such websites as www.vmsd.com and www.storesupply.com/c-609-mannequins.aspx; or attending trade shows such as GlobalShop. Although catalogs showing a manufacturer's offerings provide some indication of the mannequin's appearance, they do not provide enough to make meaningful selections. It is important to make a careful physical examination of a form to determine if it has the moveable parts that are necessary to facilitate merchandise changes, its weight, the quality of its cosmetic applications and wigs, and other details.

Table 9.1

RESOURCES FOR MANNEQUINS

Company	Specialty	Website
Patina-V (Norlaine, Inc.)	Abstract and realistic mannequins	www.patinav.com
Goldsmith, Inc.	Manufacturers of men's and women's mannequins of all types	www.goldsmith-inc.com
Adel Rootstein Ltd.	High-end mannequins	www.rootstein.com
Mannequin Service Co./Lania D'Agostino Studios	New and used antique mannequins	www.mannequinservice.com
Alternatives Plus Manufacturing, Ltd.	Manufacturer of mannequins in all materials including fiberglass, soft sculpture, cloth	www.altplusmfg.com
Almax S.p.A.	Stylized mannequins	www.almax-italy.com
New John Nissen Mannequins S.A.	Realistic mannequins	www.new-john-nissen.com
Silvestri California	Traditional and customized mannequins	www.silvestricalifornia.com
Frank Glover Productions, Ltd.	Reconditioned mannequins	www.frankgloverproductions.com

Source: Based on *VMSD* magazine, 2013.

Lighting

The narrow intensive beam of light that settles on a fashionably dressed mannequin accentuates and dramatizes it as nothing else can. The tiny, sparkling bulbs that grace the majestic Christmas trees at holiday time in store windows and interiors transform the most mundane displays into enchanting presentations. The exciting dimension attained with the use of artistically crafted **neon** designs turn interior spaces into lively sales arenas. With comparatively little expense, lighting has been successfully used by visual merchandisers to enhance otherwise unexciting displays.

Before fashion merchants select the lighting that will become part of their windows and interior environments, they must first assess what they want the lighting to do by focusing on the following goals:

- *Attract attention.* The merchandise featured in the windows and interiors must be sufficiently illuminated so that shoppers will notice it over the merchandise offered by the competition. Whether in downtown central districts, where the flagships reign; in the shopping malls; or on the fashion streets that dot the major cities, effective lighting can make the passersby stop and take notice of what the merchants are offering.

- *Create a mood.* Store windows or interior spaces that are properly illuminated create an ambience that provides a positive mood for shopping.
- *Enhance the store's image.* It is obvious that upscale, high-fashion brick-and-mortar units, and discount or off-price chains have different approaches to their visual merchandising. In terms of lighting, each must approach its goal differently. The former use subtle lighting with pinpoint spotlights to enhance their premises and create a low-key environment and the latter generally rely upon bright, overall illumination to light up the entire premises.
- *Provide flexibility.* Most of today's fashion retailing environments require different lighting for different purposes. Retailers need illumination systems that can adapt to these changes. For example, track lighting is flexible enough to enhance any type of display.

Once retailers have established their goals, the store designers, in consultation with the visual merchandising experts, choose from the many available lighting sources and systems to install the types that best suit their needs.

The plans should include general lighting designed for overall illumination and accent lighting that highlights specific targets, such as mannequins. Different light sources make the lighting both functional and mood setting. These include fluorescent lighting, the narrow cylindrical tubes that offer a great deal of light at little expense; incandescents, which are available as both spotlights that pinpoint specific targets and floodlights that provide general, overall illumination; **fiber optics**, which offer cool light such as those needed to show diamonds and other gems; energy savers such as **high-intensity discharge bulbs**, which produce more light per watt than any of the other forms of lighting; neon, a flexible offering that sculptors can use to create unusual designs; and **halogen lamps**, which are ideal for dramatic, intense lighting. It is imperative to choose lights that are low-wattage, "environmentally" safe, and are cost effective.

The systems that can deliver these light sources include track lighting, which offers a great deal of flexibility; recessed fixtures, which house both spotlights and floodlights; and many types of decorative fixtures, such as chandeliers, that help to set a mood or create an impression.

Color

Putting a single red dress in the midst of an all-white window will generate excitement and help focus the viewer's attention on the colored merchandise. The striking contrasts of reds and greens will intensify both colors in a manner that cannot easily be achieved by any other means. The feeling of warmth imparted by a color scheme that utilizes amber creates a comfortable mood for shoppers looking for swimsuits.

These are but a few examples of how visual merchandisers can properly use color to quickly and inexpensively create moods and capture shoppers' attention with windows and interiors that are attractive and distinguishable from the competition.

The visual merchandiser's cue for color selection must first come from the merchandise selected for the display. Clothing that features prints or patterns can inspire the trimmer to select a particular scheme as can seasonal colors, and the fashions worn during certain times of the year. An autumn display would naturally include the rusts, oranges, and yellows of the turning leaves, and many fall styles come in these colors. For a summer display, the colors of the American flag could inspire the display to use a nautical setting. Sometimes, proper color selection is not so obvious, and visual merchandisers need to refer to technical theories to help them choose attractive and correct schemes.

The theory of color and its appropriate selection is based upon a number of different methods. The most widely used involves the **color wheel**. When the wheel's three **primary colors**—yellow, red, and blue—and the **secondary colors**—orange, violet, and green—or variations of them are used in particular arrangements known as schemes, the results are pleasing to the eye. Most seasoned visual merchandisers are so familiar with the standard approaches the wheel has to offer that they automatically make their color selections without referring to it. The novice, however, can learn a lot about creating color harmonies of distinction by using the wheel and understanding the color guidelines. Experienced visual planners often break the rules, however, and create color schemes that are eye stoppers.

The "Rules" of Color

There are a host of color schemes or arrangements in the **rules of color** that are simple to extract from the color wheel. Each scheme is based upon a specific color or set of colors and their placement on the wheel. The simplest arrangement, which utilizes only one hue, or color, is a **monochromatic color scheme**. While at first this scheme doesn't seem very stimulating, when used properly, it has the potential for real visual elegance. By using variations of the single hue and accenting it with neutrals such as black and white, visual trimmers can produce a showstopper. They can provide extra interest in the monochromatic arrangement by using a variety of textures and patterns that stay within the single color range.

Analogous colors are those that are adjacent to each other on the wheel. Using this scheme enables the trimmer to develop a presentation that has more than one color. Because fashion designers often use analogous arrangements in their fabric designs, it is easy for the visual professional to pick it up from the featured merchandise and carry out the color story in an exciting setting. As with monochromatic harmonies or schemes, adding variations of the colors along with the neutrals can create interest.

The use of two colors that are directly opposite each other on the wheel results in a **complementary color scheme**. When reds and greens are placed next to each other in a setting, as is the case in many Christmas displays, the colors intensify. When trimmers want intensity, no other scheme can accomplish this.

Other color arrangements include **split complementaries**, which use one basic color with two other colors on either side of the color's complement; **double complementaries**, which use two sets of colors, or four basic colors, that are opposite each other on the wheel; and **triadic color schemes**, which use three colors on the wheel that are equidistant from each other.

Trimmers can use neutral ingredients such as black, white, gray, or tan to go with any color harmony and achieve more flexibility for their presentation.

The rule to follow when applying color to a window or interior presentation is that the merchandise is the most important element, and color should be used in background materials and props only as enhancements. Any other application could distract viewers from the merchandise.

Signage and Graphics

In the vast majority of brick-and-mortar establishments, signage and graphics are becoming increasingly important. Oversized graphics in particular are one of the most important tools that merchants can use to attract immediate attention. Chains such as Gap and Abercrombie & Fitch use graphics in both their windows and interiors. With a minimum of expense, they quickly get their fashion messages across to passersby and shoppers. Retailers that must restrict their visual budgets have found that graphics have made a big difference, and they are reporting that graphics are as effective as many of the traditional, more costly props.

Retailers can easily acquire both signs and graphics in a number of ways. Those that want to minimize their expenses and require immediate acquisition choose **stock houses**. These companies maintain thousands of images that cover every conceivable format. By going directly to the libraries that house the images or viewing them online, visual merchandisers can quickly select the one that is best suited for their operation. Just as advertising agencies assist retailers with their promotional needs, **stock agencies** offer sources from which the merchants can choose their images.

Retailers that want to avoid a "me-too" look choose original photography. Photographers that work for the fashion retail giants or freelancers that accommodate smaller businesses offer custom artwork on an exclusive basis.

There is a wealth of different types of signage and graphics available to the retail community. These include **backlit transparencies**, which use photographs in light boxes to provide exciting illumination; **digital images**, which offer enormous visuals that often measure 100 feet wide and 25 feet high and are used outdoors to announce the opening of a new retail outlet; **prismatic displays**, which simulate a venetian blind and automatically rotate the graphics to feature different messages; and **motion displays**, which are full-screen programmable visual offerings that can be easily changed to fit the user's needs.

Even the smallest retailers can use signage and graphics. Computerized offerings are available in every part of the country and can inexpensively be created to satisfy their needs.

By continually investigating the resources that provide the latest in materials and props, mannequins, lighting fixtures and formats, graphics, and other state-of-the art components, visual merchandisers can not only make their presentations fresh and exciting but can also create displays that will satisfactorily stand up to the competition. Table 9.1 features a sampling of the vendors that supply the visual merchandisers with their tools and includes their website addresses. Table 9.2 lists selected visual merchandising resources.

THE PRINCIPLES OF DESIGN

Once the visual team has selected the functional fixtures, mannequins, and other materials that will put the chosen merchandise in the best setting, or in the case of an institutional theme, will enhance the retailer's image, it is ready to install the presentation. To achieve the best effects, the trimmers must follow the principles of design and incorporate them in ways that will maximize the display's effectiveness.

The design principles that visual merchandisers adhere to are the same ones followed by interior and apparel designers: they strive to achieve **balance**, emphasis, **proportion**, **rhythm**, and **harmony**. When coupled with imagination and the creative use of props and merchandise, they result in presentations of distinction. The following sections discuss these design principles.

Table 9.2

VISUAL MERCHANDISING RESOURCES

Resource	Product Classification	Website
Abet Laminati	High-pressure laminates	www.abetlaminati.com
Banner Creations, Inc.	Full-service banner company that produces digital printing, dye sublimation, screenprinting, etc.	www.bannercreations.com
Bowman Displays Digital Imaging, Inc.	Modular lightboxes, vehicle graphics, photography	www.bowmandisplays.com
Coastal Woodworks & Display	Quality wood displays	www.coastalwoodworks.com
Consolidated Display Co., Inc.	Seasonal décor, Christmas displays, animations	www.letitsnow.com
Goldsmith, Inc.	Mannequins	www.goldsmith-inc.com
Gemini, Inc.	Dimensional sign letters	www.signletters.com
Hera Lighting L.P.	Stylish halogen and fluorescent lighting	www.heralighting.com
Illuma Display/Salon Sign	Curved and frameless backlit displays	www.illumadisplay.com
Laser Magic Productions	Holographic projection	www.laser-magic.com
Regal Display	P-O-P displays	www.regaldisplay.com

Balance

The concept of balance gives the impression of the equal distribution of weight. For example, a scale is balanced if both sides are at the same level and each is supporting a similar object.

Visual merchandisers are less concerned with absolute balance, which scientifically assigns exact weight to each side; they are more concerned with the impression of equal distribution on either side of a central imaginary line. Balance is accomplished either formally (symmetrically), or informally (asymmetrically).

Symmetrical Balance

Perfect, formal, or **symmetrical balance** involves the placement of identical items on both sides of a central, imaginary line. For example, placing a mannequin on one side of the window and another of the same dimensions on the other side provides symmetrical balance. While this is a safe approach to guaranteeing a balanced presentation, the results are usually monotonous. Beginner visual designers sometimes fall into this trap, because they want to make sure their display is balanced and they do not have the confidence to select less obvious symmetrical elements.

It's possible to achieve an interesting, symmetrically balanced display if the merchandise is unusually appealing, the colors are exciting, and the items on either side of the imaginary line are similar in weight but are not identical.

Asymmetrical Balance

Informal, or **asymmetrical balance** is more relaxed, and trimmers can use it to show off their design talents. While the imaginary center line still exists in this type of balance, and there is still a concentration on weight distribution, the objects on either side of it are different. Two small items on one side might be balanced with one large one on the other.

Emphasis

Every installation requires an area of interest that draws the shopper's eye. Keeping in mind that the fashion merchant is first and foremost in business to sell merchandise, the professional visual merchandiser must make certain that this area of emphasis, or the **focal point**, is the item for sale, or as in the case of institutional window displays, to motivate the shopper to enter the store. While some props are excellent attention getters, they should never steal the thunder of the products being promoted.

Emphasis can be achieved with a variety of techniques including the following:

- *Size.* Oversized graphics, which many retailers use, draw the eye immediately. When these larger-than-life images are contrasted with traditionally scaled merchandise, it achieves a positive effect.
- *Repetition.* Whether it is color, shape, pattern, or texture that is repeated, the eye quickly focuses on the repetitive aspect. This approach emphasizes the important element to the shopper. When a monochromatic color pattern is the repetitive element, the shopper quickly realizes that this is the dominant color of the season.
- *Contrast.* Using light and dark colors, or arranging certain shapes, such as cones, that contrast with the merchandise forms, accomplishes a visually pleasing effect.
- *Unique placement.* Placing an element in an unexpected position in a display can capture the shopper's attention. Suspending a mannequin from an overhead position immediately draws the eye to examine the clothing the mannequin is wearing.

Proportion

The principle of proportion involves the comparative relationship of the different design elements to each other. It is particularly important that these elements are properly scaled to their space. For example, an oversized mannequin in a low-ceiling window will make the presentation look awkward. Similarly, small jewelry pieces should never be placed in oversized spaces.

To assure appropriate proportionality, trimmers must consider the size of the window, showcase, floor case, counter, or vitrine before selecting the merchandise. Similarly, they must make certain that the proportions of the mannequins and other props enhance the merchandise featured on or near them.

Rhythm

To make the eye travel from one part of a display to another, trimmers try to achieve movement, or rhythm. This is an extremely important design principle since it guarantees that the shopper will look at the entire presentation. Trimmers can achieve it by using the same shapes in a row; using borders or moldings that will flow in a continuous line; using the gradation of line, shape, size, or color; radiating from a central point; or alternating patterns such as awning stripes.

Harmony

If the visual team executes all of the design principles, the visual offering will achieve harmony. The merchandise-oriented display that incorporates balance, emphasis, proportion, and rhythm and is augmented with appropriate lighting, fixturing, signage, and other visual elements presents a compelling whole that motivates the passersby to stop and take a closer look.

It is not difficult to master the design elements and employ them in visual settings, but the professional visual merchandisers can break the rules and achieve exciting and creative effects that will attract attention and shoppers into the store to buy the merchandise so imaginatively displayed.

MAXIMIZING THE VISUAL PROGRAM'S SUCCESS

It seems logical that when retailers budget large sums of money for visual merchandising, and significant planning has preceded the use of the funds, the end result would be distinctive installations. This is not always the case. If the visual merchandising vice president or director in the largest company, or the entrepreneur in the smallest boutique does not pay strict attention to details, the visual programs will not deliver what they are capable of doing.

For a program to achieve maximum success, the visual team needs to develop a checklist outlining basic visual rules and regulations and religiously adhere to it. The areas of concern in the following sections include some that are most often mishandled or ignored.

Maintenance of the Display's Component Parts

A chipped mannequin, burned-out spotlight, unkempt wig, or other unsightly display element can cause a distraction and minimize the effectiveness of the entire presentation. Before installing any display, trimmers need to repair and refresh the fixtures and props, check lighting to make certain that it is functioning properly, carefully press merchandise, and clean every part of the display. After installing the elements, it is necessary to have a final inspection to remove stray pins from the floor, to conceal those pins that have been used on mannequins to alter the apparel, and to carefully check if any loose threads have been left on the merchandise. These seemingly trivial details can diminish an installation. It is sinful and wasteful and bad business to present the latest fashions in settings that don't do them justice—and won't sell them.

Prompt Removal of Displays

Visual presentations must be timely to maximize the retailer's profits. Retailers that have a store window the day after Mother's Day that still features fashions for that event or interiors that still have the Christmas look long after the holiday has passed do a disservice to their visual program.

Fashion retailers are always moving from one season to the next and must use every day to alert their customers to new merchandise. While the days leading up to marquee events are big volume periods for retailers, once the events are over, displays featuring those items are not important and waste valuable promotional space.

Visual merchandisers should remove signage and graphics used for brief promotions once the event has passed. When a store offers a three-day sale and reduces prices 25 percent, it could cause problems to leave up signage that publicizes the promotion. Telling shoppers "the sale is over" if they ask for the discount is a poor way to cement customer relations and the retailer might have to sell the merchandise at the lower prices past the sale period. Figure 9.5 shows a sale sign.

figure 9.5
When a sale is over, the signage must be removed. If left in place after its usefulness, it takes up too much valuable space that could be used to display something new.

The Daily Walkthrough

With the increased concentration on in-store displays, more visual merchandisers are using mannequin groupings at selling department entrances, on free-standing islands, and on open counters. While these presentations invite shoppers to inspect them and often motivate shoppers to purchase the displayed items, passersby might also handle them.

To make sure these point-of-purchase displays appear as fresh as the day they were first installed, they must be regularly checked. Most major merchants develop **walkthrough** schedules during which trimmers refresh them and restore their original, attractive appearance if necessary. If no one does this every day, the featured merchandise will no longer be appealing, and the store will take on a poor visual image.

Maintenance of Self-Selection Merchandise

When shoppers enter fashion retailers such as Gap, Banana Republic, and Crate & Barrel, they immediately see merchandise offerings that invite handling. The self-selection method is very successful in these retail environments and not only tempts passersby to stop and touch, but also considerably reduces the expense attributed to personal sales assistance.

Store designers and planners are creating self-selection fixtures in more quantities and styles than ever before. Although this type of merchandising generates significant sales volume, it also gives the counters and other selling units a sloppy appearance. At Gap, for example, the tidiness of the stacks of color-coordinated sweaters that are merchandised in this fashion is imperative to attracting shopper attention. To keep the sweaters as appealing as when they were first placed on these risers, sales associates must constantly refold and realign them according to color.

If the self-selected merchandise is not strictly maintained, the stores will become a jumble of merchandise and the visual effect of the display will be lost.

Rotation of Merchandise

It is very important that every piece of merchandise is within reach and view of passing customers. Since some locations in the department are more accessible and visible than others, it is important to rotate the inventory so that each item can have a turn in the best location. For example, placing the new arrivals at the entrance to the department puts them within easy customer accessibility. Displaying a complete outfit, fully accessorized, at the head of the display rack might motivate shoppers to find their size in all the items and head for the try-on room.

TRENDS IN VISUAL MERCHANDISING

The concepts of visual merchandising have gone through considerable changes in the first few years of the 21st century, and continue to do so as described in the following bullet points:

- *Decrease in the use of formal window presentations.* Except for the downtown flagships, where the parallel-to-sidewalk window configurations still are prominent, the new retail structures leave much less formal window space. Except for perhaps a few exterior shadow boxes, the displays are found inside the store. The reason for this trend is the cost of retail space. Merchants lease total square footage and leave as much as possible for their selling departments.

- *Greater attention to interior visual merchandising.* Instead of just relying on formal interior displays to attract attention, more merchants are paying close attention to the way in which the merchandise is featured on racks and counters. At the end of the apparel racks, they are featuring the merchandise the rack holds and are fully accessorizing the clothing to give shoppers a better idea of how an outfit will look on them. Also, in and around store entrances, escalator landings, and elevator stops, displays are used to quickly show the shoppers what is awaiting them in the adjacent sales departments. These are changed regularly to feature the store's latest styles.

- *Increased use of low-voltage lighting.* Without having to sacrifice true colors, **low-voltage lighting** has become the ever-increasing choice of visual merchandisers because it gives off less heat and results in energy/maintenance savings. In particular, the heat produced by conventional lamps often fades the illuminated products so they cannot be sold or returned to the selling floor. With operating costs continually increasing, using low-voltage lighting is one way the retailer can minimize expenses without losing the benefits of traditional light sources. Also extremely important are the efforts to help the stores become energy-efficient and environmentally aware.

- *Significant use of graphics.* With their minimal costs and ease in production, retailers are turning to a variety of graphics for their visual programs. Available in most every size, including the larger-than-life types, companies such as Gap, Abercrombie & Fitch, and Eddie Bauer use them in place of the more costly props. Many major retail construction sites use these oversized graphics to announce an impending store opening since they are weatherproof, and can be seen from great distances. Retailers are also using more backlit transparencies to give the graphics the benefit of 24-hour lighting and to make them seem more lifelike.

- *Point-of-purchase fixturing.* The selling departments in most major fashion retail operations are becoming increasingly popular as venues for point-of-purchase displays. Replete with interactive video, gondolas, closed-circuit video, and countertop cases, these displays bring all types of fashion merchandise to the shopper's attention. Of particular importance are displays of small products such as cosmetics and hosiery that people buy impulsively or without preplanning.

- *Vendor participation in retail visual merchandising.* Many designers and manufacturers are giving retailers special fixtures and display materials to distinguish their collections from the others in the store. This way, they can control the visual merchandising of their own lines. Merchants are receptive to this arrangement since it reduces their own expenses.

Chapter Highlights

1. Department stores have their own in-house visual teams to create and install both window and interior displays. The principals in these departments are generally located in the company flagships, with a few people assigned to the branches to carry out the visual director's plans.

2. Major chain store organizations usually employ a visual program that involves developing concepts in their headquarters that are photographed and sent to the individual units to recreate.

3. Small fashion merchants either use freelancers to install their displays or create them themselves.

4. Windows are the main arenas for major visual presentations. To successfully carry out window installations, calendars are prepared six months in advance so that the visual team and the buyers responsible for ordering the merchandise can have sufficient time to plan for the presentations.

5. Interior display has become an important part of the retailer's visual environment because the traditional large-scale windows, except for those found in the downtown flagships, are not as prevalent as they once were.

6. Without question, in merchandise displays, it is the merchandise that is the most important element in the visual presentation.

7. To enhance the featured merchandise, trimmers use a host of mannequins, props, proper lighting, signage, and graphics.

8. By paying attention to the principles of design such as balance, emphasis, proportion, rhythm, and harmony, visual merchandisers can create effective window and interior displays.

9. A visual program can maximize its success by the team maintaining the display's component parts, promptly removing out-of-date displays, conducting daily walkthroughs, maintaining self-selection merchandise, and rotating the items.

Terms of the Trade

analogous colors	monochromatic color scheme
asymmetrical balance	motion displays
backlit transparencies	neon
balance	P-O-P displays
centralized visual merchandising	primary colors

color wheel
complementary color scheme
digital images
double complementaries
environmental visual concept
fiber optics
focal point
freelancers
graphics
halogen lamps
harmony
high-intensity discharge bulbs
in-house staffs
low-voltage lighting
mannequins

prismatic displays
proportion
props
rhythm
rules of color
secondary colors
signage
split complementaries
stock agencies
stock houses
symmetrical balance
triadic color scheme
trimmers
visual merchandising
walkthrough

For Discussion

1. How have display specialists of the past broadened their responsibilities in today's retail environment?

2. What type of fashion merchant uses in-house staffing for its visual merchandising function?

3. What are some of the areas of responsibility performed by the in-house team?

4. Define the term "central visual merchandising," and describe how it is employed by fashion retailers.

5. If the smaller fashion retailer wants to utilize professional visual merchandising but is unable to afford someone to work exclusively for the store, what approach should it take?

6. Why has there been a decrease in the use of window displays by department stores and other retail operations that have units in regional malls?

7. Describe the environmental concept that some fashion merchants have subscribed to, and name two companies that have used this approach.

8. List all of the elements of a visual presentation and briefly discuss the importance of each to a presentation's overall success.

9. Identify the most important element in a display and explain its importance.

10. Why has the use of graphics become so prevalent in fashion retailing?

11. In addition to the traditional fluorescent and incandescent bulbs, what other types of lighting are being extensively used to illuminate visual presentations?

12. In what way can visual merchandisers and fashion retailers get an overview of the visual market and satisfy their needs without leaving the store?

13. Briefly discuss the rules of color.

14. What device do many visual merchandisers use to make certain that their color schemes are technically correct?

15. What is meant by the term "backlit transparency?"

16. List the display's component parts and explain how they must be maintained to be effective.

17. Describe a store's trimmer walkthrough and its purpose.

Case Problem

Questions

1. Should management tamper with O & P's success by changing its approach to visual merchandising?
2. If a new method is instituted, what direction should it take? Bear in mind that uniformity and budgetary savings are essential ingredients of the plan.
3. Are there advantages to keeping the present policy?

Oxford and Pembroke is a large fashion specialty chain that has 450 units throughout the United States. It has been in business for 58 years, specializing in moderate-to-better-priced missy and junior sportswear. Most of its stores are in major regional malls.

The company's success has been due in part to the fashion-forward merchandise mix it provides for its customers and the manner in which it is featured in store windows and interiors. Most of the stores in the organization are built to "formula"—each is a clone of the others with approximately the same general square footage and window configuration. The oldest stores in the company have been refurbished to bring them up to date with the newer units.

O & P, as it is often referred to, has been a family enterprise since it opened its first unit. General management of the company has recently been assumed by one of the founder's sons, Jonathan Pembroke. With Don Oxford and the senior Mr. Pembroke now retired, the company's future is in Jonathan's hands.

Although the company has maintained a healthy profit for all of its years, the new C.E.O. believes that some changes could be made to improve the organization's profit picture. He thinks that savings could be realized in visual merchandising. Up to this point, the company has employed a number of regional visual teams to install window and interior displays. Each team of two is responsible for ten stores that it visits every week to make the necessary changes. There are 90 people on the visual staff. While they perform satisfactorily, they are costly to the company. Expense is not the only problem. The company provides no direction in terms of visual approach, and each team is left to its own judgment and expertise in deciding how to visually merchandise the stores it visits.

Jonathan would like to see the company adopt a more uniform approach which would also provide a saving.

Exercises and Projects

1. Visit a downtown shopping area or regional mall to photograph fashion-oriented window displays. Select five of the most interesting visual presentations, take pictures, and mount them on a piece of foam board. Alongside each one, write an evaluation of its elements.

2. In groups of three or four, visit small local fashion merchants to discuss with them an offer to trim a window or install an interior display. In exchange for the project, encourage the merchant to provide discounts.

3. Go online to find resources that provide visual merchandising elements such as mannequins, props, and lighting. Prepare a chart that lists ten vendors, their product specializations, websites, telephone numbers, faxes, and email addresses.

chapter ten

THE HUMAN RESOURCES DIVISION

After reading this chapter, you should be able to:

- Identify the various tasks performed by the human resources department.

- Describe the selection procedure used to assess a company's potential employees.

- Explain why different sources are used to attract employees to the company.

- Evaluate the types of testing that merchants use in their hiring procedures.

- Distinguish among the types of training techniques that are used by today's retail organizations.

- Outline the methods of remuneration that retailers use for different levels of employment.

- List the different types of services and benefits that are offered to employees, and assess their importance in attracting and retaining them.

The lifeblood of every retail organization is its staff. Without competent employees at every level, it is unlikely that the retailer will be able to function properly. Whether it is the decision makers at the organization's highest levels, the middle managers, the sales associates who directly interface with the shoppers, or those who provide the support services for the company, excellent employees are necessary to run a profitable company.

The task of attracting the best employees is no simple matter. People find many fields of business more attractive than retailing for a number of reasons. Except for the upper levels of management, retailing has an image of underpaying its workers. This, coupled with the potential for having to work long hours that extend into the evening as well as the weekends, often discourages many would-be employees from entering the field. Many of the country's most talented college graduates, when embarking on a career, opt for other means of employment. Confronted with such negatives, retail organizations must attract qualified people who are willing to take the challenges offered by a retailing career. Retailing does provide many pluses, however. Salaries at the middle-management level, for example, are comparable to those in other fields that require the same amount of formal education, fringe benefits rival those offered by other industries, and employee discounts enable workers to purchase a wealth of merchandise at well below the retail price.

The human resources (HR) department, still referred to as the personnel department in many retail organizations, has the initial responsibility of locating the best available people for the jobs. Once they are brought on board, the successful candidates must be trained to make sure they comprehend the company's mission and understand how to perform their various tasks. This department also is responsible for making regular evaluations so that employees know how they need to improve their performance, and those who perform favorably can be earmarked for promotion to higher levels. The HR team also makes recommendations on remuneration plans and employee services and benefits.

The HR department's place in the overall table of organization differs from company to company, as does its decision-making authority. In terms of hiring at the lower levels, such as sales associates, stock personnel, and maintenance people, most retailers leave the choices to the HR managers. When filling middle-management positions and those at the highest levels, however, those in HR management play the role of advisers rather than decision makers. Their primary task is to assess the various candidates with evaluation tools so they can recommend potential employees to the supervisors for further interviews. Thus, when an assistant buyer position in ladies shoes becomes available it is the shoe buyer who has the final say in the selection procedure and the HR people who have narrowed down several applicants for the position.

Each retail operation must determine the parameters of the HR department activities so that those in the department will be able to help staff the company with the best available employees and contribute to a working environment that will help maximize profits.

MAINTAINING EQUAL OPPORTUNITY

One of the problems that continues to plague retailing (as well as other businesses) concerns equal employment opportunities for women and minorities. Whereas past business practices had shown favoritism in advancing male Caucasians, the playing field has somewhat leveled in recent years. Once relegated to positions at the lower levels of employment even though they demonstrated the qualities necessary to move into upper management, employees who were formerly passed over are now making gains in reaching the upper levels.

Although the federal government has enacted such legislation as the **Equal Pay Act**, which guarantees men and women the same salary for the same job, and the **Civil Rights Act**, which protects people from discrimination, biases and prejudices have not been completely eradicated from business practices. Companies of every type, including retailing, have made the headlines because employees have accused them of discriminatory practices. Every day's headlines speak of discrimination of homosexuals in the workplace. Although strides are being made to eliminate these occurrences, it still remains a problem.

Today, retailing, more than some other industries, has demonstrated that it has become aware of the problems and has promoted minority employees and women to positions of the highest level in the field, such as C.E.O.s, general merchandise managers, divisional merchandise managers, buyers, store managers, advertising executives, publicists, and fashion directors. With each success story, the opportunity for advancement has become easier for others. Figure 10.1 features a minority business executive.

THE RECRUITMENT PROCESS

One of the most difficult tasks facing today's fashion retailers is to find prospects who have the potential to become productive employees. The difficulty becomes even greater when the economy is booming and there is more competition for workers. With fewer qualified candidates available, HR managers have to initiate new techniques in their quest for the best. When the economy falters and unemployment figures are at peak levels, however, the task is less formidable since there are more would-be employees to choose from.

figure 10.1
Minority women have reached the
C.E.O. level. Retailing was one of
the first businesses to embrace
minorities for executive positions.

There are many stages in the recruitment process. Organizations that have been in business for a number of years have well-established requirements for their jobs, but these companies may need to do some research into new requirements if they add new positions. Newly established retail operations should undergo **job analysis** research to determine the requirements and specifications of the jobs in the company's structure. Smaller companies, such as boutiques, that employ only a few people, generally have a good idea of what their needs are to run a successful business, so job analysis is not warranted. The following discussion primarily pertains to the larger retail companies that do have HR departments.

Job analysis is the study of a specific job to learn all about its duties and responsibilities. From this analysis, **job specifications** are spelled out listing the qualifications needed to perform the job. Finally, a **job description** is written, outlining the title of the job, the division in which it belongs, the specific department, the title of the immediate supervisor, and a brief description of the duties and responsibilities. Each job description is kept on a computerized file for easy access so that the recruiter can quickly examine the job description when placing an ad or preparing for an interview. When people apply for the jobs, descriptions assist the HR team in determining if the candidates are qualified for the positions. After developing the job description, the HR manager should consult the roster of personnel sources that the HR department has created to use in the recruitment of employees.

Recruitment Sources

Basically, there are two separate areas to recruit candidates: **internal sources**, which consist of people already employed by the company, and **external sources**, which consist of people outside of the company.

Internal Sources

One of the ways in which retailers may satisfy their HR needs is by talking with people already employed by the company. These workers can help in two ways. First, if they are satisfied employees, they might be willing to recommend others for employment. Because they already understand the company's mission, the way it operates, the benefits derived from being part of the organization, and the salary, potential for advancement, and so forth, they might tell friends and relatives about the position. Sometimes, the staff is rewarded for making recommendations to the company.

The other way in which a retailer uses its internal resources is **promotion from within**. New employees are frequently motivated to join an organization because they are told that they could move up to a more important position if they have good work records. In many retailer organizations, HR managers are instructed to first scour the present staff to seek candidates for higher positions before going outside the company. This approach not only motivates staff members to perform at their highest levels but also provides a pool of candidates that already know the ins and outs of the company.

The disadvantage of using the promotion-from-within policy as the only means of filling upper-level positions is that it might result in stagnation and limited ideas. Outsiders often bring a breath of fresh air to a company. Combining those already on board with those from other sources generally provides a better employee mix.

External Sources

There is a wealth of external sources that retailers use in their pursuit of excellent employees. Some have been used since retailing was in its infancy, such as classified ads in consumer newspapers and trade papers such as *WWD* and employment agencies. Newer ones include posting positions on the Internet, where merchants can also provide application forms for interested parties to complete.

Consumer Newspaper Classified Advertisements

The method once most often used by retail HR was the newspaper classified ad. Although the use of classified advertising has waned in recent years rivaled by the Internet, it is still used to attract potential employees. Typically, these ads are for lower-level positions such as sales associates or middle-management positions such as department managers. Upper-level management positions are generally advertised in a newspaper's business section such as *The New York Times* that features a separate section for executive positions in its Sunday editions. The positions are posted as either **open ads** or **blind ads**. The former lists the name of the retailer in addition to any pertinent information about the job. The latter omits the company name, supplying only relevant information about the available position. Those who use the blind format often do so because it preserves the anonymity of the company and avoids unwanted inquiries. However, sometimes blind ads discourage job seekers from applying because they fear they might be applying for their own position, thereby alerting their present employer that they are looking for another job.

Trade Periodical Classified Advertisements

When fashion retailers have positions they need filled, ads they post in trade publications often bring the greatest number of responses. *WWD*, for example, the largest of the fashion-oriented trade papers, features a section that lists a large number of middle- and upper-management retail positions. Since those with a lot of business experience generally read *WWD* religiously, it is an excellent way to reach the best and most experienced group of potential employees.

EMPLOYMENT AGENCIES

Some retailers prefer to have job applicants prescreened before they consider them for an interview. By providing agencies with job descriptions, they can limit their time to interviewing those with the most potential. Agencies usually specialize in specific industries and particular levels of employment. Fashion retailers who use the services of an agency that specializes in their types of positions are more likely to have better-qualified applicants recommended to them. They also might want to deal with different agencies for their needs at different levels. One might serve their purposes for finding entry-level prospects, another for middle-management personnel and another for upper-management positions. The latter agency is known as an **executive search firm**, or **headhunter**. It deals exclusively with people who have significant industry experience, and agency staff are professionally experienced in attracting the most discriminating employees. Unlike the first two employment agencies, where candidates go to seek leads for future employment, the headhunter pursues the industry's best candidates and directs them to clients who have specific needs. When a company needs a general merchandise manager, it contacts the headhunter to find the right person to fill the position. Headhunters are paid on a commission basis that generally runs from 20 to 25 percent of the position's salary. Most major retailers find the headhunter route the best approach to attracting the most prized upper-level employees.

THE INTERNET

Retailers at every level, from department stores such as Macy's to value stores such as Target, are using their own websites to fill their HR needs. On the same websites on which they sell merchandise, retailers include special sections that can be accessed by people seeking employment. Job seekers are led to application forms that they complete and send immediately to the retailer. Those considered to be viable candidates are contacted via email and asked to come in for an interview. The Internet also features many career websites that offer a variety of jobs, retail included, such as jobsonline.com, monster.com, headhunter.com, and salary.com. Typically they provide a **resume** service and post available jobs in a range of geographical areas. Figure 10.2 shows someone looking for a job on the Internet.

SCHOOLS, COLLEGES, AND UNIVERSITIES

Many educational institutions across America and other countries serve as excellent resources for retailers to find prospective employees. They sponsor career fairs, where merchants can meet students in a variety of formats. Merchants can make group presentations or hold one-on-one meetings to tell students about job opportunities within their companies. Companies set up booths that students visit, giving the students the chance to make quick comparisons among those companies in attendance and seek further information about those they want to work for. Colleges and universities also implement internship programs that place graduating seniors in positions with various retail operations. In this way, employment managers get a firsthand

figure 10.2
Searching the Internet seeking job possibilities. This has become one of the more important places to research jobs for prospective retail employees.

knowledge of the student interns and can assess their progress to see if they should be considered for regular employment after the internships have been completed. More retailers are entering into these programs because they find there is no better way of learning about an employee's potential than by observing that person on the job. Fashion retailers participating in internship programs include Bloomingdale's, Macy's, Stein Mart, and Lord & Taylor. Some retailers participate in **shadowing programs** where students are invited to follow executives as they perform their daily routines. The participants are able to learn about a particular company in a brief period and determine whether or not they want to work there.

Walk-ins

One of the means of staffing brick-and-mortar operations comes from **walk-ins—** people who apply directly at the store. A substantial number of sales associates are found this way and turn out to be productive employees. Stores that promote from within often find that these people work their way up the ladder. One of reasons for the effectiveness of such sources comes from the applicants' self-motivation, evident in their willingness to go from store to store, looking for work. Some stores, such as Target, utilize in-store kiosks with computer terminals in which those seeking employment may complete applications without the need to make an appointment with an employment manager. Evaluated almost instantaneously, the computerized applications provide HR interviewers with a sufficient amount of information to determine if further screening is warranted.

Industry Networking

Fashion retailers regularly interact with a host of different fashion-oriented businesses, such as the vendors from whom they purchase, resident buying offices, reporting services, and public relations firms. Each of these groups meets with retailers throughout the year and become familiar with their management employees. Fashion manufacturers and resident buying office representatives, for example, work closely with store buyers and merchandisers and are in a position to evaluate their abilities and expertise. Thus, when fashion merchants are looking to recruit a new buyer, they can use this informal **networking** route to learn the names of potential candidates for the position. Oftentimes, assistant buyers achieve buying positions with other companies through these means.

Window and Exterior Signage

Small retailers often use signs in their windows to advertise positions. Often customers of the stores are willing to work there because they are familiar with the operations. This technique is particularly effective at Christmastime when temporary part-time help is needed. Even large retailers sometimes display such signs on in-store easels to solicit for new employees.

Employment managers often keep records regarding the success of the various types of resources they use to obtain potential employees so that when they need to hire, they know which ones are the most effective.

The Hiring Procedure

Once people apply for a position, the HR department must evaluate them to see if they meet the store's employment criteria. A company generally has rigorous rules to follow when making employment decisions but at times of employee shortages, the rules are sometimes compromised so that the company needs may be satisfied.

Regardless of how urgently a retailer needs to hire, it is essential to carefully check each candidate's background. To do so, many retailers are using outside agencies, which perform such services as public records checks, fraudulent use of social security numbers, criminal background checks, and drug testing.

Hiring practices differ in terms of the position to be filled. A company seeking a divisional merchandise manager, for example, will use a different approach than when it is looking for a sales associate. The former position is at the top level of company management and requires significant decision-making ability and a substantial background in merchandising. A candidate for the latter position might merely need to be appropriately groomed and dressed and display a willingness to work. The procedure used to evaluate the candidates for the management position will be considerably more extensive than the one used to hire the salesperson.

Most retail operations adhere to similar practices in the selection procedure, although they may use them in different orders. The following sections discuss these stages.

Resumes

Except when hiring for lower-level positions such as sales associates or stock handlers, the resume is usually the initial step in the hiring process. Some fashion merchants which cater to the middle and upper social classes will require resumes for their sales positions, since these jobs sometimes require more than just meeting and greeting the shopper. In many upscale, fashion-forward operations such as Saks Fifth Avenue, Bergdorf Goodman, Neiman Marcus, and Nordstrom, where sales associates are expected to develop a customer base, resumes can show the level of customer relationships the sales associate has developed at other stores. This is important because these sales specialists are often able to establish long-lasting relationships with customers that result in a steady flow of business, which is profitable to the retailer. Those seeking employment in management, merchandising, advertising and promotion, customer service, and store operations or control are expected to provide a resume that carefully spells out their educational, professional, and personal information.

The resume serves as a document that will help the reviewer to evaluate the candidate's ability to perform the duties and responsibilities of the available position and to fit in with the company's business environment.

Application Forms

For those applying for lower-level positions, the first step is to fill out the application. One of the places in which the application is readily available for prospective employees is the in-store "station" where the forms are presented on a computer terminal. This is a very successful approach since the information is transmitted to the HR department as soon as the form is completed. For those who have submitted resumes and have been invited to provide more information, the second step is to complete the application. In any case, the application form is a basic instrument on which the candidate provides specific information that is necessary for the later stages of the employment assessment.

Places to include personal history, educational achievements, professional experience, and references are usually part of the application forms. Application forms cannot ask for information pertaining to age, height, and weight, due to the enactment of the federal Civil Rights Act of 1964. Some states also have other restrictions.

Preliminary, or Rail Interviews

After candidates submit their applications, a member of the HR team examines them to determine if these or any people applying for the positions warrant further consideration. Those who do not meet the minimum requirements established by the company are dismissed at this stage, and those who seem like good prospects sometimes are contacted for a brief interview. These are known as **preliminary interviews**, or **rail interviews** and give the employment manager an opportunity to meet the candidates and quickly assess their persona; appearance, because they should dress in a manner that fits the retailer's image; and their ability to communicate, because it is important that they convey the retailer's fashion message and provide good customer service.

The interviewer also takes the opportunity to flesh out the candidate's answers on the application form to determine if they possess the minimum requirements for the position as outlined in the job description and job specifications. Those that pass this level of inquiry will be asked to move onto the next stage in the selection process.

Reference Checks

Many HR departments spend considerable time checking the candidate's references to verify that the information they provided is accurate. HR staff contact educational institutions to determine the accuracy of the dates of attendance that the candidates state and any degrees they claim to have earned. HR staff may contact former employers to verify dates of employment and positions that the candidates say they had with the company. They cannot ask about a candidate's performance, however, because this is considered an invasion of privacy.

To get a better picture of the candidate, many HR departments, as well as other businesses are using the services of outside organizations to learn more about potential employees than they are permitted to ask themselves. For a modest fee, online agencies provide this information.

Testing

Many HR departments administer different types of tests as a means of evaluating the candidate. They include **aptitude tests**, which determine the applicant's capacity to work; intelligence tests, which determine how much the candidate has learned in the past; interest tests which indicate whether or not the candidate has a sincere interest in the type of work; personality tests, which evaluate the candidate's characteristics and personality traits; and pen-and-pencil honesty tests, which help determine the candidate's honesty and integrity.

Gallup has developed a web-based talent assessment that serves as an important step in selection processes for potential job candidates. The test may be taken online only once, so the answers should be carefully and honestly answered. The results are considered along with the other tools in the selection process.

Drug testing has become an important mainstay in most retailers' hiring process, because drug users are not generally reliable workers. There are numerous ways in which to test for drugs including urine and hair sample tests.

Final Interviews

Candidates who have satisfactorily passed through these preliminary stages usually go through at least one more intensive **final interview**, especially if the position is management-oriented.

These are lengthy and can take anywhere from a few hours to a full day, depending on the level of the position. For upper-management jobs, more than one member of the staff conducts individual interviews or participates in a group session. These sessions are generally held in the office of the supervisor for whom the candidate will work, or when interview teams are used, in conference rooms.

The Final Decision

At lower levels of employment, such as sales associate positions in off-price fashion operations, the employment manager often makes the final decision instead of the new employee's supervisor, the department manager.

In small stores the owner or store manager often makes the decision without any other input.

At the upper-level of employment, the decision is often a time-consuming one that involves a careful review of all of the candidate's background materials, including test results, references, and the various interviews. The final decision generally rests with the immediate supervisor.

In some companies, candidates are required to undergo a physical examination. If the results of the exam are satisfactory, the person is offered the position.

TRAINING

Training is important to make certain that each employee knows how to complete the amount of work at a performance level that satisfies the company's needs and objectives.

Training takes place at different stages of employee development and is accomplished in different ways, depending on the employee's position and size of the retail operation. Small specialty shops and boutiques, for example, are less formal in their approach and often limit their instruction to **on-the-job training**. Larger companies generally utilize a program that includes classroom instruction, **online training**, **vestibule training**, and on-the-job training.

The programs in the larger operations are usually developed by the HR departments and carried out by experts on their staff and members of the company's supervisory team. Small stores generally rely upon owners or managers to familiarize their new employees with the tasks of the operation; they are not cluttered with the variety of procedures and forms used by their larger-retailer counterparts, thus eliminating the need for more than an orientation to the store and familiarization with the inventory. However, it is wise for small-store owners to learn about the essential elements of training so that they can better prepare their employees for satisfactory performances.

New Employee Training

When people join a company, it is important to teach them as much as possible about the organization's philosophy, goals, and procedures. For fashion retailers, the challenges of training are even more complex and include teaching about its fashion image and direction. The level and scope of each position dictates the types and depth of training that must be provided before new staff members can tackle their jobs.

Executives

The most important groups to be trained are those that will share in the management of the company, because its success, for the most part, is based upon management's ability to develop creative ideas and programs and to make certain that the rest of the staff carry them out satisfactorily. The upper level of every retail organization performs tasks involving merchandise analysis, forecasting, customer services, promotion, visual merchandising, and so forth to make the organization more profitable. Fashion retailers face even greater management challenges since they regularly must make decisions regarding the introduction of new styles, color selection, fashion cycles, and purchasing from offshore vendors.

Even new employees who have excellent experience in other retail operations need to understand the specifics of their new company. Each organization has its own methodology as to how it will achieve its goals. Thus, training is an essential part of teaching new managers the complexities of the company.

Many of the marquee fashion retailers spend a great deal of time and effort in the training of employees who come from colleges and universities to enter **executive training programs**. Some programs, such as the ones subscribed to by Macy's and Bloomingdale's, are so extensive that they are considered to be the Harvards of executive development. Graduates of these programs are regularly contacted by headhunters with offers to join other retail institutions seeking top-level managers.

Middle Managers

Department heads and assistant managers are not called upon to make policy decisions but are given the tasks of carrying out the decisions made by top management. They are trained to perform such duties as tallying the daily receipts, organizing meal breaks, determining employee schedules, handling customer complaints, and managing sales associates in their departments.

Sales Associates

If a fashion retailer wants to make a profit, it must sufficiently train its sales associates in the role they play for the company. These associates assist shoppers by offering product knowledge, making suggestions, and making the sale. If salespeople are improperly trained, they could lose sales. People new to selling need more training in this area than those who come with previous experience. Both groups, however, must learn about company procedures, proper handling of credit cards, sending of merchandise, procurement of items from other units, and so forth.

Nonselling Personnel

Those responsible for receiving and marking merchandise, store security, customer service, accounting and control, stock keeping, and a variety of other nonselling tasks need training specific to their jobs. For example, merchandise receivers and sorters must understand how to use the computers to properly record the inventory. All employees in these support positions must learn the company's overall philosophy and procedures and apply them to their individual responsibilities.

Retraining Employees

Some people who are already on the company's payroll may need to be retrained because they are promoted or transferred, the company implements a new system they must use, or the company adds a new department that they will work in.

If an employee is transferred from one department to another, the new training might focus on familiarization with different merchandise. When an assistant buyer is transferred from menswear to junior sportswear, for example, the company's buying procedures will be the same, but the merchandise knowledge and specifics of order replenishment will be different.

With promotions come additional responsibility. A group manager who executed merchandising plans for several departments might be promoted to buyer which includes different challenges and decision-making responsibilities. This person now requires training that includes development of a model stock, pricing, negotiation with vendors, open-to-buy calculations, and other skills.

The installation of new systems requires staff **retraining.** It might be a new point-of-purchase terminal that uses different types of scanning equipment or a new automated system for moving merchandise from the receiving room to the selling floor. Some new systems require the retraining of the entire staff, such as in the case of new computer software, or just that of one department, as in the case of a new conveyor system that replaces an older model.

Sometimes fashion retailers will expand their operations by adding new departments to their companies. For example, they might establish a boutique section that requires more personalized selling and better servicing of the more affluent customers expected to patronize these departments. Consequently, the sales associates who will work in these new areas will require additional sales and service training.

Training Methodology

Different positions and circumstances require different approaches in training, including such traditional methods as **role-playing**, vestibule training, classroom instruction, and on-the-job training. Today, many new techniques have been added and include the use of DVD presentations and online training.

Role-Playing

Role-playing is one of the more effective methods of teaching sales techniques and methods. This learning tool involves two participants, one playing the consumer and the other the salesperson. The selling role is usually first demonstrated by a sales associate who has been with the company for a while. The newly hired salesperson is then asked to play this role and is assessed by people familiar with excellence in selling and using prepared forms. The results are then discussed by the trainer. Figure 10.3 is a typical form used in evaluating sales trainees during these exercises.

Another area in which role-playing is used is in customer service. A trainer might act as a customer with a complaint about such things as defective merchandise or a bad experience with a sales associate, and the newly employed customer service representative responds. This demonstration is also analyzed and assessed.

THE SALES PRESENTATION	SCORE

Evaluator's Name _____

Name of Sales Trainee _____

THE SALES PRESENTATION   SCORE

APPROACH: Evidence of preapproach preparations, confidence, poise, friendliness, sincerity, achieved interest of prospect quickly _____

SALES PERSONALITY:
Proper appearance, tact, voice, grammar, attitude, absence of objectionable mannerisms . . . . _____

BUYING MOTIVES: Skill in creating interest in product and arousing a desire to buy . . . . _____

PRODUCT AND COMPANY: Knowledge of product and company necessary to
convince prospect to buy . . . . _____

SALES STORY: Well planned and executed, thorough, held prospect's interest, believably enthusiastic, illustrated how prospect
could benefit from buying product . . . . _____

DEMONSTRATION: Imagination and appropriateness, encouraged prospect participation when suitable . . . . _____

MEETING OBJECTIONS: Skill in overcoming barriers to completing the sale, application of proved techniques to handle objections
. . . . _____

TRIAL CLOSES: Ability to detect clues or buying signals, attempted closes when feasible . . . .
. . . . _____

CLOSE: Skill in application of closing techniques, order-filling proficiency, absence of idle chatter . . . .
. . . . _____

FUTURE BUSINESS: Encouraged return visit to store . . . . _____

                                                      TOTAL SCORE _____

As an individual judge, score the sales presentation on each of the areas listed by assigning points from 1 to 10.
Total the points to get the score. A conscientious and unbiased rating helps the salesperson learn how well he or she performed and to
recognize strengths and weaknesses.

SCORING GUIDE: Excellent (10), Good (8), Fair (6), Poor (4)

figure 10.3
Evaluation form that is typically used to determine if the participant has achieved success during this practice exercise.

Vestibule Training

When teaching specific tasks such as using a point-of-sale terminal for recording sales, most retailers elect to simulate the conditions rather than train employees on the selling floor so they can learn to handle the equipment and perform the transactions without the fear of making costly mistakes. The trainer can provide the necessary information and allow the trainee as much time as necessary to comprehend the machine. This is called vestibule training, because it takes place away from the selling floor.

Classroom Instruction

Most major retailers have instructional facilities that include a classroom. Such facilities are used for different purposes: orientation sessions to introduce new employees to company systems, retraining current employees, and instructing executive trainees. For example, since newly hired executive trainees generally rotate assignments, they must learn what each division of the company offers to the operation so they will be better prepared to handle any job. These trainees regularly meet in classrooms, where they are addressed by divisional heads of merchandising, management, promotion, and control as well as by HR specialists who coordinate the training effort.

Many HR instructors create PowerPoint presentations that clearly outline the key points of the lesson. They can also incorporate a wealth of drawings and photographs to help those in the classroom sessions comprehend the text.

Most classroom sessions include lectures followed by question-and-answer periods for teaching such tasks as servicing the customer, handling suspected shoplifters, and dealing with customer complaints. Figure 10.4 shows classroom instruction for new employees.

On-the-Job Training

In most small stores, the only training that employees receive takes place on the job. The owner or manager usually familiarizes the new employee with store policy, such as return privileges, selling techniques, and anything else necessary to perform the job. Some larger stores also use on-the-job training in combination with vestibule, classroom, and other training practices.

DVD Presentations

Many major retail operations are using individualized video instruction for their managers. For example, Dr. William G. Harris, of Stanton Corporation, one of the earliest developers of video programs for instructional purposes, designed and created an instructional video for managers to use to hone their interviewing skills. One of the DVDs features a 30-minute back-to-basics lesson that reinforces the importance of the initial interview and of being prepared beforehand. It focuses on learning to ask the right questions and listen well. Although an instructor can provide such instruction in the typical classroom setting, this format enables users to examine the DVD at their convenience and to review it as often as it takes to master the skills.

Video instruction is available that deals with a number of different retailing areas. Those who are concerned with mathematical concepts that include open-to-buy and markup calculations, for example, can easily find videos that address such topics. Others concentrate on such areas as retail advertising and promotion, purchase planning, and visits to wholesale markets.

figure 10.4
An instructor training new hires in a classroom setting. This is one way that the human resources manager can provide information and observe the individual's responses.

Online Training

Many merchants are finding that the most efficient and affordable ways to train their staffs is through packaged or customized online training. It is especially good for companies with a network of smaller branches and units in many geographical locations where classroom instruction might be impractical. HR departments can access specific programs that will help train their employees no matter where they are.

By using search engines such as www.google.com, retailers can locate websites that offer packages that feature online training.

EVALUATING EMPLOYEES

Once the employees have been trained and assigned to specific jobs, they demonstrate their value to the company through their performance. Although each person may receive the same training and opportunity for advancement, not everyone is capable of the same results. Some may be outstanding in their assignments and merit future promotions, others might demonstrate the ability to perform but their current job does not sufficiently satisfy their own personal needs, and still others might show signs of incompetence or an unwillingness to succeed. Each of these situations will eventually need attention from management and result in such actions as promotion to positions of greater authority, transfers to areas that will better suit needs and abilities, or terminations.

To evaluate employee performance in a fair and equitable manner, the HR departments in the larger retail organizations develop a plan for employee evaluation. Not only does it separate the talented from the unworthy but it also serves other purposes, such as the following:

- It helps the supervisor to evaluate the employee according to certain established criteria, thus ensuring fairness to everyone.
- Salary increases can be awarded based upon the employee's commitment to the company.
- When positions at higher levels become available, those best suited can be easily recognized.
- When employees are evaluated, their strengths and weaknesses can be addressed and productivity improved.
- When employees receive regular, positive feedback about their performances, they are motivated to perform better.
- It helps to determine if the employee's present position is appropriate or if they might better serve somewhere else in the organization.

Characteristics of a Productive Evaluation Plan

Whether a company is a small venture with a few employees or one that ranks among the giants in the field, it needs to have a sound plan to evaluate employee performance. In small retail operations such as proprietary specialty stores or boutiques that have less formalized structures, evaluation procedures—if they are used at all—are often haphazardly administered. However, workers in the smallest stores will perform better if they know they are being evaluated. In these retail environments, the carefully developed rating forms and other materials used by the giants are unnecessary. The evaluation procedure should be spelled out at the time of the initial hiring, and when it occurs, might include a brief written evaluation followed by a discussion. If everyone is evaluated in the same manner, the manager will be able to address any problems, award the worthy with salary increases, and terminate those who have failed to perform according to the company's needs.

Larger organizations, because of their size and the many people charged with the evaluation process, must use formal employee evaluation systems. Not only is this a fair way to evaluate performance but in these times where disgruntled employees bring law suits, the company is better prepared to answer the charges.

The process should include the following ideas:

- Carefully structured evaluation forms should focus upon all of the major areas of importance to individual performance. There should also be space for a written summary outlining strengths and weaknesses.
- Evaluations should be taken at specific intervals, never greater than six months.
- The performance should be evaluated by the employee's immediate supervisor with a face-to-face discussion to make the employee aware of areas that need improvement. An effort should be made to discuss the person's positive characteristics as well as those that are negative. At the time of the discussion, the worker should be given time to respond to any negative comments in the report.
- If possible, rewards such as salary increases should be given to the better-performing employees.

METHODS OF COMPENSATION

The majority of people consider compensation as the most important factor when seeking employment. The HR department is involved in determining which methods of remuneration are most appropriate for the various levels of employment and what the salary range should be for each job title.

There is a vast difference in the earnings potential for people in the lower-level jobs such as selling and those in top management. Not only are the dollar figures different but so are the ways in which they are paid.

Whatever the jobs, certain considerations must be studied before any decisions in terms of remuneration are made. Good plans should consider the following criteria:

- There should be a direct relationship between productivity and salary.
- Jobs that are similar to each other should offer similar salaries. This is not only important in terms of employee fairness but it is a requirement of the Equal Pay Act, which requires equal pay for equal work.
- Additional income potential and promotion are two motivational techniques that could be part of the plan.
- Employees should receive a constant minimum amount of money each week. While this is inherent in **straight salary** programs, straight commission plans could also be adapted to include regular income guarantees.
- Salaries should be based upon the prevailing wages of the retail industry and adjusted upward to attract the most qualified people.
- All employees should understand the plans. While straight salary arrangements are easy to understand, "**quota bonuses**" are more complicated and must be carefully described.

Straight Salary

Although some fashion retailers are now moving in different directions, many of their employees are paid a straight salary. This plan is simple to understand and guarantees the same salary each week, but it does not provide the necessary incentive to motivate employees to maximize their efforts. This lack of motivation is easy to recognize, especially in sales associates, by the minimum attention they pay to their customers.

Salary Plus Commission

One of the ways of combining a salary guarantee with productivity incentives is to use the **salary plus commission** method of remuneration. Employees receive a set amount based upon the number of hours they work each week and an additional amount based upon how much merchandise they sell. In these plans, the commission usually ranges from 1 to 5 percent.

Straight Commission

The greatest amount of attention in fashion retailing compensation is now focused on **straight commission.** Simply stated, this plan offers the employee the greatest earnings potential because remuneration is based solely on productivity.

One of the leaders in this area has been Nordstrom. The company pays virtually all of its sales associates in this manner and reports that some associates have earnings that reach levels of $100,000 or more. In addition to providing members of its sales staff with the opportunity to earn as much as they are capable of, the company believes that its customers are serviced better than by any other retailer because of this payment plan.

Following the lead of Nordstrom is Bloomingdale's, as well as other upscale fashion emporiums. In these stores, employees in the departments that sell the highest-ticket items are paid on the straight commission basis.

While straight commission motivates employees more than any other plan, it does not guarantee uniformity of earnings. That is, one week's commissions might come to $1,000 and the next, $500. To enable employees to budget themselves, most stores offer them a "draw" against future commissions. Employees are given a draw, or a loan, each week and, at the end of the month, the draw is compared with the actual earned commissions. In cases where the commissions are higher than the draw, the employees receive the compensation due them. Where the draw exceeds the commissions, the difference is subtracted from the next month's commissions. In cases where the draw is consistently greater than the actual earned commission, the draw might be adjusted or the ineffective employee might be terminated.

The inability to generate sales is not always the sales associate's fault. During economic downturns, for example, such as the recession that plagued the country during the beginning of the new millennium and in the early part of 2010 retail sales were down. Those on straight commission received smaller paychecks as a result.

Quota Bonus

In the quota bonus, the retailer determines the level of sales it expects from each salesperson. Those who surpass this amount are paid additional monies. Merchants that use this compensation method employ a variety of systems and amounts. Most report that it provides the necessary incentive to improve sales but it eliminates the uncertainties of many employees who are fearful of straight commission selling.

Typically, when the employee achieves the determined amount, one of two methods is used to reward the participants. One provides for a commission on sales that exceed the established quota. If the quota has been set at $2,000 for the week and sales in excess of that amount are commissioned at 5 percent, for example, and the salesperson sells $2,500 worth of merchandise, he or she gets $25 in addition to the preestablished salary. The other method merely awards a dollar amount for reaching the predetermined goal. The goals are set in stages of success. For example, after selling $2,000 worth of merchandise, the employee might be rewarded with $15 for every additional sale of $500. This amount is added to the base salary. About 20 percent of the fashion retailers are now using quota bonus arrangements.

Salary Plus Bonus

Many retail operations offer bonuses to the management personnel who are responsible for their selling departments but they are not paid commissions or bonuses based upon what they individually sell. These bonuses are usually based upon overall sales in their respective departments. They are generally paid periodically, such as every three months, in addition to the salaries that they receive. The **salary plus bonus** incentive plan is used to reward the managers for their roles in motivating their sales associates to perform at their highest potential.

Other Methods of Compensation

Most of the previously described plans focus on compensation for the sales staff. To provide incentives to those paid on a straight salary arrangement, such as management employees, retailers frequently use a variety of plans, described in the following sections.

Profit Sharing

In many major retail operations, all of the management personnel, and in some cases, all of the company's employees, are given the opportunity to share in the company's profits. **Profit sharing** generally fosters company loyalty and discourages employee turnover.

Stock Options

Retailers often offer their management teams the option of buying company stock at prices that are lower than those available on the open market. Some companies even provide stock to their managers without cost to them. In times of prosperity, these **stock options** have contributed to employee savings. There is no guarantee about the performance of the stock during recessions.

Prize Money

In cases where retailers want to encourage the sale of slow-moving merchandise, it is common practice, especially in the smaller specialty and boutique operations, to offer **prize money (P.M.)** to sales associates. The P.M. might come in the form of a commission for each of the items sold or a preestablished dollar amount. Sometimes the rewards are in the form of free trips or other incentives instead of cash.

EMPLOYEE BENEFITS

Today, a significant number of job seekers are as concerned with employee benefits as they are with the salary potential of the positions they are applying for. In retailing, where monetary compensation generally ranks below other fields, especially at the entry levels, benefits packages seem to be the answer to attracting qualified candidates for the jobs, and these packages continue to improve.

The HR department has the responsibility for designing benefits and services packages that will not only compete with those in their own field but in other areas of employment as well.

Health Insurance

Obtaining health insurance is a major problem for most Americans. With the costs ever spiraling upward, more workers are looking for employment that offers some form of medical and dental program. In fact, some candidates take positions with companies solely because they offer such benefits.

The Affordable Care Act, which was passed in 2013, now in effect, has mandated that every citizen must purchase health-care insurance. At the time of this writing the Act had stalled because of computer glitches, and had yet to be made available to many inquirers. If the plan totally works out, retail organizations will have this action to overcome the provision of health-care insurance. Figure 10.5 shows a health-insurance claim form.

Discounts

Most merchants offer their employees merchandise discounts that range anywhere from 20 to 40 percent. In the large retail organizations, the typical discount is at the low end of the scale; small retailers often provide the larger discounts. Small fashion boutiques and specialty stores often encourage their employees to purchase and wear the merchandise that the store sells by offering it at cost. Customers often notice the clothes that store employees wear and ask if they are available in the store. This helps to make selling easier and warrants the awarding of such a benefit to employees.

Dining and Recreational Facilities

Many of the giants in the retail industry provide spaces where their workers can relax during breaks and eating facilities that feature low-cost meals. Not only do these provide

figure 10.5
Health insurance is often more important to employees than salary. In today's work market, it has become a factor in attracting good employees.

direct benefits to the employees but they enable the staff members to socialize and relate to each other away from the selling environment. Quite often friendships are established in these dining and recreation areas that help employees to work better with each other.

Pension Plans

One of the means by which companies can reduce the amount of employee turnover is by providing pension plans such as 401(k)s. The knowledge that their company offers a pension plan often encourages them to stay. Programs range anywhere from the employer making the entire contribution to those that require contributions from the employer and employee.

In the wake of the Enron and Worldcom scandals, when employees lost most or all of their pensions, most companies have entered into programs that make their pension plans relatively safe from mishandling by top management. Without this attention, employees are likely to seek employment elsewhere.

Tuition Reimbursement

As a means of encouraging their employees to improve their job performance, many merchants provide **tuition reimbursement**. Employees who take courses appropriate to their jobs are able to do so without any out-of-pocket expense. Some organizations pay according to the grades their employees receive.

Child-Care Facilities

One of the more attractive benefits offered to employees are in-house child-care centers. While the expense is considerable, the centers attract people who would otherwise be unable to work and opens up a large pool of potential employees.

LABOR RELATIONS

Although the HR department is a part of the management team, it has the responsibility of acting as the liaison between company management and employees and of working out any difficulties that may arise from disagreements between the two parties. If these problems are not resolved, staff performance could be severely hindered, which could lower company profits. The HR department also has to solve problems that range from minor everyday occurrences such as tardiness to more problematical concerns such as internal theft.

The HR department plays an important role in collective bargaining. Most retail operations have one or more unions representing the company's employees, and the senior vice president in charge of HR has the responsibility of developing salary and benefits packages for union contracts. The vice president also establishes the means of dispute resolution. Fostering better relationships between management and labor is an extremely sensitive area and those with the best skills are likely to prevent job actions such as slowdowns or strikes.

EMPLOYEE TURNOVER AND PROFITABILITY

One of the more serious problems that plague retailers today is the alarming rate of employee turnover at every level. The rates increase when national unemployment numbers are down, especially at the entry-level positions, because retail salaries are generally less than those offered in other fields. Headhunters or retail recruitment firms are also constantly contacting upper-level employees and enticing them away from their current positions with offers of better salaries or benefits.

Company profitability is affected by the turnover problem, because it is very costly to constantly retrain employees. To adequately train new hires, retailers need to maintain an in-house training staff or use the services of an off-site company. Improper training could cause employees at all levels to make costly mistakes that might affect profitability. Sales associates, for example, unfamiliar with the different types of credit plans available for large purchases, could lose these important sales.

Turnover among those with extended company affiliation such as buyers and merchandisers, could result in the store having less negotiation power with vendors for better wholesale prices and terms. *Happening Now* explores actions to be taken for slowing turnover among employees.

HAPPENING NOW

HOW RETAILERS ARE TAKING ACTION TO REDUCE EMPLOYEE TURNOVER RATES

Since the recession began in 2008, many employees realized declines in their employee turnover rates. With jobs difficult to secure, a multitude of workers decide to stay in their present positions rather than seek hard-to-find employment elsewhere. While this was considered to be a positive for retailers, the situation was about to change due to the pickup in the economy with employment opportunities starting to increase in 2013.

In early 2014 about three-quarters of retail employers started to see some changes especially at the store level and distribution centers, where hourly worker turnover is expected to increase. For them and full-time employees, retention is a must since turnover costs the retailer a significant amount of money. Some of the negatives associated with high turnover costs include the dollars spent on recruitment advertisements, employee searches, applications handling, and screening of prospective employees. Workplace dissatisfaction is also on the rise because of downsizing which often causes more job responsibilities, fewer pay increases, fewer advancement opportunities, and so forth.

A major reason for retail workers to leave their positions is to seek better career opportunities.

Another is to seek better-paying jobs. Many workers are leaving their posts to secure better health insurance. Today, turnover is increasing because of the simplicity in job searches. Those looking to make changes merely list their capabilities on social media websites, and learn about the pay packages that other retailers offer.

To combat the challenge of retaining employees, many retailers are promulgating career paths, offering incentive programs, changing remuneration practices, and so forth.

Those who are willing to address the changes will find turnover rates deceasing and better performance will occur.

Chapter Highlights

1. Federal guidelines specify that companies must not discriminate in any manner in the hiring of employees and that men and women receive the same pay for the same job.

2. The recruitment process begins with job analysis, from which job specifications are determined and job descriptions are written.

3. Employers have two major sources for fulfilling positions: internal and external.

4. Promotion from within is an excellent practice that generally helps to motivate employees in their job performance.

5. One of the more efficient ways in which to attract new employees to a company is through its website.

6. The hiring procedure is more effective when retailers utilize the services of investigative agencies to check the backgrounds of new candidates before they are considered for employment.

7. Except in the recruitment of lower-level employees, most retailers prefer that candidates submit a resume before they are called in for an interview.

8. Employees are tested as part of the hiring process in such areas as personality, drug use, aptitude, and intelligence.

9. Training programs are used by retailers to introduce new employees to the company and to retrain those already in employment in new concepts. These training techniques include role-playing, vestibule training, classroom instruction, video presentations, and online training.

10. Periodic employee evaluation is extremely important to the success of the company and should be based upon carefully developed rating forms and other materials.

11. There are numerous methods of employee remuneration that retailers use in paying their staff. The methods that offer such incentives as commissions and bonuses generally motivate better performance.

12. Health-insurance programs have become one of the more important aspects of employee benefits. In many cases, employees consider them to be more important than the salaries offered.

13. The HR department has the responsibility of acting as liaison between management and labor so that difficulties can be effectively resolved without causing unrest between the two groups.

Terms of the Trade

aptitude tests
blind ads
Civil Rights Act
Equal Pay Act
executive search firm
executive training programs
external sources of recruitment
final interview
headhunter
internal sources of recruitment
job analysis
job description
job specifications
networking
online training
on-the-job training
open ads
preliminary interview

prize money (P.M.)
profit sharing
promotion from within
quota bonuses
rail interview
resume
retraining
role-playing
salary plus bonus
salary plus commission
shadowing programs
stock options
straight commission
straight salary
tuition reimbursement
vestibule training
walk-ins

For Discussion

1. What form of protection does the Civil Rights Act provide employees?

2. In new retail operations, what type of study is undertaken before any hiring plan is put in place?

3. Why are internal recruitment sources so important to the running of a retail operation?

4. If a retail operation utilizes a system of internal sources in its recruitment plans, why is it necessary to also use external sources?

5. Why is promotion from within such an important consideration in retailing?

6. What is the difference between a blind and an open ad?

7. How do headhunters assist merchants in their pursuit of excellent candidates for their jobs?

8. In what way has the Internet served retailers in their quest for new employees?

9. Why do walk-ins often become the most productive employees?

10. How does industry networking help retailers procure some of their best workers?

11. Why are investigative agencies becoming so important in the hiring procedure?

12. How does the rail interview differ from the final interview?

13. What types of testing are most retailers using in their hiring practices?

14. Why does on-the-job training sometimes become problematical for retailers?

15. In what way can role-playing help to improve the abilities of the newly hired employee?

16. What is vestibule training?

17. Why are more merchants using online training for new employees instead of traditional methodologies?

18. Is it important for a retail operation to utilize a specified employee evaluation plan? Why?

19. Why do so many retailers offer commissions in addition to guaranteed salaries to their employees?

20. What has become the most important employee benefit in most retail operations?

Case Problem

Like most other fashion retailers, Calvert's, Inc. does more than 40 percent of the year's business during the Christmas selling period. Throughout the year, the company has well-trained sales associates who cater to the needs of its clientele. With an inventory steeped in upscale merchandise at very high price points, servicing the customer is of great importance.

Calvert's business—except for the Christmas rush, which begins the day after Thanksgiving and ends Christmas Eve—is unlike that of most traditional companies. The number of daily sales is not high, but the amount of each is significant. Companies such as Calvert's that stock such expensive merchandise have a small customer market from which to draw, but those who do patronize the company spend considerable sums.

To guarantee the best possible customer service, the HR department spends considerable time and effort in training its sales associates. Before anyone is sent to the selling floor, he or she receives a great deal of attention. Training includes extensive classroom lectures as well as role-playing, where new employees participate in simulated sales presentations. Coupling this training with high rates of commission has contributed to the company's ability to attract qualified employees.

The problem that Calvert's must deal with each year surfaces at Christmas time. During this period, the store is transformed into a different environment. Many more shoppers enter the store in search of Christmas gifts in addition to satisfying their own personal needs. To accommodate these large numbers, the store must recruit additional sales personnel. Those available are generally untrained and unfamiliar with the Calvert's customer service philosophy. With little time for traditional training, the company has not been able to staff the selling floor with competent people. With fewer and fewer people willing to work for such a brief period, Calvert's is finding it difficult to be selective. With such limitations, it has not been able to satisfactorily train the new employees to meet the needs of the company.

Questions

1. What training techniques might the company employ to deal with this group of sales associates?
2. Describe why such techniques are better for these circumstances than those traditionally used.

Exercises and Projects

1. Log on to the websites of five fashion-oriented retailers to learn about employment possibilities. Make a list of the available job titles, salaries (if provided), experience requirements, and instructions of how to apply for the position.

2. Prepare an application form that would meet the standards allowed by the government. These forms are available on search engine listings.

3. Write a list of 20 questions that might be asked during a job interview for a particular retail position. As a role-playing technique performed in front of the class, select a partner and pretend that he or she is applying for this position, using all 20 questions.

chapter eleven

MERCHANDISE DISTRIBUTION AND LOSS PREVENTION

After reading this chapter, you should be able to:

- Describe the methods used by retailers to handle their merchandise.

- Explain some of the current technology used in merchandise handling between retailers of all classifications and their suppliers.

- Differentiate between centralized and regional receiving installations.

- Discuss quantity and quality checking systems.

- Distinguish between marking and remarking merchandise procedures.

- Examine shoplifting problems and how it affects the retailer's bottom line.

- Detail the deterrents to shoplifting.

- Discuss the problem of internal theft and how it can be minimized.

Merchandise acquisition is one of the most important parts of the retailer's operation, so it is vital that it is received, handled, and secured in an efficient manner. Buyers select their products and arrange for them to be shipped to the brick-and-mortar operations, catalog companies, and Internet merchants.

Retailers must have systems in place to handle the incoming merchandise that include a variety of receiving and marking procedures. Receiving records must be established, equipment must efficiently handle and disperse the goods, quantities must be checked to make certain that they are in line with the amounts indicated on the purchase orders and invoices, quality assurance must be addressed, and merchandise must be marked to indicate prices, sizes, and any other pertinent information that will be needed for inventory tracking and future purchase planning.

Today's retailers have a significant edge over their predecessors because they have a wealth of technology that enables them to perform their merchandise handling responsibilities more quickly and efficiently. Such programs as **electronic data interchange (E.D.I.)**, quick response (Q.R.), and **vendor managed inventory (V.M.I.)**, have made the routines associated with inventory handling faster and more accurate than ever before.

Once the merchandise arrives at its retail destination, whether it is on the selling floor, a centralized or regional warehouse being readied for shipment to these selling floors, or in an off-site merchant's facility such as those utilized by catalog companies and e-tailers, it must be properly secured to reduce the losses due to **shoplifting** and employee theft. Combined, more than $13 billion worth of goods are stolen from retailers each year, so retailers face a significant task in safeguarding their inventories from those who work for them as well as from those who pose as shoppers. These two groups, coupled with vendors that cheat their retail customers, as well as theft by those that ship the merchandise to the retailers, account for significant losses that seriously affect the retailers' **bottom lines**.

Some of the facts surrounding these losses, in addition to monetary losses, include the following:

- 1 in 11 people in the United States are shoplifters.
- The stealing adds a great deal to a store's security expenses.
- Men and women shoplift equally.
- About 3 percent of shoplifters are professionals, many of whom steal to feed drug habits.

In an attempt to offset these staggering losses, merchants continuously focus on new **loss prevention** technology. The use of shoplifting deterrents, such as **video surveillance systems**, **electronic article surveillance systems (E.A.S.)**, careful applicant screening, and a host of other methodologies help to reduce the problem. There are still, however, a great deal of losses, leading to reduced profits. Few customers realize that they are actually paying for some of the losses caused by dishonest shoppers because retailers adjust their prices upward to regain the lost profits due to shoplifting and **internal theft**.

The proper handling of merchandise and its security is thus a prime responsibility of company management. While it is unlikely that the entire problem will disappear, attention to the latest innovations will more than likely help to reduce it.

MERCHANDISE DISTRIBUTION

Brick-and-mortar operations, regardless of size; catalogers; e-tailers, and home shopping outlets must all establish a **merchandise distribution** system that assures they will receive merchandise as stated on the invoice and that it will be delivered to their warehouses and selling floors in a timely manner.

Retailers must determine the way their incoming merchandise is handled, the manner in which the goods are scrutinized, how they are marked, and the ways in which they are moved to their final destinations before they can sell a single item.

By investing enormous sums in new technology, merchants are not only guaranteeing their merchandise's safe arrival at their destination points—the selling floors of brick-and-mortar operations and the warehouses of the off-site operations—but they are also benefiting from the potential for greater company profits.

In-House Receiving

The methodology and techniques used for merchandise distribution from the vendors to the retailer's premises generally depends upon the size of the retailer. Small operations with few outlets, such as boutiques and independently owned specialty stores, generally have new orders sent directly to the units; this is called **in-house receiving**. Some major retailers also subscribe to this arrangement. They believe that by using such a receiving system, the merchandise gets to the selling floor faster than it does if it made an intermediary stop at a centralized warehouse. By using a barcode system that is affixed to the outside of the delivered cartons, the units in the chain are able to determine the contents and learn if it is the same as what was listed on the purchase orders.

Centralized Receiving

Many of the larger department stores and specialty organizations, catalog operations, e-tailing ventures, and home shopping outlets receive their goods at a centralized location in which all of the products go through a receiving procedure before they are sent to their final destinations. Oftentimes, in the cases of the off-site retail operations, the receiving department is within the headquarters of the company, and the goods remain there until they are ordered by the customers.

There are several reasons why **centralized receiving** is the choice of the vast majority of large retail organizations. These include the following:

- *More space for merchandise on the selling floor.* In brick-and-mortar operations specifically, space has become so prohibitively expensive that the more that can be used for selling, the more likely the store will have larger profits. While each of the units in a large organization must still set room aside for receiving incoming goods, fewer units are involved in marking the merchandise. Space in warehouse facilities used in the receiving process is also costly, but it is considerably less expensive than store-leasing costs.

- *Better control of goods.* Retailers using centralized locations are more likely to spend on the latest technology to track their incoming merchandise. By using a variety of programs such as E.D.I. and V.M.I., the goods are carefully tracked and recorded before they make their way to the selling arenas. In contrast with store managers, who are often in charge of single-store receiving and have other duties and responsibilities to perform, those in charge of centralized receiving facilities only have to concentrate on this one role. The end result is usually a more efficient way in which to carefully handle the goods from the receiving platform to their final destinations.

- *Cost reduction.* The monies needed to invest in the latest receiving technology is extremely high so it is often impossible to install it in each of the chain store organization's numerous outlets. By using the centralized approach, large retailers can put in place the latest and most efficient systems that will not only better serve the needs of the entire organization but also do it more economically.

Regional Receiving

When a brick-and-mortar operation has a large number of units dispersed throughout a range of geographical locations, most opt for **regional receiving** departments. Instead of having a centralized facility to handle the goods for every store in the chain, regional offices cover one region. The advantage of this system is that merchandise reaches the selling floors in less time than if it came from centralized points. A company with units throughout the United States, for example, that subscribes to this decentralized arrangement will more than likely get the goods to the stores in the different regions more quickly than if they were all shipped from a centralized location that was far away from many of the regions.

The receipt of goods in a timely manner is particularly important to the fashion retailer. With fashion cycles playing such a significant role in its merchandising endeavors, every day that is saved in shipping gives the retailer more time to sell the items.

Individual Store Receiving

In the case of individual proprietorships, where just one or a few units are involved in the receiving procedure, there is little choice but to have each unit process its own incoming merchandise.

Goods are usually delivered to the front door of the store, then opened, checked, tagged, and made ready for the selling floor directly within the selling space. In some stores, small back rooms are available to handle the incoming merchandise. The latter choice is a better one, since it does not interfere with the activities taking place on the selling floor.

Since the people responsible for unpacking, sorting, and making merchandise ready for inclusion onto the racks and counters are responsible for other chores, the cartons are often left unattended until they have time to attend to them.

Merchandise Distribution Technology

Unlike the retailers of the past, who manually handled the tasks associated with the receiving and marking of merchandise from vendors, today's merchants have the benefit of technological advances to perform these steps. In fact, the vast majority of major retailers utilize technology to interface with their suppliers. Most important among the retailer–vendor innovations are electronic data interchange (E.D.I.), and vendor managed inventory (V.M.I.).

E.D.I. is a computer-to-computer exchange of data organized in a format specified by retailers and vendors. There isn't any human involvement at either end of the transactions. Inherent in the benefits of the system are better inventory management, reduced expenses, improved accuracy, better business relationships, increased sales, and a minimization of paperwork.

Retailers of all classifications use the E.D.I. system. It is especially attractive to fashion retailers, because the increased speed of transactions can extend the life of the product on the selling floor, in catalogs, in e-tail outlets, and in home shopping operations. Where time is of the essence in retail transactions, no other system can place a company in a better market position. Thus, the tasks of placing purchase orders, preparing invoices, and shipping are performed at record speed, saving time and money for the merchant.

V.M.I. involves the use of scanners at the retail operations, by which suppliers are able to gather information about the sale of their products and replenish inventories with a time lag. It places the onus on the vendors to make certain that their retail customers' inventories are stocked as needed.

These technologies, collectively known as **quick response inventory systems (Q.R.)**, are the keys to better merchandise management controls, resulting in more profitable situations for their users.

Nonprofit Supply Chain Involvement

Several nonprofit groups have been organized to improve the retail industry's merchandise supply chain: the Collaborative Planning, Forecasting, and Replenishment Committee (CPFR), and the Voluntary Interindustry Commerce Standards Association (VICS). Each offer recommendations and guidelines for retailers and vendors to follow so that merchandise delivery will be most efficient.

Receiving Equipment

After the merchandise has been delivered to the receiving platform or loading dock and has been checked to make certain that the shipment includes all of the cartons or racks indicated on the receiving invoice, it is transferred to the marking area.

In most major retail operations, outside sources such as shipping companies or the vendors from whom the retailers purchase their goods mark the merchandise. The merchandise tags are prepared by the retailers or by the outside sources that use the information provided by the retailer. When manufacturers do the actual tagging, they often also place the garments on hangers, which saves time once the goods reach the retailer's premises.

Whether the merchandise has been tagged or not, discrepancies sometimes occur at this point. Vendors may make unintentional errors when preparing their shipping records that, if undetected, will result in the retailer paying for merchandise that was not received. A great deal of pilferage takes place during the shipping procedure, and unsuspecting merchants may fall victim to such crimes. In any case, retailers need to detect the discrepancies at this point to correct the flawed invoices.

Once the receiving process has been completed, the merchandise moves from the platform to places where closed cartons are opened, unmarked merchandise may be ticketed, and any other product handling procedures can be completed. The equipment that is used in the movement of the goods includes **packaged merchandise transporters**, and conveyors.

Packaged Merchandise Transporters

There are several types of packaged merchandise transporters that move merchandise through the receiving process. Some are open, in which the goods can be seen, and others are closed, for maximum security merchandise such as precious jewelry. They all move on swiveling casters that maneuver easily around the selling floor aisles and narrow lanes of distribution centers.

Conveyor Systems

Most larger retailers have installed **conveyor systems** that move incoming goods from one handling stage to another and ultimately take them to a place in the warehouse or on the selling floor. The systems that fashion merchants use are either roller conveyors that move cartons containing flat packed items or trolley conveyors that move merchandise on hangers. In central operations, once the goods have been processed and are ready for shipment to the brick-and-mortar operations, they are placed in the merchandise transporters and taken to their final destinations.

MERCHANDISE CHECKING PROCEDURES

The actual checking of the incoming merchandise is both quantitative and qualitative. Merchants must carefully verify that the number of items they are being charged for is the exact number inscribed on the packing slip or invoice. Quality is also an important part of the process since vendors sometimes substitute lesser-quality goods for the ones they featured in the samples used by the retailers to order by. It is commonplace for a manufacturer to substitute different fabrics or less-desirable trimmings.

Quantity Checking

When checking incoming merchandise it is important to do more than count the number of cartons, because there is the possibility that the contents will not match the invoice. Thus, there are different **quantity-checking** systems, such as the following:

- *Direct checks.* In this check, which is most commonly used by retailers, the checker uses the invoice or packing slip to verify amounts and compares the actual contents to the size, color, and price specifications entered on the purchase orders. Checkers physically count merchandise, and make any adjustments at this point. **Direct checking** is the fastest technique but it also has one distinct disadvantage: dishonest employees might verify the contents without actually making the physical count. Once checkers have signed off the invoice, the company has no recourse if shortages are later discovered.
- *Blind checks.* This method is the opposite of the direct check. Merchandise checkers must prepare a list of the items that are in the packages without utilizing any invoices that accompany the packages. With the **blind check method**, the checker must account for each item. While the system is somewhat slower than the direct check, it eliminates the potential for cheating.
- *Semiblind checks.* The **semiblind check method** combines the best features of the other two. Checkers are provided with a list of the items without the quantities. Thus, they must count the items to verify the actual contents against those indicated on the invoice.

Quality Checking

More retailers are using **quality checking** controllers to inspect incoming goods and to make certain that they are exactly what has been ordered. Too often, vendors use **substitution shipping**; instead of shipping exactly what has been ordered, they substitute other products, colors, and sizes. Sometimes manufacturers run out of particular products and ship replacements in the hope that their inclusion will go undiscovered. Vendors might include items of different colors because the color on the purchase order was out of stock. Different sizes are substituted because those selected by the buyer are unavailable.

In small fashion-retailing operations, buyers are generally present to evaluate the quality of the incoming merchandise, and they do the examination. No one knows better than the buyer what the actual samples looked like at the time of the purchase or is more capable of comparing the items received against what was ordered. If the new goods aren't carefully scrutinized, retailers could end up with merchandise that is less than desirable, and therefore is difficult to sell. Figure 11.1 shows employees checking quality of merchandise.

After the goods have been inspected and any discrepancies are noted, they are sent to the marking area, unless they have been marked by an outside source.

figure 11.1
A small store buyer checking the quality of the goods with a sales associate. Oftentimes, when vendors are unable to fulfill the same quality merchandise as ordered, they will ship something of a lesser quality that will not suit the retailer's needs.

MARKING MERCHANDISE

Individual items must be marked for a number of reasons, such as the following:

- Some states require that all merchandise be individually marked with tags that feature the price to eliminate the possibility of charging different prices for different customers.
- Merchandise tags feature such pertinent information as price and size that are particularly beneficial to retailers that rely upon customers to make their own choices with the assistance of sales associates.
- Shoppers may quickly make the decision if the price is within their price range.
- It enables the merchant to evaluate the sales of the different items for inventory and reordering purposes.
- Inventory is automatically changed after each sale.

Marking Procedures

Fashion retailers use different systems to mark their merchandise, ranging from hand tagging, which is used in small stores such as boutiques, to the automated systems used in chain store organizations, department stores, catalog companies, e-tailers, and home shopping organizations.

Computer-generated tags have **bar codes** which can encode data that can be optically read and produce machine-readable symbols that can be converted to computer-compatible digital data.

Remarking Merchandise

In today's competitive fashion retail environment, there are a number of reasons that merchants must reduce prices for in-stock merchandise. These include the following:

- Styles are out of season.
- Only a few pieces in a particular style remain in the inventory.

- Buyers purchased merchandise that didn't sell as well as had been anticipated.
- Colors were selected that customers didn't like.
- Only a few sizes remain of certain styles.

To dispose of this unwanted merchandise and make room for new items, merchants take markdowns and indicate them on the price tags by **handmarking** the new price directly on the tag in a different color from the original price or using handheld machines to enter the new price.

LOSS PREVENTION

Retailers all over the globe are victim to losses attributed to shoplifting, internal theft, vendor theft, and Internet fraud. No matter how carefully they try to protect their inventories, the **shrinkage** numbers continue to climb. Retailers are combining older systems with new technology to attempt to use loss prevention measures to reduce their losses.

Because they are so vulnerable to theft, fashion merchants implement measures ranging from stationing uniformed guards at store entrances to installing vast security measures that include electronic article surveillance systems (E.A.S.). It is not only shoplifters but company employees who regularly help themselves to goods without paying for them. Whether they are on the selling floor or working somewhere in the supply chain such as warehouses, employees are often in positions to take merchandise. Vendors, to a lesser degree, are also culprits in the shortage scheme, accounting for about 1 percent of the shortages. The increased use of the Internet as a selling tool has also resulted in increased fraud that costs retailers.

The following sections address each of these groups in terms of the losses they account for and the ways in which the retail industry is acting to control their theft. In *Happening Now*, the shoplifting and internal theft scene are examined.

Shoplifting

Simply stated, shoplifters are people who enter brick-and-mortar establishments for the purpose of stealing merchandise rather than paying for it. While many think it is easy to recognize potential shoplifters, this is far from the truth. People from all walks of life have been apprehended, including members of the clergy, those in the upper socioeconomic groups, celebrities such as movie stars, drug addicts, and those with mental problems. Their dress and demeanor are generally indistinguishable from that of the legitimate shopper, making them hard to detect. Figure 11.2 shows a shoplifter in action.

The average shoplifting loss in the United States in 2012 was $207.18 per incident, the latest figure available, a significant increase over the previous year's average. European retailers are also plagued by shoplifting; overall, the losses were 88.8 billion euros with Spain, France, and the Netherlands leading the way.

SHOPLIFTING AND INTERNAL THEFT: A RETAILING NIGHTMARE

The most recent news from the latest Annual Retail Theft Survey has revealed a problem that continues to escalate all over the globe. While the statistics for shoplifting are frightening, the statistics for internal theft are even more staggering. The number of apprehensions of dishonest employees continues to escalate each year. According to the aforementioned survey, employees steal at a rate of 5.5 percent more than shoplifters. While the theft of small items such as pens, paper clips, etc. are considered internal theft, most of the stealing is attributed to more costly items. Those apprehended for the thievery of more significant items offer a variety of reasons for their actions such as being underpaid or being denied a promotion they think they earned. Other reasons include gambling debts, drug habits, and medical expenses.

At this point in time, internal theft is being addressed with the use of preemployment practices such as intensive background checks, honesty testing, reference checks, more drug testing, and careful use of the interview process.

In the case of shoplifting, the problem is not just the ordinary consumer who looks suspicious, but celebrities, sports figures, and church leaders who more easily mingle with employees are often the culprits.

Companies collectively cite these specific reasons why employee theft continues to upwardly spiral:

- economic conditions, while showing improvement, have yet to get significantly better
- poor detection strategies
- a shortage of on-the-floor supervision
- an increase in part-time help
- an increase in dishonest people

One of the ways in which loss prevention professionals suggest that retailers curtail the problem with the assistance of longtime employees is through the implementation of rewards programs such as honoring them at recognition events.

More and more companies today are increasing their efforts to minimize shoplifting and internal theft, but the inaction of the others continues to plague the industry as a whole.

figure 11.2
A customer in the act of shoplifting. This is one of the major reasons for retailers' shrinkage problem.

Deterrents and Controls

Retailers employ a wealth of deterrents and controls to address the problems of shoplifting. These include the following:

Electronic Article Surveillance Systems (E.A.S.)

With shoplifting in America accounting for almost half of their retail shrinkage, the vast majority of large retail enterprises utilize one of the many E.A.S. systems. Any one of the systems automatically protects the merchandise from theft. Commonly referred to as **tag-and-alarm systems**, industry experts say that they are the most effective antishoplifting tools available today. E.A.S. identifies merchandise as it passes through a gated area at the store's entrance. Each piece of merchandise is tagged with a hard reusable tag or a paper tag that is not used again. Sales associates deactivate the item by swiping it over a pad or scanning device, or by removing it from the item. If a tagged item has not been deactivated or removed and a customer attempts to take the item from these portals, an alarm sounds, alerting store personnel.

The most widely used electronic article surveillance systems are the **radio frequency (R.F.) systems**. In these systems, a label that is basically a miniature disposable electronic unit and antenna is attached to a product that responds to a specific frequency emitted by the transmitter antenna. The response from the label is then picked up by an adjacent receiver antenna in one of the gates at the store's exit. This processes the label response signal and will trigger an alarm when it matches specific criteria. When a package that meets this criteria moves through the gates, the alarm rings, indicating that there is an illegal removal of goods from the store's premises.

Electromagnetic (E.M.) Systems

Many retail chains throughout Europe use the **electromagnetic (E.M.) systems**. This technology uses magnetic, iron-containing strips with adhesive layers that are attached to the merchandise. Unlike the E.A.S. system, in which tags are removed once the customer pays for the merchandise, the strip is not removed but is deactivated by a scanner. An advantage of this system is that the strip can be reactivated if the merchandise is returned.

Acousto-Magnetic System

This is one of the latest entries in antishoplifting systems. Stores that use R.F. systems require the labeled transmitters in the items and the receivers in the gates to be about 8 feet apart. Retailers with wide entrances prefer the **acousto-magnetic system**. The tags and labels used in this system are detected in wide areas, so this doesn't require stores to have narrow-gated entrances. The acousto-magnetic system also responds extremely well with metal shopping carts, unlike other systems that don't work with metal objects.

Video Surveillance Systems (C.C.T.V.)

Closed circuit television systems enable security personnel to monitor store activity as it is taking place. In the newest, more sophisticated systems, retailers are able to monitor several stores in their organization, as well as distribution centers, from a single location. These remote video surveillance systems allow retailers to transmit full-frame image streams over high-speed phone lines to a variety of locations and to electronically store digital video images for review or evidence. Although the video cameras were once easily visible, today's offerings are harder to spot. They can be mounted in smoke detectors, sprinkler heads, thermostats, and clocks, making them virtually invisible to the shoplifter who might attempt to stay out of their view. Figure 11.3 shows a security guard watching TV screens for shoplifters.

MERCHANDISE ANCHORING

Locking things up is one way to secure expensive merchandise. High-ticket items such as leather apparel are secured by means of cables and wire products. These locking devices will more than likely prevent shoplifting, but they will also make it difficult for customers to try on the garments. Because clerks must open the locks, **merchandise anchoring** is a time-consuming process that may discourage shoppers in a hurry from availing themselves of the merchandise.

MAGNIFYING MIRRORS

Many smaller merchants without the budgets necessary to install sophisticated surveillance systems turn to **magnifying mirrors** to alert them to would-be shoplifters. By strategically placing these mirrors, clerks can spot the shoplifters in action. Although the system might not enable store personnel to see all of the shoplifting attempts, their existence sometimes deters shoppers from attempting to steal.

TRY-ON ROOM CONTROL

A number of different controls are put in place to deter shoplifting in the fitting rooms. One method posts an employee at the try-on room entrances to count the items and give shoppers a number to coincide with the number of items they have taken into the room. When shoppers exit, the employee counts the number of items they have to make certain that they have the same number and have not concealed any on their bodies. Of course, experienced shoplifters often exchange one of the items they brought

figure 11.3
A security guard watching a multitude of screens looking for shoplifters. This is a very successful way to see an overall picture of the selling floor and fitting rooms where most of the shoplifting takes place.

to the fitting room with one that they brought to the store. Another system requires that each try-on room be locked and not opened until the clerk counts the number of items the shopper has taken inside. Again, it is difficult to prevent the shoplifter from exchanging a new item for one worn into the room.

EMPLOYEE PROGRAMS

There are numerous programs that motivate the retailer's staff to assist in the reduction of shoplifting. These include incentive awards that reward employees with special merchandise discounts if they alert security officers of potential crimes, workshops that alert sales associates and floor managers of the magnitude of the problem and their roles in assisting the security staff in apprehending the perpetrators, and bulletin board announcements of congratulatory notes to employees who have assisted in foiling shoplifter attempts.

Internal Theft

The problem of employees stealing from their companies is often greater than that of shoplifting. Internal theft is running rampant in the United States and abroad. Although security devices have deterred shoppers from removing merchandise from the store illegally, the same devices are less successful in stopping those employed by the company for a variety of reasons including employee awareness of the systems in place, employee relationships with security guards, unsupervised spaces such as workrooms where employees are often left alone, and the company's lax prosecution of offenders. Figure 11.4 depicts a store employee handcuffed for internal theft charges.

There are many ways employees steal from their companies. Not only do they take merchandise from the store but they also engage in ticket-switching, ringing up sales at lower prices for their acquaintances, not charging for all the items in a purchase, and extending greater discounts than allowed.

Internal theft is not limited to brick-and-mortar facilities. Catalog retailers are facing problems with the loss of merchandise in their warehouses, in which significant

figure 11.4
An employee accused of theft. Internal theft is rivaling shoplifting in terms of stealing.

amounts of goods are stocked and made ready to be shipped to online, catalog, and telephone order customers. These premises are often not as carefully scrutinized as are the store operations, because shoppers do not have access to them. Unless retailers establish stringent rules and precautionary measures, merchandise losses can run extremely high.

Each of these unethical practices affects the retailer's bottom line. While total elimination of internal theft is unlikely, there are numerous ways in which it can be curtailed, as discussed in the following sections.

Deterrents

Merchants use a variety of tools, such as the screening of applicants' reference checks, drug testing, rewards programs, and the timely prosecution of offenders.

SCREENING OF APPLICANTS

The best time to weed out potential risks is when a candidate completes an application for employment. Whether the person completed the form in a company's human resources department, at an in-store computerized kiosk, or online, it is essential that every word be carefully scrutinized to alert the employment manager of possible areas of concern. Especially at peak selling periods such as the Christmas holiday seasons, when a host of part-time sales associates are brought on board for short periods of time, management is often more concerned with getting the necessary number of bodies on the selling floor than with examining the information on the form. Details such as a large number of positions held in a short time frame or the listing of companies that are no longer in business should serve as red flags for human resources personnel.

Many retailers are using the services of outside agencies to assist them with applicant screening. Companies such as www.findoutthetruth.com run background checks for as little $19.95 for local searches to $49.95 for nationwide investigations. In 24 hours or less, the merchant is able to determine whether or not job applicants are worthy of further consideration.

Many potential job candidates, especially those seeking middle-management to upper-management positions, offer resumes of their educational and professional backgrounds. These too must be diligently checked to eliminate those people without the proper credentials from further consideration. This screening process is essential, since further evaluation of the candidates is time consuming and costly.

CHECKING REFERENCES

The value of references depends upon the candidate's previous employers' willingness to cooperate. Some only verify employment histories in terms of dates employed. Other companies might be willing to offer a more complete evaluation of the former employee's work ethic and performance. Where references provide little information, especially about honesty, some retailers use outside research firms, such as USSearch.com. For a nominal fee, the companies provide a background check with information that might be helpful in early evaluation.

TESTING FOR DRUGS

More merchants are requiring the use of drug tests for new candidates. In fact, some randomly test people already in their employ to determine drug use. The reason for the increased attention to drug screening is that there seems to be a direct correlation between drug abusers and internal theft; for example, employees who need to have extra money to feed their habits often steal from their company. Search engines such as www.yahoo.com or www.google.com can provide names of a host of drug-testing agencies. Figure 11.5 is an example of a drug test.

PSYCHOLOGICAL TESTING

The use of psychological and honesty tests are increasingly part of the screening process. By administering a variety of tests, either in-house or at outside agencies, employers, regardless of size, can get yet another look at candidates before offering them positions. Some of the better-known tests are Wonderlic and Stanford–Binet.

MERCHANDISE CONTROL

Small items, such as sunglasses, hosiery, or scarves are easy to conceal, especially in large handbags that managers and sales associates may carry with them to the selling floor. To prevent the theft of such items, many retailers require employees to store personal handbags in lockers, and to take only small see-through plastic purses on the selling floor. In this way, it is difficult to conceal stolen goods.

"SHOPPING" THE SALES ASSOCIATES

Many retail establishments have traditionally used **mystery shoppers** to test sales associate honesty. Posing as customers, they pretend to be making a purchase, and carefully watch the transaction to see if it is done in an honest manner. They note if the clerk rings up the wrong amount or fails to put the cash in the register, and immediately report it to management. Often, if management suspects that particular employees are involved in illegal practices, the shoppers are told to shop in their department and carefully scrutinize their actions.

figure 11.5
A lab assistant testing for drugs by drawing blood. This test has become increasingly more important to curtail employee theft. In some companies urine tests are the norm.

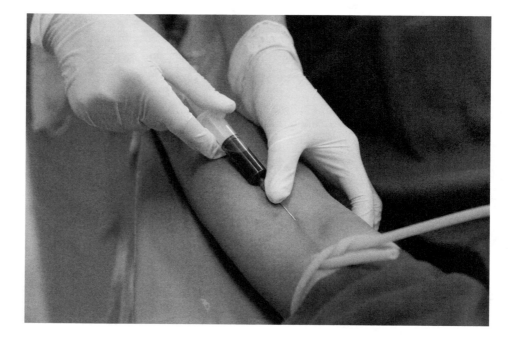

RECOGNITION PROGRAMS

To encourage employees to report those engaged in internal theft, some companies have instituted programs that reward the honest employees with monetary rewards or extra merchandise discounts. Of course, employees must be assured that their assistance will remain anonymous; otherwise, they are unlikely to participate.

OFFENDER PROSECUTION

The key to the success of apprehending those engaged in internal theft is quick prosecution. Immediate termination and repayment of cash or items stolen are necessary components of any deterrent system. Companies that have the reputation of looking the other way or taking a lax position on these criminal actions will send a weak message to employees, and internal theft will more than likely continue.

Internet Theft

Internet business for retail operations continues to increase every year. While this has proven to be an excellent outlet for selling fashion merchandise as well as other products, its success doesn't come without problems, particularly the losses due to the fraudulent activities of many Internet shoppers using stolen credit card numbers. So severe is the **Internet theft** problem that industry professionals estimate the losses to be greater than those of shoplifting and internal theft combined. Because retailers are responsible for their own losses, they are addressing the problem, as are the credit card companies that approve the sales. Customers whose numbers were stolen are protected from Internet fraud because any disputes usually result in chargebacks to the merchants. Not only does this create monetary losses for the retailer, but it can compromise the customer's faith in the company.

Forms of Fraud

Research studies from organizations such as APACS (Association for Payment Clearing Services) reveal that those who steal credit cards or their numbers are most often responsible for theft of merchandise on the Internet. The card's details may be taken from the following sources:

- Discarded cards or lost receipts.
- Card numbers that aren't carefully concealed by their owners and are written down for later use.
- Online programs that generate account numbers.

Many retailers are taking out insurance policies to cover their losses, although the expense of such policies is considerable and affects their bottom lines.

Fraud Prevention

A host of companies offers numerous ways in which merchants may eliminate Internet theft or at least reduce it. Advice for merchants includes the following:

- Be wary of purchasers who do not complete forms or provide full contact details, or who offer Post Office box or drop box addresses.
- Beware of orders from remote addresses.

- Be wary of orders that are shipped outside of your own country.
- Be wary of orders that are outside the norm such as those that exceed the value of your average orders.
- Beware of purchases made in the middle of the night.

Vendor Theft

The manufacturers and wholesalers that fashion retailers purchase goods from are occasionally the sources for merchandise and monetary losses. Some of the errors are accidental, but others are deliberate attempts to defraud their accounts.

Improper billing, while usually an occasional occurrence, does take place. Invoices may not be carefully tallied or may be deliberately misstated. Retailers should take the time to check the charges.

Similarly, merchandise shortages can be either deliberate or the result of improper order fulfillment. Those merchants that have systems in place to check quantities, as discussed earlier in this chapter, will not be the victims of such shortages. When checkers physically count the merchandise, they will discover whether or not the invoice truly reflects the number of pieces in the package. If there are discrepancies, the merchant must immediately notify the vendor of the problem.

In-Transit Theft

Once the shipment leaves the vendor's premises and the invoices have been accurately prepared to reflect the contents, there is no guarantee that the entire order will reach the retailer's destination. The items might be shipped on racks that leave them open for **in-transit theft**. In the case of closed containers, the cartons may not be carefully sealed, leaving room for the nimblest of fingers to remove some of the items. In either situation, the shipment, if not adequately checked, will could result in losses for the retailer.

Chapter Highlights

1. With the use of such programs as E.D.I, R.F., and V.M.I., retailers can handle their merchandise distribution operations more quickly and efficiently.

2. The methodology and techniques used to move new merchandise from the vendor to the retailer's premises generally depends upon the size of the retailer.

3. A centralized receiving location is generally preferred by larger department stores, specialty organizations, catalog operations, e-tailing ventures, and home shopping outlets.

4. Some major chains that have units spread throughout the United States prefer to use regional receiving facilities so that the merchandise will be closer to the stores they serve.

5. The industry's supply chain has been vastly improved due to the efforts of several nonprofit groups such as CPFR and VICS.

6. Fashion merchandise is generally moved around the retailer's location by packaged merchandise transporters and conveyors.

7. Quantity checking is essential to ensure proper record keeping, and is accomplished through direct checks, blind checks, or semiblind checks.

8. When merchandise is properly marked, it will include such details as price, style number, color, merchandise classification, and size, and each detail is pertinent to accurate merchandise inventory record keeping.

9. Shrinkage numbers continue to climb in the United States, requiring retailers to install the latest systems that will help to alleviate the problems.

10. Shoplifting accounts for approximately $207.18 per incident, causing considerable adverse effects on the merchant's bottom line.

11. Control of shoplifting is accomplished through the use of electronic article surveillance systems, electromagnetic systems, acousto-magnetic systems, video surveillance systems, merchandise anchoring, magnifying mirrors, and try-on room control.

12. Internal theft is running rampant in the United States and abroad. To deter the losses, many employers carefully screen job candidates, check applicants' references, test for drugs, administer psychological exams, control employee access to merchandise, use mystery shopping services, and offer recognition programs for honest employees.

13. Internet theft is at a level that causes losses greater than shoplifting and internal theft combined.

14. Vendor theft can come from either improper billing or shortages in shipped merchandise.

15. After the goods leave the vendor's facility, theft is often attributed to the shipping industry.

Terms of the Trade

acousto-magnetic systems	magnifying mirrors
bar codes	merchandise anchoring
blind check method	merchandise distribution
bottom line	mystery shoppers
centralized receiving	packaged merchandise transporters
computer-generated tags	quality checking
conveyor systems	quantity checking
direct checking	quick response inventory systems (Q.R.)
electromagnetic systems (E.M.)	radio frequency (R.F.) systems
electronic article surveillance systems (E.A.S.)	regional receiving
electronic data interchange (E.D.I.)	semiblind check method
hand marking	shoplifting
in-house receiving	shrinkage
internal theft	substitution shipping
Internet theft	tag-and-alarm systems
in-transit theft	vendor managed inventory (V.M.I.)
loss prevention	video surveillance systems (C.C.T.V.)

For Discussion

1. Why is it necessary for fashion retailers to invest in the latest innovations for merchandise distribution?

2. Why do some chains opt for in-house receiving at individual units instead of using centralized receiving facilities?

3. What are the advantages to the major retailer in using centralized receiving facilities?

4. Instead of using the centralized receiving plan, why do some major chain store organizations prefer to use regional receiving centers?

5. What are the two major merchandise distribution technologies that are important to retailers and vendors?

6. Why have nonprofit groups been established for supply chains?

7. What common feature do all packaged merchandise transporters have that helps in the quick movement of goods from the receiving room to the selling floor?

8. In what way does the direct method of quantity checking differ from the blind method?

9. Does the practice of substitution shipping affect the retailer's merchandising plans? How?

10. Why are computerized tags so vital to the retailer's inventory procedures?

11. Is there a particular profile for shoplifters? If not, who are the culprits?

12. What is the common name used to describe electronic article surveillance systems?

13. In what way can a video surveillance system help a retailer with their loss prevention programs?

14. How do try-on room control systems work?

15. What is the best initial step to take in the reduction of internal theft?

16. How can merchants check the backgrounds of candidates for positions without doing the "legwork" themselves?

17. Why is drug testing so important as a means of preventing internal theft?

18. What are some of the forms of fraud that Internet companies face?

19. What are the two main areas of theft as they relate to vendors?

20. What is meant by the term "in-transit theft"?

Case Problem

When Claudette Fashions opened its first store 20 years ago, it was a small operation that employed three salespeople. The buying and other decision-making responsibilities were handled by the company's partners, Jackie Andrews and Carrie Michaels. As the shipments arrived at the store, the boxes were opened on the selling floor, where the merchandise was examined by either of the partners. They checked for quality and to make certain that the invoices reflected what was ordered and that the quantities were properly charged on the invoices. The sales associates would tag the merchandise according to the partners' orders and prepare it for inclusion in the inventory. The system for handling incoming merchandise was simple and satisfactory for the store's needs.

Every few years, the company reinvested its profits and opened additional units. Today, it operates six stores that are all within a 50-mile radius. Each store receives merchandise directly from the vendors, and handling procedures are dealt with by the individual stores. At the present time, Claudette Fashions is considering an expansion that would bring its store total to ten and expand its trading area to a radius of 120 miles. Along with the plans for expansion has come a need to examine its past practices, particularly merchandise handling and distribution. Both partners agree that individual shipments to each unit are inappropriate, now that the company has expanded. In fact, discussions with vendors have indicated that a centralized approach to receiving would significantly reduce shipping expenses. With all of the merchandise delivered to a central warehouse, merchandise handling costs could be minimized.

Although Jackie and Carrie are ready to acquire a distribution center for merchandise receiving, checking, and marking, they have not yet been convinced that the new arrangement would be as good as the one they have used in the past. Their concerns involve the accuracy of the shipments received in terms of quantity and quality checking and the costs involved in the operation of the new facility.

Questions

1. Will the new facility reduce or increase the overall personnel expenses attributed to merchandise handling? Why?
2. Which system of quantity checking will be best to guarantee proper attention to the shipments? Why?
3. How can quality checking be successfully achieved if the buyers are not in attendance at the warehouse?

Exercises and Projects

1. Choose a company that specializes in receiving equipment for fashion retailers and request information and brochures on its computerized merchandise distribution systems. Through the use of a search engine such as www.yahoo.com or www.google.com, you can find a host of companies specializing in such equipment. Make contact in writing, by telephone, or through the email addresses that the companies' websites generally offer. You can also read such trade publications as *Chain Store Age*, *Stores*, and *VMSD* to get names, or check the yellow pages of your area's phone book. Prepare an oral report describing the systems available and how they are used by fashion retailers. Include brochures and photographs to provide the class with a better understanding of the equipment.

2. Visit a major fashion retailer to investigate some of the techniques and methods it employs to deter and control shoplifting. Prepare a chart and use it in an oral presentation before the class to show the different shoplifting deterrents. Use five different departments in the store.

fig 1.1

fig 1.2

fig 1.4

fig 1.5

fig 1.3

fig 2.1

fig 2.2

fig 2.4

fig 2.3

fig 4.1

fig 2.5

fig 4.2

fig 4.3

fig 4.4

fig 4.5

fig 5.1

fig 5.2

fig 5.4

fig 5.5

fig 6.1

fig 6.2

fig 6.3

fig 6.4

fig 6.5

fig 7.2

fig 7.1

fig 7.3

fig 7.4

fig 7.5

fig 8.1

fig 8.2

fig 8.3

fig 8.4

fig 8.5

fig 9.3

fig 9.1

fig 9.2

fig 9.4

fig 9.5

fig 10.1

fig 10.2

fig 10.4

fig 10.5

fig 11.1

fig 11.2

fig 11.3

fig 11.4

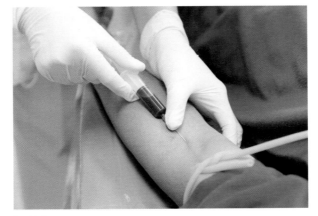

fig 11.5

fig 12.1

fig 12.2

fig 12.3

fig 12.5

fig 12.4

fig 13.1

fig 13.2

fig 13.3

fig 13.5

fig 13.4

fig 14.1

fig 14.4

fig 14.2

fig 14.3

fig 14.5

fig 15.1

fig 15.2

fig 15.3

fig 15.4

fig 15.5

fig 16.1

fig 16.3

fig 16.2

fig 16.5

fig 16.4

fig 17.1

fig 17.3

fig 17.2

fig 17.4

fig 17.5

fig 18.1

fig 18.2

fig 18.3

fig 18.4

fig 18.5

chapter twelve

PLANNING AND EXECUTING THE PURCHASE

After reading this chapter, you should be able to:

- Summarize the duties and responsibilities of fashion buyers.

- Evaluate the methodology used in the planning of each season's purchases.

- Detail several of the external support systems that are used by fashion buyers to help them with their purchase plans.

- Describe how model stocks are planned.

- Differentiate between the qualitative and quantitative considerations for purchasing.

- Assess how buyers select their merchandise resources.

- Explain the concept of open-to-buy, and how it affects purchases.

The merchandise that has been chosen for inclusion in the company's inventory is, of course, the basis of any retail operation. Those responsible for the task are generally the company's in-house buyers, or to a lesser extent, **resident buyers** who act as purchasing agents for retail operations. In any case, these people face the challenge of providing merchandise that will appeal to their clienteles. Whether the company is a brick-and-mortar operation, a catalog company, an Internet organization, or a multi-channel business that uses a variety of means of selling to the consumer, the buying responsibilities are the same.

Purchasing any product classification requires a wealth of knowledge on the buyer's part, but no classification provides the challenges of fashion merchandise. Electronics and appliances, for example, are inherently staple items that have staying power. They do not go in and out of favor in short periods and generally remain constants in their company's inventories. There are changes in design, but the volatility associated with fashion merchandise is absent. Those responsible for purchasing apparel, shoes, handbags, and the like are constantly aware that changes will take place every season and sometimes within seasons in areas such as colors, silhouette preferences, and fabric choices. Even with considerable purchase planning for each season, a buyer's best-laid plans often go awry. A wrong color selection could result in markdowns that will impact on the company's profits. With little room for error, the fashion buyer's position in a company is extremely vulnerable. Those making more than the allowable number of purchasing errors often find themselves in search of new careers. However, the most successful of the group generally move into positions of greater authority such as divisional merchandise managers; the most productive might even find themselves in the highest merchandising slot, general merchandise manager.

Buyers either work directly for retail operations or are outside consultants who work for market specialists such as resident buying offices. The former's duties and responsibilities are significantly greater than the latter's because they are the ultimate decision makers for their companies. Resident buyers, while sometimes asked to make purchases, generally work in an advisory capacity, most often assisting **retail buyers** with product selection. This chapter's material focuses on retail buyers and how they plan the purchase. Chapter 13, "Purchasing in the Global Marketplace," will explore the resident buying office's assistance when the retail buyer visits the wholesale market.

FASHION BUYERS' TYPICAL DUTIES AND RESPONSIBILITIES

The realm of tasks required of fashion buyers primarily depends first upon the size of the company and then upon the retail classification in which it falls. In small stores, for example, the buyers do everything from purchasing the merchandise, to selling to customers. Often the owner fulfills the buying responsibility as well as a host of other management duties. In the larger companies, buyers are mainly responsible for purchasing; they also interact with other management personnel such as advertising managers and department managers.

The other major consideration is the company's retail classification. Brick-and-mortar operations tend to expect the buyer to have some in-store participation such as making store visits to learn about the needs of their shoppers. Department store buyers generally have more in-store responsibility than do their specialty chain counterparts, who generally work from centralized headquarters and are often too far from the stores to makes visits viable. **Off-site ventures** such as catalog companies and Internet organizations use their buyers exclusively to purchase merchandise. As most of the larger merchants now practice multi-channel retailing, the buyer's duties and responsibilities are not as clear-cut. Some of these companies have separate buyers for each of their channels, while others make the buyer responsible for in-store and off-site purchasing. Each company proceeds in a manner that it believes is best suited toward the success of its operation.

Some of the typical duties and responsibilities of buyers are discussed in the following sections. A report by the U.S. Bureau of Labor Statistics summarizes the outlook for buying professionals as projected up until 2022. In *Happening Now* the trends are discussed for today's buyer and those in the industry until 2022.

Purchasing

Without question, this is the most important role performed by all buyers. Those in the fashion industry are concerned with choosing the best possible resources from which to purchase; previewing collections and selecting those items that seem to have the potential for widespread acceptance; determining assortments that will fit the needs of the company's **model stock**; working out arrangements that include discounts, promotional allowances, and delivery dates; and timing the purchases so that they will be ready to sell when customers want them most.

Pricing

To bring a profit to the company, buyers frequently determine at what prices the goods should be marked. Some retail operations subscribe to uniform **markups**. That is, each item carries the identical markup as the others. For example, **keystone markup**, which involves doubling the cost to arrive at the selling or retail price, is the choice of many retailers. In this case, the buyer need not be concerned with pricing. In most retail

TRENDS FOR TODAY'S AND FUTURE BUYERS IN THE FASHION INDUSTRY

Professional buyers, as researched by the U.S. Bureau of Labor Statistics, face a rather gloomy outlook with projected figures going as far out as 2022. For one, the job growth for the years up to 2022 is only 4 percent, much lower than the average. The median wage for retail buyers is $51,147, much lower than the average for all occupations. According to the Bureau's statistical report, similar occupations have greater median pay. For example, advertising, promotions, and marketing managers earn $115,750, more than double that of buyers; and sales reps average $57,870.

To achieve the buyer status in retail operations, the time it takes is approximately 5 years. Once individuals achieve this level the job at hand entails a wealth of duties and responsibilities. Their tasks today typically include evaluating suppliers in terms of their prices, merchandise quality, and speed of merchandise delivery. Extensive travel is commonplace to both domestic markets and global arenas so that they can learn about industry trends and make supplier contacts. Contract negotiation and ultimate agreements with suppliers are important to the profitability of the company. Typical duties include the maintenance of records such as past sales, product performance, on-time delivery to meet the demands of the customers, and inventory analysis.

In 2013, buyers held about 504,600 jobs, with those in the retail trade accounting for 8 percent, a low point when compared to buyers for manufacturers, wholesalers, government agencies, and management companies. In order to achieve the retail buyer position, a minimum of a bachelor's degree is necessary, at least 1 year of on-the-job training as an assistant buyer, and the personal qualities such as analytical skills, decision-making skills, math skills, and negotiating skills.

What is happening now with such a bleak outlook for the future, is that individuals who have the aforementioned qualities are seeking employment in other fields, leaving less-skilled workers for the buyer position.

operations, however, buyers determine the retail price based upon such factors as competition, inventory protection, the average time it takes for the item to sell (known as the turnover rate), probable perishability, and the buyer's judgment of the value of the individual items.

In-Store Visual Presentation

The buyer's responsibility for visual presentation is not the same as that of the professional in-house visual merchandising team, which trims windows and arranges the interior displays. The buyer's involvement in visual presentation is limited to the placement of the merchandise within the department. Where fashion products are placed and shown often affects their sales potential. For example, when a **hot number** is featured at the department's entrance, everyone entering the area will probably see it. A dress that has been touted by the fashion press, when properly accessorized by the buyer, has an even greater chance to be a big seller.

Those buyers who are far removed from the stores, such as those who work for chain store organizations and are centrally located at corporate headquarters, usually have little opportunity to directly place the merchandise in the departments. Some use emails to direct the store managers about how to place specific fashion products in the most visible locations.

Selecting Merchandise for Advertising and Promotions

No one is more knowledgeable than the buyers when it comes to the merchandise they purchase for the company. With significant promotional budgets, retailers of all classifications use advertising, special events such as fashion shows, and window displays to capture the attention of the consumer. Although buyers are not usually adept at the technical aspects of promotion—these are left to the advertising, visual merchandising, and promotional departments—they are expected to choose the products that will appear in these formats. Even when the promotions are for off-site ventures such as catalogs and websites, the buyer usually makes the merchandise selections.

Managing a Department

When buyers focus primarily on purchasing, they are rarely still responsible for department management. Some of the midsize retailers, however, still require that buyers play a role within the department they purchase for. In those organizations, buyers are involved in scheduling, handling customer complaints, and selling during peak periods. In the smaller retail operations, such as boutiques and specialty stores, the buyer is generally one of the company's principals and performs a host of management duties.

Interacting with Other Middle-Management Personnel

The goal of any retail operation is to turn a profit, and in attempting to maximize the effort, managers in every division interact with each other. Buyers in brick-and-mortar operations and off-site ventures regularly meet with advertising managers to make certain that their products are being featured in the best possible manner; visual merchandising managers to assure that their items are being displayed in the best light; and distribution managers to ensure the receipt of merchandise from the warehouse in a timely fashion.

PLANNING FASHION MERCHANDISE PURCHASES

With changes in fashion coming at a rapid pace, the buyers must always be prepared to assess their merchandise needs, using internal sources as well as those that are external to the company.

It has long been argued whether fashion merchandise selection is an art or a science. Proponents of each theory present viable reasons for their positions but, in the end, the result is usually a combination of both. On the one hand, the buyer who plans purchases based only upon last season's data is often missing the artistic element that enables some fashion buyers to select creative and unique collections for their companies. On the other hand, those who base their purchasing decision solely on whim often make impractical decisions that turn into costly mistakes.

Buyers usually begin with an analysis of the sales figures from a variety of reports, and combine them with the wealth of information culled from external sources.

Internal Preparation

By investigating past sales records, the buyer of any fashion retail operation is able to analyze the success or failure of each vendor, style, color, price point, size allocation, and other information. Figure 12.1 shows a buyer examining an in-house statistical report.

figure 12.1
A buyer is looking at past sales records to determine the next year's merchandise needs. This is one of the more important documents that help in the purchasing process.

After the merchandise has been distributed to the brick-and-mortar units, or warehouses, as in the case of catalog and online operations, it is unpacked, sorted, tagged, and entered into a merchandise record keeping system and the record is retained for use in a variety of merchandise reports. Although the information is available to the buyer anytime, it typically is presented in weekly, biweekly, or monthly presentations. By being able to go back a few months, or even a few years, buyers can make inventory adjustments based upon this data. Without question, past sales records are the backbone for any future planning.

Retailers use other sources to assist them with their merchandise acquisition decision-making. Many subscribe to various survey methods, as addressed in Chapter 5, "Retail Research Directions in Today's Retail Environment," to assist in the development of purchase plans. By determining customer fashion preferences through fashion counts, direct questioning via the personal interview or questionnaire technique, or through focus groups, the buyer is able to incorporate customer wants and needs into the buying plans.

Employee input is yet another internal source that seasoned buyers employ in the decision-making process. Staff personnel, such as fashion directors, are the experts in the field of fashion and can offer invaluable information regarding the state of the fashion market. The specialists, generally on the staffs of major fashion operations, often are at the vice-president level, which indicates their importance to the company in terms of fashion information. They often travel to the wholesale marketplaces in advance of the buyer's visit so they can obtain early information on what the trends are going to be. They also meet with members of the fashion editorial press to get their opinions on fashion innovation and design and gain significant information that they bring to the buyers.

Sales associates in brick-and-mortar units are also excellent sources of information to the buyer, because they are intimately acquainted with customer likes and dislikes. Buyers able to get to the selling floor themselves can also obtain this information.

Department managers at the brick-and-mortar units are also excellent sources of information. Many routinely meet with their staffs to elicit ideas about how to improve sales and satisfy customer needs and can share this information with the buyer.

External Assistance

Once the buyers have carefully studied past sales records and met with those inside the organization that could provide information regarding purchase planning, the next step is to make use of the many external sources. A large number of fashion merchants employ the services of a resident buying office or market consulting firm, **fashion forecaster**, or **reporting service**; join trade associations; subscribe to trade publications for information regarding the new season and its offerings, and consumer periodicals to learn about what fashions these magazines are presenting to the public.

Resident Buying Offices

The fashion industry's most important external source of market news are the **resident buying offices**, or market-consultants firms as many now call themselves. They are located within the wholesale markets, making it easy for buyers to meet with their company's representatives whenever they are visiting vendors.

The headquarters of these offices are located in New York City's **Garment Center**, and other major wholesale fashion markets in cities like Chicago and Los Angeles. Leading the pack is The Doneger Group, a company that specializes in apparel and accessories for the family and in home furnishings. Although the bulk of the business is related to the traditional resident buying office functions, its diversity has made it a one-stop place for clients throughout the world who rely upon research, analysis, and evaluation of every segment of the fashion industry's products. Figure 12.2 features Abbey Doneger, C.E.O. of The Doneger Group.

Other resident offices include Barzilay Goldberg Buying Group, Jane Dragonas, Dianne Cohan Associates, Equatoriale S.r.l., Magenta Enterprises, and Marshall Kline Buying Service. A complete list of these and other buying offices can be accessed at www.apparelsearch.com/buying_groups.htm.

Most resident buying offices primarily either assist with or directly purchase merchandise for their members. Some provide a host of other services that include the following.

figure 12.2
Abbey Doneger, C.E.O. of The Doneger Group, addressing retail clients at his resident buying office. This is the world's largest resident buying office with locations in many parts of the globe.

Locating New Resources

Buyers of every fashion retail classification, be they brick-and-mortar operations or off-site ventures, constantly look for new lines of merchandise. Since the vast majority of a retailer's in-house buyers are often faced with numerous duties and responsibilities, they don't often have the opportunity to visit the wholesale markets other than during **Market Week**, when the new season's offerings are shown for the first time. In their place, resident buyers, who have the advantage of being located in the wholesale markets, are able to visit new resources and evaluate their collections. The clout that these offices have makes them a constant target for vendors to contact, especially those that are new to the fashion industry. The recommendations that resident buyers make to retail buyers can help make the buying decision easier and potentially more successful.

Previewing Collections

When retail buyers come to market to shop for the new season, their time is often limited. Resident buyers save the retail representatives time and effort by previewing the collections and analyzing their merits in terms of their client's needs. Then, when buyers come to Market Week, they can pass over the lines that the resident team hasn't recommended and spend more time with the vendors that are recommended. Having several years of a close retailer–resident buying office affiliation makes it easier for the resident buyers to assess the retailer's purchasing preferences and needs.

Following Up Orders

Although retailers place purchase requisitions, merchandise frequently does not arrive according to the instructions on the order form. It is the responsibility of the resident buyer or assistant to visit the vendors and try to determine if a problem exists. Some resident buying offices employ follow-up interns for these chores.

Communicating with Retail Buyers

The more communication there is between the merchant and the resident buying team, the more likely it is that the retailer's inventories will be up-to-date and include the latest fashion offerings. Resident buyers contact their clients by calling, emailing, and mailing the latest hard-copy brochures and pamphlets that feature fashion information. Resident buying offices websites can post updates there for their clients to access as well.

Purchasing

Although it is the retail buyer who is most often responsible for the bulk of the company's merchandise acquisitions, some buyers pass the responsibility on to the resident buying office. Generally, however, the resident buyer's purchasing duty is limited to placing special orders, processing reorders, or buying new merchandise that the retailer has asked the office to scout. Resident buyers are asked to place reorders because they have clout with the vendors and are usually able to obtain the hot items that are in limited supply. When resident buyers place these orders, it is likelier that they will be accommodated sooner than when the retailer places them.

MARKET WEEK PREPARATION

Several weeks before the buyers come to town for Market Week, the resident buyers are at their busiest to make sure the retail buyer's trip is a success. They are busy previewing the new season's collections, obtaining sample merchandise to show the retail buyer, participating in the planning of in-house fashion shows, preparing written materials that include suggestions for the coming sales period, and taking care of all the other details that would be beneficial to their clients. In Chapter 13, "Purchasing in the Global Marketplace," the role of the resident buying office during the merchant's visit to the market is extensively examined.

ARRANGING ADJUSTMENTS

No matter how much attention the retail buyer pays to purchasing, there can be problems with the merchandise once it arrives at the retailer's outlet. For example, the fit might be imperfect, the construction could be shoddy, the fabrics might not be exactly as promised by the samples, or the customers just aren't buying it. Under such circumstances, the retailer sometimes tries to return the goods to the vendor. If these attempts are futile, the retailer often calls upon the buying office representative to act as mediator; the significant amount of business they refer to the vendors often gives them the connections to work out a deal. The resident buyer might arrange for the goods to be returned or to have the vendor offer **chargebacks**, discounts for slow-selling goods.

ANALYSIS OF MARKET CONDITIONS

Buying and suggesting purchases are not the only services resident buying offices provide. In fact, many of them have shed this traditional name and have substituted the title **market consultants**. These organizations are familiar with the state of the market because of their continuous involvement with designers, manufacturers, fashion forecasters, reporting services, trade publications, and trade associations. Through these contacts, they are able to assess the conditions of the market and apprise their member retailers of any changes or trends that might affect their businesses. This assistance allows the merchants to be better able to adjust their future purchasing plans.

PROMOTIONAL PLANNING

The success of the retail operation is essential for the resident buying office to be successful. Although many of the large retailers have in-house promotional divisions that develop special events, create unique advertising campaigns, and design exciting visual presentations, some of the smaller companies do not enjoy this advantage. Some of the full-service resident buying offices maintain promotional staffs to help these retailers prepare advertising layouts and develop promotional concepts, and present their fashion offerings in exciting ways.

POOLING ORDERS

Some vendors have minimum order requirements that the smaller retail operations cannot meet. Many of the resident offices arrange for these merchants to **pool orders** with other merchants so that they can purchase from these vendors.

INVENTORY MANAGEMENT

While all of the large and midsize retail operations have in-house staffs that develop computer programs for inventory management purposes, their smaller counterparts do not. With inventory management at every level of retailing essential to maximizing profits, some market consulting companies help these smaller retailers design the systems that could satisfy their needs and assist in training the people who will be using the programs.

Fashion Forecasters

Fashion forecasters scout markets all over the world before buyers are ready to begin the purchasing process. They visit textile mills, trimmings manufacturers, design studios, and trade associations so that they can determine **trend forecasting** in fabrication, color, and style, that will probably reach the marketplace. Some of these internationally based firms, such as Promostyl, are able to supply their clients with information pertinent to buying plans about a year in advance of the season. Promostyl offers **trend books** for textiles, women's wear, accessories, men's clothing, and children's fashions that contain a host of photographs and forecasting predictions, and the buyers find these publications valuable sources of merchandise information.

Reporting Services

Most major fashion retailers subscribe to reporting services that provide them with up-to-the-minute information on a weekly basis. Through the distribution of brochures and pamphlets in hard-copy format and online, that feature such information as the current hot sellers, which retailers are successfully selling what particular fashions, the names of the resources where the headliners in the fashion industry are available, what items are being reordered, and suggestions for inventory replenishment, fashion retailers are able to quickly adjust their inventories to reflect what is making news in fashion. One of the major fashion industry reporting services is the Retail Reporting Bureau, based in New York City. It offers a number of weekly informational reports to its clients that address such areas as the market's hottest items and includes editorial overviews. Seasonal supplements explore merchandising themes for the upcoming seasons, complete with style, fabric, and color stories, and the names of resources where the latest designs can be ordered.

Trade Publications

Each segment of the fashion industry has at least one trade periodical that explores a particular fashion merchandise classification. The leading publisher for the industry is Fairchild Publications, which produces a wealth of globally acclaimed papers such as *Footwear News*. Other trade publications for the fashion industry include the *California Apparel News*; World Textile publications, *Textile World*, and *Apparel Insiders*.

Trade Associations

Every industry has a trade association that provides its membership with vital information necessary to properly conduct its business. Retailing is no exception. In addition to many small trade organizations, many of which are regional in nature, the National Retail Federation (NRF) is an association with members throughout the world. It conducts its major meeting every January in New York City, and merchants congregate from every part of the world to learn about everything that is current in the industry. In addition, NRF sponsors a wealth of specialty regional shows in the United States and abroad. Figure 12.3 features attendees at the NRF trade show.

By belonging to these groups, buyers, merchandisers, and others in the retailing business learn about the problems facing their industry counterparts, trends, changes in consumer shopping patterns, and so forth.

Consumer Periodicals

There are numerous consumer publications that provide buyers with insights into the world of fashion. Most notable are *Elle*, *Vogue*, *Harper's Bazaar*, *Esquire*, and *Seventeen*. Even newspapers, such as *The New York Times*, have columns that address trends in the fashion world. By reading these papers and magazines, buyers become aware of the fashion information their potential customers read. Since many consumers are motivated to buy what their favorite publication's editorial staffs are touting, buyers need to keep this information in mind when they are planning their new purchases. Figure 12.4 features an *Elle* magazine event.

Miscellaneous Sources

Other external sources that are valuable to buyers are the television shows watched by their targeted markets so that they can see what clothing the characters are wearing. Viewers frequently follow the design direction of their favorite personalities. Movies and theatrical events can also influence what the public will wear, and buyers need to be aware of these potential style setters when planning their purchases.

Street fashion also provides buyers with insight into the styles that consumers are wearing now and what they may wear later. Buyers need to be alert to every fashion barometer that indicates what will be hot and what will not.

figure 12.3
The NRF trade show at the Javits Center in New York City. This is one of the world's largest trade shows where buyers come from many different countries to make their purchases.

MODEL STOCK DEVELOPMENT

A model stock is an inventory that includes an appropriate assortment of merchandise in terms of price points, styles, size ranges, color, and fabrics. Fashion buyers have a much more complicated task in developing a model stock than their buying counterparts who purchase hard goods and staple items. Fashion items are always seasonal in nature, so the model stock is constantly changing, but nonseasonal or nonfashion goods are stable, and the model stock can have a longer selling period without becoming obsolete.

The scope of the model stock is determined by those who decide which merchandise classifications will be included and how much money will be expended. In small fashion operations, this decision is made by the company owner with perhaps a manager's input. In larger organizations where formalized organization models are in place, such as those discussed in Chapter 3, "Organizational Structures," the amount spent on the model stock is determined by the upper levels of the merchandising divisions. The general merchandise manager apportions the budget among the various selling divisions. The head of each of these divisions, the divisional merchandise manager, then determines how much each buyer is to receive for product purchases. Each buyer, with these figures in hand, then sets out to develop a model stock that must stay within the budgetary limitations and address the department's merchandising needs.

The model stock of a **bridge department**, which are collections that fall between departments, such as couture and better sportswear, for example, must reflect which designers will be featured, the depth and breadth of each merchandise category, the number of tops needed for the number of bottoms, the concentration on particular sizes, the price points that must be emphasized, and so forth. The buyers' initial plans are generally preliminary programs that could easily change once they visit the marketplace and examine the vendors.

ELEMENTS OF FASHION BUYING

To construct a realistic model stock, the buyer must address specific areas known as the **elements of buying**: the qualitative and quantitative considerations, the fashion merchandise resources, and the timing of the purchase.

Qualitative Considerations

Internal and external sources give the buyer an indication of the nature of the fashion products that customers will want. The scope of fashion merchandise is so broad that it is available at every price point and quality, in styles that range from conservative to extremely fashion forward.

Each fashion operation has developed a character and image that the buyer must consider before completing even the simplest task. These are the qualitative considerations of the model stock. Buyers charged with the responsibility of

figure 12.4
Uma Thurman at *Elle* magazine's 17th annual Women in Hollywood event at the Four Seasons in Los Angeles, which gives readers of the publication information on what's in for the new season, and fashion news regarding the latest trends in the industry.

merchandising a conservative model stock will immediately know the types of styles preferred by the customers, because these customers tend to buy fashions that do not change much in style or design from year to year. They know whether their customers like man-made or natural fibers, the length of the skirt that most would wear, the preference of basic colors over new colors and the ratio in which the bottoms should be divided between pants and skirts.

It can be much more difficult for buyers who purchase extreme fashions. While size allocations and price points are generally simple to ascertain for this fashion audience, it is harder to predict style and color preferences. If the fashion editors of *WWD* are championing the micro-miniskirts, is it a safe bet to invest large sums in inventory in these items if last season's styles centered around the midi look? If wide, billowy pants are being heralded as the potential winners of the next season, should the buyer cram the inventory with such fashion designs or go with a safer streamlined look popular now? Should an investment be made in a new designer's collection over those designers who have been steady winners in the past? The answers to these questions are not simple to reach, and they are not the only types of decisions that a buyer must make before placing any orders. Even the most seasoned buyer is sometimes doubtful about making fashion decisions, particularly when the new season's offerings are a departure from what the customer accepted in the past.

Quantitative Considerations

One of the most important planning aspects is how much money the buyer has to spend at any given time for new merchandise. The established limits that have been approved by the divisional merchandise manager are based upon sales forecasts for each department. The forecasts take into account past sales, economic conditions, and the company's assessment of each merchandise classification's relative worth to the entire organization.

When a department is given a dollar amount for merchandise it will need to meet the projected sales figures, this is not solely for new purchases for the coming season but must include the present inventory. Since sales are constantly being made, new merchandise is arriving, and customer returns are placed back in the inventory, the budget ceiling must be constantly examined to make certain that it has not exceeded its limits. If a retail buyer were able to dispose of every piece of merchandise from the previous season and start fresh for the next, the job would be much easier. Since this is an impossible task it is necessary to determine the total worth of the inventory at any given time. It is standard practice for buyers to use a formula called **open-to-buy** to make these determinations. Although today's merchants have the advantage of computer programs that instantly provide them with the open-to-buy figures, it is beneficial to those using the formula to understand its different components. The following example depicts the numerous figures considered in the open-to-buy calculation.

PROBLEM

On June 1, the handbag buyer wanted to know how much she still had in her present budget to purchase additional merchandise for the period ending June 30. On this day, the following figures reflected her department's situation:

Merchandise on hand	$72,000
Merchandise on order	$18,000
Inventory planned for end of month	$90,000
Planned sales	$36,000
Planned markdowns	$3,000

What was the handbag buyer's open-to-buy on June 1?

SOLUTION

The formula for open-to-buy is:

Merchandise needed – Merchandise available = Open-to-buy

To find merchandise needed for June

Planned end-of-month inventory	$90,000
Planned sales	$36,000
Planned markdowns	$3,000
Merchandise needed	$129,000

To find merchandise available for June 1

Merchandise on hand	$72,000
Merchandise on order	$18,000
Merchandise available	$90,000

Open-to-buy ($129,000 – $90,000) = $39,000

With the use of a few additional figures such as actual sales and actual markdowns, the buyer can determine open-to-buy at any time.

RESOURCE SELECTION

Buyers of fashion merchandise have a host of domestic and foreign resources to buy from, the major locations of which are focused on in Chapter 13, "Purchasing in the Global Marketplace." Unlike other merchants who buy from wholesalers as well as manufacturers, those involved in the area of fashion generally restrict their purchasing to the producers. The principal reason for this approach is that fashion items have short lives and must reach the retailers as quickly as possible. The nature of wholesaling is to have goods warehoused until they are needed. Products such as appliances are purchased from wholesalers that store them until they are needed. Since such goods have long lives and are not subject to the **fashion perishability** factor, there is little chance for them to become obsolete before they are sold. In Figure 12.5, a buyer evaluates a new fashion collection.

Although most retailers buy from manufacturers, there are a small number of fashion merchandise wholesalers in business. They serve the needs of some very small merchants who are unable to buy directly from the producer because of certain imposed restrictions such as minimum order requirements and stringent credit requirements. Fashion wholesalers also play a role in enabling some retailers to acquire imports. To make foreign purchases, a retailer usually has to take on large commitments, visit offshore markets, commit to purchasing many months before the traditional buying period, or rely upon commissionaires, who are foreign resident buyers acting on behalf

figure 12.5
Buyer visiting a showroom to evaluate a designer's newest collection. It is in the vendor's showrooms that most of the lines are purchased.

of American retail buyers. These and other factors might be too restrictive for those with limited financial ability or whose merchandise needs do not warrant the risks involved, so they buy foreign goods from the wholesaler.

With the seemingly limitless number of available resources for every classification of fashion merchandise, the buyer must evaluate those companies from which purchases were made in the past and investigate the possibility of eliminating some of them and adding other vendors to the company's roster of suppliers.

To evaluate the retailer's current resources, the buyer must carefully inspect the retailer's past sales records. Computer-generated reports such as brand analysis details give the buyer an idea of how successful each vendor's products were. It is imperative for retailers of every size to examine each supplier in terms of **maintained markup** (how much profit the company was able to achieve over the cost of the merchandise), the number of customer returns, stock turnover (the average time it took to sell the items), reliability of shipments (whether the orders were received on time and in the same quality as the samples), fit, and anything else that might make the vendor a valuable one or a risk for another season.

Buyers should always pay attention to the external sources of information where they might discover new resources. Often a new designer is on the horizon or a new line might become hot in the industry, and their offerings could result in new, exciting merchandise. The trade papers, resident buying offices, fashion forecasters, and reporting services are in business to discover and recommend the industry's latest winners, and buyers should consider their choices.

Buyers must not only address the domestic marketplace in selecting their merchandise resources but must also scan the globe to find vendors that can supply the most suitable items for their customers. With overseas design and production ever growing, buyers must be aware of where these fashion markets are and the types of fashion merchandise they make available for export.

Chapter 13, "Purchasing in the Global Marketplace," explores the decision about whether or not to pursue global fashion resources.

Chapter Highlights

1. Company size is a major factor when it comes to the buyer's duties and responsibilities.

2. Off-site retailers exclusively use their buyers to purchase merchandise.

3. In most retail operations, the buyers determine the markup percentage for the merchandise in their department, unless the company employs standardized markups.

4. Buyers who purchase for the large department stores are often called upon to assist in the planning of in-store visual presentations.

5. To make a retail operation as profitable as possible, buyers are called upon to interact with managers in other company divisions.

6. Without question, past sales records are the primary indicators buyers use in determining their fashion purchases for the next season.

7. Merchants use a variety of research tools to assess consumer wants and needs.

8. The major external source of information used by fashion retailers is the resident buying office.

9. Among the activities that resident buyers engage in to properly advise their retail members are locating new resources, previewing collections, following up on orders, arranging adjustments, and preparing for Market Week.

10. Small merchants that are unable to meet minimum purchase requirements often have their orders pooled with other small merchants through the assistance of the resident buying office.

11. Fashion forecasters are specialists who do preliminary field work so that they can bring the pulse of the fashion wholesale market to the retail buyer.

12. Trade publications, reporting services, consumer periodicals, and trade associations are invaluable resources for buyers to research before they make their actual purchasing commitments.

13. A model stock is an inventory that includes an appropriate assortment of merchandise to meet the retail customers' needs.

14. Both qualitative and quantitative considerations must be undertaken by the buyer before making any purchases.

15. Open-to-buy is a concept that indicates how much money a department can spend for new purchases at any time of the month.

Terms of the Trade

bridge department	markups
chargebacks	model stock
elements of buying	off-site ventures
fashion forecaster	open-to-buy
fashion perishability	pool orders
Garment Center	reporting service
"hot" numbers	resident buyer

keystone markups
maintained markup
market consultants
Market Week

retail buyer
street fashion
trend books
trend forecasting

For Discussion

1. Why is it more difficult to purchase fashion merchandise than staple merchandise?

2. Buyers in the largest retail operations were once responsible for in-store management; why has this responsibility been taken from them?

3. Although most medium-sized and large retail brick-and-mortar operations have in-house visual merchandising staffs, why does the buyer play a role in visual presentation?

4. Why is it necessary for retail buyers to interact with their management counterparts in retailing's other divisions?

5. What is generally the first step that buyers take in the planning of future purchases?

6. What purpose does it serve the buyer to have such information as vendor name, style, and color listed on the merchandise tags?

7. Is there any distinct advantage to computerized record keeping for merchandising purposes?

8. How important is the role played by the resident buying office in fashion merchandising?

9. Where are the major New York City resident buying offices located, and why are they located there?

10. Why is it important for resident buyers to preview fashion collections before the retail buyers see them if it is the buyers who make the ultimate purchasing decisions?

11. What does the term "following up orders" mean, and why is this an important role played by the resident buying office?

12. Is it sometimes important for the resident buyer to intervene with vendors on behalf of the retail buyers when there are disputes? Why?

13. Why do some merchants need to pool their orders?

14. How are some of the larger resident buying offices providing their members with up-to-the-minute fashion information and visuals?

15. In what way does a reporting service differ from a resident buying office?

16. Do consumer fashion publications play an important role for retail purchase planning?

17. What is a model stock, and why is it important to determine in fashion merchandising?

18. What is the difference between qualitative and quantitative considerations in purchase planning?

19. How important is it for buyers to determine their open-to-buy?

20. What is a commissionaire?

Case Problem

Ellen Sherman has been employed in fashion retailing for the past 13 years. After majoring in college in fashion buying and merchandising and successfully completing an internship with Conway, Inc., a full-line department store, she accepted a position with that company after graduation.

For approximately 9 months, she participated in Conway's executive development program, rotating throughout the store in a number of merchandising and management roles. She was involved in a combination of formal classroom instruction and on-the-job training. After the 9 months, the company decided Ellen was ready for her first full-time assignment, assistant buyer for men's furnishings.

After about 5 years, showing considerable strength as an assistant buyer, Ellen was promoted to become a buyer of moderately priced men's sportswear. She met the challenge of the job admirably and enthusiastically carried out a successful career for another 7 years.

A few months ago, Ellen was approached by an executive search firm that specializes in fashion retailing and offered to arrange an interview for her with a major upscale fashion retail organization. Although she was satisfied with Conway's, the temptation to work for such an important fashion leader motivated her to go through the interview process and ultimately accept the new position.

Ellen Sherman became the buyer for men's designer collections at John Steven's, the Midwest's most highly regarded fashion retail empire. The merchandise for which she was now responsible was at the highest price points and was the most fashion forward. Although she was a seasoned buyer, this new venture was totally different from her previous experience. At the time of her employment with John Steven's, the company was preparing its purchasing plans for the fall season. With approximately 6 weeks before the industry's collection openings, Ellen has to develop a model stock for her department and address the elements of fashion buying. Since the new position was completely different from the last in terms of merchandise classification and customer base, she had a considerable challenge ahead of her.

Questions

1. Which information source should Ellen first investigate in initiating her buying plan? Discuss the various aspects of the source with which she should become familiar.

2. In trying to quickly familiarize herself with the merchandise classification, which external sources of information should she utilize?

3. From which people on the store's staff could she seek advice and counsel to develop a sensible buying plan? What types of assistance should she employ to help her with the purchase of menswear?

Exercises and Projects

1. Log onto the website of Fairchild Publications at www.condenast.com/fairchild to learn about the many different periodicals the company publishes. After selecting the one that seems most interesting to you, contact the publication by email to obtain a few issues and examine it for articles that would help buyers who were planning for the next season's purchases. In an oral presentation, discuss each article in terms of how it will help buyers with their plans.

2. Make arrangements to interview a store's fashion buyer to determine how he or she develops a model stock. It may be difficult to get an interview in the buyer's office; if this is the case, arrange a phone interview or one via email. Prepare your questions in advance of the interview so that you will be fully prepared; and ask particularly about the various elements that go into fashion buying. Once you have gained the necessary information, prepare a report that describes the particular buyer's approach to model stock development. In addition to the written material, include photographs or drawings (often available in newspapers) that are typical of the buyer's merchandise.

3. Using any search engine to obtain a list of resident buying offices, or going directly to a resident buying office's website such as www.doneger.com, study the services they offer to their clients. Prepare a report that highlights these services, and anything else that would help prospective members evaluate them.

chapter thirteen

PURCHASING IN THE GLOBAL MARKETPLACE

After reading this chapter, you should be able to:

- Identify the major domestic fashion marketplaces in which retail buyers make their purchases.
- Assess the advantages of purchasing in the domestic marketplace.
- Name the leading regional fashion markets in the United States and some of the important resources located within them.
- Prepare a list of the important permanent domestic fashion marts.
- Evaluate the importance of visiting resident buying offices before calling on any vendors.
- Describe how overseas fashion consultants may help buyers maximize their profit potential.
- Determine why offshore purchases are beneficial to American retailers, and list the most important offshore fashion capitals.
- Provide the reasons for the need to perfectly time the purchase.
- Prepare a list of fashion trade shows and the merchandise they feature.
- Outline the areas of negotiation that need to be addressed before any purchase order is written.

Once buyers carefully plan their purchases for the next season by consulting various internal and external sources, and develop a model stock that serves the needs of their retail organization, there is still much to be done before they are ready to put their signature on the bottom of any purchase order.

Buyers have three major areas of concern regarding their order placement. The first is the geographical locations of the vendors they are considering purchasing from. It is easier to procure products from domestic resources than from the foreign producers, but offshore fashion merchandise providers are still very important players. The second concern is how to determine the most appropriate time to have the new merchandise arrive on the selling floor or be ready for inclusion in catalog offerings or on websites. The third concern is whether or not it is best to make personal market trips to evaluate the latest fashion innovations, use Internet resources for product procurement, or rely upon the seemingly unending parade of road representatives who bring their collections to the retailers' premises.

This chapter describes the global marketplaces, as well as those that are domestically located, and discusses the various aspects of purchasing in each arena.

THE DOMESTIC MARKETPLACE

Some American buyers purchase the majority of their model stocks in one of the major U.S. wholesale markets. They flock to these sales facilities during the Market Weeks as well as other times depending upon the size of their companies and their proximity to the markets. Buyers from other countries also purchase their inventories domestically, as well as using offshore manufacturers.

However, the offshore marketplace increasingly attracts U.S. fashion retail buyers. Many leading fashion merchants such as Bloomingdale's, Saks Fifth Avenue, Bergdorf Goodman, and Neiman Marcus regularly go overseas to attend the fashion premieres of the world's leading **couturiers**, such as Armani, Dolce & Gabbana, Ferré, Chanel, and others. Companies at the other end of the fashion spectrum, such as Walmart and Target, also go to offshore markets to purchase their value-priced items. And fashion apparel bearing the names of Ralph Lauren, Tommy Bahama, and Calvin Klein, for example, are actually made in China, Hong Kong, Korea, Peru, and other distant shores where labor is generally cheaper than in the United States. In spite of this rising foreign competition, the domestic scene is still significantly important to fashion retailers for the following reasons:

- *Delivery reliability.* It is more likely that orders placed for American retailers with American manufacturers will arrive in the retail operations in a timely fashion. Although delivery problems can result no matter where the merchandise is procured, the closer proximity of the domestic vendors generally results in fewer problems.

- *Price guarantee.* When a purchase order is finalized domestically, the prices inherent in the U.S. orders are in American dollars. Products purchased overseas are listed in the country's own monetary unit. For example, the euro, the official currency of most European nations, fluctuates against the dollar every moment of every day. At the time of purchase, buyers might consider the wholesale price to be appropriate for their purchase plans, but the actual cost might not be the same as it was at the time of the order placement. The **landed cost**, which is the actual cost at the time the merchandise arrives in the United States, might be greater than the buyer anticipated, often making it too pricey to maintain the markup the buyer initially counted on for a profitable season. This concept will be fully explored later in the chapter.

- *Chargeback adjustments.* A buyer's best-laid purchase plans do not always result in the procurement of products that shoppers will buy. Price adjustments have become commonplace in the fashion industry. Buyers usually negotiate discounts from the vendors for the merchandise that didn't sell. Although this is a growing problem for fashion manufacturers, they often acquiesce so that retailers will continue to patronize them. Negotiating the **chargebacks** is a relatively simple procedure if the vendor is in a domestic market. Buyers and manufacturers are able to directly communicate with each other because of their similar business culture, common language, and their close proximity. It is more difficult to settle the details of such demands with foreign vendors for the opposite reasons.

- *Economic advantage.* For the past several years, the unfavorable balance of trade with overseas markets has caused considerable concern for Americans. Importing, more than exporting, has a negative effect on the U.S. economy. Purchasing in the domestic marketplace keeps the dollars in the United States and strengthens the domestic economy.

- *Reliability of "fit."* Although there are no standards when it comes to size uniformity, products that are purchased in the United States generally fall within a specific set of size standards. Although one manufacturer's size 6 isn't exactly the same as another's, there is some degree of standardization. Purchasing overseas doesn't usually offer the same fit guarantees. Each country has its own set of measurements that are best suited to its own population, but they do not necessarily coincide with the figures of overseas consumers. Merchandise made in the United States is less likely to have these fitting problems, thus reducing the number of merchandise returns for this reason.

Major American Domestic Wholesale Fashion Markets

Buyers who represent American fashion retail operations travel to a host of different fashion markets to preview the new collections and place orders. These markets are in many major American cities, and New York City is the leader.

New York City

The Garment Center, as it is generally referred to, is in New York City. It is home to the largest number of fashion manufacturers in the United States. Other cities traditionally have centralized apparel marts and merchandise marts that feature a host of vendors under one roof; the Garment Center is spread out among several streets, the most notable being Seventh Avenue and Broadway. Along with these main fashion arteries are the side streets from 34th Street to 41st Street. Even that doesn't perfectly describe New York City's Garment Center. With a multitude of new resources opening every year, new fashion manufacturers have opened headquarters in New York City's SoHo district, Chinatown, Greenwich Village, the Upper East Side and West Side, and lower Manhattan. A *WWD* supplement, *The Fashion Center*, reported that the Garment Center was approximately 34 million square feet and included 5,100 showrooms and 4,500 factories. Figure 13.1 shows a typical scene on Seventh Avenue.

Although the majority of the collections displayed at these manufacturers' premises are no longer produced in New York, the bulk of their sales are transacted in New York City's showrooms. That is where the designers still create their collections and the buyers come to preview them. Marquee collections such as Calvin Klein, DKNY, and Ralph Lauren are headquartered there, as are lesser-known fashion lines that hope to achieve the success of their better-known counterparts.

Buyers from all over the world come to this location, especially during each season's market weeks, when each new season's collections are introduced for the first time. Buyers visit the numerous vendor showrooms that feature everything from couture to lower-priced collections, **trade shows** that bring together a wealth of collections under one roof, and fashion presentations by such groups as the Council of Fashion Designers of America (CFDA).

figure 13.1
These shipments are moving across Seventh Avenue in New York City to a shipping facility. Shipping on these carts has been the traditional way for many years.

American Regional Markets

Other American cities have centers of their own that make them important to retailers. Some major fashion designers, such as Bob Mackie, are headquartered in Los Angeles, as are the more modest collections of Carole Little and Karen Kane, making it the second most important wholesale market after New York City. San Francisco is not far behind, with Camelia Skikos, head designer for Gap, and Levi Strauss, two of its better-known fashion brands.

In these wholesale regional markets, companies are either headquartered there or have branches there. Buyers come to place orders during their Market Weeks or any time of the year they need to order. They may patronize these markets rather than those based in New York City because they are close to the buyers' retail operations or because they want to visit more than one market in pursuit of the best merchandise they can add to their model stocks.

While New York City and the two California markets make up the lion's share of regional markets, there are others notable in the industry. Most regional markets operate primarily from marts or centers. Table 13.1 lists some of the important domestic fashion marts.

Table 13.1

SELECTED PERMANENT DOMESTIC FASHION MARTS

Mart	Location	Specialization
The Merchandise Mart	Chicago, IL	Home furnishings and giftware
California Market Center	Los Angeles, CA	Fashion merchandise and textiles
Dallas Market Center	Dallas, TX	Home furnishings, giftware, apparel, and accessories
Miami Merchandise Mart	Miami, FL	Fashion merchandise
The New Mart	Los Angeles, CA	Contemporary fashion
Concourse Exhibition Center	San Francisco, CA	Fashion apparel
Denver Merchandise Mart	Denver, CO	Apparel, accessories, gifts
L.A. Mart	Los Angeles, CA	Fashion merchandise

OFFSHORE FASHION MARKETS

With every passing season, more fashion merchants are sending their buying teams to distant shores in pursuit of merchandise that is either unique or better priced than that found at home. The competition demands of retailing are such that the **"me-too" lines** merchandised in so many domestic companies will not satisfy consumers who want products atypical of what U.S. manufacturers provide. Whether they are looking at couture-level merchandise, trendy fashion items that provide style as well as value, or something in between, buyers seem to be spending more time abroad than ever before.

To make certain that their visits to the offshore markets are merited, many American companies are members of reporting services that cover the foreign fashion markets. By using these resources while planning their purchases and visiting them once they are in the foreign markets, buyers are able to get a better feel of what's new in the marketplace.

Just as the domestic marketplace offers certain advantages to buyers, so do the **offshore production** locales for the following reasons:

- *Fashion-forward design.* Although many American designers present lines with a definite "look" to them, a season's cutting-edge fashions often appear first on the runways of Paris, London, and Milan. The creations shown in these venues typically give buyers a glimpse of what is on the fashion horizon for all price points. Figure 13.2 features a French designer making adjustments on a model.

- *Prestige.* Many foreign designers attract a segment of the fashion consumer market. Clothing by names such as Prada and Louis Vuitton, for example, immediately give the wearer a feeling of status. It is obvious that neither the unique construction nor the materials of these items account for their cost; people are willing to pay for the gratification that comes from someone recognizing the names or logos emblazoned on them. Prestige and status are extremely important aspects of upscale, fashion-forward merchandise, and buyers and merchandisers responsible for purchasing the most noteworthy of these items often find them in the world's overseas fashion markets.

- *Value.* Not every foreign resource produces prestigious apparel. Buyers who purchase merchandise for the brick-and-mortar operations, catalogs, and retail websites are more often concerned with getting a price advantage. The cost of producing goods in America is far greater than it is in many overseas manufacturing arenas except for those designed and produced in the couture capitals of the world. Eastern European countries, Mexico, China, and the Caribbean Basin countries, for example, are able to manufacture items that are similar to those made in the United States but at significantly lower prices. One need only glance at the labels of the value-oriented merchandise found in Target and Walmart to see the large percentage of items produced overseas.

- *Exclusivity.* More major retailers are in pursuit of items that are not found in their competitors' model stocks, because inventory duplication invariably affects their bottom line. When retailers need to meet last year's sales figures during a slow selling period, they might mark down certain lines. If these lines are the same that a competitor is also reducing, a price war may develop. To avoid these complications and to also provide unique styles, many buyers scour the overseas markets for products that the retailer can have to itself. Oftentimes, a manufacturer will

figure 13.2
A designer adjusts her creation on a model. This last minute maneuver is done to present a perfect model to the buyers.

produce a collection that bears the company's own label, thus making it an exclusive line. In other cases, a buyer searching for out-of-the-way resources might turn up products that the competition might not know about. When retailers place large orders from these offshore producers, they generally negotiate exclusivity agreements, enabling them to merchandise the line as they see fit, which usually results in higher-than-average markups.

- *Product quality.* Just as foreign automobiles are enticing to many Americans because of their high quality, so are fashion items from certain overseas countries. Places such as Belgium are noted for the fine workmanship on linen garments, Japan for silk products of distinction, and Spain for quality leather apparel. Professional purchasers for prestigious American fashion retail outlets are in constant pursuit of collections that feature unusual qualities and they frequently include merchandise labeled from these countries to satisfy their customers.

These advantages make offshore purchasing tempting, but as was mentioned previously in the discussion on domestic markets, the quoted prices are often in foreign monetary designations such as the euro. The daily fluctuation of the euro against the dollar makes it difficult to predict exactly what the cost of the merchandise will be when it is invoiced to American retailers. When the dollar weakens, the merchandise may actually cost more than anticipated to the point of being outside the merchant's price point structure. To this unknown are costs that are added to the initial price of the items such as packing, commissionaires' fees, tariffs, and shipping. Buyers must carefully determine the latter extras to derive the actual cost, or the landed cost, of the merchandise when it reaches their American retail operation.

Major Offshore Fashion Markets

The four corners of the world are dotted with fashion markets that produce every conceivable classification of apparel, accessories, and home furnishings that have appeal to the American consumer. These markets are in the traditional fashion capitals of Europe, in Asian countries, Canada, and Mexico as well as in obscure locations such as the Caribbean Basin countries. Each serves as a unique environment for buyers to explore and find products that best meet the needs of their clienteles.

Paris, France

Ever since the designs of Paul Poiret, Madame Paquin, and Jeanne Lanvin made headlines at the turn of the 20th century, and Vionnet, Patou, Chanel, and Schiaparelli followed, Paris became the standard for couture fashion. Today, with couturiers such as Lagerfeld carrying the torch, it is still Paris that commands the respect of professional buyers, fashion editors, and those who just love to read about the world of fashion.

Buyers come from every part of the globe to catch the heralded openings of each season's fashion couture collections. They come not only to buy the couture designs for their most affluent customers but also to get ideas about the trends that will eventually emerge from these designer creations. Also important to many fashion buyers are the prêt-à-porter, or ready-to-wear, collections that are offered at significantly lower price points. For the most part, it is these more affordable collections that eventually make their way into the American retail operations.

The Chambre Syndicale is France's regulating fashion agency in terms of when collections will be shown to the buyers, who will be accepted into this prestigious group, and the rules that govern selection.

Milan, Italy

Where Paris once stood alone as the preeminent fashion capital of the world, Milan has joined her as a fashion center of global importance. With Armani, Ferré, Missoni, and Krizia heading the list of fashion couturiers, buyers responsible for couture price points as well as those who just want to learn about fashion's cutting edge gather there to view the collections.

London, England

Rounding out the trio of European fashion leaders is London. Its popularity as a fashion center is based upon the acceptance of such notable designers as Vivienne Westwood, Zandra Rhodes, Maxfield Parrish, and Betty Jackson, and it features a variety of designs ranging from the avant-garde to the more traditional.

Spain

When American buyers are in the market for leather apparel and footwear, few countries offer them more variety than Spain. Recently however, this country has made its way onto the lists of buyers seeking to purchase women's and children's fashions. Most companies are centered in Madrid or Barcelona and feature the designs of Adolfo Dominguez, Antonio Álvarez, Margarita Nuez, and others who have gained considerable recognition in the United States.

Germany

Another rising star in the international fashion scene is Germany, with its ever-growing list of fashion designers headed by Hugo Boss and Jil Sander. So successful have their creations been with American consumers that these designers have opened flagship stores in the United States.

Japan

For upscale, fashion-forward design, Japan is one of the leading forces in Asia. In addition to being a leader in partnering with many American companies to produce their collections for consumption in Japan and other Asian countries, Japan also has a wealth of designers who have gained a great deal of attention from the American fashion industry; Issey Miyake and Rei Kawakubo being just two. Figure 13.3 depicts a Japanese fashion show.

Hong Kong

Although it has made recent strides in producing original fashion collections through the efforts of such companies as Toppy and Episode, Hong Kong's importance to the industry is based upon its ability to produce fashion merchandise at comparatively low prices. Buyers flock there on a regular basis to discover designs that they can use in their companies' private label collections.

figure 13.3
A runway show in Japan for prospective buyers. Japan has become a leader in original fashion creations.

Canada

With the implementation of the North American Free Trade Agreement (NAFTA) in 1994, Canada has started to emerge as a fashion resource for merchandise that ranges from expensive to modest, and in stylings that include sophisticated as well as more serviceable products. Although its product range includes women's and children's wear, menswear is Canada's forte.

Mexico

Also a beneficiary of the NAFTA pact, Mexico continues to increase in importance as a supplier of fashion merchandise for American retailers. Its extremely low cost of production makes it especially appealing for merchants to have their private label collections produced there.

As in Paris and the other international fashion centers, specific dates and times that collections will preview their new lines are scheduled months in advance so that the buyers will have ample time to view as many collections as possible. As most buyers have only a short time to be away from their headquarters, they must plan their trips months ahead to maximize their time spent in these fashion capitals.

The *Happening Now* feature examines a "new" fashion capital.

TIMING THE PURCHASE

As discussed in the previous chapter, buyers must make quantitative and qualitative decisions as well as resource evaluation, known as the elements of buying, before they actually make their purchases. Rounding out the details of this fundamental plan is the actual timing of the purchase so that the merchandise can reach the selling floors, catalogs, and websites in time to make the greatest impact on the consumer.

STOCKHOLM, A NEW FASHION CAPITAL

Much to the surprise of the buyers and merchandisers around the world as well as the fashion editorial press, Stockholm has become the capital of everyday fashion. Its number one ranking has made the Swedish city a must-see place for moderately priced fashion. Its collections are more affordable than that which is available in most other global fashion centers. What is happening now is that for the past few years, Stockholm has gone from a venue that was mostly appealing to the Scandinavian countries to one that is steadily gaining attention from around the globe.

Today, there's been a steady move from the French prêt-à-porter merchandise to Scandinavia to seek out the "next coveted fashion brands." In fact, in the 2014 Stockholm Fashion Week, buyers from such famous fashion emporiums as Harvey Nichols of London were seen in the front row of the exhibition.

Brands such as Acne and Whyred, fashion magazines like *Styleby*, Elin Kling's blog The Wall and website Stockholm Streetstyle, are among the reasons for the success, with the recession being another.

Up until the past two years, functionality was the keyword in Swedish fashion. While functionality is still obvious in the latest styles, the new designers are no longer playing it safe, but are experimenting with more avant-garde creations. The safety of monochromatic colors and clean lines, as in past years, is no longer the emphasis on fashion, but still plays somewhat of a role in the designs.

A vast number of fashion professionals believe this is not a short run for Stockholm, but "definitely more than a passing trend."

There are traditional purchase periods in the fashion market when the buyer begins to make selections for the next season. The time when the major companies send their buyers to the fashion industry to visit the resources is called Market Week. The number of such markets varies according to the particular merchandise classifications and the places where the markets are held. During Market Week, the buyers face a whirlwind challenge that requires their attendance at a host of collection openings.

Not every fashion retailer heads for the market during these times; most buyers attending then are the major players in the field who must get a jump on the competition in discovering what the latest offerings will be. Smaller retailers or those who are concerned with opportunistic buying, such as the off-price merchants, usually wait a little longer before they begin the process of evaluating the new season's offerings. The timing decisions are individually geared to the needs of the particular retailer, and different timing strategies have different implications.

Early Decision-Making

The many advantages afforded the fashion buyer who participates in the earliest timing of purchases include the following:

- *Seeing the line in its entirety.* A vendor showing its collection for the first time includes every design it has created. The buyers at this showing have the opportunity to see the entire line and choose what is most appropriate for their model stocks. It is commonplace in the fashion industry for lines to be edited soon after Market Week, making fewer items available for the buyers to purchase later on. The editing is often based upon early buyer acceptance, and if buyers don't place a sufficient number of orders for certain items those pieces often fall by the wayside. Thus, if buyers wait until a later time to view the collections, they do not have a role in selecting what items a vendor will stock, causing some pieces to be eliminated.
- *Guarantee of early delivery.* In the fashion game, merchandise must always be delivered on time. This, however, does not imply that every merchant requires the same delivery dates. Fashion-first retailers such as Saks Fifth Avenue, Neiman

Marcus, Bloomingdale's, and Macy's require the merchandise to be in stock as soon as it comes from the manufacturers' plants. For them, early delivery is essential so that they can have their model stocks ready to meet the needs of the customers who shop early each season.

- *Exclusivity agreements.* Almost every major player carries some identical lines, which can lead to significant problems with their competitors. When shoppers enter the selling floors of Neiman Marcus, Bloomingdale's, or Saks Fifth Avenue, for example, they see sections devoted to Ralph Lauren. While each store would prefer to avoid the potential problems associated with carrying the same labels, these marquee brands are the leaders in their fields, and customers want to buy them. Retailers can gain a degree of exclusivity even with these collections through early decision-making. Often, designers and manufacturers of such lines are willing to confine specific groups within the collections to retailers within a specific trading area. In this way, the designer label is represented in each store, but some of the merchandise is exclusively distributed to certain retail operations. Buyers who purchase early often work out these exclusivity agreements.
- *Obtaining seasonal discounts.* Early purchasing is sometimes a way to get the merchandise at discounted prices, because manufacturers love to get a jump on the season and will offer inducements to buyers who purchase early. In the swimsuit industry, for example, many producers reward their retailers with seasonal discounts if they purchase ahead of the traditional purchasing time frame. Not only is this a price advantage for these buyers but it gives them a head start on the competition and enables them to test the items with smaller quantities early in the season before the major selling period arrives. They can then eliminate the slow sellers and invest in the better styles.

Just as there are advantages to making early decisions in terms of purchase timing, there are also disadvantages for some retailers. Among them are the following:

- *Purchasing "edited" items.* All fashion designers or manufacturers produce a line that they hope will appeal to the buyers. In reality, however, this is rarely the case. Some items do not sell well enough to be considered for production. Vendors have minimum order requirements known as "**cutting tickets**" that go into effect before they begin manufacturing a style. Buyers who order very early in the season may choose one of the eliminated items, only to be notified later that it is cut from the line now known as the **edited line**. They must reexamine the collections to replace the discontinued models and make certain that their inventories are appropriately adjusted. Buying a little later in the season eliminates this problem.
- *The "winners" are yet to be determined.* While buying early affords buyers with the opportunity to be fashion first, it also makes the selection process more difficult. Early decision-making also gives the buyer the opportunity to make more mistakes. Once the lines have been seen by the buyers who attend market weeks and purchase early, the vendor's sales reps know which pieces will be edited out and which will be the season's potential winners. Buyers who sometimes rely upon the vendor sales reps to give them advice now have the opportunity to gain from the reps' insights in terms of what is going to be a hot item.

Lead-Time Requirements

One of the primary considerations in the proper timing of the purchase is **lead time**— the amount of time it takes to receive the order once it has been placed. Unlike much of the hard goods, such as major appliances, that line the floors of the wholesalers' premises and can be shipped within a day or two of an order, fashion merchandise is a different story. Vendors usually do not start manufacturing fashion items until they have processed a sufficient number of orders. Typically, fashion merchandise produced in the United States takes as long as 6 months after it is ordered until it is delivered. Buyers need to place their orders for goods produced offshore even earlier to make certain they will receive their orders on time. Seasoned buyers are fully aware of the problems associated with receiving merchandise when they want it and must place their orders sufficiently early. It is vital that the inventory is in place to coincide with catalog presentations and advertising and promotional plans.

PURCHASING IN THE MARKETPLACE

Buyers have a wealth of both domestic and offshore markets in which they may make their purchases. Buyers for major merchants, who have the luxury of visiting any of the global arenas, have a considerable advantage over those whose market visitations are more restricted. They can feel the pulse of the marketplace at the earliest possible time, enjoy the privileges of the earliest possible delivery dates, gain insight from the market representatives based within the wholesale markets, and trade information with the noncompeting merchants they meet at the trade expositions and manufacturers' showrooms.

Resident Buying Office Visits

Chapter 12, "Planning and Executing the Purchase," fully explored the relationship between the market specialists, also known as resident buyers, and the companies they represent. One of the most important services they provide is to assist the retail buyers when they come to market during Market Week by locating new resources, prescreening the fashion collections, analyzing market conditions, and so forth.

Most buyers stop at their resident buyers' office when they first arrive at the fashion markets. The resident buyers help their retail buyers' clients make the best use of their limited time in the market. They perform a variety of duties such as presenting an overview of what the buyers are about to see in the vendors' showrooms or at the trade shows, providing buyers with a list of scheduled appointments made for them at these purchasing venues, alerting buyers to new resources that have the potential for success with their companies, answering any questions buyers might have regarding market conditions, and making themselves available to accompany the buyers to the market if the need arises.

Once the resident office representative provides the buyers with all of the information they need for a successful visit, they head for the showrooms or trade shows to preview the lines in which they are interested.

Showroom Visits

In the major wholesale venues such as New York City, the vast majority of fashion manufacturers and designers maintain permanent showrooms. Buyers visit these showrooms to see a season's entire collection and meet with the sales reps who regularly service their account. In some of the more important showrooms, especially during Market Week, the premises are transformed into show facilities that feature runways on which models parade the latest offerings. In smaller showrooms, the different styles might be informally modeled so that the buyers can get a better idea of how the garments will look when they are worn. Other wholesale arenas such as the Apparel Marts in Chicago and Dallas also feature permanent showrooms for the buyers in those trading areas to visit and place their orders.

Trade Shows

Trade shows, held throughout the world, specialize in a particular fashion segment and only last a short time. Figure 13.4 features a trade show.

The value of trade shows is that buyers can see a great number of collections under one roof, saving them the time of going from one showroom to another and enabling them to compare the different lines more easily. Trade shows include the collections of smaller companies that aren't able to afford the luxury of their own sales arenas, so buyers can see their offerings as well.

Alternatives to Wholesale Market Visits

Many smaller fashion retailers have neither the time nor the financial resources necessary to visit the wholesale markets to make their purchases. Those that can, however, usually must restrict their number of market visits to Market Week openings. To assess the fashion producers' merchandise on a year-round basis and review any additions to various lines made since the season began, buyers are able to arrange for alternate purchasing opportunities.

figure 13.4
Buyers visiting a trade show to oversee the market and make purchases. This is the easiest way to compare collections and save time in the marketplace.

Fashion Representative Visits

Most major fashion manufacturers maintain a staff of road representatives that visit different retailers. The sales reps are responsible for certain regional territories, and they travel from retailer to retailer to show what is new in their line. Although this is an excellent way for merchants to see a vendor's line without leaving their premises, the reps are not able to carry the entire collection and frequently only bring what the vendor considers to be its highlights.

Business-to-Business Websites

Many fashion manufacturers and designers maintain websites to show their collections to the retail buyers. They regularly update the sites to feature the highlights of their lines and to edit them as the need arises. By logging onto these websites even the buyers from the smallest operations can feel the pulse of the fashion industry without leaving their premises.

Buyers who practice opportunistic buying for off-price ventures use numerous websites that feature fashion closeouts of items at distressed prices. Merchandise from well-known labels including Nike and Ralph Lauren are regularly offered at closeout prices.

The beauty of **business-to-business websites** for fashion merchandise is that buyers can search them at any time of the day or night without interfering with their other duties.

WRITING THE ORDER

Seasoned buyers rarely commit themselves to specific merchandise the first time they see the lines. They generally take notes on what they have seen at each showing so they can compare and evaluate each item against what they have seen at all of the resources. Once they have examined everything, they choose those fashions that best fit their model stocks.

Before they write the order, buyers must negotiate the various terms of the agreement. A purchase order is a formal contract and must be entered into with care. The negotiation involves price, a host of discounts, allowances for advertising, delivery dates, terms of the shipment, and chargebacks. Each of these areas is described in the following sections.

Pricing Considerations

In most cases, fashion merchandise pricing is fixed, with the same costs applicable to both large and small merchants. Even those who purchase in large quantities are often bound by the constraints of the **Robinson-Patman Act**. This piece of legislation was enacted to limit price discrimination and help the small retailers compete with large ones so they could stay in business. The conditions of the law are carefully spelled out and indicate that every purchaser must pay the same price except under certain circumstances. These exceptions are as follows:

- The merchandise is a job lot or closeout in which assortments are limited and reorders are unavailable.
- The manufacturer needs to meet the competition's prices.
- The savings that come from producing merchandise for specific clients may be passed on to the clients.

Discounts

Although the base prices are generally fixed, there are conditions under which a better price may be negotiated, as follows:

- *Cash discounts.* The vast majority of fashion manufacturers and designers offer small **cash discounts** to encourage prompt payment of the invoices. This usually involves a 30-day time frame in which the bills may be discounted at rates that vary from a typical high of 8 percent to a low of 2 percent.
- *Anticipation discounts.* To pay their bills even earlier than they would to receive a cash discount, many manufacturers offer an extra discount known as an **anticipation discount**. Merchants who opt to pay their invoices at this predetermined time are rewarded with additional discounts of 1 to 2 percent. Suppliers who might have a cash flow problem and need the money as soon as possible to pay for the costs of production frequently offer those discounts.
- *Quantity discounts.* Although the Robinson-Patman Act generally disallows discounts based solely on the size of the order, some **quantity discounts** are allowed if the production of the large quantity results in lower manufacturing costs.
- *Seasonal discounts.* In some fashion merchandise classifications such as swimwear and outerwear, retailers taking early deliveries sometimes receive extra price reductions. For example, coat buyers, whose season typically begins in early September, willing to take the goods as early as June, can often negotiate an additional discount. There are advantages to both the buyer and seller of this merchandise. Early delivery enables retailers to test the waters and determine what the hot sellers will be, giving them an indication of what should be reordered and what should not. Vendors enjoy the advantage of getting paid earlier and do not need to allow space for longtime storage of the items, a costly part of their budget.

Advertising Allowances

Retailers, large and small, use advertising as a means of promoting their companies and merchandise to regular and potential customers. The costs of these endeavors are comparatively high, and any assistance to defray their costs can help improve the retailers' profit margins. At the time of negotiating the terms of the purchase, buyers are often able to get monies from the vendors to help with their advertising budgets. Through the use of **cooperative advertising**, vendors contribute to costs of the retailers' advertisements as long as their companies' name and merchandise appears in the ads. Chapter 16, "The Importance of Advertising and Promotion," provides a more detailed discussion of cooperative advertising. Figure 13.5 shows newspapers that have fashion ads.

Delivery Dates

Although the timing of the merchandise delivery is important to every product classification, prompt delivery is especially important for fashion merchandise. The nature of this type of merchandise, with its relatively short seasonal life, makes on-time arrivals imperative. Buyers must make certain that the goods are promptly delivered according to the dates stipulated on the order for a number of reasons: to reap the benefits of planned advertisements, to have goods in stock early enough for peak selling periods, and to allow for special promotions of the goods.

figure 13.5
Newspapers are where much cooperative advertising is featured. This is a very common partnership between the vendor and the retailer.

The buyer must carefully note the delivery dates on the purchase order and include starting dates and **completion dates**. If deliveries are not made within these time frames, buyers must make certain that the orders are subject to cancellation. In either case, the early or late deliveries interfere with the predetermined model stocks. Merchandise received too early may result in too much merchandise for a particular selling period. Merchandise received too late may cause the inventory to be incomplete.

Shipping Terms

The cost of shipping continues to escalate. To make certain that the manufacturer chooses the most cost-effective methods for the deliveries, the buyer must indicate on the purchase order the name of the preferred shipping company and the terms of the shipment. Typically, shipping costs are the responsibility of the retailer, but in special cases where the orders are significantly large, buyers may be able to negotiate a deal where such expenses might be passed on to the vendor or shared by both parties.

The order must have terms such as **FOB shipping point** or **FOB destination** clearly spelled out to avoid any problems. The former requires that the retailer pay for the shipping charges, and the latter charges the vendor.

Chargebacks

When the merchandise doesn't sell as well as anticipated, many major retailers want the vendor to share in the problem. Although the manufacturers and designers do not want to partake in such discounts, they are inclined to do so if the purchaser represents a major retail operation. Given the competition in fashion merchandise, there is little that vendors can do to avoid the problem of chargebacks. Without these considerations, buyers are likely to find other resources that will acquiesce to these demands. The professional buyer must negotiate these terms when the order is written. Failure to do so may result in the vendor's refusal to grant these discounts.

When all of the terms and conditions of the orders have been agreed upon by both parties, the order is submitted and processed for future delivery.

Chapter Highlights

1. The vast majority of the fashion products found in most major traditional retail operations are purchased in one or more of the domestic markets.

2. Purchasing fashion products in the domestic markets affords the retailer greater delivery reliability, price guarantees, reliability of fit, and economic advantages.

3. For fashion apparel and accessories, the major domestic wholesale market is in New York City.

4. Regional markets in the United States are found in many parts of the country, with the leaders in Los Angeles, San Francisco, Chicago, Dallas, and Miami.

5. Purchasing offshore is attractive to fashion buyers in the United States because of such advantages as fashion-forward design, prestige, value, exclusivity, and product quality.

6. Paris remains the world's leading couture fashion market due in part to the efforts of its regulatory agency, Chambre Syndicale.

7. Other countries such as Italy, England, Spain, Germany, and Japan offer the collections of world-famous designers.

8. Purchase timing is essential to the success of every fashion operation.

9. Buying in the wholesale markets, especially during Market Week, affords the retailer the guarantee of early delivery, potential exclusivity agreements, the chance to see the line in its entirety before it has been edited, and the possibility of seasonal discounts.

10. When buyers go to the fashion markets, those with resident buying office affiliation head to these market consulting firms before they make any vendor visits to receive advice on what they are about to see.

11. Buyers can visit individual manufacturer and designer showrooms or go to trade shows, where a wealth of different lines are shown under one roof.

12. Retail buyers who are unable to regularly make personal visits to the marketplace may place orders with traveling road reps or through business-to-business websites.

13. Writing the order involves such aspects as pricing considerations, negotiating a variety of discounts, and obtaining advertising allowances.

Terms of the Trade

anticipation discounts	FOB shipping point
business-to-business websites	landed cost
cash discounts	lead time
completion dates	me-too lines
cooperative advertising	offshore production
couturiers	quantity discounts
cutting tickets	Robinson-Patman Act
edited lines	trade shows
FOB destination	

For Discussion

1. Why does the ever-growing list of offshore fashion merchandisers continue to play such an important role for American retailers?

2. What are some of the advantages of buying in domestic markets?

3. Define the term "chargeback" and explain why so many major retailers demand this consideration before placing their orders.

4. Which is the major fashion wholesale market in the United States, and where are some of the regional markets of importance?

5. With all of the potential pitfalls involved in offshore purchasing, why do so many American fashion retailers still choose to purchase overseas?

6. What is the meaning of the term "landed cost" and what impact may it have on purchases?

7. Who is the regulating body for fashion in Paris, and how does it serve retailers who have plans to attend collection openings?

8. Why have Mexico and Canada become more important offshore producers for retailers in the United States?

9. What advantages does early decision-making, in terms of purchasing, afford the retail buyer?

10. Is it important for buyers with resident buying office affiliation to visit their market representatives before visiting the vendors? Why?

11. In what way does a visit to a trade show benefit the buyer more than visits to different manufacturers' showrooms?

12. If buyers are unable to regularly come to the wholesale market to purchase, what alternatives can allow them to view a vendor's lines?

13. What is the purpose of the Robinson-Patman Act?

14. How does a regular cash discount differ from an anticipation discount?

15. What arrangements for advertising compensation do buyers often make with their vendors?

16. What is the difference between FOB shipping point and FOB destination?

Case Problem

Questions

1. Is there any way in which the partners can gain sufficient information on the European fashion market without spending more time abroad?

2. How might the partners devise a plan to cover the European collections without spending more time abroad?

Abby and Amanda Ltd. is a very chic, upscale retail operation. Its clientele is composed of women who are primarily in the lower upper classes. Wives of entertainers and successful businessmen, as well as being major executives in their own right, these women are extremely careful about acquiring the most fashion-forward merchandise available. Price is not a factor, only the uniqueness of the apparel and accessories.

Unlike the majority of retailers that merchandise collections at these price points, Abby and Amanda is a comparatively small company. Since it began 10 years ago in a small space that measured 1,200 square feet, it has continuously expanded its store to its present location that occupies approximately 15,000 square feet. Its merchandise assortment is primarily composed of price points that begin at the bridge level and go upward to the couture level. Its appeal to its clientele is based upon the fact that it does not carry the "me-too" lines of other merchants but deals exclusively with marquee couturier collections and prêt-à-porter lines that do not regularly have a great deal of recognition in the United States.

The need for Abby and Amanda Ltd. to maintain its level of exclusivity requires that the company's partners, who are also the buyers, visit the overseas fashion markets to make their selections. They always go together to make certain they agree on their purchases. While it has been their practice to attend the major French collection openings twice a year, their time constraints haven't allowed them to look past these lines. The 5 days in Paris is barely enough time to see the major offerings. Being aware of other European fashion capitals as potential resources, Abby and Amanda would like to expand their purchasing horizons and buy the exciting lines available there. In particular, they would like to learn more about the fashion collections in London and Milan for possible inclusion in their inventories. But with their limited time to spend overseas, they haven't been able to adequately assess the fashion capitals' offerings.

With more of their customers inquiring about the couture collections of other countries, the partners are in a quandary as to how to evaluate these fashion offerings and how to attend the openings in London and Milan without spending more time abroad.

Exercises and Projects

1. Log onto a search engine such as www.google.com to locate the websites for international fashion associations such as Chambre Syndicale. Each fashion capital has associations that provide a great deal of involvement in its respective industries. Select one of these organizations and write a report that includes the following:

   a. The name of the group
   b. Its purpose
   c. Costs of membership
   d. Requirements for inclusion
   e. Roster of members

2. Using the fashion marts located in the United States, select two and log onto their websites to gain information about them. Prepare an oral report on the two marts that includes their locations, the retail markets they serve, their product specialization, and so forth.

chapter fourteen

PRIVATE LABEL IMPORTANCE TO THE MERCHANDISE MIX

After reading this chapter, you should be able to:

- Contrast the merchandising advantages of private labeling and branding with those of the national brands and labels.

- Enumerate the different approaches used by retail operations in their pursuit of private label and brand involvement.

- Discuss the differences between partnering and the other private label routes merchants take.

- List many of the major retailers involved in private branding and labeling and their approaches to this merchandising concept.

- Define the term "The Store is the Brand," and explain why some of the country's largest retailers have embraced this plan.

- Identify the different merchandise acquisition methods retailers use in their pursuit of private labels.

Fashion retailing is a very competitive business, and the efforts to keep customers from shopping elsewhere often seriously affects a company's profitability. Because so many fashion retailers carry inventories that look like clones of each other, there is often little difference between their model stock. Walking through most department stores, for example, or looking at the offerings featured off-site in catalogs and on websites, one immediately recognizes that they all carry the same lines by fashion leaders such as Ralph Lauren and DKNY. Because so many outlets have the same stock, there is as little variety in fashion offerings as there is in the appliances that are stocked in the large home improvement stores. Although most consumers don't mind if the appliances they buy are not unique, they do want variety in their selection of fashion apparel and accessories. Fashion enthusiasts want a degree of exclusivity. Most do not want to walk into a room and find several people clad in the same ensembles.

This lack of individuality is not the only problem that results from merchants stocking almost identical inventories. With so many retailers carrying the same lines, they must frequently cut prices. Faced with a slow selling period, the overstocked merchant might slash prices, which could force its competitors to do the same, resulting in a loss of profit for them all.

More merchants are turning to creating private labels and brands to differentiate their model stocks from the rest of the field. They are either using them as a percentage of the total merchandise mix or exclusively stocking their shelves with a single signature brand. The development of these labels and brands gives retailers a degree of exclusivity and makes them less likely to be affected by the problems associated with carrying the same brands as their competitors.

This steady move toward private labeling was prompted by industry research pertaining to fashion merchandise, particularly the results of a study conducted by the market research firm NPD Fashionworld, based in Port Washington, New York. It revealed that designer apparel accounts for 7 percent of the business, private label 35 percent, **national brands** 52 percent, and others 6 percent.

Major fashion retailers such as Bloomingdale's, Macy's, and Saks Fifth Avenue have embraced this concept by developing a host of these brands that they include alongside the marquee labels that many of their customers still desire. Others, such as Gap and Banana Republic, have taken exclusive branding to an even greater stage and feature only their own products in their inventories. This concept has become known as "**The Store is the Brand**," and has freed the businesses that subscribe to it from the need to continuously check the competition to learn if their prices are in line with them.

By choosing this approach to inventory development, fashion retailers have taken on a new responsibility. Where merchandise selection was once determined by assessing the industry's offerings and selecting the best collections for their clienteles, retailers are now in the business of creating lines that bear their own signatures, producing them, promoting them, and hoping that they have the appeal to motivate their customers to purchase them.

NATIONAL BRANDS

Throughout the United States and abroad, the brick-and-mortar operations as well as the off-site ventures feature a host of national brands and labels that are immediately familiar to the consumer, such as Ralph Lauren, Calvin Klein, and DKNY. These are the brands that have been promoted through the print, broadcast media, the Internet, and social networking, and have maintained a loyal following among shoppers around the world. They are generally available in a variety of retailers' model stocks and do not feature any degree of exclusivity. Figure 14.1 shows a DKNY fashion show.

In spite of their universal appeal, these brands cause a number of different problems for the merchants that stock them. First and foremost is **price cutting**. Retailers have no protection from competitors that find the need to reduce their prices of these identical lines. They are also at the mercy of the off-price merchants, whose opportunistic purchases give them the advantage of buying for less and selling for less than the traditional merchants. There is no longer any **fair-trade pricing**, which once protected retailers from untimely markdowns. The availability of these designer brands in so many on-site and off-site ventures in turn often makes them less desirable to those customers looking for some degree of exclusivity, and they shop elsewhere in their search for unique fashions.

In spite of all these drawbacks there is still a market for these collections, and as indicated by the racks upon racks of these nationally prominent lines in most stores, retailers are not about to relinquish their rights to stock them.

Advantages of National Brands

While there are certainly disadvantages inherent in carrying national brands, there is also a wealth of reasons for retailers to feature them in their inventory, including the following:

- The amount that manufacturers spend on advertising and promoting them is significant. Whether it is the seemingly limitless numbers of ads run in fashion magazines,

figure 14.1
DKNY is one of the most successful national brands. The name itself is an incentive for consumers to buy the brand.

newspapers, retailer direct marketing efforts, broadcast commercials, and social media, the message about these brands is always somewhere the public can see it or hear it. The cost is included as part of these brands' promotional budgets.

- Visual presentations, both in retailers' windows and interiors, continue to bring these brands to the customer's attention. A walk through a major merchant's cosmetic department, for example, is enough to see that large sections of selling space have been set aside to feature extensive offerings of these brands. Estée Lauder, for example, enjoys the luxury of a large section in most department stores such as Macy's and Bloomingdale's. It showcases the majority of the brand with samples and large point-of-purchase posters and displays.

- While shoppers are sometimes suspicious about the quality and fit of the fashion merchandise they purchase off-site by means such as catalogs or websites, they are generally assured of getting what they expect when they purchase one of these marquee labels. Manufacturers with national reputations are extremely careful about quality assurance and deliver exactly what they have promised in terms of fabrications, wearability, and care. They have gained the public's trust by making certain their products meet the highest industry standards.

- Continuity of production is extremely important for retailers who discover "winners" in their industries. These are the backbones of their industry and account for their potential to maximize profits. The nationally prominent manufacturers have the capability to continue to deliver these winners in a timely manner, thereby developing positive relationships with their retail clients.

- The prestige provided by many of the national manufacturers' labels is of significant importance to fashion merchants. A considerable number of fashion enthusiasts are motivated to buy marquee labels such as the products offered by Prada. Handbags priced upwards of $1,000 soon sell off the shelves of the fashion retail leaders. It certainly is neither the fabrics nor the construction that distinguish these accessories, although they are of the highest quality, but rather the little nameplate that adorns the outside of the product. It is debatable if they would sell in the same quantities if the labels were on the inside. Prestige is something that gives the wearers of such merchandise a feeling of exclusivity, which is often the most important factor in determining whether they will purchase the product or not.

PRIVATE LABELS AND BRANDS

No matter the venue, whether the retailers are brick-and-mortar operations, catalogs, or websites, they carry a host of brands and labels that they exclusively market. Some outlets feature labels that they have developed and that account for a specific percentage of their overall model stocks, while others subscribe to the retailing strategy, "The Store is the Brand." In both cases, it is the exclusivity factor that plays an important role in the marketing of these labels and brands.

In department stores that subscribe to private label and **private brand** retailing, they frequently carry more than one collection of these exclusive names. In Macy's, for example, one of these brands is INC, which sells in significant amounts.

Private labeling and branding don't only rely on the exclusivity factor but also on the premise that the products that bear these names are equal in quality and styling to their nationally prominent counterpart.

Once a private brand is established and accepted by consumers, it is often confused with the national brands. Shoppers who are satisfied with a store's private label offerings sometimes seek these collections at other retail outlets, not realizing that they may only be found in the companies that successfully developed them. For example, shoppers frequently enter a Lord & Taylor store looking for an Alfani label, only to find that it is sold only in Macy's.

When a company embarks upon a private brand program, it is a major undertaking. Aside from the significant financial investment necessary to get into this type of merchandising, a number of other factors must be addressed to make the product a successful rival to the national brands. The factors that contribute to the success of these exclusive offerings are discussed throughout this chapter. In *Happening Now*, the outlook for private labeling at J. C. Penney Company, Inc. may be their saving grace.

HAPPENING NOW

PRIVATE LABELING IS THE APPROACH J. C. PENNEY HOPES WILL SAVE THE COMPANY

The cloud that surrounds the future of J. C. Penney is quite evident in articles that appear almost every day in trade papers such as *WWD*, consumer reports, broadcast media, social media, and the like. The news has been shaky at best for the past 2 years with declining sales plaguing the operation. With a few changes having been tried, the company plans to inject more excitement into its offerings and a great degree of exclusivity. As a beginning, J. C. Penney is turning to more private labels in the merchandise assortment to beef up sales. According to C.E.O. Mike Ullman, "What we need now is to edit things out that didn't resonate sufficiently." The plan is to offer more private branding in its merchandise mix, and "to use the freed-up prime floor space for its more-profitable exclusive private label brands."

A beginning of the new merchandising approach starts with the bringing back of its St. John's Bay apparel line, and the reintroduction of the Ambrielle lingerie collection. Under the leadership of former Apple "star" Ron Johnson, which included dumping many J. C. Penney brands, the company lost $1 billion in sales in 2012 sending the stock to a 31-year low. C.E.O. Mike Ullman renewed the company focus on private label merchandise that he envisions is a way to increase sales.

As a start, J. C. Penney's is trying to get more out of its existing private brands by expanding them. One example is the addition of sportswear to its JF J. Ferrar line of men's suits. It is also beginning to replace the floor locations of some brands with those that are private label. For example, Joe Fresh shops in its stores will see a reduction in assortment and a movement from the front-door location to give a more prominent spot to its own ana and jcp women's sportswear.

The goal in the immediate future is to introduce private brands that will produce profitability.

Advantages of Private Labels and Brands

Merchants that stock their own brands as part of the merchandise mix or use them as the only label they market are afforded certain advantages, such as the elimination of price cutting.

Price cutting is a problem that is pervasive in the world of fashion retailing. When merchants are overstocked and economic conditions warrant markdowns, they often reduce the prices of the national brands. Merchants try to get an edge on competition and show their customers that their prices can't be beaten, resulting in a lowering of profits. With the exclusive nature of private labels, this can't happen. Retailers can control the prices, and shoppers cannot comparison-shop at other venues, seeking bargain prices for these collections. Figure 14.2 shows a sale sign to rid the store of excess merchandise.

In the case of national brands, the items are produced to have the broadest appeal to their retail clients. Except in the most extreme cases, there are no changes to the

figure 14.2
An in-store sale sign. Merchandise reductions are made by the retailer so that the products that sell will make room for new merchandise.

mass-produced lines of merchandise. Since retailers that deal in private branding and labeling have complete control over the design of their products, they can make their merchandise to their specifications. For example, once a line has been created, a long-sleeve model can be changed to a three-quarter sleeve offering if the retailer believes it will sell better in that style. These and other product specifications, such as trimmings, can be adjusted until the retailer thinks it is a potential best seller.

Because there is less competition, there is the potential for greater profitability. National brands are heavily promoted, adding extra costs to the products. With private branding, this and other extra costs such as the salaries of high-profile designers are eliminated; a private brand without these expenses can often achieve a higher markup and in return realize greater profitability.

The need to adhere to some manufacturer's purchasing requirements is eliminated. For example, many of the better-known brands are prepackaged according to the dictates of the producer. That means that buyers are unable to tailor the size distribution to fit their specific needs. This can lead to an abundance of slow-selling sizes and a shortage of the sizes that sell best. Ultimately the leftovers head for the markdown racks and minimize profits.

When a private label or brand is well received by the retailer's customers, it has the potential to create brand loyalty. Satisfied shoppers often return again to purchase the same lines of goods or buy them from the company's catalog or website, and repeat business is the key to success for any retail establishment.

Vendor demands in terms of advertising requirements are eliminated. Many of the better-known manufacturers, as a condition of purchasing, set minimum amounts that retailers must spend to promote their products. This contract term adds costs to the marketing of the products, often making them less profitable for the company.

Merchandising Approaches

There are numerous ways in which retailers approach private branding. As previously mentioned, some carry a certain proportion of private labels and national brands, others subscribe to "The Store is the Brand," some utilize licensed arrangements with well-known names to bring exclusivity to their inventories, and a few engage in the innovation known as **partnering**.

The Proportional Philosophy

To have a model stock that will appeal to the widest range of customer desires generally requires retailers to mix name brands and private brands and labels. By proportioning their merchandise, these merchants recognize that some customers prefer established household names, some like private labels, and still others want to choose from a combination of both. Department stores tend to subscribe to this promotional philosophy.

Because department stores are organized to provide a wealth of different products and brands to the consumer, it can prove damaging to their bottom line to carry only private brands or only national brands. A case in point is Sears. For most of its years in business, the company prided itself on its own brands and labels. While this approach made Sears one of the more important players in retailing history, its popularity slowly eroded when customers began demanding it carry more of the nationally advertised brands. In response, in the early 1990s, Sears abandoned its private brand identity and started stocking highly visible labels. Today, it promotes numerous famous brands alongside its own, including Levi's, Carter's, New Balance, Reebok, and Adam Levine, among others. Figure 14.3 shows a Sears store.

The **proportional philosophy** of private to national brands that a retailer stocks depends upon how much customers accept each type. Past sales records are excellent indicators of the popularity of each classification. By examining these sales figures in predetermined time periods, retailers are able to determine the relative success of the two merchandise offerings and make adjustments as dictated by customer purchases. For example, if each period in a 5-year study indicates a 1 percent increase of private brand sales, the inventory plans should be adjusted to reflect this trend. If private label products are decreasing in popularity, the retailer should carry a greater proportion of manufacturer brands.

figure 14.3
Sears now carries many national brands. There was a change in management philosophy to not limit their inventories only to their private brands.

When a retailer first embarks upon a private label program, it will have no past sales records to help determine the proportions. Through various types of marketing research, which might include questionnaires and focus groups, the merchant "guesstimates" its initial private label needs and adjusts them once the label is better established and has begun to generate sales records.

The "The Store is the Brand" Philosophy

When shoppers enter a Gap location, a Banana Republic store or an Old Navy unit, they are limited to buying products that bear each store's name. Although Gap once carried lines such as Levi Strauss, today it only features its own brand. The philosophy centers upon the concept that the store and the brand are one and the same. If the retailers are successful in motivating customers to return to their stores or websites to purchase their branded products, they have achieved the ultimate in exclusivity.

Although Gap is still the leader in the "The Store is the Brand" concept, others are catching up using this philosophy. Based in Spain, Zara and Massimo Dutti are gaining prominence through this policy. Both of these companies are expanding worldwide and are achieving significant recognition from fashion shoppers. They primarily carry men's and women's styles but are starting to expand to home furnishings.

Other major retailers that successfully utilize this concept are Abercrombie & Fitch, Eddie Bauer, and the promotionally driven Jos. A. Bank Clothiers, Inc., which has made it a success in discount retailing.

Licensed Private Branding

Recognizing the power of certain signatures and relationships, some retailers subscribe to a form of private branding and labeling that involves licensing, called **brand licenses** and **brand signatures**. By contracting with well-known personalities and celebrity designers, businesses such as Kohl's have reaped significant benefits.

The entertainers that have contracted with retailers include Jennifer Lopez and Madonna. Designers include Isaac Mizrahi, Vera Wang and Liz Claiborne. Figure 14.4 shows the Jennifer Lopez brand.

Partnering Brands

The most recent innovation in privatization of brands and labels is known as partnering. Instead of developing their own brands and labels or becoming involved in the typical licensing agreements, a few major retailers are taking an approach that is similar to the concept of **leased departments**. In leasing arrangements, outside merchants occupy a portion of the store and use it to sell their own products. Oftentimes these vendors, many of whom sell precious jewelry or furs, maintain their own departments in the retail operations but do not identify themselves as the merchants, so they appear to be the same as any others in the store. Practitioners of this type of retailing may operate a number of these departments in several stores on a nonexclusive basis. In partnering arrangements, the outside vendor has an exclusive relationship with the retailer it occupies.

figure 14.4
The Jennifer Lopez brand (pictured here for Kohl's) is one of the many celebrity brands that has made a significant impression on consumers. Jennifer Lopez is important in attracting the Hispanic market.

An example of the partnering between retailers is at Sears. Sears is partnering with Two Hearts Maternity, a division of Destination Maternity Corporation.

Private Label and Brand Acquisition

Retailers that purchase manufacturers' brands have to buy either directly from them or from manufacturer representatives or wholesalers. Retailers that participate in developing their own brands and labels, however, have several choices for merchandise acquisition. They can have the goods manufactured in their wholly owned facilities; purchase them from outside contractors that specialize in tailoring private label products for specific users, buy from national manufacturers that, in addition to producing their own "name" collections also produce special lines for retailers under their own labels; participate in private label programs that have been designed and distributed by retail marketing specialists such as resident buying offices; or from noncompeting retailer groups.

The following sections describe these different choices.

WHOLLY OWNED SUBSIDIARIES

The main way that the giants in fashion retailing obtain their private label merchandise is by owning their own production companies. "The Store is the Brand" retailers in particular are merchants as well as manufacturers. These support businesses that manufacture the products for the retail outlets are **wholly owned subsidiaries**. L Brands, Inc. is one such company.

PURCHASING FROM OUTSIDE CONTRACTORS

While company-owned production facilities afford the retailer total control in terms of product design, a guarantee of exclusivity, the best possible production time frame to maximize sales, and so forth, some merchants have neither the financial resources to have their own factories nor the expertise needed for such undertakings. Instead, they choose a method that involves relationships with companies that supply everything from design assistance to the actual production of the merchandise. Figure 14.5 shows factory workers in China.

figure 14.5
Outside contractors producing fashion items in China. Offshore factories participate in garment construction because factories in the United States are more costly.

Throughout the United States and abroad, there are many manufacturers of fashion merchandise that are in business to help merchants create their own private label collections to sell at all price points in stores, catalogs, websites, and home shopping networks. The latter channel of distribution, in fact, is an enormous client of private label developers—the vast majority of the merchandise offered for sale is not standard manufacturers' brands but items only available on the home shopping programs.

In many instances, a retailer brings styles that have been successfully marketed by prominent designers and manufacturers to a contractor to have the styles adapted to its needs. The contractor then modifies the original designs by substituting fabrics, adding or deleting trimmings, or making minor modifications such as sleeve lengths, thereby creating a "new" model and producing it for the retailer to sell under a private label.

Using National Manufacturer Production Facilities

Although their primary concern is to design and market their own brands and labels, some of these manufacturers contract with retailers to produce lines that bear the retailers' own signatures. The practice was first popularized by Sears when its Kenmore brand of appliances was produced by prominent manufacturers and marketed as Sears' private brand.

In many cases, the retailer purchases the nationally known collections that bear the producer's label but also contracts to have a separate line made that is identified as its private label. Manufacturers of these established labels engage in this activity for a number of reasons: it helps to maintain a sound working relationship with a major retailer that regularly purchases the national brand; keeps factory operations running during slow periods, thus avoiding layoffs of employees; and achieves an additional profit that it otherwise would forego.

The retailer's advantages from these relationships include the guarantee of receiving merchandise with the same qualities as those from the manufacturer's own brands and maintaining servicing of its accounts because of its commitments to the national brands.

Participating in Resident Buying Office Programs

In addition to the typical benefits that they receive from resident buying offices and other fashion consulting groups, many retailers use these resources as a means of procuring private label collections for their own companies. By choosing this route, they avoid the vast expenditures associated with maintaining factories or engaging in long-term contracts with outside vendors.

The larger resident buying offices such as The Doneger Group have their own private label brands.

Those merchants that are either too small to establish their own labels or not properly versed in production matters often use this route as a means of entering the private label arena. Since the clients of the resident buying office are noncompeting, there is no chance that their private labels will compete.

Forming Noncompeting Buying Groups

Because of the potential for better profits from private label programs, a growing number of small retailers are pooling their resources and professional expertise and are entering the private label as groups, thereby avoiding the significant expense of going it alone. The concept of **buying groups** is not new; they have existed for many years. Originally their primary purpose was to combine orders so that they could buy from designers and national manufacturers who maintained minimum order requirements that were too extensive for their individual needs.

The process generally involves interfacing with freelance designers who create models that would serve the member's merchandising needs, and making arrangements with contractors for the production of the lines. Before any items are produced, the line is evaluated by the members of the group, and edited to make any necessary changes.

The degree of exclusivity that is important to private branding and labeling is sufficient to the needs of the group's participants. Since the member merchants are not in direct competition with each other, they are able to control pricing, invest in joint advertising and promotion of the label, and make any changes to suit the needs of the membership.

PROMOTING AWARENESS OF PRIVATE BRANDS AND LABELS

The advantage of having nationally prominent brands and labels in the retailer's inventory is that they are generally in the public's eye. With the vast sums invested by prominent designers or manufacturers on special promotions and campaigns, and the coverage of such collections by the fashion industry's editorial press, the individual retailers' clienteles are generally aware of their offerings. Companies like Ralph Lauren and Calvin Klein have either their own in-house public relations staffs to get their message across or use the services of outside publicity resources to make the public aware of its latest fashion introductions.

Those engaged in private label programs do not enjoy the luxury of having someone else promote their exclusive lines, but must engage in a variety of endeavors to guarantee customer recognition. Ways to achieve this recognition include advertising campaigns, special events, development of special departments, visual presentations, customer giveaways, and staff familiarization. The following sections describe those different methods.

Advertising Campaigns

When major retailers embark upon a new private label, they budget a significant sum to make their own customers and others aware of the new merchandise. Some retailers have in-house teams that develop ad campaigns involving all of media.

Retailers can easily alert their regular customer base to the new line via direct marketing. Armed with mailing lists of their credit card customers, they generally send separate mailers announcing the private label or enclose ads in each customer's monthly billing statements. Supplementing the direct mail endeavor is generally a multimedia campaign that often combines newspaper, magazine, TV, radio, their websites, and social media. The Internet, in particular, has become an extremely important tool for reaching the consumer, not only on their own websites, but on "**Internet popups**" on search engines that announce the new line and lead users directly to the retailer's website where they can further explore the products.

One-time ads are insufficient in marketing new collections, so retailers must create a variety of advertising campaigns that regularly remind shoppers of the private labels in their merchandise mix.

Special Events

The introduction of a new fashion private label requires a substantial investment in special events. These happenings include runway shows that take place either within the department in which the new line will be housed or in a special events center that most major retailers have in their flagship stores. Often, these fashion shows are dovetailed with charitable events that provide contributions for the charities while highlighting the merchant's newest merchandising endeavor.

Celebrities are often used to promote a new label. When shoppers visit the store to see them, they are also made aware of the new private label. Personality appearances are not limited to brick-and-mortar outlets; celebrities are often on home shopping cable shows to endorse particular lines, all of which have private brands that either include the celebrity signature on the label or use the personality to give the line or product a little extra clout.

Creation of Special Departments

Today's retail environments are no longer the large arenas with what seem to be never-ending departments featuring a host of different lines. Fashion retailers that subscribe to the **store within a store** concept include Bloomingdale's, Saks Fifth Avenue, Bergdorf Goodman, and Neiman Marcus. To underscore the importance of their own private labels, many retailers have designed departments that separate the products from others in the store in settings that exemplify fashion exclusivity. Macy's uses this approach with private labels such as INC and Charter Club.

Visual Presentations

Exterior and interior visual merchandising are excellent means of highlighting new private labels. Whether potential purchasers of the private brand have been motivated by advertising to come to the store or have merely walked past the premises by chance they can be attracted to the merchandise by window displays that prominently feature the items. Inside the store, strategic placement of the goods, eye-catching displays, and other visual tools of the trade can make shoppers even more curious about the new line.

Customer Giveaways

Some retailers have developed promotional plans that help keep shoppers aware of the new private label even after they have left the store. By distributing shopping bags emblazoned with the name of the new label, small items such as pens engraved with the brand's logo or signature, or reusable totes that feature the private label's name, the retailer makes it more likely that shoppers will remember the label and look for it when buying in the store, online, through catalogs, or social media.

Employee Training

It is important to train employees at all levels so they are prepared to answer shoppers' questions concerning the collection. The training may be accomplished in the following ways:

- *Special classes.* In these face-to-face sessions, product developers and others responsible for creating the new line present the salient points about the merchandise, such as pricing comparisons to similar nationally marketed lines and ease in care of the product.

- *Closed circuit TV.* In large department stores and specialty chains operating a great number of units in different regions, management often utilizes closed circuit programming and power points to offer product presentations. This technique allows staff that are far from the company's headquarters or flagship stores to ask questions of those giving the presentation.

- *Video and DVDs.* Professionally produced videos and DVDs carefully outline all of the planning that went into the creation of the new line, the final products that will reach the selling floor, and the benefits that will be passed on to the customers who purchase them. With **DVD training** employees can view these programs as often as necessary to solidify their knowledge of the private label.

Chapter Highlights

1. The use of private labels in major department stores and chains is continuing to increase and now stands at approximately 35 percent of the overall inventories.

2. While national brands still dominate the fashion retailing industry, every year their importance erodes in many retail operations.

3. Advantages of private branding and labeling to retailers include a lessening of price cutting, the ability to tailor garments to specific retailer needs, minimizing competition, the potential for establishing brand loyalty, and the elimination of the need to adhere to specific manufacturer purchasing requirements.

4. The most important approach to private labeling is known as the proportional method, where retailers set aside one portion of their model stock for private brands and the rest for manufacturer-produced brands.

5. Retailers following the "The Store is the Brand" philosophy require that the only brand they carry is the one that bears their name.

6. Partnering is a relatively recent approach to developing merchandise exclusivity, by which a major retailer forms formal partnerships with other retail companies that occupy specific shops within the store.

7. Licensed arrangements with celebrities are very important to retailers that believe their clout will help to sell the products.

8. Retailers may acquire private labels and brands through wholly owned subsidiaries, joint ventures, purchases from outside contractors and/or national manufacturers, membership in resident buying offices, participation in buying groups, and partnering.

9. To ensure that their private labels and brands become important products, retailers must significantly advertise and promote them, feature them in special events, show them in special departments, create successful visual presentations, keep the brand name in the customer's mind, and train their employees to completely understand them.

Terms of the Trade

brand licenses	partnering
brand signatures	price cutting
buying groups	private brand
DVD training	proportional philosophy
fair-trade pricing	store within a store
Internet popups	The Store is the Brand
leased departments	wholly owned subsidary
national brands	

For Discussion

1. Why do the majority of retailers carry nationally advertised brands in their inventories?

2. Does prestige ever play a part in motivating some consumers to purchase specific fashion merchandise? Why?

3. Is it possible that prestige adds a significant amount to the retail price of a garment or accessory? Why?

4. Why have more fashion retailers opted to include private label merchandise in their model stocks?

5. What philosophy does the typical fashion-oriented department store use in its private label involvement?

6. In what way does the proportional private label concept differ from the "The Store is the Brand" philosophy?

7. Why are many retail operations stocking their fashion inventories with merchandise acquired through celebrity-licensed agreements?

8. How does partnering differ from department leasing?

9. If retailers aren't able to participate in private label acquisition through wholly owned subsidiaries or joint ventures, by what other means can they acquire private label fashion products?

10. How can small retailers purchase private label merchandise when the amount of merchandise they need is often too small to produce it themselves and still guarantee a degree of exclusivity?

11. Why do some nationally prominent manufacturers that produce their own collections enter into the private label arena?

12. What types of special events do retailers of private labels conduct to promote their own brands?

13. Why is it beneficial for major retailers to create special departments for their private label collections instead of mixing the items into other departments?

14. By what means are retail employees trained to fully understand the advantages of their company's private brands?

Case Problem

Questions

1. Do any of the suggestions make sense in improving Carnegie's position? Defend your answer with logical reasoning.
2. What alternate solution might help the company achieve a new direction and ultimately increase sales and profitability?

Since the late 1880s, when it made its debut as a fashion retailer, the Carnegie Company has maintained a position in the marketing of fashion merchandise that is rivaled by few in the industry. After the success of the first store, the proprietors opened several branches, and in 1922 operated and managed the original unit, its flagship, and five other units. Business kept improving, with each year's sales and profits exceeding those of the previous.

The Carnegie brothers, eventually replaced by their offspring, continued to successfully operate the company as a private entity. They employed a management team that aided them in their decision making and left the buying and merchandising responsibilities to the buyers and merchandisers, who had gained experience from their roles in other department store operations.

In 1965, Carnegie, now the operators of 16 units, entered into direct marketing with a Christmas catalog. The response was more than it expected, and soon added numerous catalogs throughout the year to give its off-site venture more visibility. This decision was also positive, and sales continued to increase.

In 1982, the company sold its holdings to another fashion retail giant, Walker & Peck; because the Carnegie name was considered to be prestigious, the new owners kept it. The new owners continued on the expansion program. By 1997, there were 32 units, and 12 individual catalogs were produced each year.

Always ready to address any means of increasing sales, Carnegie entered the world of the Internet and established its own website. It was now a true multi-channel retailer. While online sales weren't as spectacular as those in the stores and catalogs, the website showed the potential of being accepted by consumers.

At the turn of the 21st century, for the first time in its history, the company was feeling the negative effects that department stores faced across the country. As a result of the "me-too" merchandising that was pervasive in the industry, Carnegie customers began to opt for specialty stores where the merchandise assortments were often more exciting. Even though its private label programs, first introduced in 1982, were successful, the company had a need to look for more individuality.

The company's C.E.O. held several meetings trying to rectify the falling sales and profits. Suggestions included turning the company into a "The Store is the Brand" operation, disbanding the website operation since sales only increased slightly each year, and changing the name of the company to Walker & Peck. At this time a decision has yet to be rendered to improve the company's profit picture.

Exercises and Projects

1. Visit a department store or specialty store to evaluate its private label collections. Through your own observation, and with the help of a department manager, gather enough information to develop a chart that has three sections; the department name, the private labels in it and the merchandising approach.*

   * The designation should be fully owned private label, license, partnering.

2. Visit any value retailer such as Target or Kohl's to assess its collections of private brands. You might ask to meet with the store manager, explaining what you are doing, or email the company before your visit to learn the names of these products.

Ask questions concerning the number and names of any licensing arrangements the retailer has made, the names of the brands that it has developed using names it has decided upon, the importance of these brands to the overall merchandising direction, and anything else of interest concerning this type of merchandising. With the acquired information, prepare a brief report on your findings and present it to the class.

chapter fifteen

INVENTORY PRICING

After reading this chapter, you should be able to:

- Discuss the various factors that fashion retailers consider in pricing their merchandise.

- Evaluate the importance of competition to retailers in determining their prices.

- Explain the concept of markup and perform its calculations.

- Identify the different markup philosophies that retailers use in pricing their inventories.

- List several reasons for markdowns and how they are calculated.

- Describe the nature of automatic markdown systems.

After retailers have established their merchandise mix through purchasing national brands and creating private labels and brands, the buyer, in the case of purchases from outside manufacturers, and merchandise managers or upper-management teams in the case of private labels, must determine the individual price that will be charged for each item. Whether retailers are exclusively brick-and-mortar operations, catalogs, or websites, or engage in a multi-channel approach to reach their targeted market, they all develop pricing philosophies and guidelines that they hope will bring a profit to their companies.

Retailers must consider many factors before formulating such policies, including the composition of their consumer market, the image that they wish to project, the amount of competition they face, and other elements that relate to specific merchandise. Retailers who have their own private labels and brands have additional concerns to address. Unlike merchandise that has designated specific wholesale costs, such as national brands, brands that have been designed and produced specifically for and by the retailer involve costs associated with design origination, fabric selections, construction techniques and the like, that the retailer must consider before assigning any retail price.

The buyers and merchandise managers must then apply their markups (the amount added to the cost to arrive at the retail price) based upon the guidelines established by the company's C.E.O. and upper-level management team, which depends upon the type of retail outlet and the inventory it carries. These guidelines range from the relatively simple policy of uniform markups to the more complex concept of individual markups.

Although retailers invest a significant amount of expense and time into planning their model stock, even the best plans will need some adjustments. Some merchandise will be on target and warrant reordering, and others will fall short of expected sales and might require **markdowns**. When to reduce the prices of slow sellers and how much of a reduction should be applied to these items are just two of the problems that buyers and merchandise managers must handle.

All retailers face a number of hurdles in merchandise pricing, but it is the fashion merchants that usually have the greatest challenges to confront. Fashion goods are more difficult to merchandise than any other inventory classification because retailers must contend with customer acceptance of designer whims as well as seasonal cycling of merchandise, which creates a short selling period.

PRICING CONSIDERATIONS

Before they decide on the appropriate price of each piece of merchandise, fashion merchants focus their attention on such areas as the amount of competition they face, the life expectancy of the item, riskiness in terms of customer acceptance of a trendy style, overheads, the type of promotional endeavors they need to conduct to bring attention to the product, the image of the company they wish to project, the type of customer patronage they seek, special requirements needed in the sale of the merchandise, and its vulnerability to pilferage. These areas are described in the following sections.

Competition

Fashion retailers today face greater pricing challenges than they experienced in the past. In addition to the traditional competition from the conventional brick-and-mortar retail community, there is a growing number of merchants that sell fashion for less. The off-pricers such as Burlington Coat Factory and Marshalls carry many of the well-known fashion collections but at greatly reduced prices. Figure 15.1 features a Marshalls store.

Retailers also face **online competition**. Websites of all kinds offer a wealth of the same sought-after labels such as Calvin Klein, DKNY, and Ralph Lauren. By logging onto such websites as www.smartbargains.com, shoppers can get a great assortment of the Ralph Lauren label at highly discounted prices, and at www.bluefly.com, the cream of the fashion crop, such as Fendi and Prada, is available at discounts of up to 70 percent. The big Internet giant eBay now offers fashion merchandise that customers do not bid for, at prices that are well below the traditional.

figure 15.1
Marshalls stores are competitive to traditional retailers. Price conscious customers visit this store to get the best value.

Faced with all of this value pricing, many department stores are meeting the competition by presenting several promotions throughout the year. Bloomingdale's, in particular, regularly sends discount mailers to its customers with coupons they can redeem in stores or through the catalogs.

One of the major competitive forces is the continued expansion of the outlet malls such as those operated by the Simon Property Group, which took over from the Mills Corporation. They are replete with entertainment centers and eating facilities that are above the standard. Sawgrass Mills in a suburb of Fort Lauderdale, Florida, for example, offers dining establishments such as the Cheesecake Factory to make the shopping experience a pleasant one which offers bargains at the same time.

With the growth of these retailing empires, the traditionalists have been geared to study their competition's pricing and make price adjustments to their merchandise accordingly.

Merchandise Characteristics

To a large extent, fashion merchandise has a limited life expectancy, or perishability. Not only do seasonal changes affect the salability of goods but fashions that are considered to be trendy or fad-like often decline in desirability soon after they reach the selling floor, catalog pages or company websites. In these cases, their prices must be high enough to cover the losses attributed to their sudden demise.

Some items are delicate or fragile and subject to damage. White or pastel garments often require markdowns when they become soiled after careless handling, and sheer, chiffon-like materials might be damaged after they are tried on by many customers. These perishable characteristics necessitate higher than typical markups to offset the losses caused when they are damaged.

Swimsuits and furs, because of their seasonal nature, are generally marked up more than other items to make certain that those that do sell early in the season bring sufficient profit to cover the losses of those that do not.

Small fashion items such as jewelry must be stored in cases and therefore necessitate additional sales personnel to show them. This tends to increase overhead expenses, thus warranting an additional markup.

Company Image

Many fashion retailers enjoy prestigious images that enable them to price their merchandise higher than what is typical for their industry. A markup of just a few percentage points is safe since it will rarely discourage customers from purchasing. Companies such as Bergdorf Goodman, Neiman Marcus, Saks Fifth Avenue, and Henri Bendel are typical of those that charge higher prices for their merchandise. Although value shopping is becoming increasingly important to the vast majority of consumers, price is not a factor for every customer. Many get sufficient pleasure from patronizing these companies and are willing to pay a little extra for the "privilege." Figure 15.2 features a Neiman Marcus event.

figure 15.2
Stephen Brunelle, Dwyane Wade, and Brett Fahlgren at the Neiman Marcus *GQ* fashion chat. This and other events often motivate shoppers to become customers.

Customer Profile

Chapter 4, "The Fashion Consumer," focused a great deal of attention on different types of consumers and how their fashion needs are satisfied. All retailers should recognize the composition of their markets and understand how price affects their purchases. Some classes of people are cost conscious and only shop in stores or patronize off-site ventures that feature the price advantage, while others such as those in the upper-upper and lower-upper classes are more concerned with service and quality and pay little attention to price. Factors such as income, lifestyle, and psychographics indicate to what degree price is an object; merchants need to take **customer profiles** into consideration before establishing a pricing philosophy.

Stock Turnover

A very important concern to retailers is the number of times a year most items in an average inventory are sold. The more often an inventory turns over, the less need there is for a high markup. Conversely, the lower the number of **stock turnovers**, the higher the markup to make a profit.

Off-price retailers and discounters are able to turn profits with lower markups because they expect greater turnover rates. Traditional fashion retailers that charge higher prices than the off-pricers and discounters expect fewer stock turns. In menswear, for example, the stock does not turn over as much because men do not purchase as many items, so men's items are often marked higher than women's wear, because women buy more items and thus turn over the stock more frequently.

Promotional Endeavors

Fashion retailers participate in a variety of promotional activities to attract shoppers. The promotional involvement depends upon the size of the organization, its method of operation, its budget, and its target market. Promotional dollars spent on advertising, special events such as fashion shows, and visual merchandising contribute to the retailer's overhead expenses, which in turn necessitate higher prices. The use of special events such as Macy's annual Flower Show and Thanksgiving Day Parades, and the extravagant Christmas windows featured by Lord & Taylor, and Saks Fifth Avenue, were explored in Chapter 9, "The Importance of Visual Merchandising to Stores," and will be discussed in Chapter 16, "The Importance of Advertising and Promotion."

Services

Unlike their off-price counterparts, which subscribe to a bare-bones service philosophy, many of America's better-known fashion emporiums offer a host of services to their clienteles. These include **personalized shopping**, where customers receive individualized attention for all of their shopping needs, such as the "At Your Service" program at Bloomingdale's; foreign language assistance for non-English speaking shoppers, such as the interpreters program at Macy's; corporate gift service; and bridal registries. While there are no extra costs charged to the customers for these services, the expenses incurred by offering them are taken into consideration when merchandise is being priced.

Vulnerability to Shrinkage

The attention retailers pay to shoplifting and internal theft, as described in Chapter 11, "Merchandise Distribution and Loss Prevention," underscores the severity of the problem and the losses fashion retailers sustain. Some companies are plagued by the problem more than others and must address its seriousness when determining price. These shrinkage losses are felt not only in the brick-and-mortar units, but also on websites, where shrewd thievery is taking place. The cost of losses must be considered, as must the cost attributed to the protection of the merchandise and the fraudulent order placement.

In fur departments, for example, where retailers must install sophisticated surveillance systems to protect the merchandise and include additional sales associates on the selling floor, the cost of doing business increases. Departments that are located near store entrances provide shoplifters with greater accessibility to the merchandise and ease of getaway and thus might warrant higher prices than other departments that are less prone to thievery. Figure 15.3 shows furs on racks.

While highly sophisticated systems are in place in most retail environments to curtail shoplifting and in most warehouses to deter internal theft, enough merchandise is stolen to necessitate higher prices.

Buyer Knowledge

Typically buyers apply the same markup to all of the items they have purchased from manufacturers. Occasionally, however, they may price some styles higher or lower. Collections that are likely to be carried by competitors are not going to be priced higher or lower than usual. But a particular business suit that has been obtained on an exclusive basis from a relatively unknown resource, may allow for a higher markup. A few extra dollars added to the retail price of this merchandise could result in a better profit for the company. Conversely, another suit might seem too expensive when the traditional markup is applied and the buyer will mark it lower to have broader customer appeal.

figure 15.3
These fur coats require extra security and thus higher markups. Precious jewelry, leather apparel, and other luxury goods also require special devices to safeguard them from shoplifters.

It is imperative that the buyer completely evaluate each item that is to become part of the department's model stock and make certain that the retail price applied will make it a potentially successful and profitable seller.

Exclusive Merchandise Resources

Some fashion retailers are able to charge prices that are higher for some styles because of their rights to **exclusive resources** in their trading area. For merchants involved in multi-channel retailing that extensively market their products via catalogs and the Internet, these trading areas are far beyond those of their brick-and-mortar operations, so they are usually unable to charge higher prices, except for privately held brands and labels.

As described in Chapter 14, "Private Label Importance to the Merchandise Mix," companies that create and produce their own products are not affected by the competition associated with the selling of nationally known labels and brands. Exclusivity of this merchandise enables them to gain additional markups since they have eliminated the competitive factor from the pricing equation.

Sometimes a retailer will stock manufacturer brands and labels that are rare in its trading area, giving it a degree of exclusivity. In such cases, the retailer may charge higher prices.

If a retailer is willing to purchase merchandise from a manufacturer in extremely large quantities, it may benefit from controlling the limited distribution of the items in its area. In such situations, the retailer will likely charge more than it normally would if the products were mass distributed to several competing retailers.

MATHEMATICAL CONCEPTS OF PRICING

Once a retailer's top management has analyzed all of the factors that make up the cost of its operation, it must determine the markup—how much must be added to the cost of the merchandise to arrive at a selling price that will bring a profit. While this is the beginning point in price determination, not every item sells at the original marked price, and it might have to be reduced to motivate purchasing. The amount of the reduction is known as the markdown. The following sections address the reasons for these price reductions as well as the mathematical computation involved in determining the markup and markdown.

Markups

Markups are derived from a mathematical formula. Computer programs also automatically determine the markup once the wholesale price (cost) and selling price (retail) have been considered. The basic formula is as follows:

$$\text{Retail} - \text{Cost} = \text{Markup}$$

For example, if a pair of men's trousers costs $80 and it is priced to retail at $150, the markup is $70.

$$\$150 \ (R) - \$80 \ (C) = \$70 \ (MU)$$

In this case, the buyer purchased the pair of trousers from a resource for $80, and priced them to sell at $150, and achieved a profit of $70. This situation is the best possible one for the retailer, but in reality, not every item sells at the original, or **initial markup**. Using the above illustration, assume that the trousers did not sell and were marked down to $120 and then sold. The actual markup, or the maintained markup, achieved by the retailer was $40.

$120 (price after markdown) – $80 (C) = $40

One of the factors that retailers often build into their initial prices is an estimate of how great the eventual markdowns will have to be before the goods are sold. While dollar markup gives the actual dollars achieved by the retailer once the product has been sold, markups are usually expressed in percentages. Although the markup percentages may be expressed on cost price or retail price, fashion retailers generally use the method of markup percentage based on retail price.

Before the markup percentage can be determined, it is necessary to first find the dollar markup. To determine the markup percentage based on retail price, the dollar markup price is divided by the retail price. For example, if a sweater costs $40 and it retails for $80, the markup percentage on retail is 50 percent.

Retail – Cost = Markup
$80 – $40 = $40
$$\frac{Markup}{Retail} = Markup \text{ percent based on retail}$$
$40 ÷ 80 = 50%

Markdowns

No matter how carefully a buyer determines costs and applies markups, the retailer will likely have to mark down merchandise. There are numerous reasons why prices must be adjusted. Some are attributable to retailer error and others to uncontrollable outside forces. The following sections explore the reasons for marking down the merchandise as well as the size of the reduction and when markdowns should be taken.

Reasons for Markdowns

The circumstances that prompt retailers to reduce the price of merchandise include errors committed by the buyer, management errors, sales force inattention and situations the retailer cannot control.

Buying Errors

Fashion buyers are more prone to errors than any of their purchasing counterparts because of the unpredictable nature of the industry; consequently, they must take the markdown route to right their wrongs. For example, they might misjudge the popularity of a potential fashion trend and find that shoppers do not like the new styles. They might overbuy a particular silhouette or choose the wrong color palette, incorrectly determine the proportion of private label goods to designer brands, inaccurately time the arrival of the merchandise, or place too much emphasis on an unheralded designer. All these miscalculations may require markdowns to entice customers to turn over the stock.

MANAGEMENT ERRORS

Although buyers are given the purchasing responsibility, they are guided by the decisions made by management, particularly the divisional merchandise managers and the general merchandise manager. They determine the markup percentage, for example, on which the buyer figures the retail price. Some retail operations follow the "**markup by classification**" philosophy, which mandates a specific markup percentage for each department. If the buyer lacks the flexibility to adjust the prescribed price, an item might have too high a selling price to motivate purchasing and may eventually be marked down.

INADEQUATE SALES STAFF

Many shoppers have been discouraged from making a purchase by sales staff, even when calling catalog divisions seeking assistance before placing orders or using websites where individualized help is supposedly available. Many retailers are negligent when it comes to training their sales personnel. A few days of rigorous training by in-person, classroom instruction; video presentations; or online teaching can supply the direction the sales associates need to improve their efforts.

Retailers such as Nordstrom, Bloomingdale's, Neiman Marcus, and Saks Fifth Avenue have taken the initiative to motivate their on-site sales associates by offering commission incentives. Instead of taking the traditional straight salary route, which provides no direct correlation between sales and employee income, these companies have instituted remuneration programs that require 100 percent attention to selling and servicing the customer. The result has been increased sales, fewer markdowns, and better profits.

HIGH INITIAL PRICES

Sometimes buyers misjudge the price their customers are willing to pay for specific items. Occasionally they will price them higher than they should be, and if the competition charges less for the same item, not only won't the item sell, but the "overcharging" could result in a bad reputation for the company.

EXTERNAL FACTORS

Even the very best merchandise mix that is carefully advertised, promoted, visually merchandised, and presented to the shopper by enthusiastic, knowledgeable salespeople does not always provide the company with the sales results and profits it envisioned in its planning mode. Adverse weather conditions can be neither predicted nor avoided. An unusually warm September in traditionally cold climates might discourage shoppers from buying snowsuits for their children or other cold weather fashions such as coats, gloves, and scarves. A rainy, cool summer will not provide the necessary stimulation for purchasing swimsuits. Since the merchandise affected by these unforeseen conditions is seasonal in nature, each day of the inclemency provides less opportunity for selling. Markdowns are often necessary to induce stock turnover. Figure 15.4 shows a storm that could affect retailers.

A poor or declining economy, such as was prevalent in early 2010, also plays a significant role in the poor sale of fashion merchandise. While food items and other essentials are not as seriously affected, consumers generally pay less attention to fashion-oriented items during those times. National disasters are often the causes of poor sales.

figure 15.4
A major snowstorm affects the sales at retailers. At such times, customers often browse the Internet for their needs.

One of the best examples is the tragedy of September 11, 2001. Only time would eventually help the country's social and economic life return to normal.

Because it is impossible for anyone to control these external factors, it is the responsibility of everyone on staff to reduce errors in their own jurisdictions.

While the aforementioned reasons for markdowns seem to make sense, sometimes retailers extend their reach for customers by offering them what seems to be unbelievable, and often they are. In *Happening Now*, Jos. A. Bank's markdown veracity is examined.

HAPPENING NOW

IS THE JOS. A. BANK MARKDOWN PHILOSOPHY TRUTHFUL?

It is hard to believe that Jos. A. Bank Clothiers, Inc., the company that covers the television airwaves with commercials, is the same company that began its operation in 1905 as a fine men's merchant with quality merchandise at traditional prices. About 10 years ago, Jos. A. Bank started on a new endeavor to capture a larger share of the men's market by moving into a new arena that concentrates on heavy promotion of its products. The ads have been shown on many channels depicting their unbelievable discounts and special promotions.

The idea was to inflate prices and wait for the shoppers to bite. They did so for several years and business was solid. Finally, consumers got to the point of seeing through the "manipulative" promotions. While all stores have sales, Jos. A. Bank went over the top with "buy one, get two free" and other deceptive promotions. As a result of consumer disbelief, the lawsuits started to come in. They called it deceptive marketing and went on to sue the company. Even without the lawsuits, prospective customers shied away from the retailer's "Big Sales" philosophy because they realized everything was always on sale. As soon as one promotion ended, another surfaced that seemed to be better than the one before. Realizing the store never actually sold at traditional prices, and everything was always on sale, Jos. A. Bank shoppers started to ignore the company and sales plummeted. As the recession started to improve in late 2013, customers started to shy away from the company.

With 2013 sales at an extreme low, the company has started to change its image and practices. They are still offering some promotions, but more realistic ones. The problem is to retrain the customers to think differently. It will take a major emphasis to restore customers' faith, something that they are starting to do in early 2014. This will not be a quick fix that will take a year, but considerably longer to regain its once envious position in men's fashion.

When to Take Markdowns

The seasonal nature of fashion and its unpredictability in terms of customer acceptance makes it a merchandise classification that is more complicated to manage than any other. Although many factors necessitate price reductions to turn the inventory, timing the markdown is critical to providing ample time to sell the merchandise.

Given that the goods must be sold sometime during the season, retailers take different approaches to timing their markdowns. In the recent past, the vast majority of fashion merchants subscribed to the semiannual markdown philosophy. Typically the periods following Christmas and July 4th were traditional for marking down unsold merchandise. Figure 15.5 shows a Nordstrom store that follows the markdown philosophy taking the reductions at **traditional sales periods**.

Today more fashion retailers are opting for more frequent markdown periods for the following reasons:

- Fashion items held too long will lose their market.
- Merchandise held too long will require more significant markdowns.
- By quickly disposing of less desirable goods, the retailer's turnover rate will improve and enable the buyers to purchase fresher fashion items.
- There will be less room on the brick-and-mortar selling floor to display the new season's offerings that can be sold at full markup.

Although most fashion merchants abide by these principles, some still play by the old rules of following traditional sales periods. They argue that:

- Too many "sale" periods put customers on notice to wait for the price reductions.
- Sometimes a hasty decision to lower prices is unnecessary and waiting a few more weeks will bring a better profit to the company.
- During periods of markdowns, more people crowd the store, resulting in a reduction of customer service.

figure 15.5
At Nordstrom, traditional markdown periods are still their philosophy. Its twice a year sales periods are so popular with customers that many wait until then for purchasing.

Deciding the Size of the Markdown

To make goods sell faster, the markdown must demonstrate a significant savings for the potential customer. Few shoppers would be motivated to buy a dress that originally retailed for $120 that is now being offered for $110.

The size of the markdown is usually dependent upon when it is offered in the selling season. When a buyer wants to motivate coat shoppers in early October, the discount could be much smaller than the discount offered in the middle of January, when the season has virtually ended. The early markdown decision not only affords the buyer a lower markdown percentage, so the retailer loses less profit on the discount, but also allows for a higher markdown later in the season, when the retailer just wants to move the inventory.

Early markdowns usually reflect a savings of at least 20 percent, with end-of-the season sales often producing markdowns of 50 percent or more. Markdowns of less than 20 percent rarely entice the shopper to buy.

Arithmetically, the retailers calculate markdowns as percentages of the *new* selling price. For example, a dress originally priced at $100 has been marked down $30 to retail for $70. To determine the markdown percent, the following formula is used.

$\frac{\text{Markdown}}{\text{New retail}} = \text{Markdown percent}$

$\$30 \div \$70 = 42.86\%$

PRICING POLICIES

Fashion merchants subscribe to three major pricing policies in terms of how they apply their markups: **uniform company markup**, markup by classification, and markup by individual item. The following sections describe these policies.

Uniform Company Markup

Very few retailers apply a universal markup to each item in their inventory, except for off-pricers or discounters. In these organizations, the inventory as a whole is often marked up at a specific percentage without any attention being paid to the factors discussed in the section on pricing considerations. The retailer determines the cost of running the operation and applies a markup that covers these expenses with enough left over for profit.

The uniform company markup is the simplest approach to pricing the merchandise but doesn't account for the variables that necessitate different markups for different product classifications and items.

Markup by Classification

Department store and chain store organizations generally employ a system that involves markup by classification which uses different markups for each of their merchandise classifications and carries them throughout their on-site and off-site divisions. Since each category requires different attention and costs in bringing the goods to the customers, their separate markups reflect these costs. For example, precious jewelry and furs necessitate better security systems, and furniture requires more costly warehousing. Fashion merchandise is often short lived and must bring higher prices to make up for the lower markups of highly competitive electronics. If retailers that carried a full complement of hard goods and soft goods, as most department store organizations do, and used the uniform companywide markup philosophy, some items would be profitable and others would represent losses to the organization.

For such retailers to turn a profit, they must first assess the overall markup needed to be profitable. Once all of the pricing factors have been considered, a specific markup is assigned to each merchandise classification. Averaging these markup percentages should result in the appropriate overall markup needed by the company.

Traditionally, a department store's fashion merchandise is marked up higher than most of the company's other offerings.

In many retail operations, where traditional markups are uniformly applied according to classification, keystone markup—which refers to the doubling of the wholesale cost to arrive at the retail price—was once commonplace. An extension of this concept is known as **keystone markup plus**, where in addition to doubling the cost to arrive at the selling price, an extra amount is added. This is typically today's department store pricing.

Markup by Item

More fashion buyers are given the opportunity to apply individual markups to their inventories. They must, however, consider the markup percentage mandated by their merchandise managers. By using this pricing approach, buyers are able to price certain lines, such as private labels and those that they have arranged for exclusive distribution within their trading areas, higher than they normally would and price more competitive styles, such as national brands carried by their competitors, lower. As in the case of markup by classification, where averaging is a factor, this system also requires averaging. The only difference is that the average markup is achieved within the department.

For example, consider a junior sportswear department that features a large variety of items such as sweaters, dress pants, jeans, skirts, and sweats. Some of these items are more competitive than others and might require lower markups. To offset the lower prices, other items within the department will carry greater markups.

PRICE POINTS

No one retailer is able to feature fashion merchandise at every conceivable price. With couture designs at the top of the price scale and value items at the bottom, there is an enormous range of merchandise available that different retailers can offer. Retailers select particular price ranges, or **price points**, for their inventories for a number of reasons, including the following:

- Brick-and-mortar units are too small to feature every price point.
- Higher priced fashions are merchandised differently from their lower priced counterparts.
- Different levels of customer service must be delivered for every price range. For example, those engaged in high-end fashion are more likely to offer individualized customer attention than those that sell value-priced items.
- Different price points denote different company images.
- Fashion merchandise is available in similar styles at many prices, and featuring too many price points could confuse the consumer.
- Too many price points would reduce the overall assortment.

Today, more than ever before, retailers are becoming more restrictive in their merchandise price ranges. Macy's, for example, once carried a broad variety of prices ranging from upscale to budget. In the early 1980s, it began to trade up and narrow the price points. By doing so, it was able to project a more defined image of its company and tailor the services needed to satisfy its customers. Its action, still in place today, has proven to be a good move for Macy's. Retailers that offer a narrower range of price points are also beneficial to consumers, enabling them to immediately determine if a particular retailer meets their price requirements.

Pricing is no simple matter and retailers must carefully address it so that their profits will be maximized.

Chapter Highlights

1. Before fashion retailers can make any pricing decisions, they must consider many factors.

2. Retailers must explore such pricing considerations as the level of competition they face, the image they are trying to portray, the services they deem necessary to maintain customer satisfaction, and their vulnerability to shoplifting and internal theft.

3. Today's traditional merchant is facing a great deal of competition from websites that deal exclusively with highly discounted merchandise.

4. Many major fashion merchants are facing the competitive nature of the game by creating their own brands and labels.

5. Sometimes retailers' ability to negotiate exclusive agreements within their trading areas gives them the advantage of maintaining their pricing structures.

6. After costs of running the operation have been determined, the fashion retailer decides upon the appropriate markup to cover expenses and bring a profit.

7. Markup is the difference between the retail price and the wholesale cost.

8. Fashion merchandise is marked up higher than most other product classifications due to its perishability.

9. Even the greatest amount of purchase planning doesn't guarantee that shoppers will like every product. Some items must be marked down to improve their sales potential.

10. Markdowns may be needed because of errors attributed to the buyer, sellers, or management, or for reasons such as adverse weather conditions or economic slowdowns.

11. There are three major markup philosophies used by retailers in regard to their pricing policies: uniform company markups, markup by classification, and markup by individual item.

12. Retailers must establish which price points they will carry so that they will be able to properly project their image, offer the appropriate services for that price point, and feature the largest selection of products in that price range.

Terms of the Trade

customer profile	online competition
exclusive resources	personalized shopping
initial markup	price point
keystone markup plus	stock turnovers
markdown	traditional sales periods
markup by classification	uniform company markup

For Discussion

1. Why is it more difficult to merchandise fashion items than any other classification of consumer products?

2. Briefly describe two types of nontraditional fashion retail operations that pose considerable competition for the conventional retailer.

3. Explain the effect having a prestigious image makes on pricing.

4. What is meant by the concept of stock turnover?

5. While it is obvious that knowledgeable buying often improves the retailer's merchandising mix, does it in any way affect the prices the retailer charges?

6. List three factors that constitute exclusive merchandise resourcing.

7. If a dress costs the retailer $65 and it is retailed for $125, what is the dollar markup?

8. What is the difference between initial and maintained markup?

9. What is the markup percentage on retail for a sweater that costs $30 and retails for $50?

10. Discuss some of the errors attributed to management that might cause merchandise markdowns.

11. Why are an increasing number of fashion retailers opting for earlier markdowns?

12. If a coat that was initially priced to retail for $225 was marked down to $210, would it generally sell at a faster pace?

13. Differentiate between the uniform markup philosophy and markup by classification.

14. Why do most department stores use the classification approach when pricing their merchandise?

Case Problem

Questions

1. Which management suggestion is most appropriate to solve Langham's problem?

2. Using your answer to Question 1, how would you specifically make the company a more viable retail institution?

Langham's is a traditional full-service department store that has been in business for 60 years. In its downtown flagship and 12 branches, it features a wide assortment of hard goods and soft goods. It has always offered many services to its customers who, for the most part, are considered loyal to the company, even though company loyalty is considered by many industry professionals to be a thing of the past. For all of its years of operation, Langham's has been the primary source for family needs in all of its locations.

Unlike most of Langham's department store counterparts throughout the United States, which have abandoned some of their hard goods lines, the company continues to feature major appliances, television and stereo equipment, and electronics. It is company policy that it provides one-stop shopping for the markets the branches serve. While this policy has afforded customer convenience, it has adversely affected the company's profit picture.

For the last three years, the sales volume in the appliance department has declined. The problem seems directly related to the opening of a discount appliance center in the Langham's flagship trading area and others in or near the areas of some of its branches. To combat profit decline, members of the management team have made several suggestions. Among them are:

1. Eliminate the appliances department and expand the company's fashion areas.

2. Restructure the company as a specialized department store, closing all of its hard goods departments.

3. Retain its hard goods and soft goods philosophy but adjust its pricing policies. It should be noted that Langham's has always subscribed to the uniform markup policy.

Exercises and Projects

Visit two different types of fashion retailer, one a traditional department store and the other an off-pricer, and compare the various considerations they address when determining prices. Through your own observations, examine such factors as each store's promotional endeavors, image, security, services offered to the customers, or other areas that affect pricing. Develop a form that features the image, store design, and services of a department store and an off-pricer to record your observations.

	Department store	Off-pricer
Image	_____	_____
	_____	_____
	_____	_____
Store Design	_____	_____
	_____	_____
	_____	_____
Services	_____	_____
	_____	_____
	_____	_____
	_____	_____
	_____	_____

chapter sixteen

THE IMPORTANCE OF ADVERTISING AND PROMOTION

After reading this chapter, you should be able to:

- Classify the types of fashion retail advertising.

- Evaluate the advertising media in terms of their importance to fashion retailing organizations.

- Contrast online advertising with print and broadcast media.

- Discuss the concept of cooperative advertising and how it aids the fashion retailer.

- Describe the various special events undertaken by retailers to promote fashion merchandise.

- Explain the different types of fashion shows utilized by the fashion industry.

- Identify and discuss several techniques that fashion merchants employ to promote their companies and merchandise.

Once a retail organization's management team has made the decisions concerning brick-and-mortar location and design, human resources selection, and merchandise procurement, it needs to decide how to make its potential and regular customers aware of its existence and its merchandise assortment. The primary manner in which to achieve such recognition is through **advertising**. Today, with the fashion retailing community expanding its operations through the use of websites and social media outlets, the challenge of reaching a broader customer base is another task these advertisements must meet. The wealth of advertising directed toward the fashion consumer is immediately obvious in newspapers, magazines, catalogs, direct marketing pieces, and on television, radio, fashion retail websites, and social media.

In the highly competitive fashion retailing market, it is imperative that merchants establish specific images and alert shoppers about their companies so consumers will think of them when they want to satisfy their fashion needs. Advertising is the best way to spread the word.

In addition to different advertising options, retailers can use numerous types of special promotions and events.

THE FASHION RETAILER'S SALES PROMOTION DIVISION

To promote their companies and the merchandise they carry, retailers, both large and small, set aside funds that are earmarked for advertising and promotion. The larger retail operations usually have in-house promotional divisions. For special major events, these retailers may call in outside organizations to help their own staff face the challenges of such undertakings. Small retailers usually employ agencies to carry out their promotional programs.

Once a company has determined its promotional goals, it needs to ensure that it can achieve them. While advertising generally accounts for the largest percentage of the promotional expenditures, it is not the only avenue fashion retailers take to reach their target markets. Fashion shows, demonstrations, **in-house video** programming, special campaigns and celebrations, personal appearances by designers and manufacturers, and institutional events such as charity functions are also successful means of getting a merchant's fashion message to its consumers.

Along with their advertising and promotional involvement, fashion retailers use visual merchandising in their brick-and-mortar operations as discussed in Chapter 9, "The Importance of Visual Merchandising to Stores."

Although the individual departments comprising the promotional activities are all on the same level in terms of organizational planning, the advertising department generally commands the lion's share of the promotional dollar.

ADVERTISING

As defined by the www.StudyBlue.com, advertising is a "paid-for form of non-personal presentation of the facts about goods, services, or ideas to a group." These "facts" are illustrated with the use of **copy** (the written message) and/or **artwork** that includes photographs and drawings. It is impersonal in nature because it is directed to a group rather than to a specific person, as is the case in personal selling.

The advertising programs are either internally structured, utilizing a host of in-house specialists to carry out the various aspects of anything from single ads to complete campaigns, or externally based, outside sources that encompass numerous different approaches to developing advertising plans and carrying them out.

The Internal Structure

In-house advertising departments based in the major fashion retail operations are organized in a few different ways. The majority are composed of three individual subdepartments: copy, production, and art. In this arrangement, the copy area develops the written messages; the production section carries out the technical aspects inherent in ad reproduction, proofreading, and placement; and the art section produces the artwork such as photographs or drawings that will be used in the ads.

In fashion retailing's giant operations, which use extensive advertising, the advertising department is larger and often features five departments that are divided into periodical, broadcast, direct marketing, online, and signage. Of course, copy, production, and art areas are used for all of these departments.

External Advertising Resources

Small retailers most often do not have in-house professionals to carry out their advertising programs. Instead, they rely on one or more outside sources. The large retailers also use outside sources to supplement their in-house staffs.

In each of these external organizations, specialists guide the retailer clients through their quests to become better known to the consumer or to make the public better aware of their merchandise offerings.

Advertising agencies

Whether a client needs a complete campaign to announce the opening of a new branch, an individual advertisement to recognize the accomplishments of a charitable organization in the community or anything in between, **advertising agencies** offer a full range of creative services. The agency is paid based upon a commission by the medium in which the ad is featured; the standard rate is 15 percent. For example, if the agency places an ad in a newspaper that costs $10,000, the paper will return $1,500 to the agency. It is similar to the arrangement travel agencies have; the client doesn't pay to have the agency book a cruise; the cruise line pays the agency a commission for sending the business its way.

Freelance Designers

Sometimes a retailer wishing to feature a unique advertising or promotional campaign employs the services of an outside specialist. Even when the merchant has its own staff, an outside designer might assist in developing the concept. Not only do freelancers provide creative ideas to be used in the program but they can oversee the entire advertising process which might include providing the copy and artwork.

Merchandise Resources

Some fashion merchandise manufacturers prepare a variety of aids to help stimulate sales of the lines they provided to their retail customers. Some prepare **direct mail** flyers that feature specific items and offer them to their retail accounts at cost. Retailers then include the flyers with their customers' monthly charge statements. Other manufacturers prepare complete ads that the retailer can use as designed or as guides for their own ads. Most of the major fashion designers and manufacturers participate in cooperative advertising programs with retailers in which they pay for a share of the advertisements, as explored later in the chapter.

Media Services

Fashion retailers advertise in a variety of print and **broadcast media** to whet the appetites of their customers. To assist their retail clients with their advertising needs, **media** organizations generally have staff that supply a variety of services for ad preparation. These specialists help create the entire advertisement, including writing the copy, preparing the layout, and providing information on demographics and direction in terms of where the ads might be most effectively placed. These are free services, and clients pay only for the space that their ads will occupy. This is often the route taken by small fashion merchants who otherwise would not be able to afford advertising.

Market Consulting Firms

Market consultants, such as resident buying offices, in addition to their regular services of buying and merchandise planning, sometimes offer advice on advertising. Many have in-house specialists that provide everything from suggestions to complete ad campaigns to generate business for their retail clients' upcoming season.

Classification of Fashion Advertisements

Fashion merchants must carefully assess the various types of advertisements that alert customers to their existence or to sell specific merchandise. Within a retailer's promotional budget, the funds it sets aside for advertising are often divided in some way, not always equally, to cover promotional or product, institutional, and combination advertisements. Institutional ads usually receive the least amount of funding, and promotional or product ads realize the most of the overall budget.

Promotional or Product Advertising

When a retailer wishes to sell a specific item or alert shoppers to a style that has been marked down, it uses product or **promotional advertising**. These ads are employed to provide immediate results for the merchant. For example, if a retailer advertises a hot item, the ad's effectiveness should be measured in the sales volume that the item generated immediately after the ad ran.

Institutional Advertising

Rather than promoting a particular style, an announcement of a clearance sale, or anything else that is directly related to the selling of merchandise, some fashion retailers, particularly those that are traditionally organized, such as the department stores, spend a portion of their advertising budget to promote their image. The concept is known as **institutional advertising** and is used as a means of letting the consumer know that the retailer is connected to its community and in some cases, global events, as well as trying to sell merchandise. Ads of this nature often concentrate on a number of areas such as the September 11, 2001 attacks, for example, and the death of South African president, Nelson Mandela.

At other times, retailers use institutional ads to promote their recognition of charitable organizations in their trading areas, ecological and environmental concerns of their customers and staff, their commitment to ethical practices, social responsibility, and other areas that show them as concerned businesses.

While the effectiveness of these ads cannot be measured in terms of immediate sales, as they can be with promotional and product ads, they do generate long-term results. This type of advertising is designed to gain long-term customer confidence and receive customer loyalty.

Combination Advertising

The best of both worlds is the advertisement that features promotional and institutional elements. In **combination advertising**, the retailer might choose to alert customers to the company's dedication to fashion and the community and at the same time feature a particular fashion item. For example, New York City's high-fashion retailers announce the Metropolitan Opera's opening night with ads that feature ball gowns that might be worn for the occasion.

Cooperative Advertising

Few fashion retailers have unlimited funds for advertising. Often they have a greater need to inform their regular and potential customers of newly arrived merchandise, personal appearances of designers and celebrities, or special promotions than their budgets allow. Although industry experts usually agree that advertising is worth the expenditure because it has the potential to increase sales, retailers often reduce their promotional budgets when the economy is faltering and sales have declined. The shortfall is often made up with a commitment from vendors to participate in these programs.

The concept involves a joint effort between the merchant and the vendor and the expense of the advertisement is shared by both parties. The ads feature the names of both the supplier of the merchandise and the retail operation, making them valuable to each participant. The ad is designed by the retailer, but the merchandise resource has the right to examine its contents and layout before the ad goes into production to make certain that it meets its requirements.

Under the rules of the Robinson-Patman Act, manufacturers must offer cooperative advertising allowances to all retail customers. Companies that offer such monetary compensation must do so by using a formula that is fair and equitable to both its largest and smallest accounts. Typically such arrangements are predicated on the amount of the retailer's purchases, with a percentage of sales usually used as the basis of the allowance. The following example demonstrates how the cooperative arrangement may be applied.

Beaumont Fashions purchases $300,000 worth of coats from Coleridge, Inc. The manufacturer offers an allowance of 5 percent of purchases for all its customers to use in cooperative advertising and pays up to 50 percent of the cost of the ad.

$$\$300,000 \times 0.05 = \$15,000$$

If Beaumont chooses to run an advertisement for $30,000, Coleridge will pay $15,000, or 50 percent of the cost of the ad (the amount earned on the basis of the $300,000 purchase).

The Exeter Boutique also purchases coats from Coleridge, Inc., but the amount of the sale is only $5,000. Using the same arrangement it provides to all of its retail accounts, Coleridge allows Exeter a total of $250.

$$\$5,000 \times 0.05 = \$250$$

Exeter might now be able to run an ad for $500, with each party paying $250 toward its cost. If Exeter chooses to run an ad that costs $1,000, Coleridge is only responsible for $250, the amount earned through the cooperative advertising arrangement. Thus, Exeter is responsible for $750 even though it is more than half of the cost.

Although the amounts of money contributed by Coleridge, Inc., to each customer is different, it used the same percentage allocation in the determination, a concept mandated under the provisions of the Robinson-Patman Act.

The Media

The fashion retailer's advertising needs are still best served by the **print media**, whether it is newspapers, magazines, direct mail catalogs, or shopping publications. Later in the chapter we will see the impact of social media advertising.

Print Media

NEWSPAPERS

Throughout the United States, readers of such newspapers as *The New York Times*, *The Washington Post*, *Chicago Tribune*, *Miami Herald*, and *Los Angeles Times* are exposed to ads for their favorite retail operations' merchandise offerings. Smaller localized papers are also good outlets for fashion merchants.

Most full-line and fashion-specialized department stores still spend the greatest proportion of their budgets on newspaper advertising, although the competition from digital is taking some of their financial resources. The reasons for such use include the following:

1. The timeliness of the newspaper is important to the fashion retailer. Its 7-day schedule allows advertisers to quickly reach their audiences with the latest style and fashion innovations.

2. Unlike monthly magazines, which require a significant amount of lead time for advertisement placement, newspaper ads can be inserted almost up to press time.

3. A newspaper's appeal is not limited to one family member, as are some magazines. Columns and features are directed to every person in the family, giving the advertiser exposure to more than just one segment of the population. It should be noted however, that more and more younger consumers are getting their news on the Internet, making them less likely to be affected by newspaper ads.

4. The newspaper reaches large numbers of households via subscriptions, although the number has declined in recent years, still guaranteeing the retail community a large number of daily readers.

5. When compared with other media, most notably magazines and television, the newspaper affords the advertiser lower cost per prospective customer.

6. A newspaper's **advertisement "life,"** while not as long as that of a magazine, is much greater than radio or television. The Sunday paper, which contains significant advertising, often has a life expectancy that lasts until the next week's edition is delivered. Families often read its numerous parts throughout the week, making it an excellent investment for the advertiser.

7. The major newspapers usually incorporate full-color advertising supplements in their Sunday editions. These sections are printed on high-quality **stock**, which provides the fashion retailer the opportunity to feature merchandise in a more exciting format. Some readers retain such supplements after discarding the rest of the newspaper, giving the advertiser the advantage of extended periods of customer awareness.

8. Retailers can reach specific markets, since each newspaper targets a different consumer segment. Through assistance provided by advertising agencies and the media themselves, retailers are able to assess which newspaper is most appropriate for their merchandise assortments.

9. Since most newspapers concentrate on narrow geographic areas, it is easier to confine advertising to those within reach of the company's brick-and-mortar operations. Many newspapers have regional editions that narrow the population even more strictly, giving retailers a more exact exposure. Some even publish special

sections earmarked for particular communities in the trading area. As you will read in *Happening Now*, the future of newspaper advertising for fashion retailers is still somewhat positive.

HAPPENING NOW

NEWSPAPER ADVERTISING IS ALIVE AND WELL

When one reads that newspaper advertising is dead, the future, to some, seems even gloomier. The naysayers repeatedly come to the conclusion that the days of sky-high profits are over, but neglect to address some of the possibilities of a resurgence in retailer use. Yes, the Internet has taken a significant amount from newspaper advertising, but digital has been disappointing according to industry experts.

Those who still give the newspaper a chance to regain some of its clout and survival offer some important elements in the strategy to come back again. First, the money needed has started to come from the charges for digital access to the newspaper.

Those who offer digital-only subscriptions and "bundled" subscriptions are seeing a stream of profitability that can be used to offset the costs of publishing their print editions. Second, the monies earned from e-commerce and hosting events have given them more capital to work with.

According to industry analyst Ken Doctor, author of *Newsonomics: Twelve New Trends That Will Shape the News You Get*, "We are beginning to see a glimmer of a 2018 business model, one that is at least stable and at best shows some growth." The outlines of the future were sketched out in an important report, "The American Newspaper Media Industry Revenue Profile 2012," released by the Newspaper Association of America

on April 8, 2013. Most important in the findings were that there was a flow of revenue from new streams. Ken Doctor adds that giving away content on the Internet was a mistake for many years. Today, about 400 newspapers are charging and many more will be joining that bandwagon. He says it "is the metered paywall (which allows the reader to access a number of articles before they have to pay)" that is expected to raise revenue for the newspaper.

Joining in with positive outlooks is Tom Rosenstiel, executive director of the American Press Institute, and media analyst, John Morton, a longtime columnist for *American Journalism Review*.

MAGAZINES

A trip to the newsstand immediately reveals that the fashion magazine has reached new heights in publishing. From both domestic and global publishers, a wealth of publications such as *Vogue, Elle, Harper's Bazaar, Glamour, L'Officiel-USA,* Italian *Vogue, Town & Country, Seventeen,* and *Linea Italiana* are reaching the American fashion consumer. Figure 16.1 shows a newspaper and magazine stand.

While the advertising in these periodicals mainly focuses on designers and manufacturers, more fashion retailers, national and regional, are using magazines to deliver their advertising messages. Because of the broad trading areas retailers serve, magazines' regional editions allow retailers to restrict their ads to people in predetermined trading areas. Because of the nature of multi-channel retailing, which includes the use of websites, it makes sense for retailers with limited brick-and-mortar outlets to address customers around the country, because they can include their website address in their ads. Magazines do have the disadvantages of a longer lead time necessary for ad placement and comparatively prohibitive costs.

Advantages of magazine advertising include the following:

1. The quality of the stock enables the fashion retailers to put its best foot forward. Excellent paper coupled with the high-quality color reproduction allows every item to get the best possible exposure.

figure 16.1
Fashion magazines are very important to the industry and consumer. Each issue is relevant until the next issue comes out, which makes them a great way to stay current on the latest fashions.

2. Magazines, unlike newspapers, have extremely long advertisement "life." Many subscribers keep copies for extended periods and often pass them on to others. In this way, the advertisement has the potential to be seen over and over.

3. Many fashion retailers operate branch stores throughout the country, as is the case with Saks Fifth Avenue, Lord & Taylor, Bloomingdale's and Macy's, The Limited, and Gap, making each able to reach a very wide audience. Many also have online divisions so that, when their website addresses are noted in the magazine ads, their potential for even broader markets is raised.

4. Since people hold on to magazines for a while, some fashion merchants use institutional ads to keep their names in the minds of their audiences without having to worry about the perishability factor that is a problem in promotional advertising.

5. With the women in most households now part of the workforce, magazine ads that feature telephone, mail order, and website addresses provide the means needed to shop without having to make time for on-site shopping.

6. Regional editions make it easy to market the magazine to specific groups and geographical areas.

Unlike the typical fashion magazines that feature scores of advertisements among various articles and regular columns, some fashion retailers have produced magazines that bear their own names. Two of these entries come from Bergdorf Goodman and Neiman Marcus, with editions that carry fashion newsworthy events in addition to photographs of the retailer's merchandise. Figure 16.2 shows a consumer using a catalog to make a purchase.

Direct Mail

Most people's overstuffed mailboxes are indicators of the amount of direct mail pieces coming into American households. The vast majority of these mailings are fashion

figure 16.2
Many upscale retailers publish their own magazines and catalogs from which orders may be placed. This shopper, with phone and credit card in hand, can easily place an order.

oriented with catalogs, brochures, pamphlets, and other formats, offering products ranging from apparel and accessories for the entire family, to home furnishings.

Because their shopping time is often limited, more consumers are looking at these advertising pieces. Department stores are using direct mail in ever-increasing numbers, as evidenced by the fact that they are treating these publications as separate entities from their brick-and-mortar operations. Some companies, such as Macy's, have management teams that are apart from their brick-and-mortar operations to better serve consumers who prefer to buy off-site, ordering from information included in the direct mail pieces.

Names and addresses of direct mail recipients come from a variety of places. Many are the retailer's own credit card customers, with others culled from lists the retailer purchases from marketing research firms. These can be tailored to the retailer's demographic needs in terms of age, family size, income, and profession, and the retailer's preferred psychographic segmentation as discussed in Chapter 4, "The Fashion Consumer."

Some of the reasons for direct mail's success include the following:

1. Retailers can target specific groups that appear to have the right characteristics for the company's merchandise assortment.

2. Retailers can insert small direct mail pieces in end-of-the-month statements, thus avoiding the additional expense of separate mailings.

3. Since people read each advertisement individually, it gets their attention. Ads in newspapers must vie for the reader's attention, because newspapers are full of advertisements.

4. People can examine the mailings at their leisure and order when they have time.

One of the drawbacks for some direct mail pieces is that people may perceive them as junk mail and not open them. However, if people are interested enough to open them, they are frequently motivated to purchase what the piece is advertising, proving that these are important sources of business for retailers.

Broadcast Media

Once considered impractical for most fashion retailers, the broadcast media have become important advertising outlets for some merchants with significantly large trading areas and the budgetary resources necessary to use broadcast media in addition to print media. The pros and cons of radio and TV are described in the following sections.

Radio

Of the two broadcast communications outlets, retailers, except for smaller stores, use radio less frequently than television. Although the costs involved in radio are significantly less than those required for television advertising, radio's appeal is limited, because people understand fashion merchandise best when they can see it. Verbal descriptions leave much to be desired. The radio-listening market is also somewhat restricted to a narrow segment, often the teenage or young adult population, and they tend to turn the dial when commercials are aired. Those consumers who listen to the radio do so primarily in either their automobiles or on headphones, thereby limiting the time they listen to commercials to when they are commuting to and from their jobs, or are exercising. People usually do not spend much time listening to the radio at home.

In spite of these negatives, some fashion retailers find that the radio is a good tool for announcing sales or promotional events.

Television

The old saying "a picture is worth a thousand words" is true, especially when it comes to promoting fashion merchandise. Consumers are able to see the items presented in a variety of interesting ways that might motivate them to visit the retailer's brick-and-mortar operation, log on to its website, or call in an order.

The costs associated with such presentations, however, are often considerable. Rarely do fashion merchants sponsor or co-sponsor television programming, unless they are giants in the industry such as Sears, with outlets across the country. Even they rarely sponsor programs.

Instead, retailers pay for **spot commercials**, in which their message is delivered during the programs. Often, local merchants, seeking to reach a narrower market, use the spots to reach an identified audience during the time that a program is interrupted for commercial messages or station-identification breaks. This way, a chain in the South can pay to have its ads on programs aired in that region, while another in the West, at the same time, can target its commercials to viewers in that area.

With the costs of airing television commercials generally lower on cable outlets, more retailers are opting for this exposure than using the networks. There too they can focus on regional audiences.

Although television commercials provide a great number of advantages for the retailers that run them, the advent of systems such as TiVo, which enable viewers to bypass the commercial messages whenever they choose, is beginning to diminish the value of such advertising.

Websites

Retailers are increasingly using off-site channels to sell merchandise. Major companies that engage in multi-channel retailing are reporting more sales every year. The vast majority of retailers have developed websites to attract yet another segment of the market that is either too busy to visit the brick-and-mortar operations or too unmotivated to buy through catalogs. Both multi-channel retailers and website-only merchants are generating online sales. Giants such as Amazon and eBay are involved in record-breaking sales every day.

Amazon, once primarily the marketer of goods such as CDs and books, has entered the fashion business in a big way. When people log on to the Amazon website, they see a number of different product categories they can access. Fashion classifications include jewelry, apparel, and accessories, and links to the retailers with whom Amazon has made contractual arrangements immediately appear on the screen when users choose a category. These links then lead users to retailers such as Nordstrom and Old Navy, so that they can see the featured merchandise. Both partners in the arrangement benefit from the association. Amazon gets its fee from the companies for providing them with enormous numbers of consumers who might otherwise not log on to their websites, and the retailers gain by making sales.

eBay, the leader in online auctions, has successfully moved into fashion merchandising as well. Shoppers do not need to bid on products that range from the most sought-after labels such as Prada, to lesser-known brands. Instead, eBay offers bargain prices for each item. The results have been exceptional, with sales reaching new heights every day.

Social Media

The biggest gain in the past few years of advertising has come by way of social media. A startling figure has been released by the ExactTarget blog stating that social ad spending is expected to reach $11 billion by 2017. In 2013, Facebook alone has made approximately $1 billion from its mobile revenue. For the industry as a whole, the figures for 2012 and 2013 were $4.7 billion and $6.1 billion, respectively.

The most targeted people in the United Sates are males who are 30 years old, and females who are 45 years of age, with Facebook leading the way, followed by Google, Pandora, Twitter, and Apple in their usage. These positive numbers affect print and broadcast media outlays and account for the curtailing of their use by retailers. Figure 16.3 features social media advertising.

Outdoor Media

Though not as important as the other media, some local fashion merchants use billboards, backlit transparencies, and posters to promote themselves.

Billboards

Along interstate routes and on heavily traveled streets, retailers use large photographs or hand-rendered paintings to inform potential shoppers of their operations. Billboards can be dedicated to a particular merchant or advertise a shopping mall that houses a variety of different retail establishments.

figure 16.3
Social media advertising is showing significant growth. It is one more outlet in multimedia retailing that helps the retailer with its bottom line.

Backlit transparencies

These advertisements are illuminated signs displayed in places such as bus stops and inside malls. They can be stationary, where one image is affixed to the screen, or moving, where a few different backlit transparencies are interchanged about every 10 seconds to provide additional images to the passersby. The illumination feature makes the presentation visible 24 hours a day.

Posters

These are generally smaller versions of billboards displayed on the outside of buses. They reach a large number of pedestrians who may see them as they walk to their destinations as well as people in cars who pass the buses or are next to them at traffic lights.

Collectively, outdoor advertising is modestly priced, which makes it affordable even for small merchants.

Overall Costs of Advertising

Retailers must first develop a budget for advertising endeavors so that they can determine which approaches best serve their needs. Retailers can compare the costs of the different media by consulting the **Standard Rate & Data Service (S.R.D.S.)**. Retailers generally establish their promotional budgets through one of the methods described in the following sections.

Percentage of Sales Method

Most retailers who have been in business for a number of years choose this technique to determine how much they will invest in advertising. They first analyze past sales so that they can try to determine what the sales figures might be for the next period. Once they have determined these figures, retailers assess other expenses, such as their plans for expansion in terms of additional brick-and-mortar units, and whether they should broaden the use of their catalog operation, if they have one, and their website programs, if they are part of their selling tools. Changes in merchandising policies and practices and the state of the economy are also factored into the equation and carefully assessed. After addressing these areas, retailers then apply a percentage of their anticipated sales to arrive at what they will budget for advertising costs.

Objective and Task Method

In this more sophisticated approach, the company analyzes its objectives and the tasks it must perform to achieve these goals. Today, this method is particularly appropriate for large fashion retailers that are expanding their operations from primarily operating brick-and-mortar units to creating multi-channel ventures that use off-site approaches to increase their sales potential; their advertising needs tend to grow accordingly. Other factors that often require retailers to have additional advertising expenses include introducing private brands and labels, and expanding customer services. Retailers then analyze these situations to determine how much they need to spend on advertising to reach these objectives.

Unit of Sales Method

In addition to being concerned with dollar volume, most retailers keep records on the number of units their different sales channels sell. In the unit of sales method technique for advertisement budgeting, the retailer tries to assess how much it must spend on advertising to sell each unit. In large retail organizations with numerous merchandise classifications and departments, each product type requires a different advertising investment. For example, furs will certainly necessitate greater per-unit expenditures than shoes because of the differences in prices and units sold. The retailer must then examine just how much advertising might cost for each merchandise category. Once this has been estimated, the retailer multiplies the numbers of units that are expected to sell by the factor that has been assigned to them.

Advertising Cost Differentials

There are certain costs inherent in each media classification that account for the actual charges. In newspaper, magazine, and broadcast advertising, additional charges are routinely applied if the retailer requests specific placement for its ads.

Newspapers and Magazines

When placing an ad in a newspaper or magazine, the retailer has no guarantee it will generate sales. However, placing an advertisement in a specific part of the publication will sometimes bring better results in terms of sales. It can help the retailer to know the various technical placement terminology when considering the various options.

- *Run of press.* This is the basic cost of advertising in a periodical's space. Being the least expensive rate, it does not guarantee a specific location in the publication. Placement is left to the discretion of the publisher. If a retailer chooses **run of press (R.O.P.)**, its ad might be printed in a location it considers undesirable.
- *Preferred position.* To guarantee that their ad is put in a particular place, or **preferred position**, many merchants pay a premium rate. Fashion retailers who want to get maximum exposure are often willing to pay extra for an ad to be placed near a fashion column or as close to the first page as possible, where most readers are likely to see it.
- *Regular position.* Some merchants subscribe to the theory that if their advertisements always occupy the same position (i.e., a **regular position**) in a publication, their customers will be able to find them quickly. Retailers, and other advertisers, sign long-term contracts for this right and pay additional charges for ads to occupy the same position each time.

Broadcast Media

The costs on which outlet is it vary according to:

- the time the commercial is run
- the number of times it is offered on the air
- on which stations is it used

Online Advertising

This comparatively new advertising form is gaining in the overall advertising scheme for the retailer. It helps to bring a wealth of new shoppers to the company because of its:

- ease of use
- no expense involved for the retailer and shoppers
- ability to change the message almost instantaneously if necessary, making it timely

Evaluation of the Advertisement

The purpose of advertising is to increase sales and profits. To make certain that the advertising is fulfilling its purpose and warrants the expense involved, retailers need to evaluate its effectiveness.

Small fashion retailers, because of their involvement with customers, often hear from their customers that they saw the ad in a particular location. Though this does provide anecdotal evidence of the ad's effectiveness, it is certainly not a scientific approach to advertising evaluation.

Larger retail operations that invest heavily in advertising must know if their costs were worth the investment. Most of the major companies with in-house research departments measure sales prior to the advertisement and immediately after it has run. If there was an increase in sales for the advertised merchandise, it can be assumed that the ad brought in the additional revenues. In addition to the increase in sales, some retailers determine if the additional sales brought enough business to the company to cover the cost of the ad and deliver a profit.

Some of the research tools discussed in Chapter 5, "Retail Research Directions in Today's Retail Environment," are used to evaluate advertising's effectiveness.

PROMOTIONAL PROGRAMS

Whether it is to attract new customers to their on-site and off-site outlets, make the consumers aware of their image, promote the collections of established as well as new designers, herald the arrival of a new season, or call attention to company-sponsored charities, fashion merchants are constantly developing promotional programs. While the flashier and more ambitious endeavors take place in retailing's major organizations, their small-company counterparts use numerous devices and tools with considerable success. It is not always the extravagances paid for by the seemingly limitless budgets that attract the customers' attention to the retailer but rather the creative promotions that are accomplished with small monetary investments.

Special events and regular promotional programs are planned by specialists in the major retail organizations. Under the direction of a divisional manager, the promotional efforts are usually part and parcel of a plan that includes advertising and visual merchandising, making it a multimedia collaboration. With proper coordination, the advertising captures the consumers' attention and brings them to either the company's brick-and-mortar units or its catalogs and websites, and the visual presentations in the stores enhance the promotions. The smaller operations usually rely upon the talents of their owners or managers to develop the fashion formats and tools that will draw customers to their shops.

Fashion Shows

What better way is there for retailers to dramatically present the latest styles to their customers than with a fashion show? While other devices may bring excitement to the retail arena, few incorporate the company's merchandise in the presentation as effectively as fashion shows. Ranging from formal events that demand the attention afforded professional theater and require significant budgets, to the fashion "parades" that merely employ simple runways and recorded music, fashion shows may be produced for every retailer's budget and audience.

Formal Productions

Complete with themes, live music, and commentary, formal shows are the most costly. The settings are usually in theaters that have been leased for the occasion or ballrooms that have been transformed to stage the events. Professional models wearing the clothing dance, march, frolic, or even skate through the various scenes of these shows. Sometimes the backgrounds and props rival the fashions that are being displayed.

Major fashion retailers such as Bloomingdale's and Neiman Marcus subscribe to these extravaganzas and often present them in conjunction with fund-raisers for charitable organizations. They sell tickets for these special events with the proceeds going to the charities. The retailers involved often get **free publicity** from the media's editorial press that covers such events, such as *Women's Wear Daily*, recognition from the public for their participation in worthy causes, and ultimately business from the sale of the fashions featured in the production.

Runway Parades

The more typical fashion show is presented runway style, generally in the store. The staging area might be a department that has been cleared of its merchandise for the event and refitted with chairs that are placed on either side of the runway, an in-store restaurant where the patrons may watch the show after finishing a meal, in community and special events rooms, or in shopping center malls.

Easy to organize and modest in cost, such **runway parades** concentrate on specific collections or merchandise departments. They might introduce resort wear or be organized around a **trunk show** that features a designer's collection brought in so clients can preview it and place special orders. Trunk shows are very popular with many high-fashion merchants and are equally favored by their clienteles. The designer or company representative delivers the commentary and answers questions at the show's end. Figure 16.4 shows models on a runway.

Where the magnitude of the formal show requires considerable participation from professionals and salaries that are commensurate with their talents, retailers can offer the less-structured fashion parades without incurring as many costs. College students, charity workers, or store employees could be used in place of the professional models and observers enjoy watching these amateurs walking the runway. Instead of paying a professional band or pianist, retailers could contact a school's music department with a view to using student musicians and make a small donation to the educational institution in return. Prerecorded music is also an inexpensive option.

figure 16.4
Female models in an informal runway show. This is very helpful for increased sales potential since shoppers are already in the store.

Informal Modeling

Some merchants use the least formal fashion show concept, **informal modeling**. This approach involves dressing models in specific styles and having them move throughout the store's different departments. Furs are often shown this way as are other unique collections that the retailer is trying to promote. The models carry identifying merchandise cards that list the name of the designer, price, location where the collection may be seen, and other information. This method requires little planning other than to choose the styles the models will wear and to delineate the routes that they will take throughout the store to show the clothing.

Whatever the retailer's size or budget, it can present fashion shows that will bring both **publicity** and profits.

Special Campaigns and Celebrations

The major fashion-oriented department stores are proponents of special campaigns and celebrations to attract customer attention. Companies such as Neiman Marcus, Bloomingdale's, and Macy's in the United States, and Harrods in London periodically organize these types of promotions.

Harrods, for example, kicks off its annual storewide sales with a parade that is replete with celebrities from around the world arriving at the store in horse-drawn carriages. The crowds that gather to watch them go by are much like those that witness the traditional Thanksgiving Day parades sponsored by American retailers such as Macy's.

Institutional Events

Some retailers draw attention to themselves by featuring events that are not specifically merchandise oriented but are intended to bring people to their stores, where they will be motivated to shop once they are inside. These promotions run the gamut from physical fitness-related programs to flower shows.

The annual Macy's New York flower show literally transforms the main floor of the flagship store into a botanical garden overflowing with flowers. The show heralds the arrival of spring and has been a well-received promotion since 1975. The windows feature merchandise abundantly surrounded with flowers, the street-side awnings are changed to incorporate the theme, and the interior displays incorporate flowers throughout the selling departments. The success of the show is measured by the huge crowds attending and the increase in sales during that time.

Designer and Celebrity Appearances

When a store announces that Calvin Klein is going to appear to discuss his latest collection or that Jennifer Lopez will be there to promote her new line, it is a guarantee that enormous crowds of shoppers will be on hand to see them. The arrival of soap opera stars, who have little to do with design or fashion, generally results in crowds that are often too large for the store to handle.

When Tommy Hilfiger showed up to promote his fragrance at a Belk branch in Jacksonville, Florida, the crowds were so enormous that security had trouble controlling them. Sales, of course, skyrocketed. Often, the celebrities do nothing more than show up at a store but if they have star power, they are more than likely to attract their followers and fill the store with potential shoppers.

Holiday Parades

Also institutional in nature but not held within the confines of the stores, are the numerous holiday parades that draw throngs of potential shoppers to the retailers' vicinity. The most prominent of these is the annual Macy's Thanksgiving Day Parade in New York City, which is coproduced with NBC. Crowds stand 20 feet deep and line the streets of the parade route that winds from uptown to the Macy's Herald Square flagship. Floats filled with celebrities from theater, film, sports, and television; soaring helium-filled balloons that rise up into the sky; marching bands that have competed for the right to be in the parade; and the last float carrying Santa Claus finish their participation at the entrance to the Macy's flagship. There, the television cameras are stationed to capture the numerous extravagant musical performances that have been specially staged for the event and the show-stopping scenes from Broadway musicals—with Macy's in the background. Figure 16.5 features part of a Macy's Christmas parade.

In 2013, Macy's departed from opening their New York City flagship the day after Thanksgiving, and instead, opted for an 8 p.m. opening on Thanksgiving Day to take advantage of the throngs that have seen the parade. It was a great success.

Macy's parade, with its multimillion-dollar budget and the year it takes to plan, has brought it more attention than anything else it does to promote itself.

In-House Video

Many of today's leading fashion designers produce in-house videos of their collections to be shown in the retail operations that they sell to. These productions run the gamut from those aimed at the teen market that have models dancing to rock music while wearing the latest trendy styles to those aimed at affluent adults that show sophisticated runway presentations featuring couture collections.

Retailers install video screens in the departments that feature this merchandise, and, if the videos are well produced, they capture the attention of passing shoppers.

figure 16.5
The Ronald McDonald balloon floats in the Macy's parade. It is a special event that brings enormous crowds to Macy's on "Black Friday."

Demonstrations

On any major fashion retailer's main floor are the cosmeticians who are there to show the transformative powers of their products. Stores such as Henri Bendel on Fifth Avenue in New York City always have a wealth of such "artists" on hand to demonstrate their products. Women regularly line up for the chance to have makeovers with these cosmetics. Not only do participants purchase the cosmetics, but frequently those who watch the demonstrations do so as well.

Sampling

Another promotion technique dominated by the cosmetic industry is **sampling**. Every major manufacturer has followed the lead of Estée Lauder, who first offered a free sample of her product to passersby. Today, especially around Christmas time, the cosmetics counters at every major department store are filled with sample packages of products that are beautifully gift-wrapped and modestly priced to promote their companies' lines.

Free samples are intended to introduce the products and motivate customers to purchase the items once the samples have run out.

PUBLICITY

Every major fashion retailer has a public relations (PR) or publicity department that works to gain as much favorable publicity for the merchant as possible.

Sometimes referred to as free publicity, it comes as a result of the retailer's involvement in an activity that is considered newsworthy and is technically free because the store does not pay for it. Of course, the Macy's Flower Show and Thanksgiving Day Parade cost millions of dollars to produce, but the press coverage Macy's receives as a result comes at no direct cost.

Retailer PR departments prepare press kits and releases of their promotions and send them to a variety of media in the hopes that they will find the promotional activities sufficiently appealing to mention in print or on the air.

Because of the competitive nature of fashion retailing, every bit of positive publicity that a merchant can garner will serve to attract shoppers to its retail outlet.

Chapter Highlights

1. Those responsible for the management of the advertising and promotion functions in large fashion retailing operations are specialists who limit their duties to the companies' promotional plans. In small operations, this responsibility is in the hands of the owner, who also performs a host of other duties.

2. Retailers, both large and small, employ the services of advertising agencies that plan everything from layouts to ad placement. Even the largest companies that have their own in-house staffs use the agencies either to assist them with their own presentations or to help them with major events.

3. Retailers sometimes employ freelancers who provide everything from the design concepts to the ad placement; and the media themselves employ staff to assist merchants with their advertising needs.

4. Some fashion designers and manufacturers are willing to share the expense of advertising and enter into cooperative arrangements with their retailer customers. By dividing the cost, the retailer can make better use of its budget, and the vendor can make certain that the retailer is featuring its line.

5. The most important advertising medium for fashion retailing is the newspaper. It requires little lead time for publication, can reach a defined market, and is relatively inexpensive in terms of the numbers of potential customers reached.

6. Television is used sparingly by the fashion retailer. Aside from its cost, it generally appeals to too wide an audience, unless the advertisement is shown only on a local affiliate that reaches the retailer's targeted audience. TV ads usually announce sales.

7. The fashion show is one of the more important promotional devices used by the industry. The events are usually parades that feature models on runways or informal modeling in which the action takes place in the aisles of the stores.

8. To get their names in print and on the air, the larger fashion retailers have public relations departments that send press releases and kits to area media describing their activities and events.

Terms of the Trade

advertisement "life"	preferred position
advertising	print media
advertising agencies	promotional advertising
artwork	publicity
broadcast media	regular position
combination advertising	run of press (R.O.P.)
copy	runway parades
direct mail	sampling
free publicity	spot commercials
informal modeling	Standard Rate & Data Service (S.R.D.S.)
in-house videos	stock
institutional advertising	trunk show
media	

For Discussion

1. Which departments make up a major fashion retailer's promotion division?

2. How does the typical in-house advertising department differ from the one used by many giants in the industry?

3. In addition to the advertising agencies, what other external sources are available to retailers to promote their organizations?

4. How does a promotional advertisement differ from one that is institutionally oriented?

5. What is meant by the term "combination advertisement?"

6. Is it possible for a retailer to place ads that cost double the amount allocated in the budget? How?

7. Why is the newspaper the most important advertising medium for the vast majority of major department store operations?

8. What are some of the advantages of magazine advertising for retailers?

9. How can fashion retailers without national prominence make use of television advertising?

10. In what way does the fashion retailer benefit from becoming a participant in the websites of giants such as Amazon?

11. What advantage does the backlit transparency have over the traditional forms of outdoor signage?

12. How does S.R.D.S. serve the retailer?

13. How does the percentage of sales differ from the objective and task method in determining budgetary allowances for advertising?

14. In what way is the formal fashion show different from the fashion parade?

15. What is a trunk show?

16. Why do some retailers use institutional events as part of their promotional programs?

17. Why are designers often willing to take time from their busy schedules to make in-store appearances?

18. Why has in-store video usage become an important part of the fashion retailer's promotional plan?

19. Who began the concept of sampling in the cosmetics industry, and what purpose does it serve?

20. Discuss the concept of publicity and how it differs from advertising.

Case Problem

Questions

1. Should Jim be satisfied with his modest success and forget about promotion?
2. What promotional devices would you suggest that would be within his reach?

The Kensington Kloset is a modest-sized boutique that specializes in upscale fashion for the discriminating woman. The majority of the merchandise is custom designed by its owner, Jim Sanders. Using talents that were honed by attending a well-known fashion school and working as an apprentice for a clothing designer, Jim has achieved moderate success in his own shop.

To round out his merchandise mix, Jim purchases bridge apparel and some couture products. The shop is located off the beaten path and out of sight of a potentially large market. He chose this location because those situated in better places cost more than he can afford. The only way he has earned a customer following is through client recommendations.

He believes that he hasn't reached his sales potential, but with little money to spend on advertising and promotion, his outlook for increased business is bleak. Some of his friends who work for major organizations have suggested that he use the cooperative advertising route to augment his own promotional budget. Since most of the merchandise he features is his own, this approach doesn't seem to be viable. Even with some cooperative money, major newspaper ads are out of the question because of their costs. Magazine and broadcast advertising are similarly too expensive to consider.

At this point, he would like to begin to promote his store and collection, but he hasn't been able to come up with any ideas that would fit his budget.

Exercises and Projects

1. Collect ten retail fashion advertisements from newspapers and magazines and categorize each according to type: promotional, institutional, and combination. Mount each ad on a foam board and explain to the class why it fits into the specific category.

2. Using the Standard Rate & Data Service, available at most libraries or online, look up the advertising rates for three newspapers in the same general trading area. Prepare a chart that shows the rates for R.O.P., preferred position, and regular position placement for each publication, and the circulation for each.

3. For an end-of-the-semester activity, develop as a class a runway fashion show to raise money for a charity. Many retailers will gladly provide the clothing for such a purpose if they receive the proper publicity. Divide the class into groups with each handling a different aspect of the production, such as development of the concept, model selection, acquisition of props, writing commentary, publicity, retailer liaison, and so forth. The production should take place on the campus or the retailer's premises. Sell tickets with the proceeds going to the charitable organization.

chapter seventeen

COMMUNICATING TO CUSTOMERS THROUGH ELECTRONIC MEDIA

After reading this chapter, you should be able to:

- Detail the inroads that retailers have made through the use of electronic media.

- Classify the differences among the various electronic communication systems such as the social media networks Facebook, Pinterest, and others.

- Analyze the statistics that have prompted almost every merchant to use social media in their quest for customer attention.

- Differentiate between the success of email versus social media.

- Explain the importance of in-store digital signage.

- Discuss some of the concerns with the use of electronic media.

- Explain why the WWD Digital Forums are useful for retail operations.

The new paradigm shift in retailing is a major undertaking, according to an executive at Paladin Data Corporation, a software services company that provides retail solutions. In his March 17, 2014 paper he makes the statement,

> This is the "Age of Information" in retail, and shoppers are smarter, have more choices and are more price savvy. The new paradigm in retail directly impacts businesses now more than ever as the consumers' expectations have changed, mostly due to technology. Smart phones and personal tablet devices empower casual and experienced shoppers alike with real-time information on every product ever sold. Consumers have immediate access to prices, product specifications, and alternative stores. Consumers have much higher expectations than ever before and want immediate results from cheaper and closer options (if they leave the house at all). This is the crux of the paradigm shift in retailing.

CloudTags, a company founded in the U.K. in 2012 provides personalized technology services for retailers. They have concluded that the multi-channel paradigm had shifted to cross-channel, where one channel acted as a "pivot point." Now, omni-channel (the new buzz word) includes mobile usage and social media interacting with every aspect of electronic communication. Omni comes from the Latin word *omnis* which can mean all or universal, multi-channel comes from the Latin word *multus* meaning multiple, and cross-channel, derived from the Latin word *crux*, meaning to go across.

Omni-channel is something new and notable, even revolutionary, not just a marginal evolution of existing thinking. It offers the consumer the opportunity to reach across the wealth of products in the marketplace.

As we read in the preceding chapter, "The Importance of Advertising and Promotion," there are many methods used by fashion retailers to communicate their messages to regular and potentially new customers. Those that have been examined are still being used today, although their individual importance may have significantly changed. What was once the fashion retailer's most important link to the consumer, newspapers, is no longer the case for many merchants. Of course ads are still seen in this print medium, but they no longer command the investments of fashion retailers that they once held. Magazines have primarily been relegated to those fashion merchants who retail upscale merchandise. The only print medium that has maintained significant use is direct mail. Brochures used in charge customers' statements and catalogs, in particular, still command a great deal of fashion retailer usage.

Electronic media has taken the place of radio, the first of the media, introduced in the early 1920s, and later on, television. The former is still a useful tool for local retailers, while the latter usage has declined, except for the giant merchants in the field, such as Sears, and some of the large off-price retailers such as Burlington Coat Factory and Marshalls.

The new wave of fashion retailers reach their consumer base and potential new customers through the expanding field of electronic media. For the past few years, the usage of social media, for example, continues to increase, and the types of electronic tools keeps growing.

The retailers have several problems in regard to reaching their customers, the way in which the promotional budget should be apportioned for communication purposes, how much should be spent on electronic media, and selecting which of the electronic media will more than likely bring the best results.

This chapter will explore the most recent innovations in electronic media, all of the pertinent information regarding their advantages to the fashion retailers, the current usage and future outlook for each of the participating companies, the important statistics in regard to this innovation, and how the uses of the other media have fared since this electronic media explosion.

COMPONENTS OF COMMUNICATING WITH ELECTRONIC MEDIA

In order to communicate with existing customers and prospective customers, fashion retailers have the choice of exclusively using a single approach, or a combination approach. It is the latter approach that is the most widely used. The oldest method of communication is in the print media, that includes newspapers, magazines, and direct mail. When newspapers were the only game in town, fashion retailers used them extensively. It enabled merchants to notify shoppers of the latest styles, fashion promotions, clearance sales, and so forth with very short lead time. The ability to feature photographs and drawings with copy made it especially desirable. With newspaper and magazine readership on the decline, only direct mail, primarily catalogs, has remained an important medium, with a big part of the promotional budget spent on it. The use of the newest forms of electronic communication is on the rise and has been proven in the retailing industries.

In order to better understand electronic technology, those who are newcomers to the field will benefit from a simple definition of it. As defined by BusinessDictionary.com,

> Broadcast or storage media that take advantage of electronic technology include television, radio, Internet, fax, CD-ROMs, and any other medium that requires electricity or digital encoding of information. The term "electronic media" is often used in contrast with print media.

An overview of electronic technology is explored in the remainder of this chapter.

Electronic Communication Systems

Every day, technology seems to come up with a new or updated system to make communication with shoppers more effective than the day before. Communication systems that have a digital element to it are busy determining where the action is today to take advantage of consumer spending habits tomorrow. The Internet has become the choice of many consumers too busy to peruse newspapers, and for those on the move, **smartphones**, laptops, and tablets have answered the retailer's call for communication. See Figure 17.1 for an individual at Beijing airport who is on the move.

It should be understood that electronic media, although it seems new, has been with us since the introduction of radio in 1895, followed by television in 1927, early computers in 1942, the photocopy machine in 1946, the transistor in 1947, and the minicomputer of the 1960s that used "integrated circuits" to cut down on the size of the very large sized computing machines.

This evolution brings us to today's devices and the systems they offer to people in all walks of life, all businesses and organizations, and so forth. This innovation brings a new channel that creates new ways for interaction for retail businesses, including interaction with customers and potential customers.

As we have learned, electronic media is not new, but relatively recent innovations have taken front and center for fashion retailers to communicate with their clienteles and prospective customers.

THE INTERNET

Although it has its roots in the 1960s, the Internet has only relatively recently become a valid tool for fashion retailers to use for communicating with their customers. BusinessDictionary.com defines it "as a means of connecting a computer to any other computer in the world via dedicated routers and servers." One of its unique features is that it can be accessed from anywhere by those sitting at desks in their places of business, at home when leisure time is available, or when on the move with smartphones, tablets, and laptop computers. Retailers, thus, can at any time feature messages of interest to the consumer market, including promotions, clearance sales, the arrival of new products, or the introduction of new private labels and store expansions.

figure 17.1
A businesswoman on the move using her laptop, which is often used to purchase from retailers while traveling.

One of the more widely used communication techniques aimed at consumers by retailers is the frequent use of emails. Messages or notifications can be sent to regular customers of retailers or to those who might be interested in particular products. In most cases, the email is a short statement about an impending sale, new merchandise, special promotions, and so forth. Once the recipient opens the email, and follows the prompt, the screen features text, sometimes graphics, and even sound, that is intended to pique the viewer's interest. It might result in a direct order, a telephone call to the company, or a visit to the brick-and-mortar facility if it has one. Some of the advantages of email include:

- Companies save money on postage and printing.
- The speed at which the email gets to the intended recipient is extremely fast.
- It replaces the need for direct mail.
- It provides convenience for shoppers.
- Retailers may easily reach consumers in any part of the country, and global shoppers through the opening of a network of global distributors.

Another tool that retailers and other businesses use on the Internet is the **banner ad**. It is typically rectangular, and placed on a website below or on the sides of the main content. It is linked to the advertiser's own website and very often features animated graphics and sound. These banner ads are often targeted to specific users by using data that has been gathered about their web-browsing habits, enabling retailers to reach customers that are more likely to purchase their products. Other specific benefits to the retailer include:

- Multiple messages can be used to appeal to zip codes and designated marketing area (DMA). Local store information can include maps, directions and links to "store-specific" web pages.
- Interactive overlays to banner ads so viewers can share sales announcements or store openings.

SOCIAL MEDIA NETWORKS

In 2013, approximately 1.7 billion people around the world used social media, a figure that's up 16 percent from 2012. Of the users, just about all of them have made at least one online purchase in 2013 due to their interfacing with social media. Today, it is imperative that an online retailer, or a brick-and-mortar operator with an online channel capability, makes significant use of advertising on social media, generally choosing **Facebook** above others. Without social media usage, the retailer is about to be left behind in this very competitive time. Figure 17.2 features a teenage girl updating her social network.

Facebook

The advertising component on Facebook is two-fold. A merchant can either choose to promote its business page in the hope of attracting new followers or to promote single individual posts so that it can improve its visibility. Facebook requires the advertiser to immediately list its objectives upon signing, with one of the options being "likes" and another is "boosting in-store promotions to increase RSVPs for a Facebook event," according to Bryan Shaw, an e-commerce expert in an article posted on eCommerceRules. com on October 10, 2013. With more than 500 million users, Facebook is the king of social media.

figure 17.2
Teenager checking in on her social network. The social networks are especially beneficial for retailers to announce "flash sales," special promotions, celebrity appearances in the store, etc.

Twitter

According to **Twitter**, "people who see **tweets** from retailers are more likely to visit retail websites and make online purchases. The more tweets they see, the more likely they are to buy." In a 2012 study, it was determined that 27 percent of general Internet users bought a product from a retail website, without any tweets factored in. The numbers increase to 39 percent when the user was exposed to a tweet from a retailer. As in all advertising media, the frequency of exposure on Twitter resulted in more online sales. Twitter has 135,000 new users every day and 288 million monthly active users.

Pinterest

Pinterest is a photo-based tool that enables users to collect specific ideas and "pin" them to their "walls." According to Neustar.biz, in a post on Digiday.com on January 21, 2014, "The first, most trusted real-time insights & analytics provider," "The importance [of Pinterest] to retailers has become undeniable over the past year." The data it provides comes out every day and as a social network it drives the highest percentage of traffic and sales. The "pins," its most recent addition to the information formerly offered, now add even more information for the retailer to help improve its position in the field. Major retailers that use Pinterest include Target, Overstock and Zappos. According to Pinterest consultant, Anna Bennett, in an article published on Business2community.com on February 17, 2014, this business tool has captured the market with a number of different statistics showing their importance. With major fashion-oriented retailers such as L.L. Bean, Nordstrom, Quiksilver, and lululemon athletica leading the way, the results have been significantly successful. Bennett writes that, among the favorable findings, statistics show that:

> 62% of brands have the Pinterest "Pin It" buttons on their product pages of their websites, and it is the most used button. This officially puts them in first place compared to 61% having the Twitter buttons and 59% of brands having the Facebook Like buttons. 42% of brands have the **Google+** button, all according to a study done by 8thBridge, after analyzing 872 retailers.

Another exciting fact for Pinterest is that one-third of women in the United States use it. In an Associated Press article by Mae Anderson, released on May 2, 2014, some other points are showing the importance of Pinterest. The number two discounter in the United States, Target, is pinning its hopes on this social media format. In Anderson's article, it is of interest to note that:

> Pinterest might be more valuable to retailers than some of its rivals. Data shows that Pinterest users shop more when they follow links to retailers' websites. When "pinners" buy, the average order value is $199.16 compared with $92.27 for Facebook and $58.02 for Twitter.

The most recent innovation for Pinterest ads is the offering of "rich" pins which allows for brands and retailers to add extra information to images that people pin. Of the variety of pins available, product pins are the most useful. These pins, explains the Neustar post on Digiday, "enable retailers to attach real-time pricing, inventory availability and a 'Buy this' link to their product images." One major off-price retailer, Overstock.com, makes use of rich pins to enable shoppers to check prices some days after the purchase. The site automatically sends an email to a customer notifying the price change if any takes place. It has become an excellent tool to boost company image.

Instagram

With more than 100 million users, **Instagram** enables brands to pay for their high-quality photos to appear in users' feeds. While its usage pales in comparison to Facebook, it is an opportunity for even the smallest retailer to use.

3dcart

Originated in 1997, **3dcart** is an excellent e-commerce social medium that is designed to assist e-tailers to become more profitable in such a competition-laden market. It was introduced for online merchants to easily open, operate, and maintain a successful online operation. It is a way in which global merchants, now at approximately 16,000, can become more available to shoppers around the world.

Figures on the rapid take-up of social media are widely reported online. Some recent statistics include:

- 27 percent of the total time spent on the Internet is social media driven.
- 22 percent of Americans use social networking sites several times a day.
- 56 percent of Americans have a profile on a social networking site.

In addition to attracting shoppers to purchase on the Internet, the positive impact on brick-and-mortar outlets through the use of social media is becoming more significant every day. Many retailers report that it is driving in-store traffic, and motivating purchasing there.

Dovetailing brick-and-mortar stores with social media to boost sales is sometimes an advantage. In 2013, Green Room Retail's several suggestions, the essence of some of which follows, discusses the importance of social media in prompting in-store purchasing.

- An "engage first, sell second" approach is built on the philosophy that if companies follow the rules of engagement in communication, sales will follow. A clear, concise message that has meaning to the shoppers and is relevant to their needs will often motivate them to buy in the stores or online.

- Choose the appropriate social medium to make the most of customer action. Knowledge of the differences between the various social media is essential to choose the right one(s) that will result in driving sales.
- Utilize some local marketing such as using social media to motivate shoppers to come to their brick-and-mortar outlets. A plan might include providing customers with coupons that can only be redeemed in the store.
- With more retailers branding their names, it is very important to always stress the brand name. By doing this, customers will feel they know your label, which will strengthen the relationship they have with you.
- If customers have questions or complaints, immediate response shows that there is a personal relationship with your company.
- In-store social media integration is a way in which to capture the customer's attention. It could be the tack that Nordstrom uses by adding labels to merchandise that have been "**pinned**" the most on Pinterest.

OMNI-CHANNEL RETAILING

What was once multi-channel retailing has now evolved into omni-channel retailing. A frequently cited description is that this approach is "concentrated on a more 'seamless' approach to the consumer experience through all available shopping channels." Included are all or some of the shopping channels, selected according to retailer needs. The giants in the industry use all, while smaller merchants chose those that are beneficial to their organizations. These include mobile devices, computers, television, direct marketing, catalogs, brick-and-mortar and so forth.

The use of omni-channels helps to create a more knowledgeable customer which in turn keeps the employees on their toes whether they are selling in the store, or communicating online.

Omni-Channel Strategies

While there is no one strategic approach businesses use to reach their goals, many retailers employ different strategies to improve their bottom lines and become winners. According to a report presented by CBRE Global Research and Consulting in 2013, one of the best strategies is being used by Macy's.

> Macy's is one of these winners that has performed extremely well because of investing into optimizing omni-channel strategies. The company recently reported a 3.7% year over year growth in comparable store sales, which was greater than expected. This is because they really focused on integrating online and in-store sales in a way that best meets their customer's needs. Sales on their e-commerce sites grew 41% and added 2.2 percentage points to their overall same-store sales for the year.

With these successes, Macy's has planned to spend an additional $925 million to improve omni-channel sales capabilities as well as undergoing the expansion of their brick-and-mortar division.

Others have utilized in-store multimedia displays, which are examined more fully in this text.

EMAIL SUCCESS VERSUS SOCIAL MEDIA

Email has been within the reach of retailers for many years and has proved to be a significant success, with each year beating the previous year's usage. Today, however, social media-centered advertising continues to increase with each year, since its usage began by retailers.

In an *Advertising Age* article published on September 30, 2013, several significant figures show that email is alive and well and is still the winner when compared to social media. The research on which the article is based indicates a number of findings that affect the way in which fashion retailers benefit from these two advertising components:

- 76 percent of consumers who receive email from retail operations not only read them but act upon them for shopping.
- Email is used more frequently by shoppers than social media, where they find the products they want and purchase them.
- While 77 percent go to the retail site featured in the email, according to the *Advertising Age* article, 46 percent of consumers said they never use social media for shopping.
- One of the reasons for the successes of email when compared to social media is that the former are "pushed" to consumers inboxes while social media users have to actively seek retailer messages.
- The numbers themselves are indicative of the reasons for email success. There are more than three billion active email accounts worldwide; doubling the number of Facebook and Twitter accounts combined.
- As reported in a Millward Brown digital study, half of consumers reported they receive more than ten retailer emails a week, with 20 percent receiving more than 30.

Although the email figures in the *Advertising Age* feature indicate positive success for the outlet, the numbers are from September 2013. In such a fast-changing environment, the outlook for 2014 differs somewhat. A Forbes.com article, "The Top 7 Social Media Marketing Trends That will Dominate 2014," offers some predictions regarding social media. Some are:

- *Investment in social media will become a necessity.* With the anticipated growth, businesses will see more and more of the need to hire media strategists and not rely on existing employees to do the job.
- *Google+ will become a major factor.* It is gaining on Facebook and now has 343 million monthly users. With Google's ability to collect personal information such as demographics, location, etc., Google+ will no longer be thought of as just another social network.
- ***Image-centric networks*** *will see huge success.* Visual content will become more important than just the use of text content.
- *The rise of **micro-video**.* "Micro" video apps like Twitter's **Vine** and Instagram's "video sharing feature," enable users to create and share videos from their smartphones. Instagram allows 3–15 seconds per video and Vine exactly 6 seconds.
- *The decline of **Foursquare**.* With the success of social networks such as Facebook and Instagram, and the inability for Foursquare to raise capital, it is likely that it will be absorbed into one of the better performing networks.
- ***MySpace*** *expected to grow.* With significant makeovers, MySpace seems to be getting better traction. Its emphasis will be on bands and music lovers.

TEXT MESSAGING

More and more retailers are using text messages to reach shoppers. One major benefit is the fact that 90 percent of text messages sent are opened within 6 minutes, resulting in an almost instantaneous alert to recipients. Other advantages include cost-effectiveness, highly targeted markets, and easy implementation. With 96 percent of Americans owning a mobile phone and 86 percent of them using their phones for text messaging, this is a channel that is becoming more and more important to retailers. Many merchants use text messaging for the following reasons:

- When inventories are higher than required, coupons sent via text messaging can result in unwanted merchandise "flying off the shelves."
- Sending a message to customers about promotions and contests that are on their Facebook or Twitter pages helps grow a social media following.
- To build client loyalty, text messages following store purchases thank them for their visits.
- ROI (return on investment) is higher than any marketing method.
- It builds brand awareness, especially for private label merchandise.
- It increases foot traffic.

IN-STORE MULTIMEDIA CONCEPTS

Just one of the major uses of indoor multimedia offerings is **digital signage**, which highlights whatever the store wants to alert the customer to, and anything else that is in-store newsworthy. It a great way to motivate customers to purchase.

figure 17.3
A woman text messaging on a smartphone. Text messages can be used to spread promotions of interest from one user to another.

Digital Signage

One of the fastest growing technologies for retailers is the advent of multimedia usage, making the use of paper printed signs and billboards obsolete. Once a mainstay in retailing, the paper signs are being replaced by exciting offerings of digital signage. The *Happening Now* feature explores digital signage for in-store retailers.

Other In-Store Multimedia Products and Usage

In addition to the aforementioned coverage of digital signage, there are a wealth of other multimedia products and uses for them by retailers.

Store Endeavors

One of the global retailers that have built their in-store environments with multimedia products is Uniqlo, the highly successful Japanese retailer. Its expansion to the United States has been extremely successful with some of the credit going to in-store multimedia usage. Its New York City flagship on Fifth Avenue features a show stopping attraction that can be seen from outside of the store and all of the interior.

As summarized in an article from www.digitalsignageuniverse.typepad.com, shoppers are entertained by two custom floor-to-ceiling LCD video walls with the store's glass elevators. The elevators are visible from the street to traffic and passersby on Fifth Avenue as they move up and down. The storefront's Fifth Avenue side also includes LCD displays in the windows at street level which create additional energy.

Throughout the store six large LCD video displays play motion content which is in itself motivating. This and Uniqlo's multimedia program features more than 400 LCD video displays that are arranged in "video wall" and "video column configurations." Adding to the excitement is the use of more than 175 audio speakers that, when combined with the displays, "envelop the customers in a wave of sight and sound." That arouses and motivates them to visit most every part of the store and often results in purchasing, sometimes on impulse.

While the Uniqlo foray into in-store multimedia is by and large the epitome of this concept, it should be noted that other retailers are also using multimedia display, but at a less intensive enhancement to their store's merchandise.

In London, Burberry has opened a new unit, a "digitally integrated" 27,000 square foot flagship on Regent Street, a shopping mecca for that city. The description offered by Burberry is it "has seamlessly integrated technology throughout." Some of the features include: "Full-length screens wrap the store transitioning between audio-visual content displays, live streaming hubs and mirrors." Enhancing that models are seen walking between video screens, mimicking the "Burberry World Live" experience that was staged earlier in Taipei. One of the more recent additions has been the use of radio-frequency identification chips (RFID) that have been attached to certain clothes and accessories. When the shopper approaches one of the screens in the common areas or fitting rooms, content such as "information on a bag's stitching and craftsmanship or a video showing how a skirt was worn on the catwalk," appear, all giving benefits to motivate purchasing.

Many take just a portion of what's available such as "backlit transparencies" big in the retailer's cosmetic displays, "video walls" such as seen in some American Eagle Outfitters, and "interactive screens" such as used by Harvey Nichols in London, that enables the shopper to maneuver the screen with a touch of the hands to locate specific merchandise, learn about special sales promotions, department locations, customer services, personalized shopping availability, and anything else that management has

DIGITAL SIGNAGE AND ITS IMPORTANCE TO RETAILERS

What was once a typical display staple in department stores and specialty organizations, the static paper sign seems to be coming to the end of its usefulness. Not only have some merchants such as Abercrombie & Fitch and Tommy Hilfiger switched to digital signage in their window displays, but more and more are using the technology inside their stores. Figure 17.4 shows the Tommy Hilfiger in-store digital signage.

Not only has this usage reduced the signage cost, but it has significantly translated "lookers" into purchasers. In a later section of the chapter, the WWD Digital Forum, an annual trade show that is held in different international venues, shows some of the important "digital" uses by retailers.

The digital entries use a variety of display panels, scrolling message boards, and so forth, to present video, sound, and textual materials. One of the better features of these and other systems is the ease with which the presentations can be quickly changed to meet the immediate needs of the retailer at comparatively modest costs. The digital software devices include plasma or LCD monitors with the latter becoming more prevalent.

Some of the advantages of the digital signage offerings include:

- Capturing the shoppers' attention and often motivating them to buy right at the point of purchase.
- The elimination of the high costs of paper signage production and the delivery of the printed materials.

- The ability to immediately change the signage to feature various products. For example, an incoming snowstorm could lead to featuring merchandise such as warm coats and boots to motivate purchasing.
- Income from suppliers for advertising space purchases.
- The benefit for retailers to introduce new private label collections that are exclusively featured in their merchandise mix.

Some of the retail users for digital signage include a host of upscale and fashion forward retailers around the world. These include:

- *Tommy Hilfiger* who has used store window images in some stores that enable passersby or window shoppers to leave their images for future contact by the merchant.

figure 17.4
One of Tommy Hilfiger's newer stores in Germany features digital signage. It is often a motivational tool to prompt consumer purchasing.

- *Nike FuelStation* in its interactive store in London uses **motion-sensitive monitors** to display footage of local runners wearing the store's products to motivate passersby to purchase as they walk past.

This is only a smattering of ideas of in-store digital signage usage. Just about every day new concepts are available, as seen in the aforementioned WWD Digital Forums.

assessed as important to the user. With the benefit of avoiding time-wasting to have their needs addressed, this is a plus for the consumer with little time to shop. For the retailer, it offers more information which can result in sales.

With its time having come, multimedia displays are being enhanced with new concepts and products to enable even the smaller retailers to become users.

PROS AND CONS OF ELECTRONIC COMMUNICATION

As with every communication medium, the electronically-based has many advantages to the user, as well as disadvantages.

Advantages

1. With the need for only a few seconds to communicate, it gives the user the quickest form of communication. This is especially beneficial when communicating with people across the globe.

2. The costs are comparatively low when compared to media that requires purchase of paper, printing, postal expense, and so forth. Hard copies are not in the picture.

3. Transmissions can include visual images as well as text.

4. The messages sent can be permanently stored as hard copies, or on disks or thumb drives and are easily retrievable.

5. Social media is becoming the biggest bargain for fashion retailers who have traditionally used newspaper, magazine, television, etc. to communicate their messages. With less time available for readers to use traditional print and broadcast media, using their smartphones and tablets has become increasingly important.

Disadvantages

1. The non-electronic forms of communications systems have become costlier than ever before, which is making the investment unlikely for certain businesses.

2. **Computer hacking** is becoming a prevalent issue for retailers. At the very end of 2013, many millions of Target accounts, and more recently, Neiman Marcus were hacked causing great concern for users. Often, people will intentionally use viruses that will cause great concern for email users.

3. Occasionally data is lost or undelivered due to system error, causing problems for both senders and intended recipients.

MAJOR RETAIL SOCIAL MEDIA USERS WITH FASHION MERCHANDISE ORIENTATION

There are few, if any, major retailers that feature fashion merchandise in their operations that do not use social media to promote their products. According to www.socialmediatoday.com the statistics show that businesses that fail to employ social media will soon be out of business. It should be noted that the mere usage of the media doesn't guarantee success, but those that spend significant time in developing a good approach have been making tremendous strides with the use of social media.

Table 17.1 shows the top five fashion retailer users and the specific social media they use, as extracted from Top Ten Retail Social Media published by socialmediatoday. com. The fashion retailers are listed in order of importance.

Table 17.1

TOP FIVE FASHION RETAILERS AND THEIR SOCIAL MEDIA CHOICES

Facebook	Twitter	Google+	Pinterest	YouTube
Walmart	Victoria's Secret	Neiman Marcus	Nordstrom	Victoria's Secret
Target	Urban Outfitters	Amazon	Victoria's Secret	Coach
Amazon	Target	Guess	Urban Outfitters	Abercrombie & Fitch
Macy's	Amazon	Macy's	Neiman Marcus	Foot Locker
Kohl's	Abercrombie & Fitch	*	Target	*

* Non-fashion retailer.

As you can see, many of the merchants make use of more than one social network. For example, Target uses three as does Victoria's Secret. As in print and broadcast media usage, social media requires savvy selectivity to reach the potential customer. The same message on each of those social networks used will often not bring positive results. It is imperative that each of the social media has an ultimate goal for the user. It is not always sales, but sometimes it is image building.

In the case of Kate Spade, chief marketing officer Mary Beech has introduced a yearlong plan that contains seasonal strategies. As reported in a *WWD* November 13, 2013 article, Beech uses specific social media to achieve certain goals. In the article Beech explained that:

> Facebook is about a customer who wants information on products and to be kept in the know about sales, events, and new store openings; Instagram is the visual story of the Kate Spade approach to life in New York City, and Twitter is the verbal view of this girl—whether she's tweeting about local goings-on or something great she just saw on the street.

The same article reports of Quynh Mai, C.E.O. of the digital agency Moving Image & Content, that, "there are smaller, more personalized platforms—such as Path and Vine—that Mai thinks could be interesting for brands looking to develop a deeper relationship with a niche consumer."

With the wealth of media available—such as Facebook, Instagram, Pinterest, Google+, Tumblr, YouTube, and LinkedIn—the social platform scene has become cluttered, and the concept of one-size-fits-all no longer holds true.

RETAIL PARTNERING WITH SOCIAL NETWORKS

In order to take advantage of the social media phenomenon, several approaches are being used by brick-and-mortar retailers for **partnering with social networks**. Nordstrom, for example, has become associated with Pinterest and has placed its holiday catalog on Pinterest. In all of its full-line stores, signs that feature merchandise that has been "pinned" are available for sale. Similarly, Sears uses Instagram and Walmart used both Facebook and Google in 2013. The success of this marriage has prompted Walmart to use seven or eight social networks in the future.

This action seems to be the beginning of the retailer-social platform arrangement, but with the most recent success it seems to be heading for more participation.

MAJOR SOCIAL MEDIA CONFERENCES

One of the ways in which to learn about social media is to log on to different websites that discuss the positives for the use of particular media such as Facebook and Pinterest, the costs involved, membership, and so forth. While this is a time-consuming exercise, it does provide the potential user with useful information.

In order to do a timely, exhaustive study of the numerous available social media, a preferable method for evaluation purposes is attendance at a social media conference. With approximately 40 conferences in the United Sates alone, and more globally, it becomes necessary to determine if the locations are within the company's geographical location, the costs of attendance, the conference speakers, and so forth. The lengths of the conferences vary as do the prices to attend. Some are regularly held at the same time and place at least once each year.

A major conference that is held each year is the fashion and retailing entry, "WWD Digital Forum," that can be attended at several different global venues such as New York City, London, and Los Angeles. On January 29, 2014 in Los Angeles such topics as "Creating and maintaining a devoted community online," "Preparing for the next generation of digital savvy shoppers," "Fast fashion in the digital age," and "Understanding social media's impact online and off" were the spotlight topics.

For the first time, the 2014 event featured hands-on workshops concentrating on Instagram and Tumblr. Executives from Nordstrom, Gap, Target, Zappos, Neiman Marcus, BCBG Max Azria, J.Jill, Tommy Bahama, and numerous other fashion-oriented retailers were in attendance, indicating the importance of the conference.

Table 17.2 features the top ten social media conferences of 2014, which address issues for a wealth of businesses including, but not limited to, fashion retailers. You can find the schedules for these conferences on the Internet, including the topics to be discussed, a list of presenters, and so forth.

Table 17.2

TOP TEN SOCIAL MEDIA MARKETING CONFERENCES — 2014

Conference	Location	Date(s)	Cost
Social Fresh	Tampa, FL	April 18–19	$400–700
Social Fresh	San Diego, CA	September 12–13	$400–700
SXSW Interactive	Austin, TX	March 9–12	$700–1,200
SMX Social Media	Las Vegas, NV	November 20–21	$900–3,300
NMX by Blog World	Las Vegas, NV	January 4–5	$700–1,300
Content Marketing World	Cleveland, OH	September 9–11	$495–2,395
Social Brand Forum	Coralville, IA	September 25–26	$375
Inbound Marketing Summit	Boston, MA	September 15–18	$800–1,200
Social Media Week	New York City, NY; Washington D.C.; Miami, FL	September 23–27	Free
MIMA Summit	Minneapolis, MN	October 15	$450

For those retailers, and most other businesses, attendance of at least one of these conferences is a must in order to keep up with suggestions for social media marketing efforts, industry changes, and new technology, to learn from other businesses, and so forth.

TRENDS IN ELECTRONIC MEDIA

A number of new trends have taken the spotlight for electronic media. The range of changes is significant for both the companies that use them and the customers they are trying to reach. Some of these are:

- *LinkedIn: Rich media.* A visual component has been added to LinkedIn, providing images, videos, documents, etc., to the written message. For example, artists can post photographs of their works to their profiles and then promote the posts to their LinkedIn network.

- **Pinterest rich pins**. A new feature has been added to Pinterest called rich pins that includes more detailed information than a typical Pinterest pin. Of the variety of rich pins available, product pins are most useful. As we saw before, these pins "enable retailers to attach such real-time pricing, inventory availability and a 'Buy this' link to their product images." One major off-price retailer, Overstock.com, makes use of rich pins to enable shoppers to check prices some days after the purchase. The site automatically sends an email to the customer notifying them of the price change. It has become an excellent tool to boost company image. It is expected that this new feature will "ultimately have the potential to lead to more shares and discoverability by users on the site," according to a post by Tiffany Monhollon on DMNews.com on November 19, 2013.

- *Instagram video.* In this new concept, businesses can add 15 seconds of video for such things as the introduction of a retailer's new private brand or a tour of a store that has been renovated. The concept helps to tell a story. With ownership of Instagram by Facebook, users can post their "InstaVideos" to their Facebook page. Figure 17.5 shows a portion of an Instagram video at the Pitti Immagine Uomo trade show.

figure 17.5
This photo from Florence, Italy, was taken using the iPhone Instagram application. Instagrams can add 15 seconds of video often making it more effective than those tools that don't employ "action" in their messaging.

BLOGS

Blogging has become an important tool in most industries for the distribution of news and concepts as envisioned by bloggers. It must be understood that the "articles" are merely the opinions of those interested in a certain area, such as fashion and fashion retailing. They are not necessarily factual or verifiable, but nonetheless have become informative opinions which have gained considerable publicity and have a wealth of followers. If the opinions of the blogger have proven to turn out correctly, readers often become followers.

The blogs featured below are some of those with significant followings according to Humayun Khan in Physical Retail posted on March 28, 2014:

- *Retail Adventures Blog.* This blog features the latest insights on merchandising, customer service, etc. that retailers of all sizes can read and consider the suggestions made by the blogger. It also helps other industry professionals such as resident buyers and consumers who would like to be alerted as to what might be on the retail horizon.

- *The Retail Doctor.* Featuring the thoughts of Bob Phibbs, a nationally recognized expert with more than 30 years of experience. One of the major topics covered is employee training and retention. It is particularly interesting to human resources specialists, who might be made aware of new recruitment techniques, employee turnover improvement, promotional concepts, etc. Those looking to make better judgments regarding employment often use this blog to improve their job potential.
- *Retail Minded.* Where small retailers are often left out in the cold because they can't afford outside resources for assistance, they often turn to this blog, which caters to independent retailers. Employees of small retailers sometimes use this source to gain an edge on other employees.
- *National Retail Federation Blog.* The world's largest retail trade organization publishes its "Retail's Big Blog", which covers trends, offers prediction, etc. for its membership.
- *Retailing in Focus.* It is the brainchild of 30-years retail veteran Dick Seesel who has run a successful consulting practice. It enables merchants to learn about new ideas and those entering the field to know the ins and outs of retailing.

Benefits to Retailers

In addition to benefits to retailers, including the publicity they get from independent blogs, many retailers are finding it beneficial to create their own. Some of these benefits include:

- having it as a link to their home page, it immediately brings the blog to the customer. Not only does it work with web traffic, but also on advertisements, direct mail, letterheads, etc.
- providing a way for a shopper to interact with the merchant if the blog is properly organized
- bringing exciting news to the customer and potential customer.

SHOWROOMING

"**Showrooming**" as a phenomenon continues to soar, often putting brick-and-mortar operations in peril. Many report that the practice of the online shopper coming into a store to check prices has caused falling sales. Today, more and more retailers are combatting showrooming problems by meeting the prices of the online site, carrying more private label merchandise that is exclusive to the store, offering immediate delivery that is generally unusual for online merchants, adding visual merchandising that could motivate the in-store shopper to purchase something other than the online products, and so forth.

On the other hand, many merchants are turning this negative into a positive. They are using many approaches to make this happen. *Stores* magazine, the NRF periodical, shared these approaches in their March, 2013 cover story. Some of the highlights included:

- A good omni-channel strategy can turn the showrooming shopper into one that might purchase in the store.
- With increased customer service, the showroomer might be motivated to buy in the store.
- Touching and trying-on the sought merchandise could convince the shopper to make the purchase in the store.

- The use of showrooming motivates some customers to walk into the store which increases in-store traffic and potential sales.
- Showrooming provides immediacy for the shopper.
- The salesperson is the "foot soldier" on the selling floor, and if armed with the latest technical and other information, can be the one to make the sale.

Store Applications

More specifically, some retailers are fighting back with their own plans such as:

- Target, which uses price matching when shoppers appear with web offers, finds that this very often turns the "showrooming" into an in-store sale.
- Moosejaw Mountaineering, specializing in outdoor gear and apparel, has sales associates find the products through a mobile device and matches competitive prices. It has resulted in larger sales than if purchased on the Internet.
- At Victoria's Secret, they "mine data to determine who visits their stores but doesn't buy a bra." They could figure out which people have purchased bras, and lure that group with emails to lure them into their stores.
- Discounters like Target, department stores like Macy's and specialty giants like Gap fight the battle by selling their own brands which cannot be bought elsewhere. Once a shopper becomes a purchaser, they often forgo showrooming and become in-store regulars.

In-Store Video Usage

Since the eye often detects motion immediately, the use of video offers greater color stimulation as compared to print media or signage. With the costs of implementation relatively modest, the usage is expected to increase in the brick-and-mortar operations. H&M's 42,000 square foot high tech flagship store, at 4 Times Square in New York City, has two 30 by 20 foot LCD screens located above the main entrance to the store. A curved 40 by 109 foot LCD screen is located above the main entrance that includes the H&M logo. Light boxes with messages are found throughout the store. In total, there is more than 7,000 square feet of LCD screens in use.

Information terminals

The use of these terminals is increasing in stores. When the shopper sits down at and uses an **in-store information terminal** that is easy to navigate, it is the beginning of an important step in increasing sales. The computer terminals have many applications such as price promotions, new product offerings, and sales. At Target it is a way to attract new employees by offering applications and the route to follow if interested in a position.

Shoppers may receive more information about products, be alerted to surprise sales, learn about similar products than the ones being sought, and so forth.

Chapter Highlights

1. In the past few years, the use of electronic media to reach customers has steadily grown. Innovative concepts seem to be challenging the retail industry almost every day.

2. The Internet continues to be a major method for retailers to reach their existing customers and potentially new customers.

3. The frequent use of email messaging continues to become more important to the retail industry. Once the recipient opens the email, he or she is generally led to the retailer's website. Immediate sales, motivation to visit the store, or a telephone call to the company are often the end results. In 2013, approximately 1.7 billion people around the world used social media, a 16 percent increase from the previous year.

4. Facebook is the king of social media with more than 500 million users.

5. The importance of social media to retailers is that 56 percent of Americans have a profile on a social networking site, making it very easy to reach a large number of people through this channel.

6. "Showrooming," once considered a deterrent for retailers, has now been rediscovered as potentially advantageous to brick-and-mortar stores.

7. 76 percent of consumers who receive email from retail operations not only read them but act upon them.

8. It is expected that there will be major positive changes in social media, such as Google+ becoming a major player and there will be an increase in the use of image-centric networks.

9. In-store digital signage is gaining momentum monthly to help boost sales.

10. Some of the advantages of electronic communication include speed, comparatively low costs, transmissions can include visual images as well as text, and so forth.

11. The top fashion merchants that use social media include Victoria's Secret, Neiman Marcus, Nordstrom, Coach, and Macy's.

12. The major digital conference that is held in a number of global venues is WWD Digital Forum.

Terms of the Trade

3dcart	micro-video
banner ads	motion-sensitive monitors
computer hacking	partnering with social networks
digital signage	"pinned"
electronic media	Pinterest
Facebook	Pinterest rich pins
foursquare	showrooming
Google+	sidebar ads
image-centric networks	smartphones
Instagram	tweets
in-store information terminals	Twitter
LCD monitors	WWD Digital Forum

For Discussion

1. How has electronic media affected print media?

2. In this era of newspaper decline, is there one print medium that is still capturing the attention of shoppers and is producing sales for the retailer?

3. What are some of the advantages for retailers to use email to reach their customers?

4. Is the number up or down for people around the world using social media?

5. Which of the social media is considered to be "king?"

6. What is the most recent innovation that Pinterest has added in their advertising?

7. Describe "showrooming" and discuss its use.

8. What is in-store digital signage, and how does it benefit retailers?

9. Will the problem of computer hacking be a deterrent for retailer usage? Why?

10. Which industries are the beneficiaries of attending the WWD Digital Forums?

11. What is retail partnering with social networks, and what are its benefits?

12. How does the typical Pinterest pin differ from the Pinterest rich pins?

Case Problem

The use of electronic media by fashion retailers continues to grow at a rapid pace. Through the pages of such journals as *WWD*, the information brought to merchants at such trade expositions as WWD Digital Forum, which are held several times a year at a variety of venues, and the exploration by fashion retailers in their own online research or meetings with resident buying offices continues to pique the interest of small fashion entrepreneurs who have yet to join the world of electronic media.

The partners of a small fashion boutique, The Contemporary Model, started their business 20 years ago, and have built the one-store operation into an extremely successful business by tripling its size and space. They have often considered expansion by opening new units and adding a wealth of private label goods to their merchandise mix. At this point in time, having spent 20 years running the business, Amanda and Abby are considering the possibility of their respective daughters, Sophia and Helen, joining the business as executives, and playing a less important role in the running of the company. Among such duties as product acquisition, customer relations, and evaluation of return on investment, they are also being charged with a change in their promotional endeavors.

To date, customer attraction has been through the use of direct mail, newspaper advertising, radio participation, and some telephone contacts. Having just attended the WWD Digital Forum, Sophia and Helen have been motivated to add the use of electronic media to their methods of communicating with their customers.

In addition to having little expertise in the matter, they are concerned with costs, learning the various choices available to them to use in their operation, the present merchandise mix and if it should be expanded to make the company more profitable, and so forth.

Questions

1. Is it feasible for a small merchant to make use of electronic media to communicate with their customers? How?

2. Should the use of traditional print and broadcast media be abandoned? Why?

3. Which tools would you use to enter into the world of electronic media?

At this point in time, the partners and their new management-level employees are discussing the ways in which communicating with customers through electronic media is a possibility for such a small operation.

Exercises and Projects

1. Visit three small fashion brick-and-mortar shops to determine if they make use of any electronic media to communicate with their customers. The interview should center on three different systems such as social media networks, the email, digital signage, and so forth. In the outline provided, record your findings.

	Company Name	System(s) Employed	Cost of System
1			
2			
3			

2. Log on to a search engine such as Yahoo or Google and enter the keywords, "social media." Proceed to search for five social networks that retailers use. In the layout provided, insert the advantages and disadvantages of each.

	Social Networks	Advantages	Disadvantages
1			
2			
3			
4			
5			

chapter eighteen

SERVICING THE FASHION SHOPPER

After reading this chapter, you should be able to:

- Discuss the role of the fashion sales associate in brick-and-mortar operations.

- Describe the sales associate's role as intermediary between the company's buyers and the customers.

- Differentiate between on-site and off-site selling.

- List the essentials of successful fashion retailing selling techniques.

- Identify and discuss the nature of rewards programs offered by fashion retailers.

- Describe the different types of customer services offered by retailers, and why many go to such extents to offer them.

- Summarize the different types of credit arrangements that retailers offer to their clienteles.

As has been continuously noted throughout this text, competition in the retailing industry continues to increase significantly. Fashion merchants, in particular, are facing challenges never before realized in the history of retailing. They must be concerned with the problems associated with merchandise distinction from other retailers and the best location and design of their brick-and-mortar operations. Competent staffing is especially important for retailers—both the long-term maintenance of employees from the upper-management levels to those who interface with shoppers, either in person, or through catalog or online inquiries but especially in ensuring that these frontline employees properly service their customers.

The key to the success of any retail operation, no matter how large or small, is the development of positive relationships with customers so that they will return to shop in their stores, catalogs, and websites and ultimately to become loyal patrons of the organization. Achieving this regular patronage depends a lot upon the product mix that the company offers; but the manner in which the company services its customers is equally important.

Are customers greeted properly when they enter the brick-and-mortar selling departments? Does the merchant provide sufficient services to make the customer's shopping experience a pleasant one? Is the catalog **order taker** helpful in answering questions? Are the sales associates knowledgeable about the merchandise they sell? Is the website equipped to allow customer service representatives to interact with shoppers? Merchants that provide these types of services are able to expand their customer bases, increase sales, and maximize profits.

Upper-management executives are more likely to spend time developing their company's image, directing merchandise acquisitions, developing standards, and attending to other operational details than dealing with actual shoppers. They leave this crucial task to sales staff, who are at the lower levels of the company organizational structure. Often, those at the top spend little time studying the problems associated with customer satisfaction, and those at the bottom of the ladder are often inadequately trained to make the customer's experience a pleasant one and satisfactorily close sales—which is what ultimately brings profits to the company.

Focusing attention on providing better services to customers in all aspects of the multi-channel shopping experience will enable these retailers to compete more favorably. This chapter addresses personal selling and describes different types of services that companies can use to distinguish themselves from their competitors and gain customer satisfaction and loyalty.

PERSONAL SELLING

In this age of multi-channel retailing, personal selling goes far beyond the confines of the brick-and-mortar operations. Many websites have links that directly connect the shopper with a responsive salesperson. Catalog users calling in their selections are greeted by company representatives who are not only there to take orders but also to answer questions and perhaps use "**suggestion selling**" for additional merchandise to expand the purchase.

While there are some sales techniques that salespeople can use in each of the multi-channel divisions, others are unique to only one or two types. The sections that follow address each retail category separately to show the most effective sales techniques for that channel.

Brick-and-Mortar Operations

Except for those organizations that are strictly website- or catalog-based, retailers generate the bulk of their sales in their stores. Advertising, promotions, and previous successful experiences attract significant numbers of shoppers to their premises. Once shoppers are inside the store, the sales associates are expected to provide all of the assistance necessary to transform them into satisfied customers. However, in an ever-growing number of retail outlets, especially those that offer value pricing, there has been a decrease in the number of salespeople on the selling floor, and in some cases, a complete absence of them. Fashion merchants that base their operations on traditional pricing rely upon their sales force to make shopping a pleasant experience and achieve the sales figures they need to turn a profit.

Fashion emporiums such as Nordstrom, Neiman Marcus, Bloomingdale's, and Saks Fifth Avenue, are proponents of excellent customer service and make certain that those on the selling floor are not only properly trained to sell but also to provide any other assistance that will make the shopper's experience a positive one. When salespeople at Neiman Marcus, for example, successfully complete a sale, they often follow it up with a personal note showing their appreciation. A sales associate who offers refreshments to the shopper who needs time to come to a decision is providing the quintessence of professional selling.

All too often, however, shoppers are totally ignored when entering a store or are merely greeted with the typical, routine question, "May I help you?" If the customer's response to the question is negative, the associate has little chance to recapture the customer's attention and make the sale.

The retailer's indifference to satisfying customer needs is a problem that plagues a large number of retail organizations. Except for the upscale fashion operations, providing service to the customer has become a rarity. Today, when many people work full-time and have little time to shop, it is essential that sales staff receive proper training to help customers in their stores make their selections quickly. Except at holiday shopping periods, most stores do not experience the hustle and bustle of the crowds, because many shoppers opt to use off-site outlets for their personal needs and only come to the stores when they can't be satisfied by these other means. Figure 18.1 features a salesperson completing the sale.

The Role of the Fashion Salesperson

When salespeople deal with shoppers, they must make every effort not only to sell the products but also to provide customer service, promote the company's image, and act as the intermediary between the shoppers and the company's buyers.

Selling the Product

What is the difference between a sales clerk and a professional retail sales associate? The former simply assists shoppers with selections by directing them to the try-on room, retrieving unwanted merchandise and replacing it on the racks and shelves, and performing cashiering and wrapping services for goods that the customer has chosen. The latter is a different player in the game. Sales associates try to determine the customer's needs through specific questioning techniques, suggest merchandise that might meet the customer's requirements, solve problems when the need arises, and coordinate and accessorize outfits to show how they might be enhanced while at the same time increasing the size of the purchase and cementing a relationship that will bring future business to the store. For example, those in fashion retailing shoe departments who have been professionally trained rarely bring only the style that the customer asks for but also return with a number of different styles in case the requested one doesn't fit the bill. Similarly, the service-oriented menswear seller brings a shirt and tie that would complete the suit that the customer has selected.

This is professional selling of the highest order, and it not only helps the store achieve its sales figures but also has the potential to build a private clientele for the sales associate.

figure 18.1
A salesperson in a fashion shop makes the sale. This is one of the more important customer services that often brings the customer back to the store.

Providing the Service "Extras"

Those who sell are more likely to be successful if they offer more than just their sales assistance. Simple courtesies such as providing a chair for a husband to use while his wife is trying on clothing, taking a shopper's coat and storing it until the shopper is ready to leave, tending to small children when their parent is in the try-on room, ringing up merchandise from other departments so that the shopper doesn't have to make numerous trips to different register stations, and assisting customers to their car if their packages are too cumbersome to handle are all actions that make customers feel special. Not one of these services is difficult to offer, and each could result in customer satisfaction and loyalty to the store.

Promoting the Store's Image

People frequently say, "I dislike that store; I'll never shop there again." It is usually not the store they mean but the salespeople they encountered there. Many retailers try very hard to project a positive image by assembling an appropriate merchandise mix, developing creative advertisements and promotions, and constructing visual displays that present their stores in an exciting manner. All of these expensive enhancements can mean little if sales associates are inattentive and careless. Why should people bother to shop in a store where those working on the selling floor are improperly dressed and groomed, discourtesy is a routine event, and tactless outbursts are prevalent? When people have so many other places to shop, retailers need to avoid these obstacles.

Acting as Intermediaries Between the Customer and the Buyer

Chapter 12, "Planning and Executing the Purchase," and Chapter 13, "Purchasing in the Global Marketplace," described how a company's fashion merchandising team researches the market, develops a buying plan, and purchases the goods that seem most appropriate for its clienteles. While the buyer receives scores of informational reports to get direction on future purchasing and also engages many external sources such as resident buying offices, fashion forecasters, and reporting services for additional input, only one source interfaces regularly with the shopper—the salesperson.

Computers can report which styles sold best, which colors outdistanced all of the rest, which price points brought the greatest profits, which sizes remained for markdowns, and which silhouettes were preferred. They cannot provide information on what the customer requested that the store did not stock and why sales were lost. The salespeople are the intermediaries between the shopper and the buyer. They hear about customers' likes and dislikes, their merchandise wants and needs, and anything else on their minds.

Savvy buyers understand the vital role sales personnel play in terms of merchandising, and they regularly approach these associates to learn information about the customers that other sources cannot provide.

Characteristics of the Successful Professional Fashion Sales Associate

Specific qualities and characteristics separate the average salesperson from the outstanding performer. The best of the lot could have natural ability and be born salespeople, but others can learn to refine their craft by investing time and effort to acquire the characteristics that are obvious in the most successful sellers. The following sections describe the attributes that enable successful professional sales associates to produce revenue for the company.

Appropriate Appearance

Most retailers have established dress codes that mandate a certain appearance for their staff. These codes are not formulated to force all sales associates to look alike but to make certain that sales staff favorably enhance the company's image.

The first impression that salespeople make is not with motivational greetings or through the display of product knowledge but by their clothing and grooming. If customers find their appearance offensive, they might not want to shop in the store.

Fashion retailers in particular are very concerned with the way their staff dresses. Since fashion is the essence of their business, they must insist that their staff have proper wardrobes and grooming that will enhance their merchandise offerings and make their customers feel comfortable. Although there are certain standards for acceptable dress in fashion-oriented stores, there are variations on the theme. A conservative men's retailer such as Brooks Brothers might be more rigid in terms of ensemble design and hairstyle, whereas an upscale, avant-garde organization such as Barneys New York will allow a more contemporary look. Because beards have become fashionable, many traditional merchants have adjusted their once conservative philosophies on appearance and begun to permit these once taboo styles.

Some fashion merchants encourage their sales associates to wear their merchandise by allowing them a significant discount. Ralph Lauren, in his flagship store on New York City's fashionable Madison Avenue, goes one step further to motivate the staff to purchase and wear Lauren-designed apparel and accessories in the store. All employees are given a monthly dollar allowance toward the purchase of anything that they can wear to work. Not only does having staff wear the company's clothing ensure proper appearance but it promotes the Lauren image and at the same time shows the prospective purchaser how the merchandise looks when it is worn. Shoppers will often ask the salespeople where they bought their outfit. If it is in stock, the salesperson is likely to make a sale.

Communication Excellence

Salespeople who can clearly articulate their selling points have a distinct advantage over those who can't. Of course, it is possible to learn good communications skills that will better assist shoppers with their purchases.

There are many ways sales staff can improve these skills. Colleges offer various courses in their regular degree programs as well as in their continuing-education offerings that cover everything from correct language usage to proper pronunciation. For those who have little time for formal course work, there are a wealth of audio presentations, videotapes, CDs, and DVDs that they may use at their convenience that address every aspect of proper voice and speech.

Since selling requires effective communication, it is essential that sales staff refine their language skills.

Product, Company, and Consumer Knowledge

Salespeople must have the proper appearance and communication abilities to successfully approach the shopper. Salespeople must also possess sufficient knowledge about the product classification they are selling, the company, and the customer to make selling easier and, if they are working on a commission basis, financially rewarding. Armed with such information, sales associates can immediately answer questions, handle potential customer objections, and successfully close the sale.

It is important for sales staff to understand consumer behavior so they can assess the shopper's needs and be prepared to motivate the shopper to buy. Chapter 4, "The Fashion Consumer," describes what motivates people to buy and how retailers can use this knowledge to appeal to more consumers.

Salespeople need to know the company's philosophies in terms of fashion direction, pricing, and services so they know how to handle special orders, delivery, credit, merchandise returns, alterations, prices, and special customer services, and finalize the sale. Having this information at their fingertips makes a positive impression and helps gain the customer's confidence. Retailers can provide their sales staff with new-employee orientations, handbooks and manuals, and video presentations to teach them their philosophy.

At the core of any sale is product knowledge. While articulate and well-groomed salespeople can talk to shoppers to encourage purchasing, if they don't have the right merchandise information, they may fail to close the sale. Bluffing to cover up lack of knowledge and misrepresenting the merchandise might convince the customer to buy it, but these lapses might also result in merchandise returns and loss of **customer loyalty** when the customer realizes the item is not what the salesperson said it was.

Sales staff can acquire product information by consulting a variety of sources. Designers of fashion merchandise sometimes provide retailers with videotapes and DVDs that feature their latest collections in fashion parades.

Some manufacturers provide press kits concerning their latest collections. Oftentimes, these not only address the latest in fashion innovation and collection highlights but also include photographs of models wearing the garments. Some manufacturers also generate brochures, pamphlets, and other literature that carefully spell out which styles are best suited to which body types. The swimsuit industry often provides such information.

Some colleges offer product information courses that provide technical insights of such fashion classifications as shoes, apparel, gloves, jewelry, and other accessories. Not only do these courses address style but they also discuss the manufacturing methods and the key benefits of each to the consumer. On a less formal basis, the company's fashion director can conduct seminars to bring the latest in fashion news to the store.

One of the simplest ways sales staff can gain insight into various fashion product classifications is to examine both consumer and trade publications. Magazines such as Elle, Vogue, and Harper's Bazaar regularly feature the latest and hottest trends along with commentaries by their editorial staffs. Since these publications are aimed at consumers, salespeople can learn what they are being tempted to buy and can be prepared with this information. Trade publications such as WWD include news on men's and women's fashions from the industry's point of view. Such information as color trends, fabric innovation, and texturing are regular features of these journals.

Salespeople who can discuss why one shoe manufacturing process is better than another, which fabrics will perform better, how garments should be cared for, why 14-karat gold is more costly than gold plate, and which product will provide more comfort will find it is easier to make sales and help the shopper to gain more confidence in them.

Company Loyalty

All too often, sales associates lack the integrity for success in such a career. They jump from one company to another to gain small salary increases or better hours. While salary and time commitments are important, the better way to succeed in any company is to become a loyal member of the "family." Sales staff who move around not only do disservice to themselves by not being on board long enough to make a positive impression but also cause problems for the company itself.

Staff who establish longevity with a merchant and capably spread the message of the company's image will benefit in two ways. One is the likelihood of a promotion, and the other is having the personal experience of becoming an important part of the organization. Companies that promote from within generally seek those employees who have demonstrated staying power.

The Sales Presentation

In stores that depend on personal attention to be profitable, sales associates play an important part. Those who are prepared to sell and follow specific stages that are fundamental to any selling endeavor will more than likely make the register ring. These stages are used by all successful sellers, and once learned, they become second nature.

The sequence of events inherent in most selling situations is described in the following sections.

Approaching the Customer

The timeworn opening question, "May I help you?" frequently brings a negative response, leaving the seller little room for additional conversation. More successful are approaches that begin with, "Good morning, sir," or "What a lovely day it is." These are just pleasantries that could be the beginning of a meaningful dialogue.

Determining Needs

If shoppers ask for a specific item, the salesperson knows exactly what they want. There are times, however, when salespeople need to ask questions to uncover the customer's wants. Asking brief questions or making statements might produce results. For example, if the department is one that features designer labels, the seller might bring up the focal points of the best-known designer collections, which could elicit a response from the shopper that could be used to carry on the conversation. Another question might ask the shopper about the purpose of the proposed purchase: "Will you need something for a particular occasion, or is it just to add excitement to your wardrobe?" This type of questioning usually generates an answer. After spending a great deal of time on the selling floor, experienced sales associates individualize their needs assessment techniques to particular types of shoppers and use questions or other methods that become second nature to them.

Presenting the Merchandise

When showing particular styles and models to prospective customers, salespeople need to discuss their features and selling points. This might include talking about the newest fashion trends and how this item is at the center of the concept, or focusing attention on the item's color and how it is being featured in fashion magazines such as *Elle* and *Harper's Bazaar*. If the shopper is purchasing something for travel, the salesperson could stress an item's ease in care and wrinkle resistance. If the price has been reduced, the associate should call attention to the value of the garment.

The associate should try to convince the shopper to try on the merchandise, if that is appropriate. Once the shopper is in the fitting room, the associate could bring other styles that might motivate purchasing. In such circumstances, professional sellers are often able to suggestion sell, which could result in a larger sale.

It is important to involve the shopper wherever possible. "Feel the quality of this fabric. Doesn't it feel like silk?" This is another way to bring the sale closer to completion.

Overcoming Objections

After spending considerable time with a salesperson, looking at the merchandise and asking questions, many people are simply not ready to commit themselves to a purchase for real reasons, such as the price being higher than they are willing to spend, or for other reasons that could be explained away. Whatever the situation, the seller must attempt to try **overcoming the objections** and satisfy those that are real.

There are several methods a salesperson can use to bring the sale closer to a conclusion when the customer has raised objections. The **yes, but method** involves agreeing with the customer's objection but offering alternatives that might turn the objection into a selling point. If the price seems higher than the shopper expected to pay, the seller might say, "Yes, it is a little higher priced than you might have anticipated, but the quality and versatility of the garment will serve you in many different ways. You could wear the dress to the office and, when properly accessorized, you could use it for social occasions."

Other comments using this type of objection intervention include:

- You are right, the style is very basic, but jewelry and scarves could enhance it.
- The cost of the gown might be more than you intended to spend, but you could alter this type of style for street wear, giving it longer life.
- You may have to wait longer for the delivery date of the color you want, but it will be smashing in that color.

Some salespeople prefer to handle objections by asking questions about the objection, such as, "Why isn't the color right for the party?" "Which types of fabrics do you prefer to the ones I've shown you?" and "What price would you consider your limit for a pair of shoes?"

Occasionally there is no basis for the shopper's objection. In such cases, the seller can deny the objection, although only when the seller knows with absolute certainty the shopper is incorrect. For example, "No, we do not charge more for the same items that are carried by Petite Woman," or "No, the dress will not need pressing; it is constructed with a wrinkle-resistant fabric."

The seller should handle objections in a positive manner and not one that is offensive to the customer. Some objections simply cannot be overcome, and the seller should always leave the door open for future business.

Closing the Sale

After going through the natural progression of the different stages, the seller should attempt to make the sale. Closes that are attempted before the right time are known as **trial closes**. Sometimes the attempt is successful, other times the seller has to do more selling. Some shoppers close the sales themselves, but this is not always the case.

Throughout the selling process, the salesperson should listen for signals that indicate the shopper is willing to buy, such as:

- May I leave a deposit on the shoes and pick them up at another time?
- Can it be ordered in my size?
- Can you locate it in my size in one of your other stores?
- Will there be a charge for delivery?
- Can this be changed for another item?
- Can I get a refund if I change my mind?

Many times the closing signals are not so obvious. In such cases, the professional seller uses an assortment of questions or statements, such as the following, to determine if the shopper is ready:

- Would you like to pay cash or have it put on your credit card?
- Could I give you a card to enclose with the gift?
- How much time do we have to dye the shoes to match your dress?
- Would you like the black or navy blue skirt?
- This new ivory shade would be perfect with the ensemble.

Even when the seller has made many closing attempts, the sale might never come to fruition. Sometimes the shopper simply cannot be satisfied. Other times, the approach could be to involve someone else in the store who has higher standing. In a boutique, it might be the buyer, or in a department or specialty store, it might be the department manager. When a store representative who has more authority becomes involved in the transaction, customers might feel that they are receiving special attention and may be prepared to buy as a result.

The most experienced sales associates know that not every sale can be completed no matter how many selling techniques they employ. If this is the case, they handle the shopper in a courteous manner to encourage future business.

Essentials of a Successful Sales Program

To attract the most talented people to join its sales staff and to motivate company loyalty, the retailer should consider the essentials for running a successful program.

Incentives are often the key to success. At Nordstrom, which pays its sales staff a straight commission, sales associates try their best to make the sale: only completed sales provide them with their income. Promotion from within is another means of reward for satisfactory service. Recognition seminars, prizes for the highest weekly sales, and extra staff discounts on purchases when they have achieved certain sales goals might motivate sales staff to try harder.

Proper staff training, as discussed in Chapter 10, "The Human Resources Division," is another essential in a sound selling program. It gives the seller the feeling of self-confidence that can translate into bigger sales.

Periodic evaluations are also a necessity to help sales associates learn about their positive as well as negative characteristics. A good evaluation program can help build morale and foster employee longevity.

Finally, an occasional pat on the back may go a long way in motivating the seller to try harder.

Selling on the Internet

Although the amount of consumer sales transactions accomplished over the Internet pales in comparison with those accomplished in the stores, website selling is increasing every year. More people are turning to this channel not only for books and CDs, as they did in the early stages of this medium, but also for a variety of fashion merchandise ranging from value-priced items to the likes of Prada, Ralph Lauren, and Calvin Klein. In *Happening Now*, online personal shopping services are examined.

While a great deal of purchasing on the Internet does not require selling techniques, some merchants have recognized that some selling effort might be required to complete the sale. Pictures or descriptions of items aren't always sufficient to close the sale.

Personal selling comes about in two ways. One involves interaction by telephone between the online selling agent and the customers and the other by **chatting online** or interactive relationships. Figure 18.2 shows a live chat about merchandise on the Internet.

figure 18.2
Retailer representative holding a live chat with a customer. This availability to shoppers enables those who need more information to have their questions answered.

THE LATEST ONLINE PERSONAL SHOPPING SERVICES

Since online shopping began, each year has seen more sales than the year before. The outlook for the future seems even brighter. With ever-increasing numbers of shoppers shying away from the brick-and-mortar operations because of time constraints, a desire to compare the offerings of retailers in less time than it would take to visit the stores, to price compare, and so forth, often the help of a professional to make purchasing decisions is in order.

Many upscale fashion merchants offer personalized shopping in their stores, some without cost and others with some expense to the customer. Customers who have continued success with their purchases at a single fashion merchant would likely stay with that company for their personal assistance when shopping online. What is happening now is increase in private personal shopping services. Some of them are free to the user while others charge a fee for their services. According to the Association of Image Consultants International, there are about 1,400 such personal shoppers with the list continuously growing. Davidowitz & Associates, Inc.'s C.E.O. offers this reason for its success: "People are time-poor and it can save people time."

An example of the success is evident with Stitch Fix's success. According to its C.E.O., "we have had a growth rate of seven times what we were doing the prior year," a good growth picture for personal shopping. They offer such services as creating a style profile for each individual shopper, an ability to keep what the customer has ordered and free returns for unwanted items, styling tips on how to accessorize apparel received and if the order of five or more items are kept, the shopper receives a 25 percent discount on the entire order.

Other companies, of which there are many, offer similar services.

Catalog Selling

Chapter 1, "The Nature of the Fashion Retailing Industry," discussed how catalog purchasing is alive and well and is big business for many of today's fashion merchants. Catalogs provide users with significant benefits in terms of convenience and retailers with significant benefits in terms of profits.

Shoppers buy from catalogs in three ways. They either complete order forms included in the catalogs and mail them in to the merchant, call the company and place their order with a knowledgeable order taker, or use the company website to place the order. The second method of contact gives companies an opportunity to offer selling assistance. Catalog retailers supply their telephone divisions with all the different catalogs they offer, which are identical to the ones consumers receive. When callers know exactly what they want to purchase, no "selling" is required. When callers have questions before they decide to purchase, the representative must be fully versed on such matters as additional color availability, size variation, delivery dates, shipping costs, and return procedures. It is then that the reps may need to do some selling to close the sale.

There are major differences in the sales presentation that sellers use in the brick-and-mortar operations and in catalog operations. Unlike the former, which requires the sales associate to dress appropriately and have skills in customer approach, the latter requires neither. These shoppers never see the "seller" nor do they need a special approach. Catalog users initiate the transaction by making the telephone call. The goods are not physically presented; they consist of catalog photographs and descriptions. The seller does not even have to assess the caller's needs except when the caller wants some additional information about such factors as product durability and care.

The similarities between personal and distant selling come at the overcoming objection and closing the sale stages. Here, the order takers assume the role of sellers. They must be able to overcome any objections that callers might raise and attempt to close the sale whenever the objections have been overcome. They might also, as do on-site sellers, suggest additional products to increase the size of the sale.

CUSTOMER SERVICE

When Henri Bendel, founder of the famous fashion institution that bears his name, personally greeted customers at the door and directed each one to a sales specialist who would satisfy their needs, he displayed the epitome of customer service. Today, Walmart, the epitome of value shopping, continues that concept with the use of **store greeters** at the stores' entrances to provide the same personal attention. While these two companies are at the complete opposite ends of the retailing spectrum, they each, nonetheless, have recognized the value of customer service. They, along with just about every fashion merchant, offer a host of services that they believe assists them in gaining their fair share of the marketplace and gives the shopper a reason to shop in their stores for reasons other than merchandise procurement.

This text has made many references to the highly competitive nature of fashion retailing and the sameness of the merchandise carried throughout the industry. It has focused attention upon some of the ways in which retailers attempt to separate themselves from the rest of the pack, including the design of elegant surroundings for their brick-and-mortar operations, innovative and imaginative visual merchandising, creative advertising, special events, the development of private brands and labels, and professional and dedicated sales associates.

Being able to have a personal shopper preselect merchandise that is appropriate for any occasion, have garments altered in a minimum of time, make gift selections without having to go to the store, and enjoy the assistance of a sales associate who can converse in a language other than English are all things that make shopping more pleasurable and appealing. Retailers that offer these services, and many others, are able to count on customer loyalty where shoppers regularly return to their different retailing channels whenever the need arises.

The first part of this chapter addressed what many consider to be the most important of the customer services: personal selling. This alone, however, is not where service ends. Customer service encompasses a whole host of offerings that help motivate customer loyalty.

Many of the services retailers feature in their stores, catalogs, or on their websites are fairly traditional to the industry, while some merchants customize services to better fit their own clientele's needs. The multi-channel phenomenon has caused merchants to offer a variety of services in all of their distribution outlets, and they attempt to tailor the type of services to accommodate the shoppers using those different channels.

On-Site Services

Merchants provide the greatest number of customer services in their brick-and-mortar units. The following sections discuss several traditional services offered by many retailers.

Rewards Programs

Just as the airlines try to gain consumer loyalty by providing frequent-flier miles that regular passengers can put toward free flights, companies such as Saks Fifth Avenue and Neiman Marcus have established **rewards programs** that reward shoppers every time they purchase from them. These programs also benefit those who purchase from the companies' catalogs or websites, but shoppers earn the bulk of these points in the brick-and-mortar outlets.

The InCircle rewards program at Neiman Marcus and Bergdorf Goodman gives shoppers two points for each dollar charged to their credit card. Those who accumulate 10,000 points are recognized with a distinctive charge card, giving them extra shopping status. Participants can redeem the points for merchandise as well as for use in such frequent-flier programs as American Airlines and United Airlines.

SaksFirst, the rewards program Saks Fifth Avenue offers, is similar to that of Neiman Marcus and Bergdorf Goodman. It requires a minimum of 5,000 base points before it awards membership. Those enrolled in the Saks program also benefit from double and triple point events, exclusive promotions and giveaways, complimentary companion ticket offers from British Airways, and special offers from the Ritz-Carlton hotel chain and Cunard Cruises.

Registries

Just about every fashion retailer offers bridal and other gift **registries**. Couples making wedding plans or expecting the birth of a child visit a store and preselect items that they would like to receive as gifts. The registries provide selection assistance from specialists who accompany the registrants throughout the store to help with their decision making. Once the registrants have chosen what gifts they would like to receive, they fill out forms listing their choices can consult. This helps the registrants avoid receiving duplicate gifts and ensures the retailer offering the registry receives a lot of business from the people who are buying gifts for the registrants.

Corporate Services

Most major fashion merchants provide **corporate buying programs** for businesses. Business representatives can choose from gifts of every price point and type. In addition, the retailers offer corporate discounts, engraving services for more personalized giving, and signature packaging featuring their logo. This service is especially appealing during the Christmas selling season, when businesses can select gifts for their clients and staff without any additional expense.

Personal Shoppers

With less time to spend shopping, many consumers are turning to personal shopping to quickly and efficiently choose fashion products to fit their needs. A customer contacts a merchant and gives the personal shopper pertinent information such as style and color preferences, price points, size, and the event to which the garment will be worn. The personal shopper then combs the store's premises for items that fit the customer's request.

Next, the personal shopper schedules a convenient time for the customer to visit the store and try on the selected items, and a fitter is also present to make alterations if necessary.

Some customers prefer to have a personal shopper accompany them to the various merchandise departments and help them find things or make suggestions. Figure 18.3 shows a personal shopper selecting merchandise for a client.

figure 18.3
A personal shopper goes through the rack to pick merchandise for a customer. It is an especially valuable service for shoppers with limited time.

Macy's was one of the earliest proponents of personal shopping. Its MBA, or Macy's By Appointment program, was the one other fashion retailers emulated when they developed their own programs.

Interpreters

Some fashion retailers have the advantage of being located in areas that are regularly visited by tourists. In London, Harrods provides interpreters who speak just about any language. The Macy's Herald Square store in New York City has a similar program in place.

At no additional charge, store employees who are fluent in many languages will accompany shoppers throughout the stores. They arrange for immediate alterations, provide currency exchange information, and offer any other translation assistance that shoppers require to make their visit to the store successful and enjoyable.

Visitor Services

Out-of-town visitors patronizing certain fashion retail operations receive a host of different services. At Macy's New York City flagship, the visitor is treated to a free tote bag, reservation assistance for local attractions, and city maps and directions. Bloomingdale's offers a 10 percent discount for out of the area shoppers.

Many retailers also provide concierge services for these visiting guests which enables them to spend their time more productively.

Merchandise Alterations

Often, the fact that a retailer supplies an alteration expert is enough to convince some customers to patronize it. Many shoppers with little time to spend seeking alterations opt for in-store help so they can quickly and easily get their finished product. Figure 18.4 shows a seamstress at work.

figure 18.4
A busy seamstress at a retail store. Alteration services often motivate customers to buy in a particular store.

Small specialty stores and boutiques, in particular, find that this service enables them to compete with their larger fashion retailing counterparts. The personalization of such a service often brings customers back again and again, contributing significantly to their customer loyalty.

Exclusive Shopping Hours

Some of the high-fashion retailers, such as Henri Bendel in New York City, set aside specific shopping hours for the exclusive use of particular segments of the market. For example, they feature "Girls' Nites" that offer workshops on beauty, wedding planning, shopping, and other fashion-oriented topics to women only.

Others set time aside for "men only" hours at peak holiday times in which this population segment receives individual attention, times for the disabled who cannot easily move through crowded aisles during regular shopping hours, and special shopping periods for disadvantaged children so they can spend time in the store without parental supervision.

Credit Cards

Although almost all merchants accept credit cards as means of payment, the cards are still technically considered to be part of their service package. Most retailers offer a host of different plans for their customers to use including **bankcards**, travel and entertainment cards, and **cash rewards cards**. These cards are described in the following sections. Figure 18.5 features a credit card transaction.

Company Cards

All major fashion merchants offer one or more of their own cards. The most widely used is the **revolving credit card**, which allows shoppers to purchase up to preset spending limits. Shoppers can pay the bill in full at the end of the billing cycle, for which there is no extra interest charge, or can spread their payments out over a period

figure 18.5
A shopper uses a credit card to make a purchase. The credit card offers shopper protection, eliminates the need to carry cash, and often provides the customer with different rewards.

of time. Those who opt for the latter option are charged interest on the unpaid balance. This arrangement enables shoppers to make additional purchases whenever necessary, as long as they haven't reached their credit limits. **Charge accounts** are offered to those customers who agree to pay their bills at the end of 30 days. These accounts also have credit limitations that are preestablished by the company but do not carry any interest charges. Most retailers that sell large-ticket items offer installment credit. Each of these **installment purchases** are treated as individual sales, and the retailer sets monthly payments that shoppers make until they have paid off the entire bill in a certain amount of time.

BANKCARDS

MasterCard and Visa are typical of these cards. They are issued by banks that set credit limits for card holders based upon their ability to pay. Users are expected to pay at least a minimum amount of the outstanding balance once a month, for which there is an interest charge, or they can pay off the total, and no interest is charged. Basically, bankcards are revolving credit cards.

TRAVEL AND ENTERTAINMENT

American Express is the major issuer of this type of credit card. While it was once primarily used for travel, entertainment, and dining, now it is one of the major cards used for retail purchases. No interest charges accrue on these cards, but users must pay the entire month's charges in full at the end of the billing cycle.

CASH REWARDS CARDS

The major cash rewards card is the Discover Card. The difference between this and the typical bankcard is that the user is rewarded with a cash rebate at the end of the year. The American Express Company has an exclusive arrangement with Costco, which features a special platinum card that, like the Discover Card, provides a cash rebate feature.

Miscellaneous Services

Other services retailers offer include dining facilities that range from restaurants to snack bars; leased departments, such as travel agencies; gift wrap facilities; child-care centers that provide babysitting services for shoppers in their stores; and kiosks that feature products that are unavailable in the store but are obtainable from company catalogs.

Off-Site Services

Many of the services offered by brick-and-mortar stores are also featured in catalogs and on retailer websites, such as credit purchases, gift boxing, limited alterations such as pants hemming featured by L.L. Bean and Lands' End, and gift registries. Many websites make interactive communication available between the shopper and the retailer for personal shopping services, such as L.L. Beans' "Live Help" program.

More websites provide a feature that creates and constructs **virtual models** of the shoppers using the information they supply. With this feature, companies can offer personal shopping assistance.

Recognizing that shoppers will continue to use off-site shopping sites in significant numbers, making them valuable revenue-producing channels, retailers that have these outlets are continuously refocusing their efforts on customer service to stay ahead of the competition.

Chapter Highlights

1. The role of professional fashion salespeople is not only to sell the product but also to provide service "extras" to help differentiate their store from the rest.

2. Sales associates are the intermediaries between the customers and the company's buyers, so they can pass on any information to the buyer that might make the company's merchandise mix better.

3. Professional sales personnel in brick-and-mortar operations must be properly dressed and groomed since they are the ones that make the company's first impression with the shopper.

4. A salesperson's knowledge of the merchandise, company, and the consumer will lead to more sales and also has the potential of developing customer loyalty.

5. Since not all shoppers who enter a store know exactly what they want to purchase, it is up to the sales associate to assess needs and present merchandise that has the potential to suit those needs; by doing so, shoppers are motivated to become purchasers.

6. Closing the sale is one of the most difficult steps in a sales presentation. Those with the most selling experience use a host of means to determine when it is the right time.

7. Off-site selling is more than order taking. Some major fashion retailers have made provisions for interactivity between shoppers and their reps so that the reps can do some actual selling while talking to the shoppers.

8. Customer service involves more than personal selling and includes such areas as rewards programs, personal shopping, gift registries, corporate buying programs, interpreter programs, and merchandise alterations.

9. Retailers accept credit cards in many different formats including company cards, bankcards, travel and entertainment cards, and cash rewards cards.

10. To make online shopping more successful, some retailers have used such customized approaches as virtual models and live help programs.

Terms of the Trade

bankcards
cash rewards cards
charge accounts
chatting online
corporate buying programs
customer loyalty
installment purchases
order takers
overcoming the objections

registries
revolving credit card
rewards programs
store greeters
suggestion selling
trial closes
virtual models
yes, but method

For Discussion

1. What is meant by the term "suggestion selling?"

2. What are some of the service extras that the sales associate can provide to increase the potential for making the sale?

3. When shoppers say, "I don't like that store," what are they actually referring to?

4. How can a fashion sales associate assist the company buyer?

5. Why is appropriate appearance so essential for the sales associate in a fashion retailing operation?

6. Which three knowledge areas are generally essential to making the sale?

7. From which sources may a sales associate acquire product knowledge?

8. What is the first stage in a sales presentation, and how should it be addressed?

9. List and describe two techniques that are used to overcome customer objections.

10. When is it appropriate for a seller to try to close the sale?

11. What are some of the closing techniques used in sales closes?

12. Is there any actual personal selling on websites, and if so, how is it accomplished?

13. Does catalog usage ever afford a shopper the opportunity to do anything more than place an order?

14. Why have rewards programs become important service features in major fashion retailing operations?

15. What special service is afforded by most fashion retailers' personal shoppers?

16. Why are visitor services for out-of-town shoppers offered by major retailers?

17. Differentiate between charge cards and bankcards.

18. What is meant by the term "revolving" credit?

Case Problem

Caroline Fredericks owns a small fashion boutique of the same name that specializes in apparel for "that special occasion." Brides, members of the bridal party, and invited guests to such affairs comprise the major portion of the store's market. Many of the garments are especially designed and created on the premises, while others are offerings from prestigious designer collections.

The success of the store has been based upon the uniqueness of the merchandise, excellent individual attention to the customer, and fine service. Since the store is located off the beaten path, business is generated through word of mouth. Satisfied customers send their friends and relatives whenever the occasion of a wedding or other formal event arises. Business has been brisk since the store opened 5 years ago, but Caroline believes it could improve if she took steps to promote the store.

She believes that a catalog and perhaps a website that feature some of her merchandise could be used to sell to those who might not have the time to shop in person. She is prepared to call upon a marketing specialist to prepare such an approach to increasing sales volume.

Questions

1. Does Caroline's operation lend itself to off-site marketing? Defend your answer with logical reasoning.

2. What tool might she use to reach people in their homes?

Exercises and Projects

1. Choose any fashion merchant that is involved in multi-channel retailing. Using its website, assess five different customer services offered in its stores, catalogs, and websites. With the information gathered, prepare a chart to record your findings.

2. Visit three different fashion brick-and-mortar operations and evaluate their approaches to greeting the customers. For each store, indicate the method used. After you have collected the information and recorded it, select the best of the three and explain why you think its approach is advantageous over the others.

CAREERS IN
FASHION RETAILING

Today's retail scene offers a great deal of opportunity for those seeking to enter the field at home and abroad. The globalization of retailing, especially in the fashion arena, has enabled retailing hopefuls to seek positions in almost every part of the world. With the expansion of foreign companies here in the United States, and the continuous explosion of America's pursuits in a host of countries, has made the playing field one that offers the retail employee population challenges and opportunities never seen before in this field.

In addition to the actual careers in retailing, opportunity exists in parallel fields such as resident buying offices (now often referred to as market consulting organizations), fashion forecasting operations, and retail reporting agencies.

With such diverse offerings, it is best to explore the opportunities, advancement potential, and the numerous positions that the field has to offer.

SMALL STORE OPPORTUNITY

The dream of many of those pursuing careers in fashion retailing is to fulfill their ambition by opening a small store. Being ones own boss has its advantages such as pride of ownership and looking forward to financial rewards. It is, however, as a small store employee, that the chances for significant advancement are slim. In most of the small companies, all of the major chores such as buying, management, merchandising, promotion, etc., are generally performed by the owner. If selling is the goal, then the small store might be the place to be. Little else is a reality.

ENTREPRENEURSHIP

The dream of some entering the field, or moving from a paid position to ownership of a company is usually just a fascination. Beginning a retail operation, and thinking down the road towards expansion, is very challenging. The number one problem associated with entrepreneurship is the capital requirements to begin the operation. Undercapitalization has long been the downfall of these hopefuls. A startup requires an investment to cover such areas as rent, construction of the store, fixturing, design plans, advertising and promotion, and so forth. While some of these individuals have the necessary resources to fulfill their wishes, the vast majority does not. Another significant problem is finding an appropriate location that will be favorable to the new company. The field is so crowded with chains, that getting a good location is almost impossible. The chain organizations generally have the location advantage.

That is not to say the desire for entrepreneurship is non-existent. Some people have formulas that make the risk less obvious. Those with special design ability, for example, might use this talent to develop a loyal customer base. Custom tailoring is another plus for those planning their own shop.

One way in which individuals enter the field of ownership is through franchising. Some companies franchise locations to franchisees. In these cases, the managerial skills needed for success are delivered to the participants. They have worked out every detail of running a business, and for a startup fee and other monetary requirements, the potential franchisee has the basics for success. Of course, startup fees are often out of the reach of many, so that this entry into ownership is often unachievable.

Whatever the approach for entrepreneurship, care must be exercised to diligently examine all of its pros and cons.

LARGE COMPANY MULTICHANNEL OPPORTUNITY

Today's retailing environment has witnessed the expansion of bricks and mortar organizations into multichannel operations, making the employment opportunities greater than ever before. Off-site divisions that include catalogs, etailing, mobile selling and social media, often need separate staffing from the bricks and mortar stores, and offers a wealth of more career opportunities.

The jobs in all of the large companies, whether multichannel or not, are the same. Buyers, merchandisers, and management employees perform the same tasks no matter the type of company.

In the following section, the fashion retailing job classifications are explored and provide insights into the duties and responsibilities of each one.

FASHION RETAILING JOB CLASSIFICATIONS

The world of retailing generally classifies jobs according to a number of specialized categories. These include, but are not limited to merchandising, management, store operations, advertising and promotion, and finance. In small operations, there is rarely such specialization with most employees assigned to selling, and the owners performing all of the management and merchandising functions.

Merchandising
While the mid management and upper management make the decisions, those in the merchandising division provide the lifeblood of the company. Without the proper merchandise, failure is almost a certainty.

General Merchandising Manager (GMM)

At the helm of the merchandising division is the GMM who oversees and makes decisions concerning the company's merchandising philosophy and future plans. The GMM is part of the company's management team. He or she is responsible for the company's merchandise mix, pricing structure, fashion focus, and other details. It is the top position in the merchandising division, and since there is only one in an organization, it is extremely difficult to reach this position.

Divisional Merchandising Manager (DMM)

Next in command in the merchandising division is the DMM. In department stores and most chains, there are almost always a few of them. They divide duties and are charged with the merchandising of a particular department. For example, the departments for a full-line department store are generally for menswear, ladies wear, children's, furniture, etc. Each department is divided into sub categories with buyers at the top. The DMM reports to the GMM and receive budgets for purchases in his or her departments, which they divide into budgets in their departments.

It is an achievable job since there are more than one in the company.

Buyer

The company's purchasing agent is the buyer, who is responsible for merchandise selection, market visits at home and abroad, resource evaluation, model stock development, and in more and more cases, the development of private label products. It is not a terribly difficult position to reach since there are a wealth of buyers in most retail operations. Recruited from a training program or obtained from other companies, the buyer is one step over that of the assistant buyer.

Assistant Buyer

This is the entry-level position in the merchandising division. His or her job is to assist the buyer after having demonstrated some expertise in their company's executive training program.

Fashion Director

Often an advisory position, but more and more the fashion director works with the buyers to determine future fashion purchases. They are charged with the responsibility of determining market conditions, fashion forecasting, seeking out new resources, and the like. Most are also responsible for fashion shows, trunk shows, and the accessorizing of apparel headed for displays.

Private Label Designer

Many retailers are either exclusively producing their own labeled merchandise or are making private label goods for a portion of their inventories. These individuals work with the GMM, DMM, Buyer or Fashion Director to bring new concepts and designs to offer them for exclusive products for their company's inventories. It is essential that these people have significant design experience.

Management

In fashion retailing operations there are many different areas in which managers operate. The following are some of those typically found in retailing:

Store Manager

Large retailers as well as some small retail operations utilize store managers to oversee all of the management activities in their units. Depending upon the type of operation, their duties often include management of the human resources department, selling departments, customer services, traffic, security, and maintenance as well as seeing that the company's procedures are carried out. In chain organizations, the different units have store managers who perform some other duties such as employee scheduling, hiring assistant managers, handling customer complaints, preparing daily sales figures, preparing inventory reports and other tasks that upper management requires.

Department Manager

In both on-site and off-site ventures, individual managers are assigned to specific departments. Each is assigned to a specific merchandise department and performs such duties as employee scheduling, merchandise changes in in-store visual presentations, selling during peak periods, inventory replenishment, and so forth. In some stores there are group department managers in which the individual is responsible for two or more departments.

Assistant Department Manager

Usually, the road to management begins with becoming an assistant department manager, except in cases where the individual performed department manager duties in other stores. His or her role is to sell merchandise and help the department manager as expected.

Human Resources Manager

The human resources director or manager has the responsibility of either direct or indirect providing of competent employees. In small companies, this task is performed by the company owner or manager. In large companies in addition to employee procurement, they engage in training and retraining, involvement in promotions, and anything that has to do with the betterment of those hired. For this position, a background in retailing and psychology is preferred.

Promotion

Those in the promotion division are responsible for advertising, special events, visual merchandising, and publicity.

Director of Promotion

The person at the helm of this division has the responsibility of coordinating all of the activities in the different promotional departments. They prepare the budgets and divide them according to the needs of each department within promotion. The end result of their efforts is to bring a cohesive look to all of the departments within their division.

Advertising Manager

Most large retail organizations such as department stores spend significant dollars to attract potential customers to their companies. The ad manager sets the tone of the advertising for print, broadcast, social media, Internet usage, and so forth. In companies that have their own staff, the tasks are fulfilled in-house. For companies with lesser self-involvement they work together with advertising agencies for the development of their programs. Candidates for this position generally have an advertising degree.

Visual Merchandising Director

In order to bring shoppers into the stores and motivate them to look at the merchandise is the visual merchandising director and his or her staff. Their work entails window presentations, interior displays, preparing annual window calendars, and overseeing the various projects. They are in charge of trimmers, sign makers, painters, artists and carpenters. It is important for theses indivduals to have a knowledge of display and art.

Special Events Manager

This person is responsible for the development of conceptual ideas such as holiday parades, fashion shows, celebrity appearances, institutional offerings, and so forth that will provide publicity for the company.

Publicity Manager

These create press kits and press releases regarding store events, and send them to the editorial press in the hope that they will be featured in print, broadcast, and social media.

Operations

The operations division is responsible for taking care of the facilities and making certain they are functioning well. Two of their chores are securing the merchandise from shoplifters and internal theft.

Operations Manager

The person who heads this division has the responsibility for managing employees engaged in property maintenance, merchandise receiving, security, equipment and supplies purchases, and workrooms.

Security Chief

This manager comes with a wealth of expertise regarding the securing of the company's premises. They develop appropriate programs to deter shoplifting and internal theft. They are always seeking information on new anti-theft systems to minimize losses.

Receiving Manager

In the retail industry, there are numerous methods for the receiving and distribution of merchandise. In the larger chains and some department stores the centralized receiving department is most dominant. With these retailers, as well as those that are catalog companies and website operations, the merchandise is marked and ticketed and dispersed to the many units in the organization.

Maintenance Manager

The role for this individual is primarily to maintain a company's physical premises that includes keeping the facility clean, heating and ventilation, maintenance of mechanical equipment, and the assessment of the latest innovations in equipment and supplies used in the organization's environments.

Purchasing Manager

This type of purchaser, unlike the merchandise buyers, buys the equipment and supplies necessary to run the operation. These include computers, electronic equipment, lighting fixtures and bulbs, and paper bags and boxes.

Finance

In order to maximize profits, the running of the operation either gains or loses profits. Accounting practices, credit plans, payroll, and inventory management comprise this division.

Credit Manager

Today, more than ever before, customers are opting for the use of credit cards rather than cash. The credit manager is involved in every aspect of credit, oversees credit policies, and credit authorization. This position has become extremely important especially with the increased use of the Internet for purchasing.

Accounting Manager

Developing different programs and procedures used in accounting are the main task for the credit manager. The individual should have a degree in accounting and be familiar with the latest techniques for credit management.

Payroll Manager

With the numerous remuneration systems generally in place, the payroll manager is there to make certain the appropriate amounts are paid to the employees in a timely manner.

Inventory Control Manager

The maintenance of inventory is mandated by the Federal Government for tax purposes. Assessing profits and losses can be determined by the methods the inventory control manager oversees the people in his or her employee.

Miscellaneous Careers

In addition to the aforementioned, there are other rules that are important to the success of the company.

Sales Associates

While selling is a major function in retailing, some use it as a stepping-stone for higher positions. Others in companies such as Nordstrom where sales associates often earn more than six-figure salaries, use this position as a place to stay to earn their livelihoods.

Personal Shopper

In shops that cater to upper middle class and upper class clienteles the personal shopper is an important position. They help shoppers coordinate outfits, make suggestions for apparel and accessories to be used for specific occasions, and offer a wealth of personalized services. Those who develop loyal customer lists often earn sums that exceed six figures.

Ancillary Careers

In addition to the careers directly in the field of fashion retailing, there are also positions that are similar in nature. These positions are with companies such as resident buying offices, market specialists, fashion forecasting companies, retail research operations and the like.

For the most part, these operations are more advisory than decision-making. Their tasks are to assist the fashion merchants with information about the state of the industry, color and style forecasts, fashion promotions, new resources, etc.

Looking back to previous chapters, these titles and duties are explored to give the reader the breadth and depth of the ancillary careers to retailing.

THE PLANNING STRATEGY FOR A SUCCESSFUL CAREER

In order to fully reach the opportunities that prospective retailing students should take, it is necessary to develop a plan that will translate into successful employment. Those who don't are less likely to find their career opportunities.

Pre-planning: Pursuing a college degree

Completing a post-secondary degree, and then going on to higher education, provides a better understanding for success in fashion retailing. It also develops decision-making skills and the acquisition of technical information.

Four-Year Colleges and Universities

For those seeking the higher levels of merchandising and management in fashion retailing, a four-degree equips them the best. In addition to courses in fashion retailing, those in four-year programs learn to become experts in decision-making and those skills needed to become problem solvers and future planners.

Community Colleges

The associate degrees generally concentrate on providing the knowledge necessary to better understand industries such as fashion retailing. Graduates are prepared for mid-management positions and often the opportunity for entry into executive development programs. Courses such as merchandising, buying, promotion, computer usage and management are often the courses taught. In some cases the community colleges offer internships as part of their curriculums. Students completing these programs are often invited to remain as permanent employees.

Proprietary Schools

Throughout the country proprietary institutions offer two-year degrees as well as certificate programs in fashion. Those with a flair for fashion and desire to work in ancillary organizations such as resident buying offices often find this type of education satisfying.

Preparing a Professional Résumé

One of the more important documents needed to obtain an interview is the résumé. Those in human resources carefully examine them to determine qualifications and if they are potentially good candidates for positions in the company.

Since competency in résumé writing isn't within every person's realm of capability, checking with reliable sources may be the right approach. There are books and online websites that offer professional ways in which to prepare one. By logging onto a search engine such as www.google.com, numerous sites come up that provide a wealth of résumé preparation.

Writing a Cover Letter

Simple, straightforward cover letters should accompany the résumé. It is redundant to list the candidate's strengths since they will be on the résumé. It is the perfectly prepared package that usually gets the attention of the company representative. The same websites as those procured in their résumé searches generally provide ways in which to write a good cover letter.

Gaining an Interview

There are several ways in which to gain an interview. The best one is through networking in which those connected to the company help to arrange an interview. These networks include friends, relatives, educators, or anyone else with whose name might open the door to gain an interview.

Classified ads in prestigious journals such as WWD often feature jobs of interest. Websites of some companies often feature the jobs available and the requirements for such positions. Some even offer applications that can be downloaded and transmitted back to the organization.

Interview Preparation

Going into an interview without any preparation is almost certain to fall short. Candidates must be prepared with technical and product information to impress the interviewer. This information can be obtained by reading major trade journals such as *Chain Store Age* and *Visual Merchandising and Store Design*. Role-playing is also an excellent tool to "test the waters." One other approach is to visit the company to assess how the employees dress and approach the customers.

The Follow-up Letter

Immediately after the interview, the candidate should send a letter of appreciation to the interviewer. Not only does this show courtesy but it also serves as a reminder that the candidate is interested in the job.

glossary

3dcart – Software that allows one to build one's store online

Acousto-magnetic system – Shoplifting deterrent used for store entrances that are about 8 feet wide

Advertisement "life" – The time the ad is still viable

Advertising – A paid-for form of nonpersonal presentation about goods and services

Advertising agencies – For a fee, these groups provide the finished ads

Analogous colors – Colors that are adjacent to each other on the color wheel

Anticipation discounts – An additional cash discount

Aptitude tests – Tests that predict future success

Arcade windows – When frontage is narrow, some merchants choose windows that are on both sides of the property extending from the street to the store's entrance

Artwork – Photographs and drawings in an advertisement

Asymmetrical balance – A less formal arrangement that uses different props and merchandise to create balance

Baby boomers – The group of individuals now in their 50s and 60s born in the wake of World War II

Backlit transparencies – Display fixtures that give illumination and reality to graphics

Bait and switch – Advertising one product and attempting to switch the shopper to a more profitable product

Balance – When a display is equal on both sides of an imaginary line

Bankcards – Third-party cards such as Visa to whom the monies are owed for the store purchases

Banner ads – Graphics that appear within articles that advertise something

Bar codes – A series of lines that are computer read

Big box retailers – These are merchants that sell such

merchandise as computers, furniture, appliances, etc.

Blind check method – This system requires that the merchandise is counted without seeing the invoice numbers

Blinds ads – Classified ads that omit the name of the company

Bottom line – The final profit or loss

Boutiques – Small retailers that specialize in high fashion limited offerings

Boutiques on wheels – Shops that are located on moving vehicles

Branches – Smaller versions of the flagship store

Brand licenses – Brands that are licensed to retailers

Brand signatures – This is the practice of using a famous personality or designer label

Brick-and-mortar operations – Physical, on-site stores

Bridge department – Fashion merchandise that is priced between designer and moderate collections

Broadcast media – Radio and television

Business ethics – Moral principles and rules of conduct that apply to business

Business-to-business websites – Sites on which businesses trade with each other

Buying groups – A concept of non-aligned merchants buying together

Cash discounts – Deductions from invoice charges for prompt payment

Cash reward cards – Credit cards that pay a certain percentage to the user

Casual Friday – A dress mode that is less formal than the standard dress requirements

Centralization – Concept that uses management and merchandising from a central office

Centralized receiving – Used mainly by chains; sorts and marks the merchandise and redirects it to individual stores

Centralized visual merchandising – In some large chains there are displays accomplished at central headquarters that are photographed and disseminated

Chain store organizations – Retailers with numerous units that typically operate from a central location

Charge accounts – Store accounts that enable shoppers to make purchases without paying interest

Chargebacks – The amounts that vendors return to retailers for poor sales performance

Chatting-online – Telephone attention between seller and customer

Chief executive officer (C.E.O.) – Chief decision maker

Chief financial officer (C.F.O.) – Chief financial decision maker

Chief operating officer (C.O.O.) – Person in charge of operations such as warehousing, security, etc.

Civil Rights Act – A federal law banning discrimination

Codes of ethics – Moral rules that are used to describe the company's conduct

Collection areas – Well-known collections that are featured in one area

Color wheel – A tool that features the primary and secondary colors

Combination advertising – The combination of both promotional and institutional messages

Company divisions – The different divisions show the main duties of the people within them

Company functions – The different tasks that the company is responsible for

Company producers – Employees that are directly involved in making a profit for the company

Complementary color scheme – Colors that are opposites on the color wheel

Completion dates – Final dates that a purchase order can be shipped to the retailer

Computer hacking – Illegal use; e.g., altering a computer user's message and using viruses to destroy information

Computer-generated tags – Merchandise tags that are printed by the computer

Conflicts of interest – Refers to an individual who has interests in more than one company and thus could influence decision making

Control division – Financial division

Controlled shopping center – A shopping area, generally the malls, where the realtor controls the number of merchants in each product category

Conveyor systems – Automated merchandise moving systems

Cooperative advertising – Ad costs that are shared by sellers and retailers

Copy – The written words in an ad

Corporate buying plans – At holiday times such as Christmas, the business corporation may make purchases that are geared to them and often at discount prices

Couture boutiques – Recognized couture stores that represent individual couturiers

Couture design – Fashion design that is meticulously created at the uppermost price points

Couturiers – Designers of high fashion merchandise

Customer loyalty – The restriction of consumer purchases to one retailer

Customer profile – Such distinctions such as age, employment, income, etc.

Cutting tickets – The number of pieces of a style necessary for production

Decentralization – When duties and responsibilities are handled by stores

Decision making – Factors that help individuals make purchasing decisions

Demographics – The various figures such as income, locations, education, etc.

Department stores – Stores that usually offer a variety of hard goods and soft goods

Designer boutiques – Stores that represent specific designers

Designer salons – Major high fashion departments that separate their styles from the other merchandise

Destination location – This is a retail location that shoppers will seek out even if it is out of the way

Digital images – Signage and graphics produced by computer, up to 100 feet across in some cases

Digital signage – Signs that change their images from one to another in an animated fashion

Direct checking – A procedure that is used to check if the contents agree with the invoice

Direct mail – Advertising literature that are sent directly to the consumer

Discounters – Retailers that sell their goods at reduced prices

Discretionary income – Our money after taxes and living expenses, that is free for us to choose how to spend

Double complementaries – Two sets of colors that are opposites on the color wheel

Downtown central district – A major shopping location where most department stores have their flagship stores

DVD training – Employee training with the use of DVDs

Eco-friendly – A term used to describe products that do not adversely affect the environment

Edited lines – Reduction in the styles featured in a collection

Electromagnetic systems (E.M.) – One of many deterrent systems to stem shoplifting

Electronic article surveillance system (E.A.S.) – A system that reads the merchandise tags and alerts retailers to shoplifting

Electronic data interchange (E.D.I.) – Computer to computer exchange of data

Electronic media – Social media, television, etc.

Elements of buying – The quantitative and qualitative, resources, and timing of purchase

Email selling – Sending retailer messages via email

Emerging markets – Countries that are beginning to have retail prominence

Emotional motives – Motives that are considered in order to achieve status

Energy-efficient lighting – New bulbs that last longer and are less expensive to run

Environmental visual concept – The idea of using a single theme to visually present the store

Equal Pay Act – A federal government law that requires equal pay for equal work

E-tailing – Selling on the Internet

Ethical dilemmas – While codes of ethics may be in place, individuals' interpretations of them may be influenced by different views of the circumstances making it hard to choose the right course

Ethics – Moral principles

Ethnic market segments – Minority classifications

Exclusive resources – Wholesalers that limit their lines to only one store in an area

Executive search firm – An agency that specializes in executive placement

Executive training programs – Those that are used to prepare select individuals for executive positions

Expense account falsification – The act of misrepresenting expenses for better reimbursement

External sources of recruitment – These are classified ads, Internet listings, employment agencies, etc.

Facebook – This is one of the more popular of the social media

Fair-trade pricing – An agreement for all retailers to sell at the same price

Family life cycle – A breakdown of all the possible households such as single, married with children, etc.

Fashion count – The recording of the specific styles that people are wearing

Fashion forecaster – Someone who predicts fashion trends

Fashion perishability – The length of time a fashion is viable

Fashion streets – Upscale streets where high fashion reigns

Fast fashion – Merchandise that is produced quickly to capture the latest trends

Faux finishes – Paint that has been manipulated to resemble other materials

Festival marketplace – Retail locations that have been transformed from historical venues to those that sell retail merchandise

Fiber optics – Bulbs that feature cool lighting

Final interview – One that is conducted by the candidate's potential supervisor

Fine print – The information present in ads that often use tiny fonts to hamper customers' reading

Fixed leases – These are leases that run for a period of time that have no other costs

Flagship store – The main store of a retail operation

Flash sales – Brief unexpected sales periods

Flea markets – Temporary locations where bargain merchandise is for sale

Fluorescent lighting – Tube-like bulbs that are low cost to operate

FOB destination – Shipping charges paid for by retailers through to the destination of the merchandise (FOB is a shipping term meaning free on board)

FOB shipping point – Shipping charges assessed from where the merchandise is shipped (FOB is a shipping term meaning free on board)

Focal point – The main feature of a display

Focus groups – Panels of people who are brought together to evaluate and recommend specific ideas

Foursquare – A one-time form of social media that is almost out of business

Franchisee – Individuals who purchase the rights from franchisers to operate a specific location

Franchiser – Owner of a company that sells rights to others to use that company's name

Franchises – Companies that sell parts of their operations to outside investors

Franchising – A concept where a company (franchiser) sells the rights to outsiders (franchisees) to operate specific locations

Free publicity – Promotional tools that are of no cost to retailers

Freelancers – Those who are in their own businesses, for instance in advertising or display, who work for many different stores

Freestanding stores – Retailers that open in locations that they have all to themselves

Full-line department stores – Stores that sell a wide selection of hard goods and soft goods

Garment Center – The name given to New York City's wholesale market

Generation X – Those born from 1966–1976

Generation Y – Follows generation X but is given no specific birth dates

Google+ – A social medium that is expected to surpass Facebook usage

Graduated leases – Leases that spell out the different costs for specific periods of time

Graphics – Blowups of pictures used in display

Green – A term used interchangeably with "eco-friendly"

Halogen lamps – Lights that throw the most direct high illumination

Handmarking – Individual marking of merchandise by hand

Hard goods – Merchandise such as appliances, computers, electronics, etc.

Harmony – This is when all of the display principles are well coordinated

Headhunter – Another name for executive researcher

High-end fashion leaders – Designer manufacturer collections that specialize in upscale fashion merchandise

High-intensity discharge bulbs – Also known as HIDs, these bulbs offer bright illumination

Hot numbers – Products that sell in great abundance

Human resources division – The division that oversees hiring, employee problems, etc.

Ideal other – The perfect image of ourselves

Ideal self – The perfect image one would like to project

Image-centric networks – A type of social media where the visual content is more important to the text content

Informal modeling – Involves models wearing the items and walking through the store to show them to customers

In-house receiving – Departments that are inside the store

In-house separate shops – Stores or departments within stores that feature a specific brand

In-house staffs – Staffs maintained by the retailers

In-house videos – Videos that are produced for the purpose of showing them inside the store

In-store information terminals – Places in the store where computers are set up for shoppers to learn about the merchandise

In-transit theft – Stealing merchandise that is being moved to delivery points

Incandescent lighting – Bulbs that are traditional in retailing to illuminate windows and interiors

Initial markup – The first markup before markdowns are taken

Insider trading – Using advance information to manipulate investment

Instagram – A form of social media that can use video

Installment purchases – For big ticket purchases, retailers set up accounts that the consumer can use to pay monies owed in installments

Institutional advertising – Ads that are used to promote the image of a company

Intercept surveys – Carried out by interviewers who are stationed at specific sites to question individuals

Internal sources of recruitment – Include employee recommendations

Internal theft – Theft by employees

International prominence – Retailers who have global operations

Internet popups – Announcements or ads that appear on the Internet in the midst of articles, etc.

Internet theft – Using false information to steal on the Internet

Job analysis – The study of jobs to determine their duties

Job description – The presentation of the facts about jobs

Job specifications – The "specs" that come from job analysis for job requirements

Joint ventures – A concept where more than one company joins together for better exposure

Keystone markup plus – Doubling the cost plus a little more to arrive at the selling price

Keystone markups – Doubling the cost to arrive at the retail price

Landed cost – The real costs of merchandise after shipping charges, etc. have been added to the purchase price

LCD monitors – Indoor light boxes that deliver messages throughout the store's premises

Lead time – The time necessary to produce a line from start to finish

Leased departments – See **Partnering**

Lifestyle profiling – Different lifestyles according to employment, wealth, etc.

Limited line stores – Companies with two or more units, but today it is considerably higher

Line and staff organizations – A structure that has both decision makers and advisory staff

Line positions – Decision makers for the company

Line relationships – The order in which decision makers report to each other

Line structure – Organization of company producers

Lines of authority – The reporting order for employees

Loss prevention – Installations of systems that curtail losses

Low-voltage lighting – Bulbs that are long lasting and cost efficient

Luxe goods – Luxury items

Magnifying mirrors – Convex mirrors placed at the rear of a store so that cashiers and front managers can observe shoppers

Maintained markup – The actual markup achieved after markdowns have been applied

Mall anchors – The major stores, at least two, that are the drawing attractions to the centers

Mall intercept – In-person interviews conducted at malls

Mall walkers – Those people who routinely walk the malls for exercise

Mannequins – Figures that range from realistic types to contemporary types

Manufacturer's outlets – Manufacturers that operate outlet stores

Markdown – The amount deducted from the selling price

Market consultants – See **Resident buying office**

Market specialists – Companies also known as resident buying offices

Market Week – This is major buying period when the retailers come to the wholesaler market to purchase

Markup – The amount added to the cost to reach the selling price

Markup by classification – A practice where each merchandise type is marked up the same amount

Marquee labels – The most easily recognized labels or brands

Maslow's Hierarchy of Needs – A concept where different levels of needs are satisfied according to income

Mature markets – Countries that have achieved worldwide retail recognition

Me-too lines – Collections that are similar to other collections

Media – The different outlets such as newspapers, magazines, television, etc.

Megamalls – The giants of the malls, such as Mall of America

Merchandise anchoring – A system that locks merchandise in place to prevent shoplifting

Merchandise distribution – The movement of merchandise to desired locations

Merchandise mix – Assortment of products sold

Merchandising division – Division responsible for merchandise purchases

Micro-video – This is social media that will use video apps for their participants to use

Minimalist interior design – Premises that are sparsely decorated

Mixed-use centers – Shopping arenas that also have some housing, office buildings, etc.

Model stock – An inventory that features a range of prices, styles, colors, sizes, etc.

Monochromatic scheme – One color that is used in visual presentations

Motion displays – Moveable displays

Motion-sensitive monitors – Devices used by retailers as a means of showcasing particular products

Multi-channel retailing – A form of retailing that utilizes many formats

Multicultural consumers – These are minority groups that include African Americans, Hispanics, and Asian Americans

Multilevel store – A retailer's premises that is on more than one floor

Multiple-member/shared households – This is a designation that includes same sex households, same sex marriage, two or more single parents with children who live with them, etc.

MySpace – An international social networking site that offers email, a forum, communities, videos, and webbing space

Mystery shoppers – Outside individuals who pose as customers for the purpose of testing employee honesty

Nation Retail Federation (NRF) – The largest retail trade association

National brands – Brands that are widely known

Neighborhood cluster – A group of stores that are usually privately owned and are situated on neighborhood streets

Neighboring tenants – Stores that are adjacent to each other that offer products that will bring business to each other

Neon – Color designed lighting that is bendable to form many different shapes

Networking – Calling on friends and relatives who might have job leads with specific retailers

Nonselling departments – Departments such as human resources that are far from the selling floors

Observation technique – Viewing people and recording such things as clothing worn, etc.

Off the beaten path – Retail locations that are far from the heavy traffic route

Off-price center – A retail location where off-pricers are the tenants

Off-pricers – Retailers that are opportunistic purchasers who sell below the traditional prices

Offshore production – Merchandise produced overseas

Off-site operations – Catalogs, Internet selling, etc.

Off-site ventures – Retailers that operate catalogs and websites for selling purposes

Online competition – When online merchants compete on pricing

Online only companies – Companies that sell exclusively online

Online training – A relatively new concept that uses programs to train individuals

On-site classifications – Brick-and-mortar operations

On-the-job training – Occurs when a new employee is actually trained on the selling floor

Open windows – Small windows that jut into the store without any backing

Open-to-buy – The amount needed to purchase based upon inventory

Opens ad – Ads that clearly spell out the name of the company seeking employees

Opportunistic purchasing – Buying at prices that are below original wholesale prices

Order takers – The use of a catalog in which the store rep merely places the order

Organization chart – A graphic presentation of a company's structure

Organization chart boxes – The boxes on an organization chart that spell out the different employee positions

Organization structure – The manner in which a company is divided by divisions and duties

Other self – How others really see us

Outlet center – Shopping centers that house markdown outlets for retailers

Overcoming the objections – Methods used to change objections of merchandise into sales

"Owned" retail operations – Manufacturers that operate their own retail outlets

Packaged merchandise transporters – They move merchandise through the receiving process

Parallel-to-sidewalk windows – These are the windows that front most every merchant flagship's store

Partnering – Similar to leased departments where outside merchants "lease" space in a major retail establishment

Partnering with social networks – Retailers sometimes align themselves with specific social networks to expand their market reach

Patronage motives – Purchasing regularly from one company

Personalized shopping – When a retailer has employees whose only responsibility is to either take the shopper on a tour of the merchandise and help in the selection, or preselect items and then present them to the shopper

Pinned – An added benefit to Pinterest users where certain products are pinned the show greater interest

Pinterest – One of the most widely used form of social media

Pinterest rich pins – A new Pinterest feature that provides more detailed information than typical pins

P-O-P displays – Point of purchase displays: fixtures that are generally freestanding and are placed in busy traffic areas in stores

Pop-up shops – A new concept where retailers open shops for a limited time period

Pool orders – When retailers get together to combine purchases if they don't have the ability to order minimum requirements alone

Population shifts – A situation when the population of one area moves to another

Power center – A type of small mall where big box retailers are located

Preliminary interview – The first interview

Preferred position – Choice positioning in a newspaper

Prêt-à-porter – Ready-to-wear

Price cutting – This is a practice of a retailer selling below the prices charged by competing retailers

Price point – This is the major price that retailers charge for their goods

Primary colors – The three colors from which all other colors are made. They are red, yellow, and blue

Primary data – Data that is original and never used before

Print media – Newspapers, magazines, direct mail pieces, and catalogs

Prismatic displays – These simulate a venetian blind that changes from one image to another automatically

Private brand – See private label

Private label – This is merchandise that belongs to, and is sold exclusively at, one retail operation

Prize money (P.M.) – A reward for selling certain slow-moving merchandise

Profit sharing – A method used to provide employees with extra income

Promotion from within – This is when the company moves employees to higher positions

Promotional advertising – Ads that feature merchandise

Promotional division – Division responsible for advertising and promotional activities

Proportion – This is when the sizes of the display parts are in good size relationship to each other

Proportional philosophy – A practice where a merchant's merchandise mix is that of private and national brands

Props – These are the display pieces that that enhance the merchandise

Publicity – The tool that retailers use to reach the editorial press

Quality checking – This assesses if the merchandise received is of the same quality as what was ordered

Quantity checking – This is used to determine if the merchandise direct checking agrees with the invoice

Quantity discounts – A discount for large order

Questionnaire – A research tool used to gather information

Quick response inventory systems (Q.R.) – The technologies that are in place to increase profits

Quota bonuses – Systems that reward employees with bonuses when they reach certain specified sales quotas

Radio frequency systems (R.F.) – A system that uses a label to detect illegal movement of merchandise

Rail interview – The first interview, used to weed out individuals from consideration

Rational motives – Real motivations that affect purchasing

Real self – Our image

Regional malls – These shopping venues house the major retail operations and serve the surrounding trading area

Regional receiving – In very large chains, the operation is divided into specific regions and then sent on to stores in that region

Registries – These are for items that have been placed on a list with the hope that they will be bought e.g., for a wedding or a baby shower

Regular position – Placement of ads in the same place in every issue

Reporting service – A company that provides retailers with hot-seller information, new products, etc.

Research sample – A percentage of people researched in a survey

Reserves of merchandise – Goods that are stored in "back rooms," ready to be sold

Resident buyer – Works for resident buying office

Resident buying office – Company that assists retailers with buying decisions

Resume – A graphic presentation or snapshot of an individual's background

Retail buyer – Buyer who purchases for stores and off-site outlets

Retailing research – Research that retailers use to investigate all areas of the retail organization

Retraining – Used when companies install new systems

Revolving credit card – A plan that sets a customer limit that can be carried over for several months to be paid off

Rewards programs – Rewards to customers such as points that can be used for discounts, etc.

Rhythm – A concept that ensures a movement of the eye throughout the visual presentation

Robinson-Patman Act – A federal law that prohibits price discrimination

Role-playing – A training technique that involves a seller and a customer

Rules of color – The different concepts for color usage

Run of press (R.O.P.) – Placement of ads at the discretion of the periodical

Runway parades – A type of fashion show where models walk on raised platforms

Salary plus bonus – Provides an incentive for salespersons to sell more

Salary plus commission – An incentive-based remuneration method that hopefully improves selling

Sampling – The act of giving away free items, generally with a purchase

Satellite departments – These are departments that feature one merchandise classification in more than one location

Secondary colors – Orange, violet, and green

Secondary data – Information already available to use in research

Self-concept theory – A concept that includes how we see ourselves, how others see us, and how we would like to be seen

Self-selection – A term used to describe "open fixturing." These are counters and racks that provide shoppers the ability to examine and choose their own merchandise

Semiblind check method – This is a combination of direct and blind checking

Shadowing programs – Some retailers use a concept that has an executive being followed by a trainee to learn the duties of the jobs

Shoplifting – Theft by people posing as shoppers

Showrooming – This is when online shoppers come in the store to compare prices

Shrinkage – A term used to describe merchandise losses

Sidebar ads – Advertisements that appear on the sides of stories that are on the Internet

Signage – Signs that are used in windows and interiors

Silent sellers – A term used to describe the benefit of displays

Smartphones – The latest in phones that perform a variety of tasks in addition to telephoning, particularly the ability to access the Internet

Social class – The different groups of people, from upper class at the top to working class at the bottom

Social media – A relatively new form of communication that alerts users to retail offerings, among other messages

Social responsibility – A company's commitment to specific social programs

Soft goods – Merchandise that includes apparel, sportswear, etc.

Specialized department store – A major retail operation that specializes only in soft goods, and not both hard and soft goods as full-line department stores do

Specialty stores – Another term used to describe limited line stores

Spin-off stores – Stores that belong to department store organizations but carry on classification of merchandise

Split complementaries – The two colors that are on either side of the color wheel facing one color

Spot commercial – TV ads that are used by different advertisers during a broadcast

Staff positions – Advisory personnel

Standard Rate & Data Service (S.R.D.S.) – This is an agency that shows the different costs of advertising

Stock – This is the paper that is used in advertising

Stock agencies – Another term for stock houses

Stock houses – Companies that supply images to retailers

Stock options – Used to increase management's potential to earn more in the future

Stock turnover – The number of times inventory is sold in one year

Store greeters – This is where a store rep is at the front door to meet and greet the shoppers

Store management division – Division responsible for all management functions

Store operations division – Division responsible for the maintenance of the facility, including housekeeping

Store within a store – Individual stores that are in major retail shops

Straight commission – Pays individuals on the sales they make

Straight salary – Pays employees a particular salary, with no commission

Street fashion – The fashions people are wearing on the street

Strip centers – Local small "strips" that house minor retailer operations

Subspecialty stores – Specialty stores that concentrate on one merchandise classification

Substitution shipping – Vendor shipments are not the same as ordered

Suggestion selling – Increasing the size of the sale by suggesting additional items to purchase

Sustainable fashion – Products that are made of quickly replenished raw materials and avoidance of the use of dyes that affect the environment

Sustainable Fashion Coalition – It has more than 30 major retailers who oversee sustainable fashion practices

Symmetrical balance – When two sides of a display are mirror images of the other

Tables of organizations – Charts that depict the organization's structure

Tag-and-alarm systems – These are systems that set off alarms if a shopper is illegally trying to remove merchandise from the store

Target research – Investigation of a specific market

Targeted market – A group of potential customers that retailers try to address

The Store is the Brand – This is when a retailer sells only its own brand

Town centers – Outdoor malls that are filled with a wealth of major chain stores and some department stores

Trade associations – Business associations within specific industries

Trade shows – Where a wealth of manufacturers' and designers' collections are shown under one roof

Trading area – The surrounding areas to which retailers appeal

Trading up – Increasing the price points of a retail operation

Traditional sales periods – Sales that run at the same times every year such as after Christmas

Traffic count – Automobiles that pass by certain locations are counted and recorded

Transportation terminal centers – Airport and railway terminals where merchants set up shop to appeal to the waiting travelers

Trend books – Produced by Promostyl to feature the latest fashion trends

Trend forecasting – Predicting the future fashion trends

Triadic color scheme – Three colors that are equidistant from each other on the color wheel

Trial closes – Early close attempt to make the sale

Trimmers – Display people who actually do the display installations

Trunk show – A promotional concept where company representatives bring their collections to retailers for customer viewing and buying

Tuition reimbursement – A plan that pays all or part of an employee's college tuition

Tweets – The term given to the messages on Twitter

Twitter – Social media that allows for up to 140 characters in the messaging

Uniform company markup – Everything in the inventory is marked up the same amount

Vendor managed inventory (V.M.I.) – Scanner systems used in stores for suppliers to keep track of their merchandise levels

Vendor standards – This applies to producers who sell to retailers

Vertical malls – High-rise malls that are erected in areas where there is little ground space

Vestibule training – Simulates actual on-the-floor situations

Video surveillance systems (C.C.T.V.) – Centralized store area that features a wealth of video screens that monitor shoppers

Vine – Twitter's Vine is a new mobile service that lets users capture and share short videos

Virtual models – These are models of a customer on store websites that help to personalize shopping

Visual merchandising – The art of displaying merchandise in windows and interiors in eye-catching ways

Volunteerism – Programs that are in place to volunteer to serve specific organizations

Walk-ins – People who, on their own, come into a store seeking employment

Walkthrough – A necessary observation of interior visual presentations to make certain they haven't been tampered with

Warehouse clubs – Fee-based retailers who sell to their customers at low prices

Wholly owned subsidiary – This is when a company totally owns the name of another retailer for the purpose of opening stores in new areas

Windowless storefronts – This is a type of enclosure that does not offer window space to show wares

WWD Digital Forum – A major conference that can be attended at several global venues

Yes, but method – Also known as agree and counterattack, the seller agrees with shopper but offers new advantages

credits

Chapter 1
1.1   Joe Ravi/Shutterstock
1.2   testing/Shutterstock
1.3   DmitriMaruta/Shutterstock
1.4   Dan Dalton/Getty Images
1.5   Tupungato/Shutterstock

Chapter 2
2.1   wavebreakmedia/Shutterstock
2.2   Andrey Arkusha/Shutterstock
2.3   Dan Breckwoldt/Shutterstock
2.4   testing/Shutterstock
2.5   Alexander Supertramp/Shutterstock

Chapter 4
4.1   Toronto Star via Getty Images
4.2   Filipe Matos Frazao/Shutterstock
4.3   JStone/Shutterstock
4.4   Bloomberg via Getty Images
4.5   baranq/Shutterstock

Chapter 5
5.1   GC Images/Getty Images
5.2   wavebreakmedia/Shutterstock
5.3   monkeybusinessimages/Istockphoto
5.4   LDprod/Shutterstock
5.5   wavebreakmedia/Shutterstock

Chapter 6
6.1   © James Leynse/Corbis
6.2   Lisa S./Shutterstock
6.3   swinner/Shutterstock
6.4   © ZUMA Press, Inc./Alamy
6.5   © Ed Endicott/Alamy

Chapter 7
7.1   flickr Editorial/Getty Images
7.2   FilmMagic/Getty Images
7.3   Karramba Production/Shutterstock
7.4   Aleph Studio/Shutterstock
7.5   amnachphoto/Shutterstock

Chapter 8
8.1   Bloomberg via Getty Images
8.2   Bloomberg via Getty Images
8.3   Rrrainbow/Shutterstock
8.4   TonyV3112/Shutterstock
8.5   Goodluz/Shutterstock

Chapter 9
9.1   Kotin/Shutterstock
9.2   littleny/Shutterstock
9.3   Christian Mueller/Shutterstock
9.4   ariadna de raadt/Shutterstock
9.5   hxdbzxy/Shutterstock

Chapter 10
10.1   Monkey Business Images/Shutterstock
10.2   OtnaYdur/Shutterstock
10.4   juniart/Shutterstock
10.5   phasinphoto/Shutterstock

Chapter 11
11.1   michaeljung/Shutterstock
11.2   Steve Lovegrove/Shutterstock
11.3   Viappy/Shutterstock
11.4   Tim Large/Shutterstock
11.5   THALERNGSAK MONGKOLSIN/
        Shutterstock

Chapter 12
12.1   Hasloo Group Production Studio/Shutterstock
12.2   WireImage/Getty Images
12.3   Getty Images
12.4   s_bukley/Shutterstock
12.5   Dikiiy/Shutterstock

Chapter 13
13.1   AFP/Getty Images
13.2   CandyBox Images/Shutterstock
13.3   AFP/Getty Images
13.4   Stefano Tinti/Shutterstock
13.5   Bloomberg via Getty Images

Chapter 14
14.1   Susan Law Cain/Shutterstock
14.2   Felix Mizioznikov/Shutterstock
14.3   Canadapanda/Shutterstock
14.4   s_bukley/Shutterstock
14.5   Lewis Tse Pui Lung/Shutterstock

Chapter 15
15.1   Toronto Star via Getty Images
15.2   Manny Hernandez/Getty Images
15.3   junrong/Shutterstock
15.4   Dainis Derics/Shutterstock
15.5   Northfoto/Shutterstock

Chapter 16
16.1   racorn/Shutterstock
16.2   Alliance/Shutterstock
16.3   dboystudio/Shutterstock
16.4   lev radin/Shutterstock
16.5   gary718/Shutterstock

Chapter 17
17.1   auremar/Shutterstock
17.2   DWaschnig/Shutterstock
17.3   Oktay Ortakcioglu/Getty Images
17.4   U. Baumgarten via Getty Images
17.5   Stefania D'Alessandro/Getty Images

Chapter 18
18.1   wavebreakmedia/Shutterstock
18.2   LDprod/Shutterstock
18.3   racorn/Shutterstock
18.4   Stephen Chung/Shutterstock
18.5   wavebreakmedia/Shutterstock

index

Locators for Figures and Tables appear in *italics*.